# THE HISTORY OF WEAPONS
# OF THE AMERICAN REVOLUTION

# THE HISTORY OF
# AMERICAN

Drawings by George C. Woodbridge

BONANZA BOOKS

# WEAPONS OF THE REVOLUTION

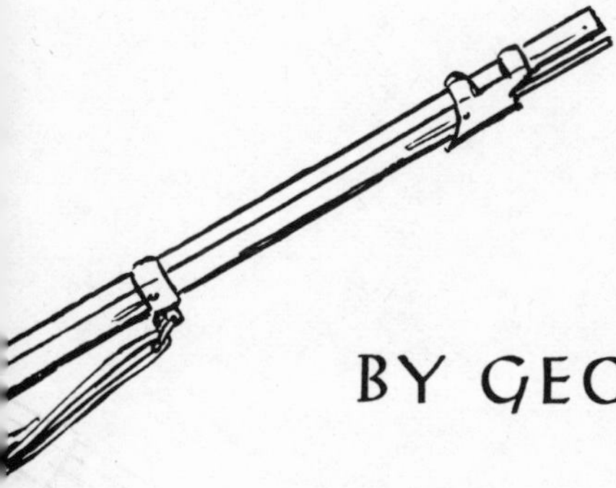

BY GEORGE C. NEUMANN

NEW YORK

To My Wife

DIANA

Copyright © MCMLXVII by George C. Neumann
Library of Congress Catalog Card Number: 67-20829
All rights reserved.
This edition is published by Bonanza Books
a division of Crown Publishers, Inc.
by arrangement with the author
a b c d e f g h
Manufactured in the United States of America

# CONTENTS

Washington, D.C.

The Company of Military Historians through its Review Board takes pride in sponsoring *The History of Weapons of the American Revolution* as an accurate and useful reference work in American military history.

F. Brooke Nihart
*President*

# Preface

AMID THE GROWING AWARENESS and interest in various aspects of the American War for Independence, it is surprising how little is known of the weapons used—despite the fact that they were our early means of survival, and our final means to freedom. This unfamiliarity is due, in large part, to the limited number of specimens remaining—of which the overwhelming proportion are preserved, not in public institutions, but by interested individuals in their private collections. This work is an effort to present a representative sampling of these arms. Over 90 percent of them have never been photographed before for publication.

The principal period covered begins with the flintlock's acceptance as the major military arm about 1700 and ends with America's emergence as a new nation in 1783. Most weapon types from this span of years saw service during the Revolutionary War. Although the majority of European muskets were supposedly standardized by the second half of the 1700's, they still varied in many ways—as did the multiplicity of pieces used by the colonists. For this reason, it is important that the interested collector or student go beyond memorization of official pattern dimensions and develop a sensitivity to contemporary styling. Toward this end, more than twelve hundred illustrations are included.

Tracing the evolution of the five categories chosen for the book (muskets, rifles, pistols, swords, and polearms) provides additional insight into the development of colonial industry—the techniques and facilities which paced our awakening productive capacity. It also indicates the extensive international trade already flourishing in the eighteenth century.

This work is a simple presentation of the best information known to the author at this time and place. New sources are constantly coming to light, and undoubtedly will lead to modification of some of the data included here.

It would be impossible to list all of the people who generously contributed to the assemblage and interpretation of this material. Those who permitted the inspection and photographing of their weapons are gratefully acknowledged under each description. Additional appreciation is extended to the following individuals:

To Harold L. Peterson for his encouragement and counsel; Lewis H. Gordon, Jr., who opened his extensive collection, library, and background sources; Joseph E. Fritzinger, who provided his file of firearm information compiled over years of contact with hundreds of weapons.

To Colonel Frederick P. Todd and Philip M. Cavanaugh of the New Windsor Cantonment; Gerald C. Stowe and Robert Fisch of the West Point Museum; Craddock R. Goins, Jr., at the Smithsonian Institution; Thomas E. Hall of the Winchester Museum; Theodore S. Sowers at the Morristown National Museum; John M. Graham II and S. Daniel Berg in Colonial Williamsburg; Christine Meadows of the Mount Vernon Ladies' Association; Anthony D. Darling, Glode M. Requa, Edmund W. Budde, Jr., Richard C. Vogt, Wayne M. Daniels, and Donald R. Toppel.

To Thomas Murtaugh, Richard De Angelis, and Raymond Pankowski who helped a new photographer-author with his camera indoctrination.

GEORGE C. NEUMANN

# THE HISTORY OF WEAPONS
# OF THE AMERICAN REVOLUTION

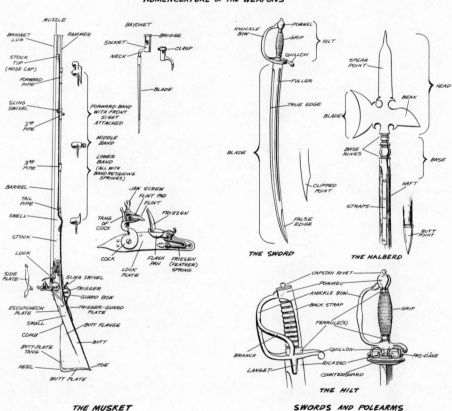

NOMENCLATURE OF THE WEAPONS

THE MUSKET

THE SWORD

THE HALBERD

THE HILT

SWORDS AND POLEARMS

# 1 | FIREARMS COME OF AGE ...
## LAST OF THE PIKES

ALCHEMISTS AND APOTHECARIES of western Europe's thirteenth century—diligently searching for new potions and occult powers—set in motion a revolution far beyond their most grandiose dreams. It apparently came from Arab writings which described mixtures of saltpeter, charcoal, and sulfur used for pyrotechnics by the Chinese. One can imagine the surprise of these early scientists in their lonely cells as gunpowder roared to life across Europe. Its potential for hurling projectiles was soon evident, and guns are known to have been in use by the fourteenth century.

For the next five hundred years, gunpowder's mixture proportions and granulation were varied but showed little basic change. The great evolution of firearms during this period was essentially a series of improved methods for ignition. Spears, bows, crossbows, pikes, and swords were eventually struck down one by one until the firearm stood as the unchallenged infantry arm by 1700.

## FOUR BASIC IGNITIONS

The hundreds of improvements in hand firearms from 1300 to 1700 can best be classified into four fundamental ignition systems:

1. Hand Ignition       circa 1300-1500
2. Matchlock           circa 1410-1700
3. Wheel Lock          circa 1500-1700
4. Flintlock           circa 1550-1840

Each of these methods was superseded as more efficient types appeared. Like today's weapon procurement, they were usually judged in terms of two criteria: ease and cost of production, and actual performance in the field. The former naturally changed as production skills, equipment, and materials improved. Field performance included many considerations, e.g. accuracy, loading speed, ignition dependability, safety, projectile impact, weight, size, and ruggedness. A detailed study of these early weapons demonstrates their growing importance as they closely paralleled man's progress in mechanical aptitude and manufacturing capacity.

**HAND IGNITION:** The first firearms known to us were crude cannon. By the early 1300's, however, reduced versions were in use (about one foot

1

long), mounted on wood or iron poles (four to five feet). These shorter and lighter arms were cast in iron, copper, or bronze and are known as "hand cannon." For the first time, they gave the firearm real mobility and permitted the individual soldier to transport and operate his own weapon.

The powder and projectile (such as a stone, arrow, or iron ball) were loaded from the muzzle. According to early illustrations, the operator usually held the weapon with one hand, bracing the extension under the arm or on the shoulder. Firing was achieved by inserting a hot wire, live coal, or match into a touchhole near the breech.

The hand cannon was not considered a primary weapon, and appears to have been in use from about 1300 to 1500. Its advantages included portability, one-man operation, ease of manufacture, and the psychological impact from its smoke and flame. Among the disadvantages were poor accuracy, unreliability, and the danger of a bursting barrel.

**THE MATCHLOCK:** The cumbersome nature of the hand cannon led to the development of the matchlock early in the 1400's. Initially, an S-shaped lever, or "serpentine," was attached by a center pin to the side of the barrel near the breech. The touchhole was then moved from the top to the side of the barrel, and a small pan fastened outside to hold "priming" powder (finer granulation). The top half of the serpentine held a smoldering length of "match" rope. When the lower half was pulled by the soldier, the upper part pivoted the match into the pan of priming powder, igniting it and sending flame through the touchhole into the loose powder inside for final ignition.

The matchlock principle afforded control of the weapon by both hands. This, in turn, resulted in the pole of the hand cannon being changed into a flat wooden stock attached to the barrel tightly. Its shape improved the grip, provided a more secure rest against the body (chest, cheek, or shoulder), and established the basic pattern for mounting shoulder arms, which still persists today. The matchlock ignition principle advanced through three basic styles: the arquebus, musket, and caliver.

ARQUEBUS MATCHLOCKS: This is the earliest known form of matchlock. Developed about 1410, it was a light weapon with a short curved stock, usually held against the chest for firing. Averaging 3 to 3½ feet long (barrel about 24 to 30 inches), it weighed close to 10 pounds. The bore was large (approximating .72 caliber) to provide great striking power against body armor. In competition with standard weapons of the 1400's and 1500's, it was slow to operate and afforded limited accuracy (under 50 yards). England's contemporary longbow, for example, was exercised at a popular distance of 220 yards. Yet a recruit could be taught to operate the arquebus in a few days, while many years of intensive training were required for the bowman. (Note: "arquebus" also referred to the wheel lock in the 1600's.)

**MATCHLOCK MUSKET:** The matchlock reached its most formidable development in the mid-1500's with the introduction of the musket. Originated by the Spanish, it was a long, heavy gun, fired with the barrel resting on a forked pole. Total weight approached 20 pounds, with the bore averaging .77 to .83 caliber. By the mid-1600's this had been generally reduced to about 12 to 16 pounds, with a bore approximating .78 caliber. Ammunition for the musket was usually carried in a bandolier, which consisted of a broad leather shoulder belt having horn or wooden cylinders of powder hanging from it. (Note: By the 1700's the term "musket" had evolved to include any smooth-bore shoulder arm.)

**CALIVER MATCHLOCK:** "Caliver" was the name used during the late 1500's and early 1600's to indicate a light version of the matchlock, or occasionally the snaphaunce.

As the matchlock gained in importance, refinements occurred. First, the priming pan was fitted with a hand-pivoted cover so that the weapon could be carried already primed. In addition, the crude serpentine was changed to a more controlled ignition action which attached it through a series of catches and levers to a trigger (Fig. I.1). Initially, the trigger consisted of a bar extending out and back under the stock (Fig. I.2). The modern vertical style with the protective guard made its appearance during the early 1600's (Fig. I.3).

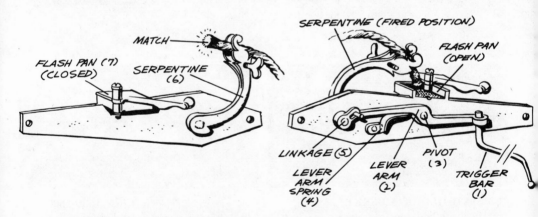

**I.1 EARLY MATCHLOCK ACTION:** Squeezing of TRIGGER BAR #1 upward rotates LEVER ARM #2 on PIVOT #3 (controlled by pressure from LEVER ARM SPRING #4). The Lever Arm then rotates the LINKAGE #5, attached by a horizontal axle to the outside SERPENTINE #6. This rotation slowly lowers the Serpentine and its lighted match into the PAN #7 (filled with priming powder) attached to the barrel outside the touchhole—sending a flash into the barrel's main charge.

## I.2 MATCHLOCK MUSKET                    Circa 1600-1630

This style of matchlock, used by the early English colonists, includes a trigger bar to activate the serpentine. Its straight stock with the flared butt was typical of contemporary military arms. Also interesting is the long thin lock plate, pivoting flashpan cover (with a short handle), and underneath screw reaching to the tang of the round barrel. German markings appear on the lock.

Length: 53½″            Butt Tang: 7¾″            Furniture: Iron
Barrel: 39⅜″; .73                                  Weight: 7.8 lbs.
Lock: 9″ × 1″

*Author's Collection*

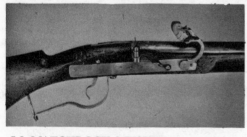
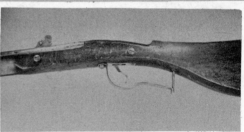

## I.3 MATCHLOCK MUSKET                    Circa 1630-1660

The evolution toward a narrower butt and full trigger guard is illustrated here. Weapons of this type saw service in America until the last quarter of the seventeenth century. Its round barrel is pinned to the stock and includes a double incised ring. The "SVL" lock marking identifies its origin as Suhl, Germany.

Length: 59½″            Tr. Guard: 7½″            Furniture: Iron
Barrel: 44½″; .69                                  Weight: 7.6 lbs.
Lock: 8¼″ × ⅞″

*Author's Collection*

Over its three-hundred-year span, the matchlock watched the gradual demise of medieval warfare. Originally inferior to the established longbow and crossbow, it had surpassed both of them in acceptance by the late 1500's, and established firearms on an equality with cold steel. Nevertheless, its problems in the field were still many: slowness to fire, inaccuracy, bulky size, and undependability in bad weather.

**THE WHEEL LOCK:** The wheel lock dates from about 1500, and appears to have come from the clock-making areas of southern Germany and northern Italy. It was the first system to strike fire by mechanical means (Fig. I.4). Although faster and more reliable than the matchlock, it was far more complicated to produce. These manufacturing and cost limitations never permitted the wheel lock to achieve widespread military acceptance. However, it did provide horsemen with their first practical pistol and carbine. Most wheel locks saw use as sporting arms among the noblemen, but by the late 1600's they also had given way to the new flintlock system.

In retrospect, the primary advantages provided by the wheel lock were greater reliability, added safety, transportability while loaded, and the ability to be fired from horseback. Its inherent problems included the need for precision manufacture and expensive maintenance.

**THE FLINTLOCK:** About 1550 the ignition principle of "flint on steel" began its development in the Low Countries of Europe. This new action was essentially an extension of the contemporary method of striking the two together to make fire. The lock action was simple—a pivoted cock held a piece of flint between two jaws; when the trigger was pulled, this cock snapped forward to hit a steel face and shower sparks down into an open pan filled with priming powder. Like the matchlock, the powder then ignited, shot flame through the touchhole, and set off the main charge. Although a seemingly haphazard arrangement, it was far more reliable than might be supposed. This new mechanism was to be the basic weapon of the American Revolution and to remain the principal military arm in North America and Europe until the 1840's. During these three hundred years, the flintlock appeared in four basic variations:
1. The Snaphaunce
2. The English Lock
3. The Miquelet
4. The French or "True" Flintlock

THE SNAPHAUNCE: The earliest flint and steel system of which we are aware is the snaphaunce. It came into being in the Low Countries about 1550 and quickly spread through the rest of Europe. The basic action of the lock was similar to the flint style described above. Its fundamental difference was that the steel battery which the flint struck was separate from the pan cover. The flat cover was slid clear of the pan at the time of firing—initially by hand, and later by mechanical means. The word "snaphaunce" is believed derived from the Dutch word *schnapp-hahn* or "pecking fowl" (referring to the pecking action of the cock). Originally this term applied to all flint ignition arms, but its current meaning (i.e., this type of lock only) will be used here.

Advantages of the snaphaunce included less cost to produce and maintain than the wheel lock; greater reliability and faster firing than the matchlock; and the fact that it could be carried while loaded and primed. Among its drawbacks were the still complicated lock action and the absence of a safety position for the cock while loading. Rapid advancements in the flint system by the new "English Lock" soon eclipsed the snaphaunce by the 1620's.

THE "ENGLISH LOCK": Refinements in the flint system accelerated firearm development during the early 1600's. One of the major steps forward was the "English lock," which ushered in two innovations. First, the separate frizzen and pan cover of the snaphaunce were combined into one piece on a single pivot. Secondly, features were added to secure the cock in a locked

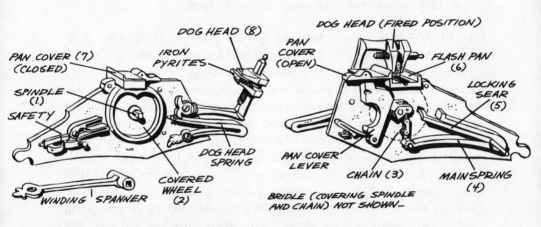

**I.4 WHEEL LOCK ACTION:** A "spanner" is fitted over SPINDLE #1 and turned to wind up WHEEL #2. This turning wraps CHAIN #3 around the Spindle, pulling up on the MAIN SPRING #4. SEAR #5 also moves sideways through the lock plate into a hole in the Wheel, locking it under tension. The DOG HEAD #8 (holding an iron pyrites in its jaws) is then lowered against the top of the sliding PAN COVER #7, which covers PAN #6. Pulling the trigger retracts SEAR #5, allowing the Wheel to spin—automatically sliding back the Pan Cover. The Dog Head's pyrites is now forced down through a slit in the Pan and against the rough edges of the spinning Wheel. This sends a shower of sparks into the priming powder of the flashpan, igniting the main charge through the touchhole in the barrel.

6

## I.5 WHEEL LOCK MUSKET                                  Circa 1600-1630

This early German-made military wheel lock includes a heavy flared butt plus a simple trigger guard. Its barrel is octagonal at the breech (ending after 17⅜″ at an ornamental ring), and is pinned to the stock. The elaborate lock mechanism required for this system is seen in the photograph.

| Length: 60¾″ | Tr. Guard: 7½″ | Furniture: Iron |
| Barrel: 47⅛″; .76 | Butt Tang: 1⅞″ | Weight: 15.5 lbs. |
| Lock: 9½″ × 3¼″ | | |

*Jac Weller Collection*

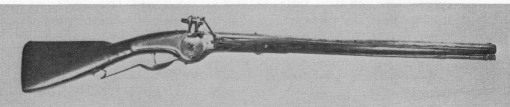

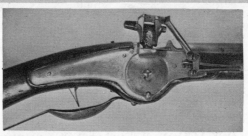

## I.6 WHEEL LOCK CARBINE                                 Circa 1670-1680

The wheel lock provided mounted troops with a weapon they could carry in a loaded state and fire from horseback. This example has a German stamping, but is typical of many used in England and the Low Countries. Notice the encased lock and cupped trigger guard.

| Length: 38⅜″ | Tr. Guard: 9″ | Furniture: Iron |
| Barrel: 25⅛″; .62 | | Weight: 4.5 lbs. |
| Lock: 7½″ × 2⅜″ | | |

*John K. Watson Collection*

position prior to firing. One of these was a sear moving horizontally out through a hole in the lock plate to hold the cock back in its firing position until the trigger was pulled. The more popular method was to mount a small dog catch on the outside of the lock behind the cock. This "dog" was then hooked manually into a notch in the rear of the cock to prevent it from slipping forward for a premature discharge while loading (Figs. I.11-I.13). The sear type of arrangement lost favor about 1650, but the dog-lock feature continued in use by the British even on later styles of locks until about 1720 (Figs. M.1-M.4).

This "English lock" found wide acceptance with the military, especially the English, because of its simpler, more reliable, and safer mechanism. It was still complicated by its many moving parts, however, and lost popularity after 1650 to the new flintlock system from France.

MIQUELET: Coincident with the evolution of the encased lock action, another variation came into being along the shores of the Mediterranean. It has since been called the "miquelet." Believed to have been introduced by Spain about 1620, it quickly found popularity in Italy by the 1650's. Like the English lock, it combined the pan cover and frizzen in one piece. The most noticeable difference, however, was the location of a mainspring on the outside of the lock plate. This meant that less wood had to be cut out of the stock for the lock's internal mechanism, and permitted a larger spring to

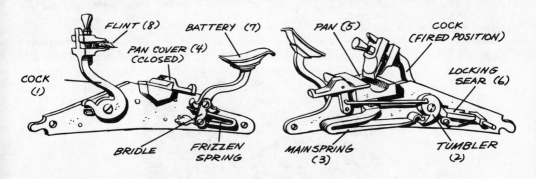

**I.7 SNAPHAUNCE LOCK ACTION:** Pulling back COCK #1 rotates its pivot (through the Lock Plate) and the attached TUMBLER #2 inside. This turning compresses the MAIN SPRING #3, and closes PAN COVER #4 over the PAN #5. When the Cock is pulled back into a cocked position, LOCKING SEAR #6 moves sideways to catch in a hole on the Cock's underside. Next, the BATTERY #7 is lowered into position over the Pan. Pulling the trigger retracts the Locking Sear, allowing the Cock to snap forward (automatically sliding back the Pan Cover) to hit the Battery with its FLINT #8. The resulting sparks spray into the priming powder of the Pan, firing the main charge through the touchhole in the barrel.

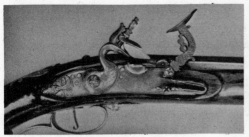

## I.8 SNAPHAUNCE LOCK                                    Circa 1610-1630

The snaphaunce lock of an Italian musket is shown at the left. Its large steel battery and thin flashpan cover are visible. Arms of this type saw only limited service in America.

*Edmund W. Budde, Jr., Collection*

## I.9 MIQUELET LOCK                                      Circa 1740-1760

The miquelet lock (right) continued in use by the Spanish through the eighteenth century as pictured on this musket (see M.50).

*Jac Weller Collection*

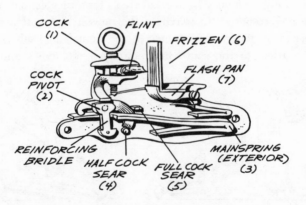

**I.10 MIQUELET LOCK ACTION:** When COCK #1 is pulled back, it rotates on PIVOT #2 and compresses MAIN SPRING #3 (on outside of lock). This cocking action causes two sears to move sideways through the lock plate to the outside. The lower HALF-COCK SEAR #4 comes out under the Cock's lower arm, locking it in a "safe" or "half-cock" position. When rotated further for firing, the Cock's lower arm catches on the higher FULL-COCK SEAR #5. As the trigger is pulled, both sears retract, and the Cock snaps forward—hitting the FRIZZEN #6. The blow springs the Frizzen upward, as the sparks from hitting the flint drop into the priming powder of the PAN #7 below. The resulting flash reaches the main barrel charge through the touchhole.

better utilize the poorer quality flint available in those countries. The miquelet continued in use until about 1825, and flourished even longer as a trade lock for the nations of the eastern Mediterranean.

"TRUE" FLINTLOCK: What was to prove the ultimate flint action and reign for more than two hundred years is believed to have been perfected by Jean or Marin LeBourgeoys (brothers) of Lisieux, France, between 1600 and 1610. It simplified existing actions in two principal ways: the horizontally moving safety sear of the English lock was replaced with a new vertical sear, which operated wholly within the lock to engage notches cut into the tumbler (attached to the cock). In addition, a second notch was provided in the tumbler to permit a safety half-cock position (Fig. I.14). There is little evidence to show that this new action was made outside of France prior to 1640, but by 1660 it had gained recognition throughout Europe as the new military lock.

## AMERICAN COLONIAL FIREARMS

To the early American colonist, weapons were vital for survival. While in Europe firearms were used for sport or for formal warfare by professional armies, in America the early settler required them for feeding and defending his own family. Evidence from excavated sites indicates that many stretched their meager resources to purchase the newest and best arms available— often ahead of general acceptance in the homeland itself. Although early Spanish settlers to the south first employed crossbows and varied arms,

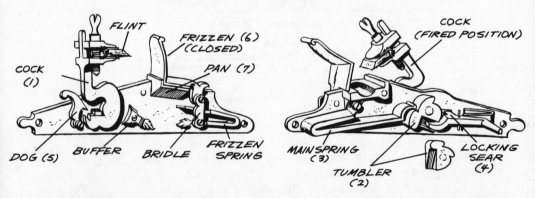

I.11 ENGLISH DOG-LOCK ACTION: First, the COCK #1 is pulled back, rotating its pivot and the attached inside TUMBLER #2. This compresses MAINSPRING #3 and allows LOCKING SEAR #4 to move sideways through the lock plate and engage the end of the Cock. The outside DOG #5 is also latched onto the tail of the Cock. To fire, this outside Dog is disengaged by hand. Pulling the trigger retracts the Locking Sear letting the Cock spring forward, striking and lifting FRIZZEN #6, and sending sparks down onto the priming powder in the PAN #7 below.

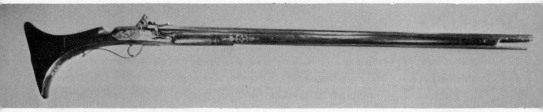

## I.12 DOG-LOCK MUSKET                                    Circa 1650

The full-length photograph shown here is a "middle"-period dog lock on an English flared-butt ("Spanish style") military musket. It has a three-screw lock, no side plate, and an octagonal barrel.

*Lewis H. Gordon, Jr., Collection*

## I.13 DOG LOCK                                          Circa 1630-1650

These close-up pictures show an early English dog lock, which includes both the horizontal sear and the dog latch. Notice, too, the simple trigger-guard construction.

*Anthony D. Darling Collection*

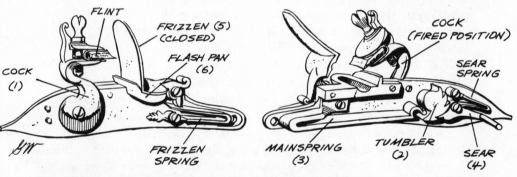

**I.14 TRUE (FRENCH) FLINTLOCK:** Pulling back COCK #1 rotates its pivot and the attached TUMBLER #2. This compresses MAINSPRING #3, and when reaching the half-cock position, the sharp edge of SEAR #4 slides into the first notch of the Tumbler (loading position). For firing, the Cock is pulled back further until the Sear catches in the second notch of the Tumbler. Squeezing the trigger raises the horizontal arm of Sear and disengages its edge from the Tumbler notch. The Cock then snaps forward, hitting the FRIZZEN #5 with its flint, and dropping sparks into the priming powder of the PAN #6. Its flash ignites the main charge through the touchhole in the barrel.

the English colonists arriving in the 1600's relied principally upon match-locks. Apparently the expensive wheel lock also found limited use here. Little evidence of the snaphaunce has been uncovered, however. Some believe that its development was followed so closely by the English lock that it did not have time to gain acceptance.

Dependence upon the matchlock as the colonists' major arm seems to have ended by 1630, as the new dog-lock flint musket proved its superiority. Continual local warfare soon led to virtual abandonment of the matchlock by the 1680's. The French version was gaining distribution in Europe and promptly received consideration in the colonies. It replaced most English dog locks by 1690. (The mother country did not achieve this until after 1700.)

## FURTHER WEAPON DEVELOPMENTS

As the eighteenth century approached, the rash of firearm innovations was reaching a climax. The new French type of lock was proving relatively inexpensive to produce and far more trustworthy in the field. Muskets were better balanced and lighter to carry; bore diameters were becoming standardized, while russetting (or browning) provided better anti-rust protection. The internal bridle for strengthening the lock's tumbler action also made its appearance.

These weapon improvements led, in turn, to revisions of standard European military tactics. The old clumsy bandolier too gave way to paper cartridges, which increased firepower as much as three times. The major change, however, began with the introduction of the bayonet by the French about 1660. It was essentially a large knife with a round tapered grip. The soldier simply forced it into the muzzle of his gun for use as a spear. The firearm and blade were now combined. Until this period the classic European formation had been built around cold steel. Musketmen had been only supplementary to the hard core of shock troops—solid lines of pikemen, massed six ranks deep behind sixteen-foot pikes.

With the end of the 1600's, these last vestiges of medieval days vanished from the scene. The new flintlock musket and bayonet were now acknowledged rulers of the field, destined to shape empires for the next 140 years.

# 2 | EIGHTEENTH-CENTURY WARFARE ... LINES OF MUSKETS

THE GREAT MOTIVATION drawing most colonists to America during the 1600's was land—the opportunity to own a farm or shop of their own. Tightly held estates and the traditional law of primogeniture in Europe helped induce many of these ambitious individuals to risk everything in the New World. For more than three centuries, this insatiable hunger for self-betterment would push settlements ever westward across three thousand miles of continent.

Their first opponents were the Indians, and then the French. As trails unraveled to the west, it was only a matter of time before they began to threaten France's coveted north-south line of control. Beginning in Canada, it extended from Lake Erie, down the Ohio and Mississippi rivers to New Orleans. The inevitable result in the eighteenth century was protracted warfare with France until 1763. Even then, a "proclamation line" by the English themselves prohibiting further settlement west of the Alleghenies proved futile, and evoked bitter fighting during Pontiac's Uprising (1763–1765), and the final Revolution itself.

**TWO SOCIETIES:** As Europeans poured into America, the population burgeoned from 250,000 in 1700 to some 2,500,000 in 1775. From about 1710 to the outbreak of the Revolutionary War, Germans and Scotch-Irish formed the bulk of this western movement. The coastal areas by now were relatively civilized—land had been cleared, the Indians had retreated, and a pseudo "Old World" atmosphere began to emerge in the growing cities. The existence of two such radically different ways of life between the frontier and coastal settlements was to continue until the early 1900's—affecting politics, living habits, weapons, and military tactics. The eastern seaboard now found little need for the fighting methods they had first developed against Indians, and emphasized use of the smoothbore musket with the standard formations of European armies. The frontiersman, however, had no choice—fighting more as an individual, using natural cover, and favoring his long rifle.

## NEW MILITARY TECHNIQUES

The coming of a new century in 1700 also brought with it revised military standards throughout Europe. Chiefly responsible was final abandonment of

13

the pike as the basic infantry weapon. The flintlock musket, with its new socket bayonet, was now the maker of kings. Its characteristics of performance evolved new linear tactics, which because of their need for absolute discipline, led to the supplanting of local militia by standing armies of professionals.

**FLINTLOCK MUSKET CHARACTERISTICS:** The infantryman of the 1700's usually carried a long-barreled (40 to 46 inches), large-caliber (.65 to .80), smoothbore flintlock musket. It was easily loaded from the muzzle (3 to 5 rounds per minute), heavy (8 to 12 pounds), with a stud on the end of the barrel for its bayonet. An indication of accuracy is the fact that virtually none of them were ever equipped with a rear sight. Although the ball it fired could theoretically carry for some 300 yards, the average long arm provided little accuracy past 80 yards, and was not very effective against massed troops beyond 150 yards. This limitation was due in part to the black powder. In addition to changing performance according to the local temperature and humidity, it would cake inside the barrel with successive shots, steadily reducing the effective diameter and the ability to reload quickly. As a result, the ball used was generally cast substantially smaller than the bore size (.05 to .10 inch less). This allowed it to better slide down the barrel, but permitted gas leakage around the circumference during ignition. The bullet's glancing against alternate sides of the smoothbore barrel on the way out was the final guarantee of an erratic flight.

The cartridge used was simply a measured amount of loose powder and a round ball wrapped in paper (Figs. IV.10–IV.12). The soldier would normally tear the paper with his teeth, tap a small portion of powder into the flashpan of his lock (with the cock at the half-cock "safety" position), and then pour the main part of the charge down the muzzle of his weapon, followed by the lead ball. He might leave the paper wrapping around the ball to act as a better gas seal, or tamp it above the bullet as a protective wadding (if the weapon was to be carried for a period before firing). The total charge was then "seated" against the breech with his rammer. Next, the cock was pulled back to full-cock position and fired.

Because of the many motions required for loading and ignition, each step was rigidly defined and inculcated into the soldier. The firing was done together and "by the number."

**LINEAR BATTLEFIELD TACTICS:** As would seem natural, troop formations and maneuvers were adjusted in the early 1700's to best profit from both the advantages and defects of the new flint smoothbore musket. What evolved from the old massed formations is called "linear tactics." They consisted of long lines of opposing men firing in volleys and then closing to clash with bayonets. The usual procedure called for infantry to march onto the battlefield in columns and deploy into a line. This line was normally made up of three closely grouped ranks (Americans often used two ranks), with a thin line of "file closers" about six feet to the rear as replacements for casualties. Locations on the flanks were considered posts of honor and jealously sought after. During the American Revolution, the British grenadier and light infantry regiments were usually given these positions. Artillery was placed in line with the infantry, while the cavalry would be kept in the rear or on the extreme flanks until needed. By the time of the War for Independence, light troops were also employed as frontal skirmishers or scouts on the flanks.

The infantry stood erect, shoulder to shoulder, and fired together by command, after following the formal loading procedure. The second and third ranks would fire separate volleys. This massed firing to the front or to either oblique stressed patterns of firepower, and actually de-emphasized individual aiming.

The battle usually opened with the two lines 300 to 600 yards apart. Artillery would then commence firing, followed by one of the forces moving forward. Ranks were continuously dressed during the advance. When only 50 to 100 yards away from the defenders, they would halt and deliver a volley, which was answered by the other line. Firing then continued (3 to 5 rounds per minute) until one force decided to charge with the bayonet. This close-quarter fighting, coupled with the timely use of the cavalry and reserves, would finally decide the winner. The key to this type of warfare was speed—the ability to deliver a greater shock to your enemy than he could inflict upon you. This demanded speed in firing and speed in advancing—to minimize the number of volleys he could pour into your formation.

**PROFESSIONAL TROOPS:** To maintain control of a line standing up to continuous musket fire or a bayonet charge required iron discipline. The result was a de-emphasizing of the traditional militia forces in favor of full-time professional armies. These regulars were bound to a brutally inflexible system built around close-order drill. The soldier literally received a worse fate from his own superiors if he turned and ran than he did by facing the enemy. (British disdain for the colonists' discipline early in the American Revolution often led them to charge without firing a shot.)

**COLONIAL MILITIA:** During the 1600's no regular troops were available in the colonies, and "train bands" were formed for defense. By the 1700's, areas of danger had followed the frontier westward, and they evolved into local militia units. Although such standard British texts as *A Treatise of Military Discipline* and *Norfolk Discipline* were used in their drills, most units had a minimum of training. Each colony considered the militia as its own separate army, and muster days often deteriorated into community holidays.

As the fighting broke out with France in the 1700's for control of North America, more and more reliance was placed upon the British regulars—while the individualistic American provincials gradually found themselves relegated to supporting roles. The British, too, were learning about the differences between fighting in the open fields of Europe and the American wilderness. In the 1750's and 1760's, new light infantry and light dragoons were created to better provide intelligence and security in wooded country. For extended campaigns, colonial troops were usually recruited as individuals from among the militia (by inducements of bounties, high pay, weapons, freedom from further impressment, clothing, etc.). Although loosely organized, the militia system did provide a hierarchy of command and a universally armed citizenry, which served as the nucleus of the Continental Army in 1775. Furthermore, most of the American leaders had been trained with British troops during the French and Indian Wars. The task before them was to build a disciplined force to face the English regulars in the linear tactics of open battle, while the British were working to add more light troops to meet the colonists in rough country.

**STANDARD WEAPONS:** Acceptance of the flintlock as the basic weapon of the eighteenth century also led toward standardization of military muskets. The first recognized French model appeared in 1717; Britain's Brown Bess was adopted in the mid-1720's. Prior to this time most European governments had bought arms from individual contractors, letting them arrange the details of manufacture. As a rule, only the barrel length and approximate bore size had been specified. Now the complete pattern, including the stock and furniture, was being given standard dimensions.

**EARLY MARKINGS:** Early weaponmaking was mostly in the hands of individual armorers and gunsmiths, many of whom stamped their own devices into the finished arm. These markings varied from animal and human figures to initials and heraldic insignia. As the use of firearms increased, controls toward greater uniformity and safer construction evolved. Initially, standard marks were adopted by the individual guilds or arms-making centers, e.g. Belgium's Liège, Germany's Suhl, France's Saint-Étienne, Spain's Eibar, Russia's Tula, or Italy's Brescia. By the 1600's, many of these stampings had come to signify certain proofing procedures. Yet, the growth was gradual, and some countries did not adopt a real system of control until the nineteenth century. Because of this it is difficult to trace properly the source of many of the weapons used during our colonial period.

ENGLISH PROOFING: Britain was the first nation to really adopt a standard proof house. In 1637, the Gunmakers Company of London was incorporated, and authorized to "search for and seize" any firearms within ten miles of London which were considered below standard. In 1672, a new charter was granted them to enforce proofing in all of England. Their marks signified specific tests for the barrel during two stages of its manufacture. First was the firing of a charge when the barrel had just been bored in the rough state (mark: a crown over V for "viewed"); the second test came with the barrel in its finished state (mark: a crown over the connected letters GP, for "gunmakers' proof"). In each case, the test load was a powder charge of twice the normal amount, with a standard-size ball.

Since these regulations applied to firearms which were sold commercially, most early military weapons were not affected. By the time of the Brown Bess (1720's), however, government requirements included another mark showing a broad arrow under a royal crown. This was stamped on the lock plate beneath the flashpan to denote government ownership. A crown above "GR" and a broad arrow served as a government view stamp on the barrel—along with a crown above crossed scepters as the proof. Inside the lock plate usually appeared the inspector's or "viewer's" mark (a crown above his number). In the center of the lock on most military arms was inscribed a large royal crown with the initials of the reigning monarch (e.g. George I–George III used "GR" for "Georgius Rex"). On the tail of the lock plate was the name of the maker or armory, with the date of the lock's manufacture (note: often assembled into a weapon much later). In 1764, this marking of dates and individual contractor names was ordered stopped. Subsequent guns carried only the word TOWER (for the Royal Proofing House in the Tower of London). Many of these English arms also include in the rammer channel the initials of the stocker, plus a Roman numeral or "assembly number."

The gunmakers of Birmingham lacked an official proof house during the eighteenth century, and established private proofing facilities with their own marks. They were granted official recognition in 1813. Marks adopted at that time are a helpful way to identify postcolonial weapons (see Fig. II.2).

FRENCH PROOFING: The first testing procedure for French commercial guns dates from 1700 at Saint-Étienne. In 1728 and 1729, a formal proofing was also specified for military arms. It consisted of two shots from the barrel: the first had a powder load of the full weight of the ball (plus the ball and wadding); the second charge reduced the powder by one-fifth. The inspector then marked the barrel with his stamp (usually his initials). Final approval

17

# FRENCH MARKINGS

A        B        C

II.1 (*a*) Lock markings: "AR" for Inspector DESJARDINS (1718–1755); "MBE" for the Royal Manufactory at *MAUBEUGE*. (*b*) A Charleville mark. (*c*) "SE" for Saint-Étienne Manufactory.

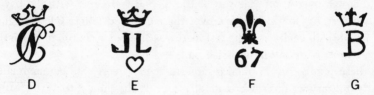

D        E        F        G

(*d*) *Ca.* 1728 barrel marking. (*e*) *Ca.* 1728 barrel marking. (*f*) The "67" indicates the last two digits of the year of manufacture, i.e., 1767. (*g*) A controller's mark (lock and barrel); B is his initial.

# OTHER EUROPEAN MARKINGS

H        I        J        K        L

(*h*) Liège, Belgium, 1672–1810, and 1835–present. (*i*) Liège, Belgium, 1810–present (a crown was added in 1893). (*j*) Amsterdam control mark (on barrels). (*k*) Denmark and Norway (*ca.* 1746–1766). (*l*) HEN—county of Henneberg; "SVL"—marking for the city of Suhl (Henneberg county, Germany).

M        N        O

(*m*) Typical Spanish marking (on barrel). (*n*) Running wolf mark; originally Passau and Solingen (Germany), later copied across Europe (sword blades). (*o*) Shotley Bridge (English sword blades).

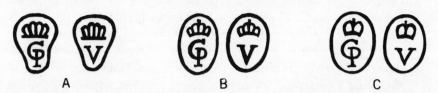

II.2 (a) London proofmarks, 1637 (usually on the barrel). (b) London proofs, 1672-style. (c) London proofs, 1702 version. Note: The "V" stamp signified the first "rough proofing ("viewing"); "GP" ("gunmaker's proof") was the final proof.

(d) Barrel proofs used in the Royal Armory. (e) Typical Birmingham private proofs prior to 1813. (f) Birmingham proofs adopted in 1813.

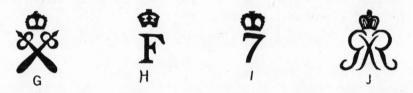

(g) Board of Ordnance "private" proof (struck twice on barrel), Tower of London (for a fee). (h) "Foreigner's" mark; proof by London Gunmakers for nonmembers [used with two regular proofs (a)-(c) above]; post-1741. (i) "Viewer's" (inspector's) mark for government arms (the number indicates the inspector). (j) Ordnance Storekeeper's stamp; usually on the side of the butt; used after 1770 (but retroactive to many earlier weapons).

(k) Board of Ordnance ownership mark (mostly on stock); replaced by "WD" (War Departme₁ ₍) in 1855. (l) Government ownership stamp (mostly on lock plates). (m) Royal cipher for *Georgius Rex* (George I–George III); used under a crown on lock plates and on sword blades. (n) Royal cipher during Queen Anne's reign (1702–1714). (o) East India Company "bale" mark (usually on the stock or barrel). Note: The sizes of these illustrations are not to scale.

in the second half of the 1700's consisted of striking the barrel with the last two digits of the current year. In 1766, new rules further required the marking of the gun's model year on the barrel tang (e.g. "M1777"), plus the name of the respective manufactory on the face of the lock plate. There were three principal manufacturing sources supplying the French arms used by Americans in the 1700's: Saint-Étienne, Charleville, and Maubeuge.

AMERICAN PROOFING: Virtually no formal proofing regulations existed in the colonies previous to the American Revolution. Even then, they varied by state, and most arms remained unmarked.

Among marks believed to have seen some use during the war were: "CR" (Rhode Island); "MB" (Massachusetts Bay); "SC" (Connecticut); "SP" (New Jersey); "NH" (New Hampshire). The popular mark "CP" is now considered by most collectors to be a post-Revolution stamping from Pennsylvania.

On February 24, 1777, Congress authorized the marking of all government-owned arms and accouterments. The ones most commonly seen on surviving weapons are US, U:STATES, and UNITED STATES (on both stock and metal components). This practice did not apply to state or personal weapons. Note: "US" stampings continued in use into the nineteenth century (although usually smaller in size).

# 3 | THE AMERICAN REVOLUTION ... ANY LOCK, STOCK, AND BARREL —THAT FIRES

AT THE OUTBREAK of the American War for Independence, the colonists' basic difficulty was the lack of an effective central organization to harness their available resources. Most colonies adopted constitutions which assigned the basic powers of government to their own state legislatures. Congress could do little more than request and persuade. Without any real authority, it had to rely upon boards and committees to perform its executive functions. This led to decisions by compromise—further compounded by the colonists' traditional fear of creating a strong military class. The result of these diverse and uncoordinated efforts was a Continental Army which undoubtedly could not have survived without the equipment supplied by France.

**MILITARY ORGANIZATION:** The American forces were basically modeled after the British Army, consisting of infantry, artillery, and some cavalry. The regiments usually served under one of three classifications. The "Continental Line" were the dependable regulars—controlled and paid by Congress (usually for a period of two or more years). The "State Forces" were regular troops supported by the individual states. Their periods of service usually ran from one to two years. The third group were the militia, which mustered from their homes for a few weeks or months when danger threatened locally. Although they were not reliable in pitched battles, their large numbers helped to keep the English from trying to occupy much land beyond the major cities.

The British troops, consisting of their own regulars, mercenaries from several German landgraves, and the locally recruited Tory regiments, were well organized, but had to depend upon a three-thousand-mile supply route. Their officers usually followed the established practice of purchasing commissions. On the other hand, American company officers were mostly elected by their men, while the regimental officers were appointed by the state raising the unit. General officers above colonel were normally commissioned by Congress.

21

**WEAPON PROCUREMENT:** The muskets carried by American troops during nine years of fighting came from four principal sources:

1. ARMS ALREADY OWNED BY THE COLONISTS: This category included a great variety of weapons, ranging from long-barreled fowling pieces and Pennsylvania rifles to European military muskets acquired during the French and Indian War. Many were the products of American gunsmiths, but most of them still included some European parts. To the practical colonist it was still far cheaper to import or reuse foreign components (especially locks and barrels) than to make them himself.

2. CAPTURED WEAPONS: Many arms were seized from Royal Arsenals and military installations at the start of hostilities. These, with personally owned British muskets from the French and Indian Wars, made the Brown Bess our principal infantry weapon until about 1778, when the French Charleville became the most common shoulder arm among line regiments.

3. MILITARY MUSKETS CONTRACTED FOR BY THE VARIOUS LOCAL COMMITTEES OF SAFETY, STATE GOVERNMENTS, AND THE CONTINENTAL CONGRESS: Specifications by the various governmental bodies varied in such things as barrel length and bore size, but most were close copies of the familiar Brown Bess pattern. In spite of all of these efforts, however, by the latter part of 1775, procurement agents were eagerly gathering almost any gun that could be fired. Even in the spring of 1776, many in Washington's army had not yet acquired muskets.

4. FOREIGN ARMS IMPORTED FROM EUROPE: Early in 1776, Congress sent Silas Deane to Paris, where he was shortly joined by Benjamin Franklin and Arthur Lee. They, with other state agents, made arrangements wherever possible to purchase and ship arms to America. The greatest number (totaling over 100,000) was sent from France. By March of 1777 the first delivery of 12,000 French muskets arrived in Portsmouth, New Hampshire, and another ship with 11,000 came into Philadelphia. It is interesting to note that Britain also found it necessary to purchase arms on the Continent during this period. A great proportion of the German mercenaries, for example, carried Dutch weapons.

## III.1 AMERICAN MILITIAMAN                                              Circa 1775

This farmer is typical of the militiamen who answered the call at Lexington-Concord, and whenever an enemy threatened their locality. He wears civilian clothes, including an old military waistcoat from the French and Indian War—plus a British double frog (*ca.* 1751) suspended from his waist belt (with a hunting sword replacing the usual hanger). Note too the common flat-brimmed hat, long semimilitary fowler, powder horn, and hunting bag.

**III.2 PRIVATE, AMERICAN LINE REGIMENT**                    **Circa 1777**

This member of the 3rd New Jersey Line Regiment has the black felt cocked hat turned on his head to minimize interference when shouldering his newly arrived French musket. Other accouterments are a single-strap knapsack (painted), leather cartridge box (linen sling), plus a bayonet and canteen. The dark blue coat has red facings, cuffs, and turnbacks. His breeches are also dark blue; the waistcoat and yarn stockings vary in color.

G. WOODBRIDGE

**III.3 OFFICER, AMERICAN LINE REGIMENT**          **Circa 1779-1783**

This captain of the Massachusetts Line wears a uniform of the style sent from France late in the war. His state uniform was dark blue with white facings, lining, cuffs, and turnbacks. The black fur felt hat includes the American black cockade plus the white one added when France entered the war. His overalls would be of white wool, bleached linen, or canvas; the officer sash is scarlet. Note too the typical small sword and long spontoon.

G. WOODBRIDGE

## III.4 AMERICAN RIFLEMAN                                     Circa 1778

The classic frontiersman is illustrated here. He wears a round hat (note buck's tail) plus a fringed linen hunting shirt and overalls. Arms include the famous Pennsylvania long rifle (with a wooden patch box), a knife, and often a belt ax. The powder horn, hunting bag, and bullet-loading block are also shown. A wooden "barrel-type" canteen hangs from a shoulder sling, and he carries a nondescript fur tote bag. Note: The coonskin hat was a rarity in the Revolution.

### III.5 AMERICAN SEAMAN

**Circa 1776-1783**

Most American naval fighting was done by privateers. This seaman is dressed in a contemporary manner—the flat black hat, short jacket (probably gray or green), waistcoat, loose trousers, and a kerchief about the neck. He is armed with an English sea service pistol (held to the waist belt by a belt hook) and an American copy of the standard British straight-bladed cutlass.

## III.6 AMERICAN LIGHT DRAGOON

Circa 1779

An American horseman is pictured here in the uniform of Moylan's 4th Regiment. His hard leather helmet has a crest of white horsehair (frequently bearskin). Arms include a cut-down Brown Bess musket (suspended from a white buff leather carbine sling), an American saber (note the sword knot to slip over the wrist), and a "belly" cartridge box. He wears a green coat (faced with red), a red waistcoat, green cloth or deerskin breeches (with knee wrappings), and heavy boots.

## III.7 PRIVATE, GERMAN GRENADIERS
Circa 1776

The Grenadier Regiment Von Roll was one of the units surprised at Trenton. Their uniforms were apparently poorly made. This one includes a typical metal-fronted grenadier cap. He is also wearing a blue coat with applied red facings and turnbacks, a white waistcoat, light buff breeches, and black linen or wool leggings. His arms include a Dutch-style musket, large pommeled German hanger, and a leather cartridge box (formerly for grenades)—mounting a "cipher trophy plate" and grenade insignia.

G WOODBRIDGE

## III.8 ROYAL HIGHLAND REGIMENT                                Circa 1776

Shown here is a battalion company man (private) of the 42nd Regiment. The bonnet is dark blue, with black ostrich feathers. His red coat is faced with dark blue, its turnbacks and lining are white, and the braid is white with a red stripe. Notice too the government (tartan) belted plaid, red and white diced hose, red garters, and leather purse (sporran). His arms are a shortened musket and bayonet—plus the famous Highland backsword, dirk, and pistol (discontinued for active campaigning here in 1776).

## III.9 SERGEANT, BRITISH GRENADIERS                    Circa 1776

This grenadier sergeant in the 17th Regiment of Foot wears a black bearskin cap. The red coat (grayish-white facings, cuffs, and turnbacks) includes grenadier shoulder "wings" (bottom fringe denotes a sergeant). His waistcoat, breeches, and stockings are white, while the spatterdashes are of black linen (later wool). Also note the braided hair tucked under the cap (a grenadier and dragoon practice); a red worsted sergeant's sash; the traditional matchbox on a white buff leather crossbelt; plus the Brown Bess musket, "1751" hanger, and bayonet.

# 4 | MUSKETS AND OTHER SHOULDER ARMS

THE PRINCIPAL WEAPON of the eighteenth century was the flint-lock shoulder arm. Basic types believed to have been used in America from 1700 to 1783 are described and illustrated in this chapter. They are grouped into five general categories:

1. Military Muskets
2. Carbines
3. Fusils
4. Blunderbusses
5. Wall or Rampart Guns

## MILITARY MUSKETS

**BRITISH MUSKETS:** During the last decade of the seventeenth century, King William III sought every available source to arm his troops fighting on several fronts. The muskets which flowed from Germany, Austria, Italy, Scandinavia, the Low Countries, and England herself were generally close to .75 caliber, but varied considerably in other specifics. With the beginning of Queen Anne's reign (1702–1714), this conglomeration of military weapons began to evolve toward a system of controlled patterns. Major British steps in this development will be outlined chronologically by decade. It should be remembered, however, that most changes were in motion for years prior to and following the dates listed:

(1700-1710)
• The pike was finally discarded as the chief infantry arm in favor of the musket and bayonet.
• (1707) A standard 46-inch barrel length was specified; the old requirement for a combination octagonal-round barrel was rescinded. (Most British musket barrels would be round for the rest of the century.)
• The dog lock was losing favor, as the new "true" flintlock with its goose-neck cock gained popular acceptance.
• The entire stock and barrel was still painted black in many cases, although more barrels were now being browned ("russeted").

32

(1710-1720)

• New iron-mounted Queen Anne muskets marked a step closer to the final Brown Bess pattern of the 1720's.

• The dog lock virtually disappeared, and most flat-lock plates were changed to a rounded surface.

• Other innovations included: an escutcheon plate, a rammer tail pipe, and a cast butt plate (to replace the flat nailed style).

(1720-1730)

• (1722) The regimental colonel was instructed to supply his men with long arms equal to or better than standard specifications. Until the 1750's, this officer usually functioned as a contractor; i.e., he would recruit a regiment and equip it himself with a financial grant from the government. In fact, he seldom took the field with his men, leaving active command to a professional lieutenant colonel. These regiments were often named after the colonel. (Numerical designations were required by the 1750's.)

• (1722) The first official mention of a 42-inch barrel was recorded, but apparently found little acceptance until the 1740's.

• (1720-1725) At about this time emerged the famous Brown Bess musket, which would serve as the standard arm until the 1830's. Although its furniture initially appeared in iron, the familiar brass fittings were already established before 1730. This first model (46-inch barrel) is called the long-land pattern (M.7-M.10).

(1730-1740)

• Remaining pieces of the early iron furniture were used up by about 1736, and brass continued as the accepted style.

(1740-1750)

• (1741-1745) Wartime demands forced England to buy more than eighteen thousand muskets and bayonets from other European countries.

• (1741) The raised carvings around the locks began to disappear (war production).

• (1741) Orders stated that no further military muskets would be accepted lacking outside bridles. (Most old ones were then sent to the colonies.)

(1750-1760)

• By this decade the button-headed iron rammer had replaced most of the earlier brass-tipped wooden style, and a large flared forward pipe had been added (to speed return of the rammer).

• The curved banana-shaped lock was steadily getting straighter along its bottom edge.

• Muskets with 42-inch barrels were rapidly gaining acceptance. Early versions had simply shortened the existing 46-inch barrels, but now the furniture was also being modified. Two early variations appearing in this trend were the militia and marine model (M.19) and the naval musket (M.20–M.23).

(1760-1770)

• (1764) The names of contractors and dates of manufacture were ordered dropped from lock plates. Only the word TOWER was allowed to remain on the tail. (Note: Judging from several examples, many earlier markings were apparently filed off and TOWER reinscribed at this time. Stampings also began to replace engraving in this period.)

• (1768) The 42-inch-barrel version of the Brown Bess was officially adopted as the new infantry arm (flat side plate, shorter butt tang; see M.11-M.13). It is referred to as the short-land pattern. (Actually, some 46-inch-barrel-length long-land muskets were still assembled until 1790.)

(1770-1780)

• A flat-sided tang on the cock, and a flared second rammer pipe appeared. The bottom edge of the lock was now almost a straight line.

• Although the short-land pattern was the recognized official arm of the period, most earlier styles also saw service on both sides during the American Revolution.

**FRENCH MUSKETS:** Unlike the British Brown Bess, French muskets of the 1700's underwent continual modification. To best understand these innovations, specific models will be described:

(MODEL 1717) This was the first officially standardized French shoulder arm. Like virtually all of their muskets, the furniture was iron, and the bore, .69 caliber. Other details included the lock: flat, 6½ inches long, gooseneck cock, distinctive vertical bridle between frizzen and frizzen spring screws; barrel: octagonal-round, 46¾ inches long, pinned (one center band), top bayonet stud; furniture: four rammer pipes, flat curving side plate, butt tang about 6 inches; sling swivels on side (one behind side plate, other on side of lone barrel band), iron-strip nose cap; high comb on curving butt; wooden rammer (iron-tipped). (See M.24.)

(MODEL 1728) The above dimensions also applied here, except that three bands were now used to secure the barrel, and a new horizontal bridle extended from the pan to the frizzen screw (M.25).

(MODEL 1746) In this year, the flat lock with the gooseneck cock continued, but the outside bridle was dropped. A new button-headed iron rammer replaced the earlier wooden one. Other dimensions remained similar to the 1728 model (M.26).

(MODEL 1754) The sling swivels were now moved under the stock, and a retaining spring was added behind the middle band. Its iron rammer was trumpet-shaped (M.27).

(MODEL 1763) This musket ushered in the style most familiar to Americans during the Revolutionary War. For the first time since the seventeenth century, the barrel length was cut (to 44¾ inches). Also included were the lock: flat, 6¾ inches long, reinforced cock, faceted pan with horizontal bridle; barrel: round (side flats at breech), 44¾ inches long, .69 caliber, bottom bayonet stud; furniture: three barrel bands (sight on rear strap of forward band), bottom lip on middle band, rear retaining springs for two upper bands, a long rammer spring extending back along the channel from the forward band to the middle one, a flat curved side plate, butt tang 2½ inches long, sling swivels underneath; stock outline squarer; trumpet-headed iron rammer (M.29).

(MODEL 1766) Within this two-year span, the lock was reduced to 6¼ inches, the stock was slimmed, its middle band's lower lip removed, the iron rammer reverted to a buttonhead style, and a sloping tail was added to the forward band (M.30).

(CIRCA 1768) A retaining spring now appeared behind the bottom band, the comb of the stock was thinned, and the bayonet stud was moved to the top. This pattern was copied for the American postwar 1795 model (M.31).

(MODEL 1774) By 1774, the lock plate and cock had acquired rounded surfaces, a rammer spring was attached to the bottom of the rear band, the middle band added a lower lip, its iron rammer became trumpet-shaped, the trigger guard was shortened, and the butt profile was lowered (M.33).

(MODEL 1777) This pattern was a major change. Its innovations included a noncorrosive brass flashpan, finger ridges on the trigger guard behind the bow, and a recessed cheek rest cut into the comb. A screw from the outside secured the upper band, while the middle band was friction-fitted. Its bayonet stud was also relocated underneath (M.34).

**AMERICAN MUSKETS:** Although it is estimated that one-third of all arms in the colonies just prior to the Revolutionary War were made locally, there was no standardization. Barrels varied from bore sizes of .50 to .80, and lengths often exceeded 50 inches.

Despite official dimensions issued by most states in 1775, the colonists fought with whatever they had. The line troops used a preponderance of British-style weapons at first, but acquired a majority of French arms after shipments began to arrive later in the war. Militia and state forces, in turn, employed a wide variety of firearms—from long hunting fowlers to early dog-lock muskets (M.53-M.88).

**DUTCH-GERMAN MUSKETS:** The leading military power in Germany during the mid-1700's was Frederick the Great of Prussia. He relied heavily upon the Potsdam Arsenal, but most of the smaller landgraves who furnished troops to England for fighting in America (e.g., Hesse-Kassel, Hesse-Hanau, Brunswick, Anspach-Beyreuth, Anhalt-Zerbst), had little in the way of manufacturing facilities. Their mercenaries appear to have carried a variety of arms ranging from Prussian to Dutch patterns, including castoffs of their own arsenals (M.38-M.49).

## CARBINES

Today the carbine is considered a short-barreled shoulder weapon. During the 1700's, however, the term often referred to the inside diameter of the barrel. The English, for example, had three standard bore sizes: the musket (.75), the carbine (.65), and the pistol (.56). English barrel length for carbines ranged from 28 to 42 inches. Four typical types are described below:

1. The Light-Infantry Carbine
2. The Cavalry Carbine
3. The Artillery Carbine
4. The Heavy Dragoon Carbine

**BRITISH CARBINES** (Prior to 1756) Before this date there was no standardized shoulder arm for British cavalry. Their needs were usually met by cutting down the length of existing infantry muskets (barrel lengths apparently varied from about 28 to 42 inches). (M.94.)

(Light-Infantry Carbine) As a result of costly lessons learned from fighting against the French in North America during the 1740's and 1750's, new light-infantry units were formed. Their uniforms, accouterments, and weapons were simplified to facilitate operating in rough country, and led to the new light-infantry carbine by the mid-1750's. It was actually a slimmer version of the Brown Bess. The barrel remained at 42 inches, the stock was thinned, and the bore was reduced to .65 caliber (with a mounting stud for the bayonet). Some Highland regiments were also reported to have used carbines (M.92-M.93).

(CAVALRY OR LIGHT-HORSE CARBINE) The Warrant of 1756 added new troops of light dragoons to each regular dragoon regiment. It also specified their first standard carbine pattern. The total length was 51 inches, with a .65-caliber bore, plus a side bar and ring for attaching to the swivel on a shoulder belt. Some were made to carry bayonets (M.95-M.97).

In 1764, reference was made to a shorter cavalry arm with a 28-inch barrel. This apparently meant the Elliott carbine, which was officially recognized in 1773 (M.99). Other versions of horsemen's carbines were improvised for use during times of war, and some are pictured later in this chapter.

(ROYAL ARTILLERY CARBINE) A reliable contemporary description of this model does not seem to be available. It was apparently developed in the 1750's, and is believed to be of the type in illustration M.98. It is essentially the cavalry carbine of 1756 without the side bar.

(HEAVY DRAGOON CARBINE) This was an early 42-inch-barrel variation of the Brown Bess used by the dragoons from the 1740's until 1770. It usually had a regular musket bore (.75), wooden rammer, no nose cap, and long-land-pattern furniture. (Some received iron rammers, nose caps, and flared forward pipes in the 1750's and 1760's.) (M.101.) In 1770 they were exchanged for a light infantry style of carbine with a side bar whose forward end bent under the stock to fasten on the opposite side.

FRENCH CAVALRY CARBINES: Unlike England's three standard bores, France set the size at .69 caliber for muskets and .67 for carbines and pistols. This greatly eased production and supply problems. Their carbines were basically short arms, carried by mounted troops. Three typical cavalry styles (*mousquetons de cavalerie*) will be reviewed here.

(MODEL 1733) It measured 42½ to 45 inches long and was brass-mounted. The stock extended to the muzzle of a pinned barrel (30¾ inches; .67 caliber). Its flat lock had a gooseneck cock, with sling swivels mounted on the rear of the trigger guard and just behind the middle rammer pipe (M.105).

(MODEL 1766) This carbine followed most of the basic alterations seen in the muskets of the mid-1760 period. It was stocked to the muzzle and included three barrel bands of which the center one had two top straps (M.104).

(MODEL 1777) The major pattern innovations of the 1777 infantry musket were reflected in the carbine. Among them were the new brass flashpan, shorter trigger guard (with finger ridges), and the outside screw holding its forward band. The final eight inches of the barrel was left unstocked, and a side bar was included. These weapons were believed carried by France's Lauzun Legion, which fought here during the last years of the American Revolution.

**AMERICAN CARBINES:** Apparently there were no standard American carbines produced prior to or during the Revolutionary War. The light-infantry and mounted colonial units seem to have used British or French weapons, regular muskets, or simply cut-down long arms (M.102, M.103).

# FUSILS

The fusil (or "fusee") was lighter, shorter, and of smaller caliber than the regular shoulder weapon. It was essentially an officer's arm, made privately for him. Many were richly embellished, but did retain a basic resemblance to the prevailing infantry pattern. During the French and Indian Wars it gradually replaced the spontoon as the officers' weapon on both sides, and by the 1770's had also supplanted most of the sergeants' halberds (M.14–M.16; M.35–M.36; M.47–M.48; M.89–M.91).

# BLUNDERBUSSES

These short shoulder-stocked weapons with large bores and flared muzzles were mostly civilian arms. They found initial acceptance in the mid-1600's, and became more popular as growing overland travel increased highway banditry in the eighteenth century. Usually loaded with small shot, they were ideal for stopping a close group of men, or defending a door or stairway (although it has since been demonstrated that the size of the muzzle flare had little control of the shot pattern).

Their greatest military use was aboard ship, where the blunderbuss proved a handy weapon on crowded decks. The infantry, too, apparently employed limited numbers of them for such things as sentry duty, signaling, etc. (M.106–M.116).

# WALL OR RAMPART GUNS

Many fortified locations of this period used a semi-shoulder firearm called the "wall" or "rampart" gun. It was usually a heavy-barreled, large-bore version (smooth or rifled) of a musket, which could carry across water or cleared land for considerable distances. Some were mounted on swivels, while others included flat metal studs underneath to hook over a parapet. Shorter types were also used, with many being mounted on ship decks or longboats (M.117–M.120).

## IV.1 MUSKET, SWORD, AND POLEARM (see p. xi and back flap of jacket)

Drawings illustrating and labeling the parts of a musket, sword, and polearm.

---

## IV.2 EVOLUTION OF BRITISH MUSKETS (left to right)

(1) **Circa 1700-1710:** This flat-lock style was virtually the same as the late dog lock, with the "dog" removed. Notice the reinforced cock, the squared top of the frizzen, its crude iron furniture, and the flat nailed butt plate. Three screws hold the lock (there is no side plate). The round barrel usually measured 46"-48"; the bore, .75-.80.

(2) **Circa 1710-1714:** The iron-fitted Queen Anne musket marked a step toward the eventual brass-mounted Brown Bess. Its "banana" lock has a rounded face and now requires only two screws. The furniture includes a convex side plate, a cast butt plate with a long tang, plus an escutcheon plate. The barrel averaged 46", the trigger guard included a pointed front tip, and the bore measured .75–.80.

(3) **Circa 1756-1780 (Naval):** The Sea Service musket included several early characteristics when adopted by the senior service in the 1750's. Although the fittings are brass, they have a flat butt plate and rounded trigger guard of the Queen Anne style (see No. 1 above). Its flat side plate is contemporary with mid-century styling (Barrel: 40"-42"; bore: .75-.78.)

(4) **Circa 1750-1770:** This long-land-pattern Brown Bess evolved in the 1720's. Its early features included a rounded "banana" lock, a long butt tang, tapered ends with finials on the trigger guard, and a convex side plate. This specimen has a straighter lock plate than was used prior to 1750. (Pinned barrel: 46"; bore: .75.)

(5) **Circa 1760-1775:** The short-land-pattern Brown Bess was the standard British arm during the American Revolution. Its round barrel had been reduced to 42" (bore: .75), the side plate flattened, the butt tang shortened, and the trigger guard narrowed.

(6) **Circa 1797-1810:** This India-pattern musket is not considered a Revolutionary War weapon by most collectors, but is illustrated here for the reader's information. The barrel is now 39", its convex side plate lacks a tail, the trigger guard has been simplified, the escutcheon plate is gone, its cock has acquired a flat tang, and the stock is thinner. This style was made by the East India Company in the last quarter of the eighteenth century and officially adopted by the government to meet wartime demands in 1797. (Bore: .75.)

**40**

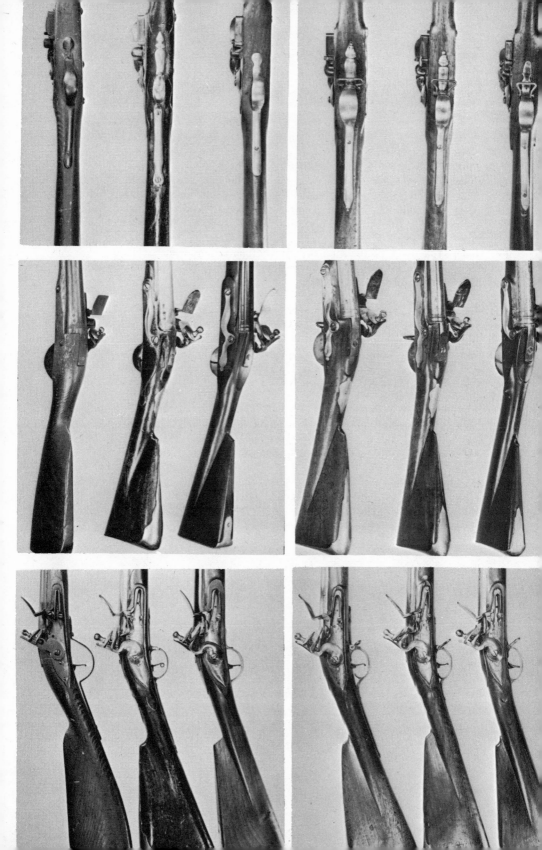

## IV.3 EVOLUTION OF FRENCH MUSKETS (left to right)

(1) **Model 1728:** French muskets were traditionally iron-mounted with a .69-caliber bore. This early style had a 46¾" banded barrel, long butt tang, plus sling swivels on the side of the middle band and next to the side plate. The flat lock included a goose-neck hammer, while the barrel was octagonal at the breech.

(2) **Model 1763:** By 1754 the sling swivels were moved under the stock, and with this model a new reinforced cock made its appearance, the butt tang was reduced to a lobe, and the banded barrel shortened to 44¾".

(3) **Model 1766:** The earlier pattern was basically retained in this year, but its stock was slimmed and the lock reduced in size. (Banded barrel: 44¾"; bore: .69.)

(4) **Circa 1768:** This is the style later copied by the United States for its first postwar musket (1795). It is very similar to the 1766 model, except that the comb of the stock has been lightened and a retaining spring added to the rear of the bottom band. (Barrel: 44¾"; bore: .69.)

(5) **Circa 1774:** By this date a rounded surface had appeared on the lock plate, cock, and flashpan. The established tapering trigger guard has been shortened and a rammer spring is now fastened under the rear band. (Barrel: 44¾"; bore: .69.)

(6) **Model 1777:** This was introduced during the American Revolution. A recessed cheek rest has been cut into the comb, finger ridges added to the reduced trigger guard, and a brass flashpan included in the convex lock. The forward barrel band is held by a screw from the outside. (Barrel: 44¾"; bore: .69.)

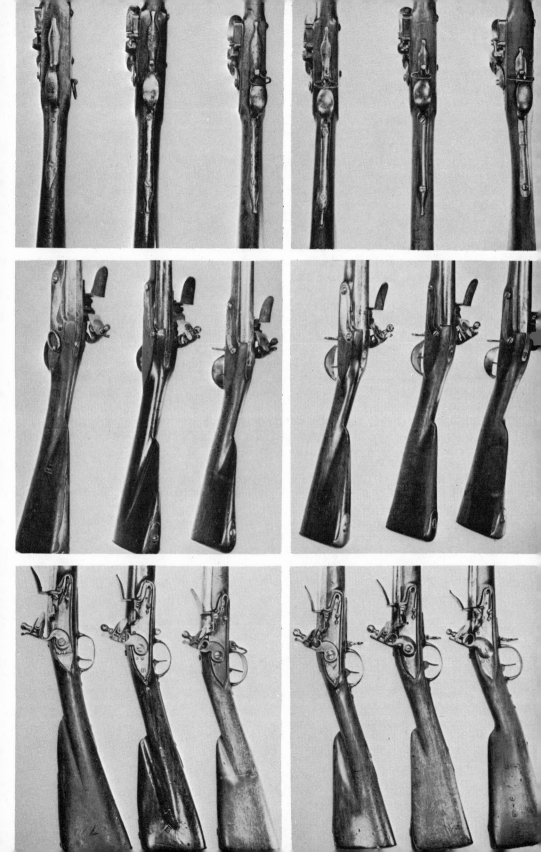

## IV.4 EVOLUTION OF DUTCH-GERMAN MUSKETS (left to right)

(1) **Circa 1750-1782:** This style of musket was used by Prussia and other German states from about 1720 to 1782. Notice the flat beveled lock and the decorative heavy brass furniture. Raised stock carvings were also common. (Pinned barrel: 41"-43"; bore: .75-.80.)

(2) **Circa 1765-1780:** This fusil illustrates the popular squared butt plate with two rounded screwheads protruding, the pointed Germanic-type trigger guard, and the flat lock face. (Pinned barrel: 39"; bore: .73.)

(3) **Circa 1770-1780:** Dutch influence is seen in this bulbous trigger-guard design, pointed butt tang, and rounded side plate (notice similarity to Brown Bess). (Pinned barrel: 44"; bore: .75-.80.)

(4) **Circa 1750-1780:** This high comb, blunted trigger-guard ends, wavy side plate, long butt tang, and flat lock were common in many mid-century Dutch arms. Three brass bands hold the 40½" barrel. (Bore: .75-.80.)

(5) **Circa 1765-1780:** The tail of the side plate was dropped from many of these later muskets. Note the flat beveled lock, squared cock jaws and frizzen top, plus the heavy brass furniture. (Banded barrel: 43"; bore: .78.)

(6) **Circa 1775-1780:** This is typical of the Dutch arms made and sold to both sides during the Revolutionary War. The lock is now convex and the flat butt plate has two rounded screwheads visible from the side. The resemblance of the trigger guard and side plate to the English Brown Bess suggests possible manufacture for them by the Dutch. Note: The comb seems to have been shaved down by someone to permit better aiming along the barrel. (Banded barrel: 40¾"; bore: .74.)

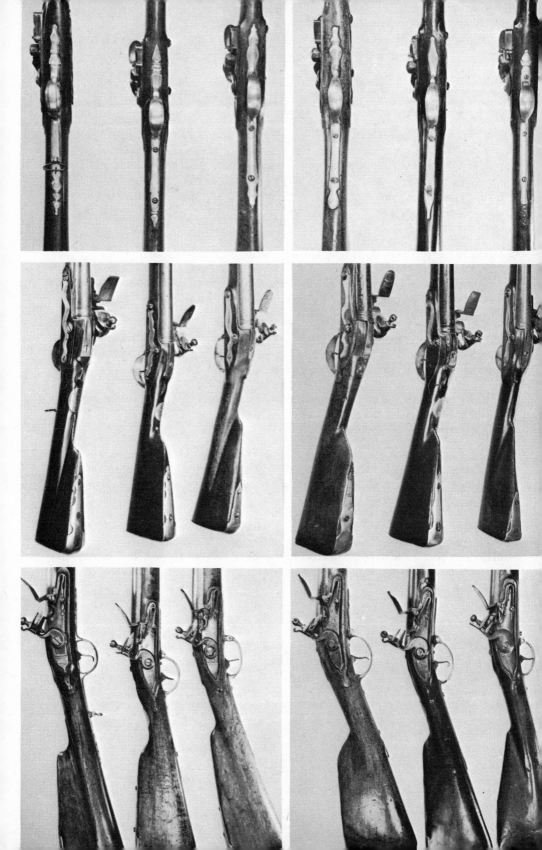

## IV.5 EVOLUTION OF AMERICAN MUSKETS (left to right)

(1) **Circa 1700-1720:** This early "Hudson Valley" fowler illustrates the common use of the Dutch-style lock, open side plate, and brass furniture. Also notice the raised carving around the fittings, and its typical "squared" butt profile. (Pinned barrel: 60"-68"; bore: .69-.80.)

(2) **Circa 1740-1750:** Club butt fowling pieces such as this were popular in New England. The side plate has become a flat piece of cast brass, and the trigger guard is a copy of the Brown Bess pattern. The flat lock with reinforced cock, and the absence of a butt plate are additional indications of an early date for this piece. (Pinned barrel: 50⅝"; bore: .72.)

(3) **Circa 1760-1770:** These "semimilitary" muskets usually served both as hunting guns and militia arms. The lock and pinned barrel (46½"; bore: .75) are both of English origin, while the simple brass furniture is American.

(4) **Circa 1760-1778:** This is an American military musket with a flat lock copied from the early French style, and its brass furniture made to reproduce the Brown Bess longland pattern. (Pinned barrel: 46"; bore: .79.)

(5) **Circa 1775-1780:** Muskets of this type were produced in the colonies early in the Revolution. The rounded lock and barrel are of Dutch origin, while the flat side plate, trigger guard, and butt plate are copies of the contemporary short-land-pattern British musket. (Pinned barrel: 42"; bore: .75-.78.)

(6) **Circa 1777-1783:** Although the trigger guard and pinned round barrel continue the English style, several French influences in this example indicate its manufacture here in the later part of the war; e.g. the curved side plate with no tail, plus the rounded lobe-like butt tang. (Barrel: 41½"; bore: .67.)

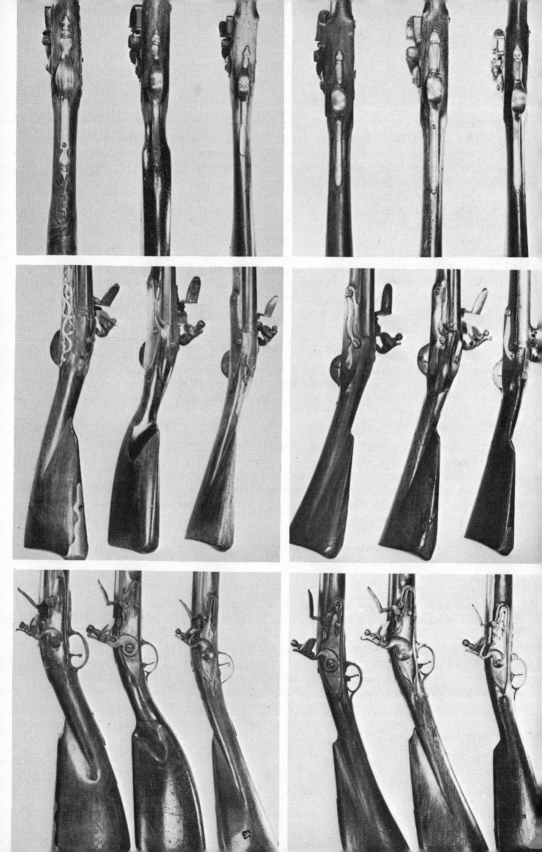

## IV.6 BRITISH BAYONET STYLES (left to right)

(1) **Circa 1680-1710:** This military plug bayonet had its tapered wooden grip inserted into the muzzle of a gun to act as a spear point. Notice that the crosspiece is a screw driver on one end and a hammer on the other. Its total length is 21¼″; the single-edged blade measures 13⅝″ (false edge, 4¾″).

(2) **Circa 1710-1720:** Socket bayonets of this type allowed the musket to fire while they were mounted on the barrel. The over-all length is 22½″, while its double-edged tapering blade (with the slight median ridge) extends for 18½″.

(3) **Circa 1710-1720:** This is an early version of the triangular-bladed bayonet used by the British well into the nineteenth century. The rear end of the socket has been repaired and the front end shows the joining ridge where the neck is attached. Total length is 20¾″; the triangular blade and neck measure 17″.

(4) **Circa 1750-1810:** Bayonets of this basic pattern, with the 4″ socket having a lip around the rear edge ("bridge") and a 17″ triangular blade, are the type used here in America during the French and Indian Wars and the Revolution. Earlier versions had a slight ridge where the neck joined the socket, and were a bit wider at the base of the blade. Note that British bayonets are cut for mounting on a top barrel stud. (The blade should always be at the right of the barrel.)

## IV.7 FRENCH BAYONET STYLES (left to right)

(5) **Model 1754:** Most French bayonets of the eighteenth century had a triangular blade (plus neck) measuring about 14⅞″, as in this case. Prior to the 1770's they also included a short central fuller on the flat upper face. This type was common among those shipped to the Continental Army, and was copied for many American muskets after the war. (Total length: 17¼″.)

(6) **Model 1763:** The socket has a straight slot for a bottom stud, and early locking clasp. Its two bottom blade faces are concave, with sharp shoulders at the base. (Total length: 17⅜″.)

(7) **Model 1774:** This model is again cut for a top mounting stud, and has a rounded bridge at the back edge of the socket. (Total length: 17½″.)

(8) **Model 1777:** Just as the 1777 musket set the pattern for French arms throughout the Napoleonic era, its bayonet was also changed substantially. The socket now mounts a centered locking clasp, and there is a long wide shallow fuller in the upper face of the triangular blade. (Total length: 17½″; blade and neck: 14¾″.)

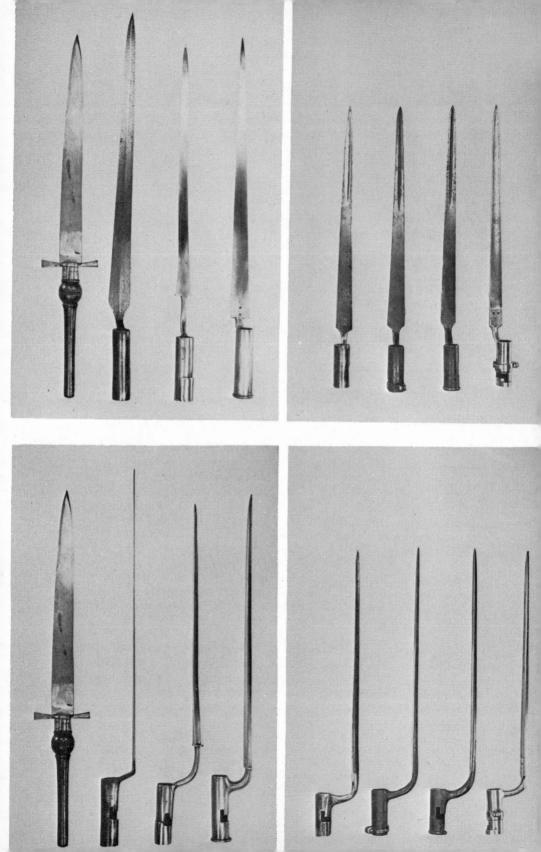

## IV.8 AMERICAN BAYONET STYLES (left to right)

(1) **Circa 1750-1765:** Most American bayonets were made locally, and varied as much as the colonists' muskets. Each was fitted to a specific weapon. This example has a short socket (2¼″), with a rear bridge, thin neck, and a flattened triangular blade. (Total length: 17½″.)

(2) **Circa 1750-1770:** This long double-edged tapering blade includes a slight median ridge on each side. It is fitted for a top stud. (Total length: 19⅝″.)

(3) **Circa 1760-1783:** The triangular blade with the raised base in this case is roughly forged in the British style. The slotting is cut for a bottom barrel stud. (Total length: 19″.)

(4) **Circa 1775-1780:** Here is another colonial specimen patterned after the English model. The triangular blade is quite wide at its base and attaches to the socket with a crude rectangular neck, which flares at the top. (Total length: 18¼″.)

## IV.9 AMERICAN AND GERMAN BAYONET STYLES (left to right)

(5) **American, circa 1760-1780:** This short fusil bayonet is also a copy of the English style. Its triangular blade has a base flange, and the socket includes a bridge around its rear edge. (Total length: 15″.)

(6) **American, circa 1750-1770:** The crude workmanship and alignment of this piece identify another blacksmith-made American bayonet. Its frail neck and thin short blade suggest manufacture at an early date. (Total length: 15¼″.)

(7) **German, circa 1750-1780:** Socket bayonets of this pattern were one of two styles used by the Germans here during the Revolution. The simple socket attaches to a neck which leads to a wide-hilt-like base at right angles to the six-faced, double-edged blade. (Total length: 16¾″.)

(8) **German, circa 1750-1780:** This type is also found on German-Dutch muskets believed to have been used here in the 1770's. It is similar to the British version, but is slotted for a bottom stud and has a shorter blade with a projecting flange underneath at the base. (Total length: 18⅛″.)

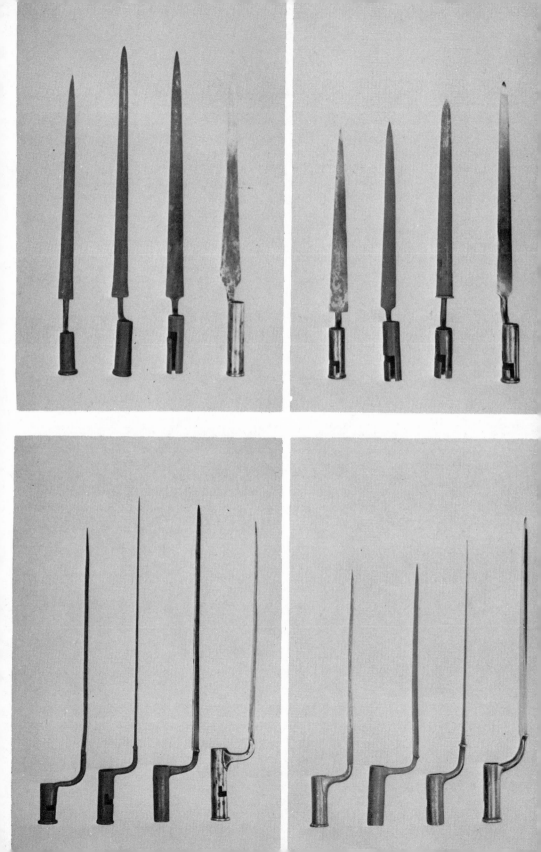

# SMOOTHBORE CARTRIDGES

**IV.10 BRITISH CARTRIDGES:** Illustrated (left to right) are English musket, carbine, and fusil cartridges of the type used just after the war. They consisted of loose powder and a round ball, wrapped in whitish-brown paper. It was tied with a string just below the ball, and twisted to seal the other end. The bullet generally measured .05″ to .10″ smaller than the actual barrel diameter to allow for powder fouling. The musket powder charge was approximately 6 drams (164 grains).

**IV.11 FRENCH AND EUROPEAN CARTRIDGES:** This ammunition includes (left to right) French musket and pistol cartridges, plus two European musket cartridges. They were made of rolled paper which had one end below the ball and the side seam pasted shut. The remaining end was then folded into a long or short "tail." (Note: The third cartridge shown is fastened with sealing wax.) These were all made for a .69-caliber barrel.

**IV.12 AMERICAN CARTRIDGES:** Early in the Revolution, many of the American troops made their own cartridges or loaded directly from a powder horn and shot bag. Eventually contractors filled most of the needs. But the wide variance in bore sizes limited their interchangeability. One Pennsylvania Committee of Safety complained about still having to supply balls of seven different diameters in 1777. The colonists employed both English and French wrapping techniques and utilized many sources of paper—including newspaper. Smaller shot were often included with the large bullet to make a "buck and ball" combination.

*Maurice E. Zubatkin Collection*

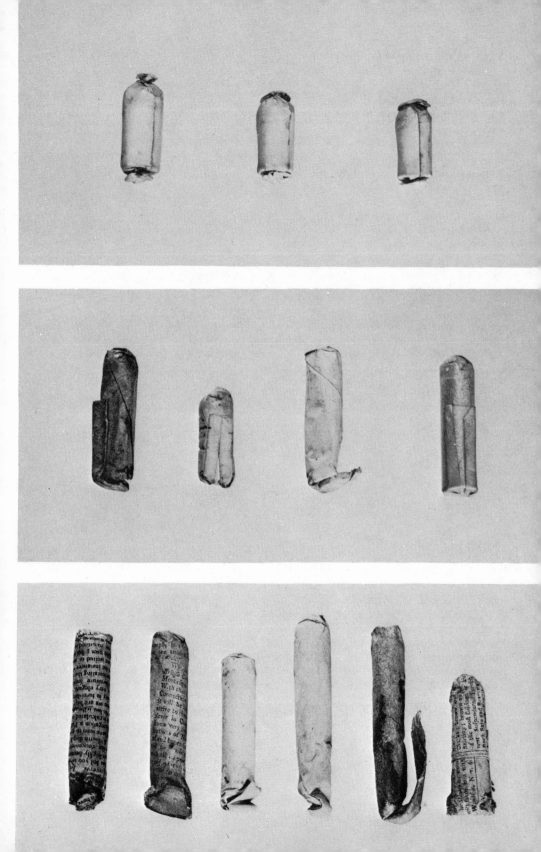

## M.1 ENGLISH DOG-LOCK MUSKET          Circa 1690-1710

This is a late style of British dog-lock musket. The pinned barrel was probably stocked to the muzzle originally (later cut back for a socket bayonet). Note the squared top of the frizzen and the absence of a tail pipe. The lock has three side screws, a flat surface, and two cocking notches in the tumbler (no interior or exterior bridle). Its side plate is cast, while the butt plate is of sheet brass (fastened with square-headed nails). There is no escutcheon plate. Barrel markings include a "P" under a crown, and "51."

| | | |
|---|---|---|
| Length: 61½" | Tr. Guard: 9⅝" | Furniture: Brass |
| Barrel: 46⅛"; .79 | Butt Tang: 2¾" | Weight: 8.9 lbs. |
| Lock: 7" × 1¼" | | |

*Author's Collection*

## M.2 ENGLISH INFANTRY MUSKET          Circa 1705-1710

Muskets of this type were apparently turned out under the pressure of war and dispensed with most of the refinements. The "dog" has been removed from the flat lock (although it still has three side screws and no outside bridle). Notice the absence of a side plate, and the early practice of holding the barrel tang with a screw from underneath the stock (its head is just forward of the trigger). The barrel bears the 1702-style London proofs, with the number "31."

| | | |
|---|---|---|
| Length: 62⅞" | Tr. Guard: 9⅞" | Furniture: Iron |
| Barrel: 47⅛"; .80 | Butt Tang: 2¼" | Weight: 8.6 lbs. |
| Lock: 7⅛" × 1⅛" | | |

*Lewis H. Gordon, Jr., Collection*

## M.3 ENGLISH INFANTRY MUSKET          Circa 1710

This marked Queen Anne musket has a flat three-screw dog lock and a squared frizzen top. The pinned barrel is stocked to the muzzle (requiring a plug bayonet). Other characteristics include a curled trigger and a flat nailed butt plate. The trigger guard is of the type readopted for sea service muskets in the 1750's (see M.21). Its lock face bears an engraved crown above the royal cipher "AR," plus the maker's name on the tail: WOLRIDGE 10 (i.e., 1710). Barrel marks are "AR" over a broad arrow, and crossed scepters under a crown.

| | | |
|---|---|---|
| Length: 61½" | Tr. Guard: 9⁹⁄₁₆" | Furniture: Brass |
| Barrel: 45⅝"; .78 | Butt Tang: 2⅞" | Weight: 9.0 lbs. |
| Lock: 7⅜" × 1¼" | | |

*Jac Weller Collection*

54

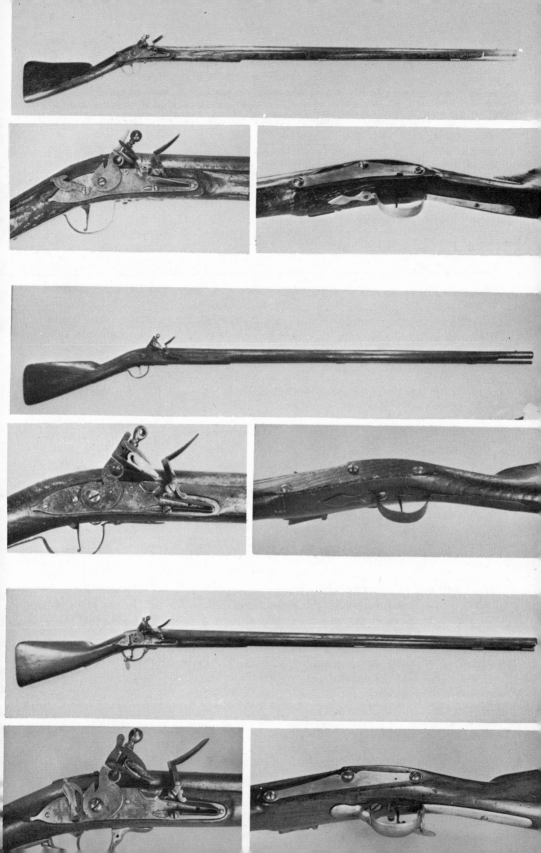

## M.4 ENGLISH DOG-LOCK MUSKET
### Circa 1710-1720

This type of all-purpose gun was used extensively in the colonies because of the shortage of "Queen's Arms." Although mounting a dog lock with three side screws, it has evolved closer to the Brown Bess style—adding a tail pipe, a nose cap, and a slender side plate (with a developing tail). The brass sheet on the small of the stock is a repair. Its lock bears the name of a private contractor, WILSON; the barrel has London proofs and his initials.

Length: 57"          Tr. Guard: 9"          Furniture: Brass
Barrel: 41"; .77     Butt Tang: 1⅞"         Weight: 8.0 lbs.
Lock: 6⅞" × 1³⁄₁₆"

*Anthony D. Darling Collection*

## M.5 ENGLISH QUEEN ANNE MUSKET
### Circa 1707-1714

Still further progress in the evolution of Britain's arms under Queen Anne is seen here. Note the rounded lock (with two side screws), its "banana-shaped" lock plate, and the gooseneck cock. Also visible are the developing side plate tail, new escutcheon plate, and cast butt plate (having a characteristic long tang). The lock bears the maker's name, W PREDDEN.

Length: 61¼"         Tr. Guard: 11"         Furniture: Iron
Barrel: 44⅝"; .82    Butt Tang: 7"          Weight: 9.1 lbs.
Lock: 6⅞" × 1¼"

*Lewis H. Gordon, Jr., Collection*

## M.6 ENGLISH INFANTRY MUSKET
### Circa 1710-1714

This iron-mounted musket has its pinned barrel shortened to 40", as was often done for early light troops in the colonies, or aboard ships. Some of the black paint which covered many early arms still remains on the stock. A tail pipe is included, and its forward pipe is slightly flared to speed entrance of the wooden rammer. Note the typical raised stock carving around the fittings. The maker's name, T GREEN, is engraved on the lock; the barrel shows early proofs and faint remains of a colonel's name (denoting the regiment).

Length: 55½"         Tr. Guard: 10½"        Furniture: Iron
Barrel: 40"; .78     Butt Tang: 7"          Weight: 8.3 lbs.
Lock: 7" × 1¼"

*Author's Collection*

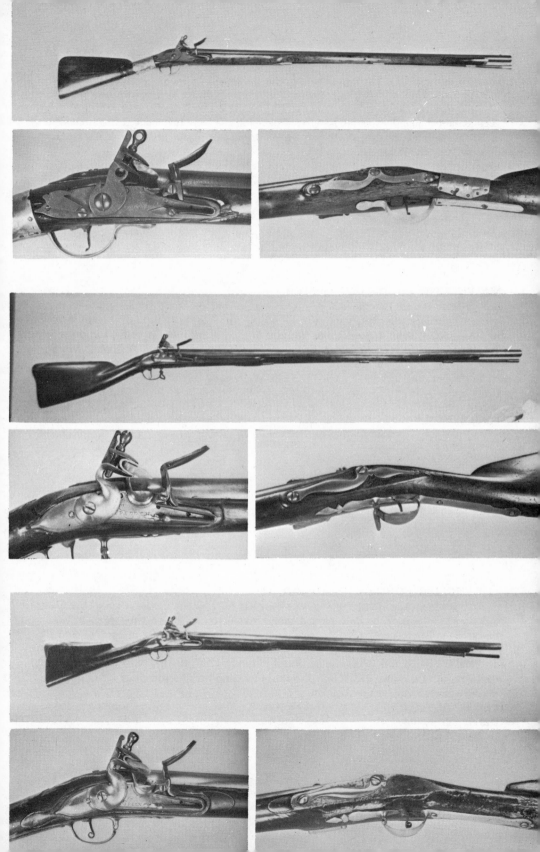

## M.7 ENGLISH LONG-LAND MUSKET

Circa 1721

This is one of the earliest known examples of the "Brown Bess" pattern, which finally emerged in the 1720's. These preliminary versions usually had iron instead of brass furniture, plus the blunt-ended trigger-guard design seen here. Its lock bears a crown above "T," the maker's name, WILSON, and "C 10," "N 21." The barrel is engraved with the regimental commander's name, HAWLEY, Colonel of the 33rd Regiment at this time. The metal rammer and "iron strip" nose cap appear to be part of the original weapon, but are possibly later additions.

Length: 61¾"           Tr. Guard: 12¼"           Furniture: Iron
Barrel: 46"; .77       Butt Tang: 7¾"            Weight: 10.0 lbs.
Lock: 6⅞" × 1¼"

*Author's Collection*

## M.8 ENGLISH LONG-LAND PATTERN

Circa 1728

This later Brown Bess now has brass furniture, but the early trigger-guard design persists (although the final style was already in use by this time). The large bulge in the stock just behind the tail pipe and the single stem at the rear of the trigger bow are other early features. Lock markings include a crown above "GR," plus TOWER 1728 (Royal Arsenal in the Tower of London). Its barrel is inscribed ROYAL WELSH, while the butt tang bears the name "Lt Colo. Waite" and the escutcheon "B/N9."

Length: 62⅛"           Tr. Guard: 11½"           Furniture: Brass
Barrel: 46"; .77       Butt Tang: 6"             Weight: 9.4 lbs.
Lock: 6¾" × 1¼"

*Author's Collection*

## M.9 ENGLISH LONG-LAND MUSKET

Circa 1733

By this time, the familiar long-land pattern has fully emerged: the convex "banana" lock (with an outside bridle), pinned round 46" barrel, tail pipe with three forward pipes (none flared, i.e., for a wooden rammer) and heavy brass furniture. The added spur on the rear stem of the trigger bow and the absence of a nose cap are also typical. The maker's name and year of manufacture, JORDAN 1733, are inscribed on the tail of the lock, with the crown and "GR," plus the crown and broad arrow (indicating government ownership) under the flashpan.

Length: 61⅛"           Tr. Guard: 11⅜"           Furniture: Brass
Barrel: 45½"; .80      Butt Tang: 6"             Weight: 9.6 lbs.
Lock: 6⅞" × 1¼"

*Winchester Museum Collection*

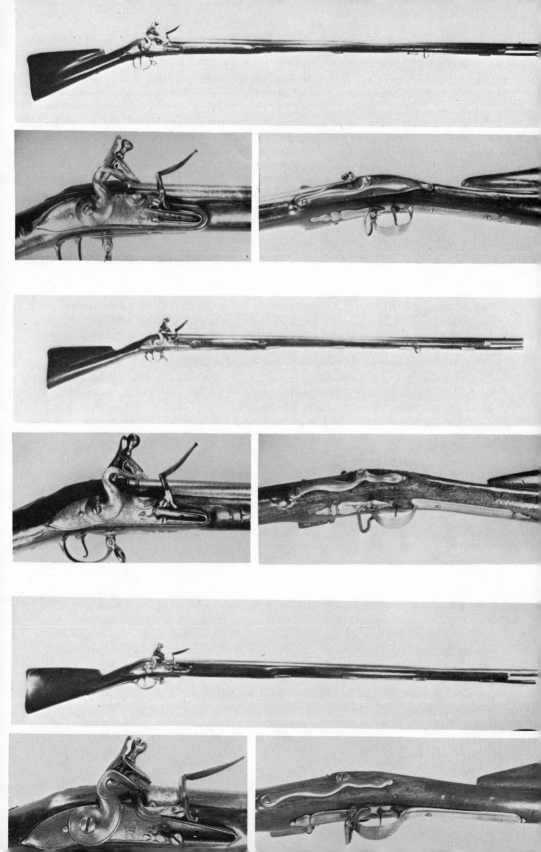

## M.10 ENGLISH LONG-LAND MUSKET                    Circa 1762

This later example of the Brown Bess illustrates a style in common use during the French and Indian War and the Revolution. Notice the addition of a button-headed iron rammer, along with a nose cap and flared forward pipe. The lock plate has evolved a straighter bottom edge, and the raised stock carving around the fittings has gone. VERNON 1762 is engraved on the lock, CONN on the escutcheon plate, and "GR" with a broad arrow, crossed scepter proofs, plus "RE" (barrel maker) on the barrel.

Length: 61⅞"                  Tr. Guard: 11⅛"              Furniture: Brass
Barrel: 46"; .80              Butt Tang: 5⅜"               Weight: 10.5 lbs.
Lock: 6⅞" × 1¼"

*John K. Watson Collection*

## M.11 ENGLISH SHORT-LAND MUSKET                    Circa 1765-1775

The short-land pattern was a shorter version of the Brown Bess (42" versus 46" barrel) which evolved in the 1740's and 1750's, and was accepted as the official infantry arm in 1768. Other changes from the long-land model include a flattened side plate, a shorter butt tang, and a straighter lock. It can also be seen how the stock swelling behind the tail pipe has diminished. The standard engravings include TOWER on the lock (required after 1764), for the government proof house in the Tower of London.

Length: 57¾"                  Tr. Guard: 10⅜"              Furniture: Brass
Barrel: 42"; .78              Butt Tang: 3¾"               Weight: 10.3 lbs.
Lock: 7" × 1¼"

*Author's Collection*

## M.12 ENGLISH SHORT-LAND MUSKET                    Circa 1770-1780

Here is a Brown Bess typical of those issued to many British troops during the 1770's. There are two indications of this modified short-land pattern: the cock tang is now rectangular and enclosed on three sides by the top jaw (note also the two screw ends visible behind the cock versus the previous one screw end), and the second rammer pipe is beginning to expand at its forward end. The 14 REGT engraved on the barrel was active here in the Revolution. Its escutcheon is marked "1/27" (believed to designate the company [top] and the rack number [below]).

Length: 57¾"                  Tr. Guard: 11⅜"              Furniture: Brass
Barrel: 41⅞"; .77            Butt Tang: 3¾"               Weight: 10.8 lbs.
Lock: 6⅞" × 1¼"

*Lewis H. Gordon, Jr., Collection*

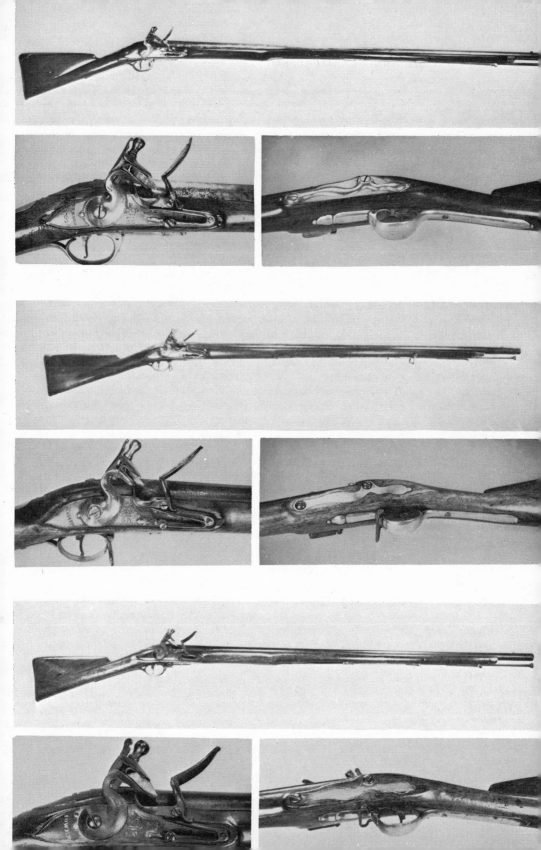

## M.13 ENGLISH SHORT-LAND MUSKET  Circa 1775-1783

The continued evolution of the English musket during this period is indicated here. Notice that the cock tang now has an unbroken rounded profile at the top (it eventually became standard for the later India pattern), and the second rammer pipe has acquired a wider flare at the forward end. An escutcheon plate is present, but was beginning to disappear. The barrel is marked 46 REGT—this unit fought here in the Revolution—and a large "US" surcharge behind it also testifies to use by American forces.

Length: 58"                   Tr. Guard: 11¼"              Furniture: Brass
Barrel: 42⅛"; .78            Butt Tang: 3¾"               Weight: 10.0 lbs.
Lock: 7" × 1¼"

*Author's Collection*

## M.14 ENGLISH FUSIL MUSKET  Circa 1744-1750

Royal warrants of the 1740's and 1750's suggest that while fighting in America, officers might replace polearms with fusils of their own preference. This early example's pinned barrel is shorter, lighter, and of smaller bore than the infantry musket. Its forward rammer pipe is not flared (indicating probable original use of a wooden rod), and the flat brass strip embedded near the end of the stock is an early form of nose cap. I LUDLAM appears on the lock, and COLLUMBELL LONDON NO 2 on the barrel.

Length: 52⅝"                  Tr. Guard: 10⅛"             Furniture: Brass
Barrel: 37⅛"; .68            Butt Tang: 4⅛"               Weight: 6.5 lbs.
Lock: 5¾ × 1"

*Author's Collection*

## M.15 ENGLISH FUSIL MUSKET  Circa 1760-1770

The brass furniture on this specimen is smaller but similar to the regular musket. Its trigger guard is simplified in design, however, while the forward pipe is elongated and the nose cap omitted. Inscribed on the lock is WILSON. Two 1702-type proofs (London) plus the initials "GR" and "RW" appear on the barrel. A typical top bayonet stud is present.

Length: 52¾"                  Tr. Guard: 10⅜"             Furniture: Brass
Barrel: 37"; .66             Butt Tang: 4¼"               Weight: 7.5 lbs.
Lock: 6⅛" × 1⅛"

*Gerald C. Stowe Collection*

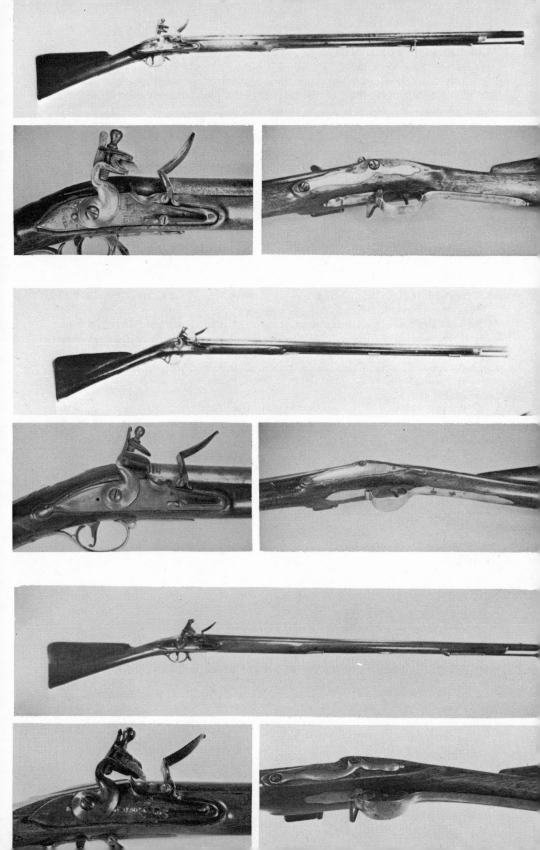

## M.16 ENGLISH FUSIL MUSKETS    Circa 1770-1780

These two fusils (numbered "3" and "4") were obviously made for officers. Engravings on the brass furniture reflect the expense and care of personal weapons. Their solid side plates have a short third screw near the tails, plus an inscribed flag motif. The trigger guard's acorn design was a popular device in England from about 1750 to 1780. Each lock is marked KETLAND & CO (the prodigious British lock producer and exporter). The iron rammer and flared pipes are also typical of this period.

Length: 49½″             Tr. Guard: 10½″              Furniture: ᴗrass
Barrel: 34⅛″; .68        Butt Tang: 3⅞″               Weight: 6.5 lbs. per
Lock: 5⅞″ × 1″

*Lewis H. Gordon, Jr., Collection*

## M.17 ENGLISH TRADE MUSKET    Circa 1770-1785

Other shoulder arms in early America were the ones made for trading with the Indians. At first, shortened infantry muskets were used. Later models retained many early characteristics: a "dragon" side plate, a flat nailed butt plate, and a stock extending to the muzzle (mostly of poor-quality materials). This style actually persisted into the mid-1800's. The trade gun here is typical of the usual pattern. Its lock is marked WILSON, and the barrel bears the 1702-style London proofs plus the initials RW between them.

Length: 51¾″             Tr. Guard: 10⅜″              Furniture: Brass
Barrel: 35¾″; .60        Butt Tang: 2¼″               Weight: 5.1 lbs.
Lock: 6″ × 1″

*Foster Tallman Collection*

## M.18 ENGLISH TRADE-UTILITY MUSKET    Circa 1700-1759

Apparently many muskets such as this one had their barrels shortened (the base for an original pin is still evident under the present muzzle) for use as trade or general utility arms in the colonies. This three-screw dog lock is marked WALKER, while the brass furniture includes a flat lobe-ended butt plate held by square-headed nails and a large dragon-shaped side plate (copied for later trade guns; see M.17). Several numerical stampings appear on the butt. The earliest is "L59" (probably for 1759).

Length: 57⅝″             Tr. Guard: 9″                Furniture: Brass
Barrel: 42″; .77         Butt Tang: 2¾″               Weight: 8.1 lbs.
Lock: 6¾″ × 1¼″

*Author's Collection*

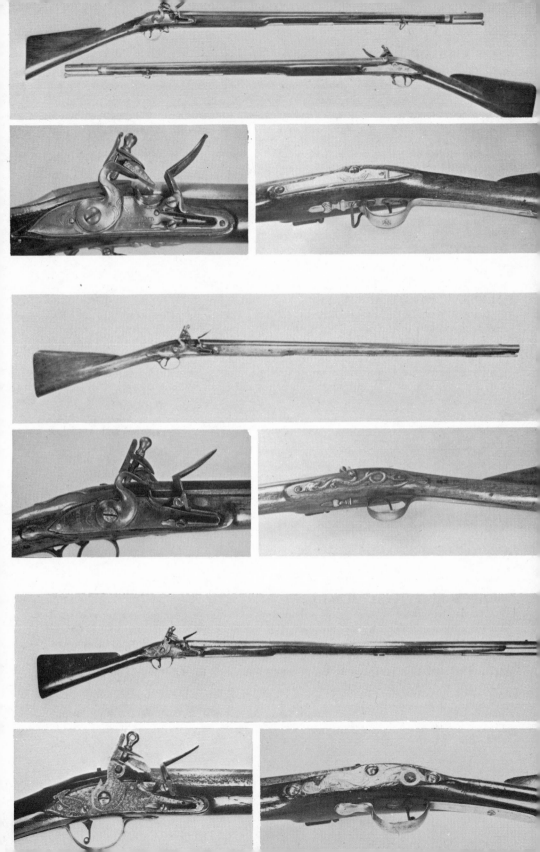

## M.19 ENGLISH MILITIA AND MARINE MUSKET          Circa 1756

This early naval variation of a 42"-barrel musket is like the short-land pattern (M.11) except that it uses a wooden rammer and omits the escutcheon plate, tail pipe, and nose cap. In addition, the butt tang is secured with a top screw (not present on the infantry model). Other known examples (same decade) are equipped with iron rammers and tail pipes. The lock plate is marked with the usual crown and "GR," plus the maker and date of manufacture, GRICE 1756.

Length: 57½"               Tr. Guard: 11⅛"               Furniture: Brass
Barrel: 41⅞"; .78          Butt Tang: 3⅞"                Weight: 10.0 lbs.
Lock: 7" × 1¼"

*Author's Collection*

## M.20 ENGLISH NAVAL MUSKET          Circa 1756

Normal practice in the eighteenth century was to relegate poorer quality and salvaged muskets to the navy. During the 1750's a more distinctive naval arm began to appear. Their initial effort was the militia and marine model (M.19 above). Those following continued to show variations, but normally mounted a 42" barrel and components patterned after the Queen Anne era, e.g. a flat butt plate with a lobe-shaped tang, circular trigger-guard tip, no escutcheon plate, and often no sling swivels. This lock is marked GRICE 1756.

Length: 57¾"               Tr. Guard: 8½"                Furniture: Brass
Barrel: 42"; .78           Butt Tang: 2½"                Weight: 9.3 lbs.
Lock: 7" × 1¼"

*Author's Collection*

## M.21 ENGLISH NAVAL MUSKET          Circa 1759

The flat lock face, as well as the rounded style in the preceding example, was used for sea service muskets. Notice, however, this model's close resemblance to the Queen Anne lock (M.3), as well as the early rounded trigger-guard tip, flat butt, and lack of an escutcheon plate. Virtually all of these naval models had a top stud for a bayonet (required after 1752). The nose cap, iron rammer, and flat side plate follow the contemporary short-land pattern. Its lock plate reads EDGE 1759.

Length: 57¾"               Tr. Guard: 9½"                Furniture: Brass
Barrel: 42"; .78           Butt Tang: 3¼"                Weight: 9.8 lbs.
Lock: 7" × 1¼"

*Foster Tallman Collection*

**66**

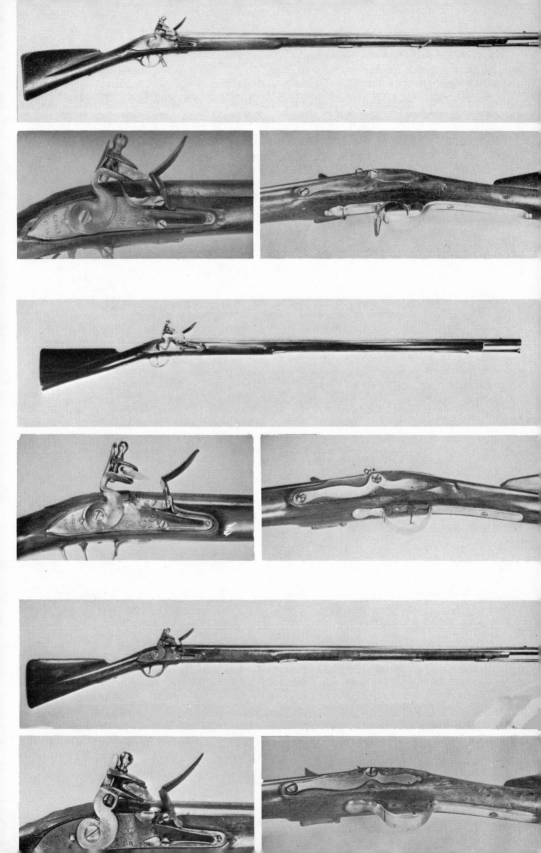

## M.22 ENGLISH NAVAL MUSKET                    Circa 1755-1765

The sea service musket shown here is slightly shorter and has a heavier stock than most others. Its brass furniture is typical, and the lock is an early "banana" style, engraved TOWER 1742 (although the arm was probably assembled later). Barrel markings show the "GR" and scepter proofs plus the number "14." Two inspector ("viewer") stampings are inside the lock—a crown above "7" and another above "1."

Length: 55⅝″                 Tr. Guard: 8½″              Furniture: Brass
Barrel: 40″; .78             Butt Plate: 2½″             Weight: 9.6 lbs.
Lock: 6⅞″ × 1⁹⁄₁₆″

*Author's Collection*

## M.23 ENGLISH NAVAL MUSKET                    Circa 1765-1775

Here is a short version of the naval musket. Although its middle and flared forward pipes (no tail pipe) appear to be in their original positions, the barrel (37″) was possibly cut down from a longer length. The rammer is wooden, and a brass strip serves as the nose cap. Note the rounded tang profile on the cock. Probable use by the Americans during the War for Independence is indicated by the butt tang inscription, NO 23 MASSACHTS BAY.

Length: 52⅞″                 Tr. Guard: 9½″              Furniture: Brass
Barrel 37″; .79             Butt Tang: 3½″              Weight: 8.9 lbs.
Lock: 6⅞″ × 1¼″

*Author's Collection*

## M.24 FRENCH MUSKET                              Model 1717

The first standardized French infantry musket was this Model 1717. Its 46¾″ barrel was pinned to the stock (plus one band) and octagonal for 7″ from the breech. The bore was .69 and the rammer was held by four pipes. This illustration is actually a rampart variation (length and pattern typical, but bore is .79). The model's distinctive features are the vertical supporting strap on the lock and the oval sling swivels at the side (normally behind the side plate, and on the side of the lone barrel band).

Length: 62¾″                 Tr. Guard: 11⅞″             Furniture: Iron
Barrel: 46¾″; .79           Butt Tang: 6¾″              Weight: 9.6 lbs.
Lock: 7⅛″ × 1⅜″

*Author's Collection*

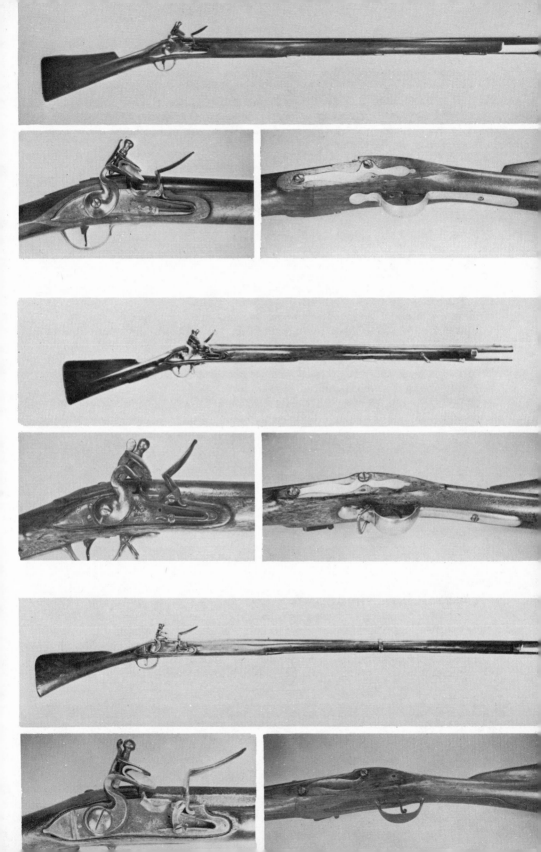

## M.25 FRENCH INFANTRY MUSKET          Model 1728

This model parallels the "1717" except for the use of three barrel bands (two rear ones held by friction) and the exchange of the lock's vertical strap for a horizontal bridle. The iron furniture includes the traditional flat side plate, tapered trigger guard, plus a long butt tang. It has a top bayonet stud; the rammer was originally wooden. This style was common in the French and Indian Wars here, and included in the arms shipments during the Revolution.

Length: 62¾″  
Barrel: 46¾″; .71  
Lock: 6½″ × 1¼″

Tr. Guard: 11⅜″  
Butt Tang: 5¾″

Furniture: Iron  
Weight: 9.5 lbs.

*Author's Collection*

## M.26 FRENCH INFANTRY MUSKET          Model 1746

During this period French muskets underwent continuous modification. The Model 1746 maintained the same dimensions, high comb, iron furniture, three barrel bands, side sling swivels (missing here), and octagonal breech (7″) as the Model 1728. Yet there were two principal changes: the horizontal lock bridle was dropped and the first official iron rammer appeared. (Note: Many of the earlier rammers were apparently changed to iron in the French and Indian Wars here.)

Length: 62¼″  
Barrel: 46½″; .72  
Lock: 6½″ × 1¼″

Tr. Guard: 11¾″  
Butt Tang: 5″

Furniture: Iron  
Weight: 8.8 lbs.

*Author's Collection*

## M.27 FRENCH INFANTRY MUSKET          Model 1754

The Model 1754 marked another step toward the important patterns of the 1760's. Notice that the sling swivels are now underneath, the flat lock has a bridle, the middle band includes a retaining spring, and the butt tang is shorter. This weapon illustrated apparently saw extensive service in the Revolutionary War. It is surcharged "US" on the lock and barrel, with U:STATES on the stock behind the trigger guard. The butt and barrel were shortened at one time.

Length: 59⅝″  
Barrel: 44½″; .70  
Lock: 6¾″ × 1¼″

Tr. Guard: 12½″  
Butt Tang: 4″

Furniture: Iron  
Weight: 8.5 lbs.

*Author's Collection*

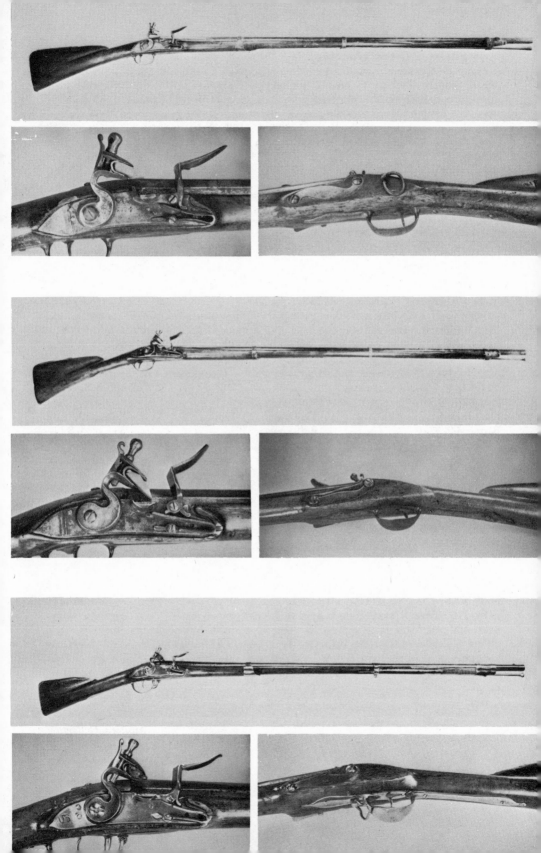

**M.28 FRENCH INFANTRY MUSKET**                           Circa 1746-1763

Many of the arms from this period are "mixed," i.e. contain parts from different official models. The barrel here is probably a shortened 1754 style. Its side plate appears to come from a 1746 pattern, and the butt plate has a Model 1763 lobe-like tang. The bottom swivels indicate that the bands and trigger guard are of 1754 vintage. Note the squared butt profile of the 1760's. Its lock and barrel are surcharged "US," while the lock is also marked "MBG" (Maubeuge Arsenal).

Length: 57"                    Tr. Guard: 13"              Furniture: Iron
Barrel: 42¼"; .72              Butt Tang: 1¼"              Weight: 8.8 lbs.
Lock: 6½" × 1¼"

*Winchester Museum Collection*

**M.29 FRENCH INFANTRY MUSKET**                              Model 1763

The Model 1763 set a new basic pattern for French arms. The barrel was cut to 44¾" (with a round surface), but the standard bore remained (.69). A new flat lock and reinforced cock appeared (cock screw not original), plus a short lobe-shaped butt tang, and a lower lip on the center band. Its stock was straighter and a long rammer spring extended back along the channel from the forward to the middle band. "M1763" appears on the barrel tang, CHARLEVILLE on the lock, plus "US" also on the lock and behind the side plate.

Length: 59¾"                   Tr. Guard: 12⅝"            Furniture: Iron
Barrel: 44½"; .70              Butt Tang: 2½"             Weight: 9.3 lbs.
Lock: 6¾" × 1¼"

*Hermann W. Williams, Jr., Collection*

**M.30 FRENCH INFANTRY MUSKET**                              Model 1766

By 1766, several modifications appeared: the forward band's rear edge now slopes back, but retains the brass sight on the second strap; its lock remains in the 1763 style although smaller in size. The stock, too, is slimmer, and the lip on the middle band has disappeared. Engraved on the lock is CHARLEVILLE, while barrel markings include "NH 2B NO 30" (believed to be New Hampshire designations).

Length: 60⅛"                   Tr. Guard: 12¾"            Furniture: Iron
Barrel: 44¾"; .71              Butt Tang: 2⅜"             Weight: 8.0 lbs.
Lock: 6¼" × 1¼"

*Author's Collection*

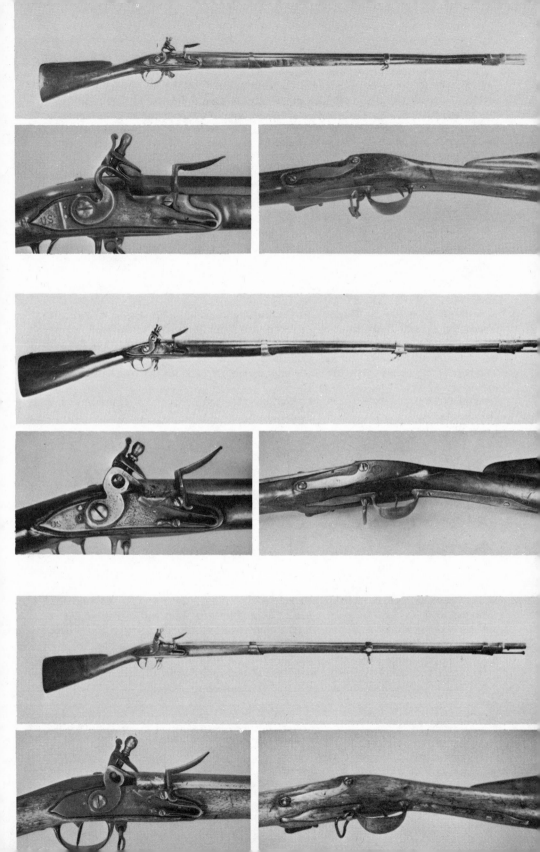

## M.31 FRENCH INFANTRY MUSKET — Circa 1768

This appears to be the pattern actually copied by the United States for its first musket in 1795. The French use of earlier barrels with "M1763" on the tang probably explains previous references to that date. This piece keeps the basic dimensions, lock, and furniture of the M1766. Yet, a rear retaining spring appears behind the bottom band, the comb is narrower, and the bayonet stud moves back on top of the barrel (put underneath in 1763). "US" surcharges are on the lock and barrel, with U.STATES behind the trigger guard.

Length: 59¾"  
Barrel: 44¼"; .70  
Lock: 6⅝" × 1¼"  
Tr. Guard: 12¾"  
Butt Tang: 2½"  
Furniture: Iron  
Weight: 8.4 lbs.

*Author's Collection*

## M.32 FRENCH INFANTRY MUSKET — Model 1772

By the early 1770's the French lock had become rounded, a bit shorter, and had replaced the faceted flashpan with a circular one (still bridled). Notice that a lower comb gives the stock a smoother outline. The trigger guard's forward end has also been shortened. Its lock marking, ST ETIENNE, identifies the source of manufacture. The barrel tang is inscribed "M1772"; other stampings include "US" surcharges on the lock face and barrel top.

Length: 60¼"  
Barrel: 44¾"; .69  
Lock: 6¼" × 1¼"  
Tr. Guard: 11¼"  
Butt Tang: 2½"  
Furniture: Iron  
Weight: 9.1 lbs.

*E. Norman Flayderman Collection*

## M.33 FRENCH INFANTRY MUSKET — Model 1774

In the Model 1774, the trigger guard has a shortened front end, a bottom lip reappears on the middle band, and a new rammer spring is attached to the lower band. A small clip spring usually protrudes from the end of the stock to secure the new bayonet (with a raised rear ring). Its lock plate is inscribed CHARLEVILLE, while the barrel is marked "P74" (i.e. made in 1774), and its tang "M1774." Behind the trigger guard is a UNITED.STATES surcharge; "US" is stamped in the lock, barrel, and side stock.

Length: 59¾"  
Barrel: 44⅝"; .71  
Lock: 6¼" × 1¼"  
Tr. Guard: 11⅜"  
Butt Tang: 2⅜"  
Furniture: Iron  
Weight: 9.2 lbs.

*Foster Tallman Collection*

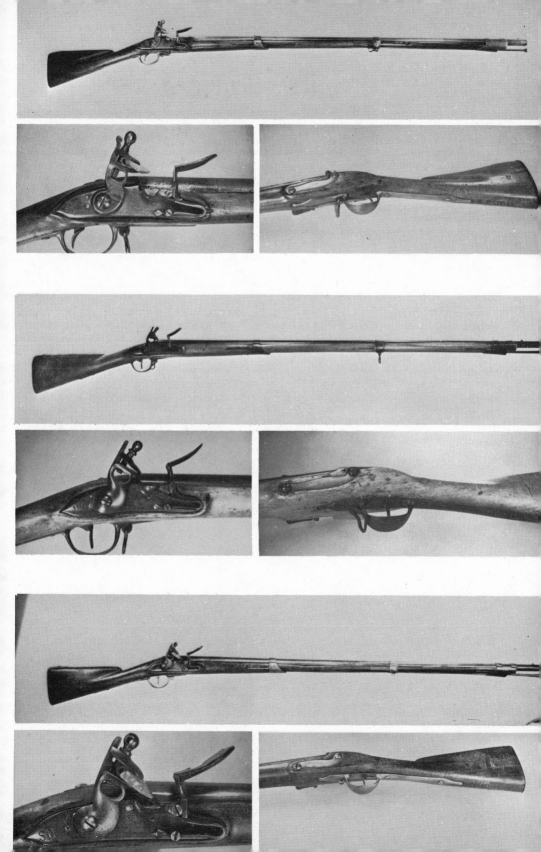

## M.34 FRENCH INFANTRY MUSKET                    Model 1777

The year 1777 marked a major change in the French pattern. Its rounded lock acquired a noncorrosive brass flashpan, the trigger guard shrank to 10″ and added finger ridges, while a recessed cheek rest was cut into the stock comb. A screw from the outside now held the forward band, and the retaining spring moved forward of the bottom band (middle band held by friction). This model was probably not shipped to the colonists, but undoubtedly saw service with French troops here in the Revolution.

Length: 59⅝″    Tr. Guard: 10″    Furniture: Iron
Barrel: 44¾″; .69    Butt Tang: 2⅜″    Weight: 8.8 lbs.
Lock: 6¼″ × 1¼″

*Author's Collection*


## M.35 FRENCH SERGEANTS' MUSKET                  Circa 1728-1733

This smaller version of the Model 1728 is believed to have been an early sergeants' weapon. Its furniture and lock follow the standard 1728 musket, including an oval swivel on the far end of the middle band. Apparently the weapon was carried over the shoulder (muzzle down) so that the sling passed through the trigger guard (no rear swivel). The rounded cock on the lock is a replacement (usual rule: round cock on round lock, flat on flat). A crown over the "SE" lock marking indicates its Saint-Étienne manufacture.

Length: 47¾″    Tr. Guard: 11½″    Furniture: Iron
Barrel: 23¾″; .70    Butt Tang: 3″    Weight: 7.4 lbs.
Lock: 6½″ × 1¼″

*Joseph E. Fritzinger Collection*


## M.36 FRENCH FUSIL MUSKET                        Circa 1758-1763

The first official fusil design appeared in 1754. It followed the infantry pattern, but included embellishments on the mountings. This slightly later and plainer specimen "mixes" a 1754-type lock and trigger guard, with 1763 parts (butt plate, round barrel, side plate). Engraved borders can be seen on the brass barrel bands. The distance between the two forward bands suggests that it was shortened at one time. U:STATES surcharges appear on the butt face and forward of the trigger guard.

Length: 55″    Tr. Guard: 13″    Furniture: Brass
Barrel: 39½″; .72    Butt Tang: 2½″    Weight: 8.3 lbs.
Lock: 6⅝″ × 1¼″

*Author's Collection*

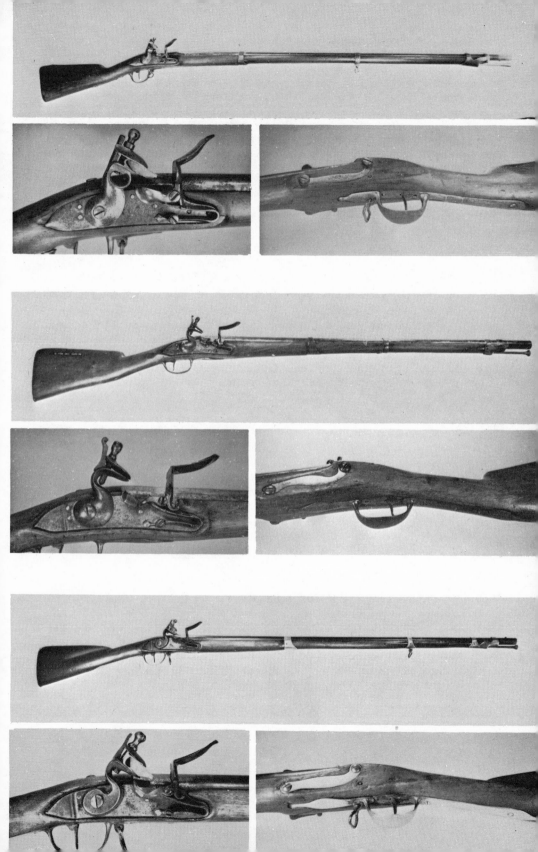

## M.37 FRENCH ARTILLERY CARBINE                                     Circa 1768

This short musket is the type believed carried by the French Artillery. Its typical iron furniture follows the 1768 pattern (see M.31). The lock is full-size and the rammer is trumpet-shaped. It was made at the Maubeuge Manufactory (lock marked MANUF MAUBEUGE). Also present is a crown over the inspector's mark "B." Note how the piece of flint in the cock was usually held in a strip of lead or leather.

Length: 53¾″                   Tr. Guard: 12⅞″                  Furniture: Iron
Barrel: 38¾″; .72              Butt Tang: 2½″                   Weight: 7.8 lbs.
Lock: 6¼″ × 1¼″

*Lewis H. Gordon, Jr., Collection*

## M.38 GERMAN INFANTRY MUSKET                                   Circa 1750-1782

The high comb, heavy brass furniture, and massive lock (cock jaws and frizzen top are squared) help to identify this German musket. It was a pattern used by Prussia and other states from about 1720 to 1782. Note the typical long butt tang, four octagonal and flared rammer pipes, plus raised carving. Its lock is engraved POTSDAM MAGAZ (Potsdam Arsenal); the lower beveled edge is marked "SAD" (probably the lockmaker). An oval escutcheon plate bears Frederick the Great's royal cipher ("FR" under a crown).

Length: 57½″                   Tr. Guard: 12¼″                  Furniture: Brass
Barrel: 41″; .75               Butt Tang: 5½″                   Weight: 10.9 lbs.
Lock: 6¾″ × 1¼″

*Author's Collection*

## M.39 GERMAN-DUTCH INFANTRY MUSKET                             Circa 1750-1780

While this weapon is very similar to the one just above, it does have a shorter and plainer lock, a wider side plate, and a trigger guard typical of the Low Countries. For this reason, it is thought to be one of the arms made under contract for German states. Guns of this pattern were believed carried by Brunswick and other troops during the Revolutionary War. The pinned barrel has the popular elliptical brass front sight, and a bottom bayonet stud.

Length: 59″                    Tr. Guard: 12″                   Furniture: Brass
Barrel: 43″; .79               Butt Tang: 5″                    Weight: 10.5 lbs.
Lock: 6½″ × 1¼″

*Lewis H. Gordon, Jr., Collection*

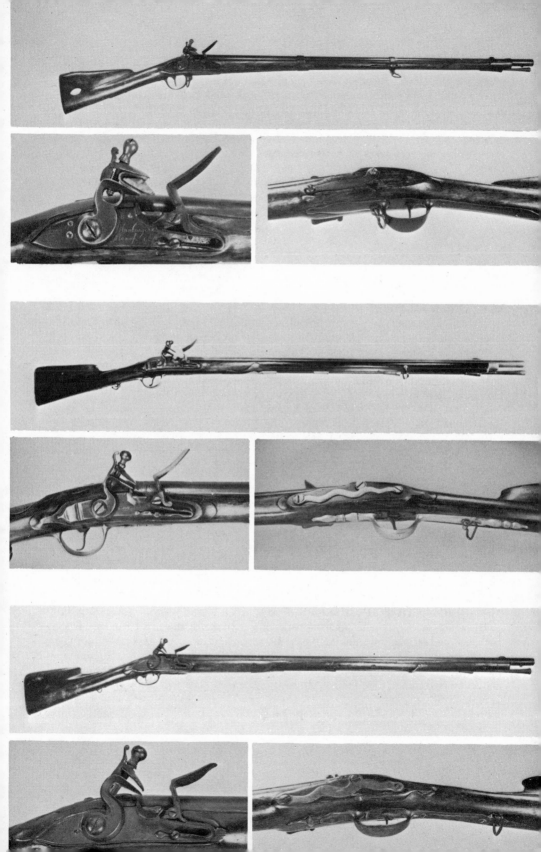

**M.40 GERMAN-DUTCH MUSKET**  Circa 1760-1780

Among the German landgraves providing troops for the British forces in America, there were few large weapon-manufacturing sources—thus little standardization of arms. A large proportion of the muskets apparently carried by them have Dutch characteristics or markings. While the majority were banded, some had pinned barrels, as in this case. The trigger guard, side plate, and raised carving seen here are typical. This jaw screw and possibly the cock were early replacements.

Length: 57½″  Tr. Guard: 11¼″  Furniture: Brass
Barrel: 42″; .78  Butt Tang: 4¾″  Weight: 8.8 lbs.
Lock: 6½″ × 1¼″

*Author's Collection*


**M.41 GERMAN-DUTCH MUSKET**  Circa 1750-1770

The very high comb on this butt is believed to be an early style of the Dutch musket. The flat beveled lock has a faceted flashpan (but no connecting bridle), and its cock jaws and frizzen top are not squared. The forward band includes two straps and a rear retaining spring; the other two barrel bands are held by friction. Its blunted trigger-guard ends are a type found on many Dutch fowlers and trade guns sent to America before the Revolutionary War.

Length: 56″  Tr. Guard: 12″  Furniture: Brass
Barrel: 40½″; .76  Butt Tang: 5½″  Weight: 9.4 lbs.
Lock: 6½″ × 1⅜″

*Author's Collection*


**M.42 GERMAN-DUTCH MUSKET**  Circa 1765-1780

There are several popular characteristics apparent here: the usual flat lock has its cock jaws and frizzen top squared, typical blunt tapered ends are present on the trigger guard, and the tail has been dropped from the side plate. Its forward band is unusual, having only one top strap (mounted with a brass sight), while the bottom bayonet stud and trumpeted rammer are normal. An oval escutcheon plate is held by two brass pins.

Length: 57¾″  Tr. Guard: 12⅛″  Furniture: Brass
Barrel: 42⅞″; .78  Butt Tang: 5⅜″  Weight: 9.3 lbs.
Lock: 6″ × 1¼″

*Author's Collection*

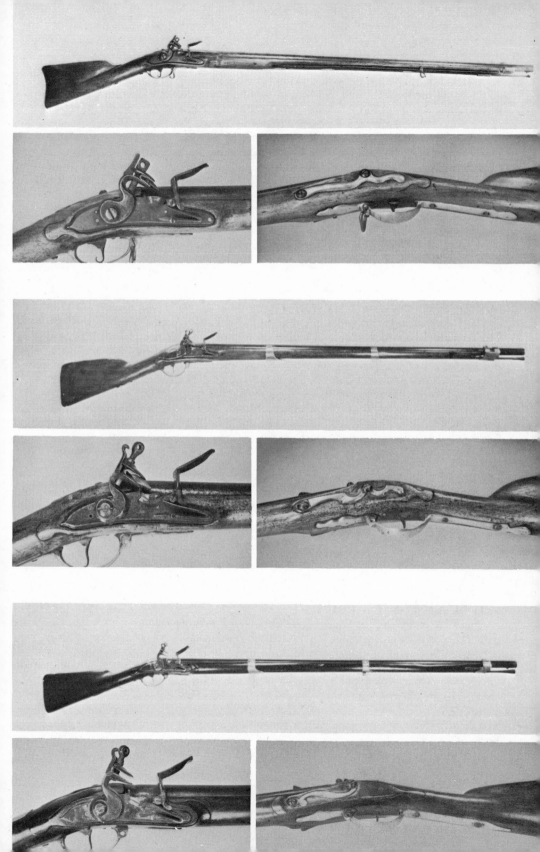

## M.43 GERMAN-DUTCH MUSKET                                    Circa 1770-1780

Several of this pattern are known, and most of them bear a "GR" cipher under a crown on the tail of the lock. They are believed to be products of the Low Countries, supplied to German units for use in America—possibly through England. Notice the similarity of the side plate (small rear screw missing) to the Brown Bess style. All four rammer pipes are flared at their forward ends. The butt tang is inscribed "2RT G B," and the round pinned barrel is stamped with several small arrow-shaped marks.

Length: 58⅜"            Tr. Guard: 11⅞"            Furniture: Brass
Barrel: 44"; .78         Butt Tang: 4"             Weight: 10.5 lbs.
Lock: 6" × 1⅛"

*Morristown National Historical Park Collection*


## M.44 DUTCH CONTRACT MUSKET                                 Circa 1775-1780

This Dutch musket is marked A. ROTTERDAM and N TOMSON on the bevels of the lock. The similarity of the side plate and trigger guard to the contemporary British pattern suggests that this might be one of the arms produced under contract for them in Holland during the mid-1770's. The long lower pipe under the forward band is interesting, and the comb has been shaved by someone to help in aiming. There is no escutcheon plate. The round barrel is marked NO 79 near the muzzle.

Length: 56¼"            Tr. Guard: 10⅜"           Furniture: Brass
Barrel: 40¾"; .74        Butt Tang: 3¾"            Weight: 8.3 lbs.
Lock: 6¼" × 1¼"

*Author's Collection*


## M.45 DUTCH CONTRACT MUSKET                                 Circa 1775-1780

Among the many colonial arms contracts made in Europe beginning in 1775 was one with Thone of Amsterdam (probably by Benjamin Franklin for Massachusetts). This is believed to be one of the styles of arms he supplied. Notice the double-strapped long forward band; the two rear bands are held by friction. Its rounded lock is a typical Dutch style of the 1770's, and the trigger guard is of British styling. On the lock face appears THONE AMSTERDAM.

Length: 55"             Tr. Guard: 9⅝"            Furniture: Brass
Barrel: 40⅜"; .67        Butt Tang: 3⅞"            Weight: 7.4 lbs.
Lock: 5⅝" × 1⅛"

*Lewis H. Gordon, Jr., Collection*

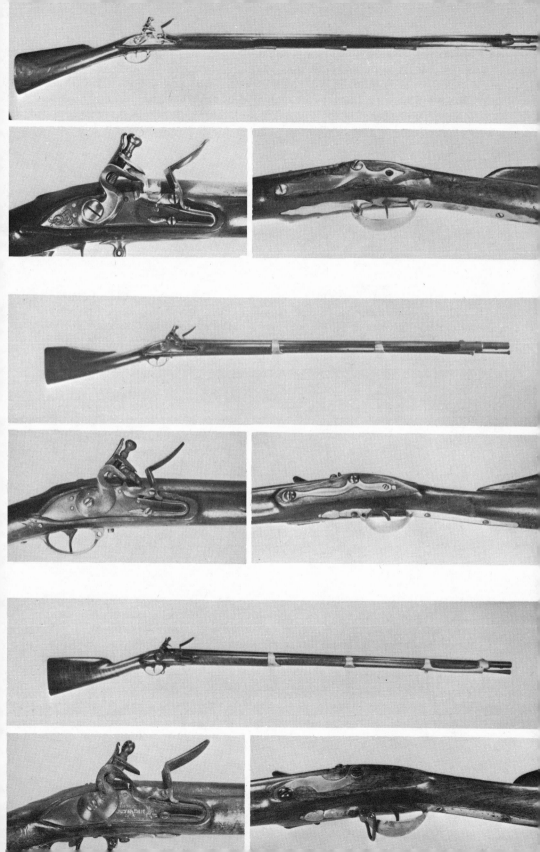

**M.46 DUTCH MUSKET** **Circa 1770-1780**

This is a typical Dutch musket of the 1770's. Its lock has a convex surface, plus a rounded flashpan and outside bridle. The side plate is without a tail, while the trigger guard has narrowed ends. Its round barrel is held by three brass bands. This is one of several known specimens with the barrel inscription GENERALITETT. The oval escutcheon plate (held by two pins) is engraved NO 4098. Other markings include JB, and a small sunburst design stamped behind the trigger guard.

Length: 58¼″ | Tr. Guard: 10¾″ | Furniture: Brass
Barrel: 43¼″; .77 | Butt Tang: 4¼″ | Weight: 9.6 lbs.
Lock: 6⅞″ × 1¼″

*Author's Collection*

**M.47 GERMAN FUSIL MUSKET** **Circa 1765-1780**

An officer or light infantryman probably carried this fusil. It has several Germanic characteristics of the period: the trigger guard includes an arrow shape at each end, the side plate (broken) has an uneven tail, a straight groove in the stock parallels the rammer channel on each side, and the long decorative butt tang extends along a high comb. Its four rammer pipes are octagonal with flared forward ends. The lock is stamped KULENBURG.

Length: 53″ | Tr. Guard: 11⅞″ | Furniture: Brass
Barrel: 39″; .73 | Butt Tang: 5¼″ | Weight: 7.5 lbs.
Lock: 6⅛″ × 1⅛″

*Author's Collection*

**M.48 DUTCH FUSIL MUSKET** **Circa 1775-1780**

This Dutch fusil is marked THONE AMSTERDAM and has a long front-barrel band of the type found on arms believed supplied by Thone to Massachusetts (see M.45). Engraving on the furniture indicates that it was probably an officer's weapon. Checkering was not very popular during the Revolutionary War period, and might have been added here at a later date. The reinforced cock indicates French influence, while its side plate and trigger guard resemble contemporary British styling.

Length: 53⅞″ | Tr. Guard: 9¾″ | Furniture: Brass
Barrel: 39″; .67 | Butt Tang: 3¾″ | Weight: 6.9 lbs.
Lock: 5¼″ × 1″

*Author's Collection*

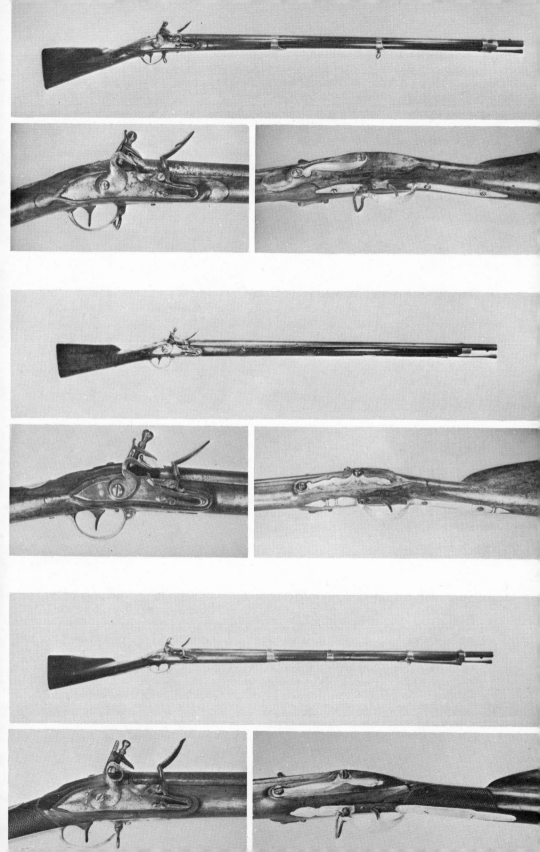

**M.49 GERMAN-DUTCH CARBINE**                        Circa **1770-1780**

The short-barreled arm shown here has a known history of American use during the Revolution. Being of a Dutch-German pattern, it might have been purchased abroad or acquired from Hessian troops in the colonies. Its short (39″), large-caliber (.76) barrel suggests a probable artillery or light-infantry weapon. The use of four brass barrel bands is quite unique. Its lock is of the earlier flat style, with no exterior bridle. A small silver American oval escutcheon plate is held by two pins.

Length: 52⅝″             Tr. Guard: 9¼″              Furniture: Brass
Barrel: 37¾″; .76        Butt Tang: 3″               Weight: 8.1 lbs.
Lock: 6⅛″ × 1¼″

*Author's Collection*

**M.50 SPANISH INFANTRY MUSKET**                     Circa **1740-1760**

The miquelet lock was used by Spain as late as the nineteenth century. This musket is of the type their infantry carried during the mid-1700's. Its flat brass side plate, thin trigger guard, and three-pointed butt tang are typical of the Spanish pattern. The barrel is held by three bands (forward one missing here). Although octagonal at the breech, it flows into a round form after 7″. There is no escutcheon plate.

Length: 55¾″             Tr. Guard: 10⅞″             Furniture: Brass
Barrel: 40⅛″; .72        Butt Tang: 4¼″              Weight: 7.7 lbs.
Lock: 5⅞″ × 1½″

*Jac Weller Collection*

**M.51 SPANISH INFANTRY MUSKET**                     Circa **1750-1791**

The Spanish arm in this case is the pattern produced from the 1750's until about 1791. Its lock has been changed from the miquelet to a French style which was manufactured in Spain (note the Spanish cock jaw screw ring). These muskets were undoubtedly used by the Americans—some acquired in the Havana expedition during the Seven Years' War, and others through the West Indies and Florida in the Revolution. The furniture remains similar to the previous model shown.

Length: 59⅝″             Tr. Guard: 11¼″             Furniture: Brass
Barrel: 43½″; .72        Butt Tang: 4¼″              Weight: 8.6 lbs.
Lock: 6¾″ × 1⅜″

*Author's Collection*

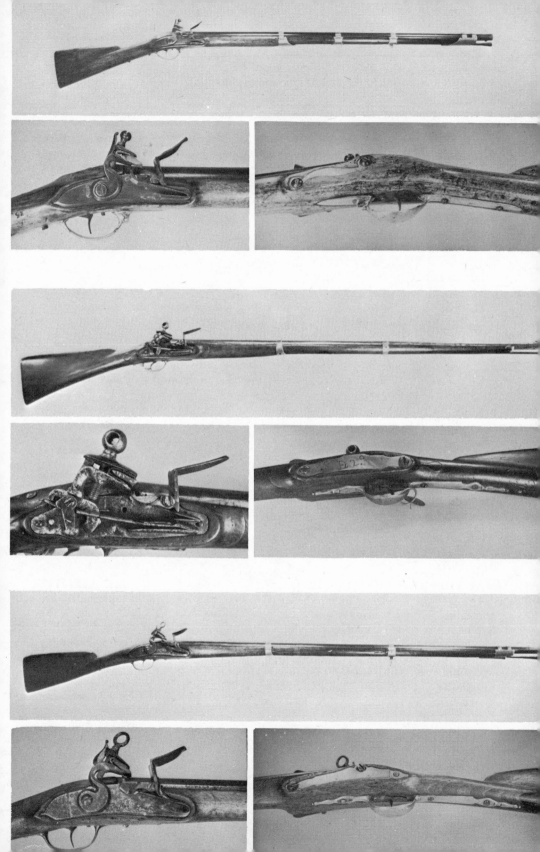

## M.52 EUROPEAN INFANTRY MUSKET $\qquad$ Circa 1740-1760

This is one of the many types imported from Europe by the American colonies. The round lock, convex side plate, and trigger guard are all similar to Dutch styles (but are made of iron notwithstanding their preference for brass). The butt too has acquired a downward cast. It is probably of Low Countries origin—possibly from Liège. The trumpet-shaped rammer is held by four ribbed pipes, and the bayonet lug is on top of the barrel (octagonal-round in shape).

Length: 59¾"　　　　　Tr. Guard: 13½"　　　　　Furniture: Iron
Barrel: 44¼"; .70　　　 Butt Tang: 6⅝"　　　　　Weight: 8.7 lbs.
Lock: 6¼" × 1¼"

*Howard B. Greene Collection*

## M.53 AMERICAN HUDSON VALLEY FOWLER $\qquad$ Circa 1690-1710

This long fowling piece, which stands some 6½' high, is typical of the hunting weapons used along New York's Hudson River Valley during the late seventeenth and early eighteenth centuries. They usually had imported barrels and locks, Dutch-pattern furniture, and stocks of native American woods. Notice the open side plate (early dragon form), plus the raised carving around the trigger guard and lock. Its round barrel (Amsterdam-proofed and "ringed" 12½" from the breech) is pinned to the stock, and mounts a front brass sight (no rear sight).

Length: 78½"　　　　　Tr. Guard: 11"　　　　　Furniture: Brass
Barrel: 61½"; .69　　　 Butt Tang: 5½"　　　　　Weight: 11.7 lbs.
Lock: 6" × 1¼"

*Glode M. Requa Collection*

## M.54 AMERICAN LONG FOWLER $\qquad$ Circa 1725-1740

This 7' fowler is believed to have belonged to the Samis family on Long Island (New York), and to have seen some use in the Revolutionary War. The barrel bears seventeenth-century London proofs, while the banana-shaped lock is a typical early English specimen. Its open side plate, pointed trigger guard, curled trigger, and raised carvings are all indicative of this era. A tail pipe plus four plain forward pipes hold the wooden rammer. The stock is of American maple.

Length: 84"　　　　　　Tr. Guard: 11¼"　　　　　Furniture: Brass
Barrel: 67¾"; .76　　　 Butt Tang: 6¼"　　　　　Weight: 16.0 lbs.
Lock: 7" × 1¼"

*Anthony D. Darling Collection*

88

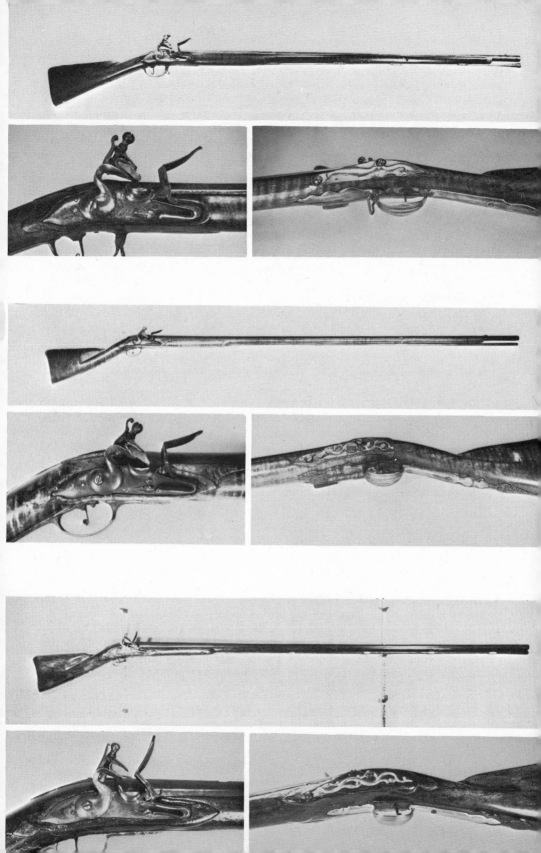

## M.55 AMERICAN LONG FOWLER

**Circa 1730**

This example has a Spanish barrel (octagonal breech, blending into a round surface after 18¾"). Its butt end in this case is flat, and covered with sheet brass (instead of a cast plate) fastened on with small square-headed nails. Raised carvings again appear around the Dutch-style lock and trigger guard. The striking American striped maple stock is also visible. Its simple escutcheon plate is fastened with two brass pins.

Length: 78"  Tr. Guard: 12"  Furniture: Brass
Barrel: 61½"; .71  Butt Tang: 6½"  Weight: 9.6 lbs.
Lock: 6¼" × 1¼"

*Glode M. Requa Collection*

## M.56 AMERICAN LONG FOWLER

**Circa 1750-1760**

As the century progressed, the long fowler barrels were gradually shortened. In this specimen of the 1750's the total length is under 6'. Although the raised carving in the stock is still prevalent, a flat, solid side plate is now evident, an exterior lock bridle has appeared, and the curl of the trigger is less. Its rounded barrel (slightly flared at the muzzle) is of English manufacture (1702-style proofs), and the British lock is marked WILSON.

Length: 70¾"  Tr. Guard: 11½"  Furniture: Brass
Barrel: 55"; .71  Butt Tang: 6"  Weight: 10.5 lbs.
Lock: 6½" × 1¼"

*Glode M. Requa Collection*

## M.57 AMERICAN LONG FOWLER

**Circa 1745-1755**

By the middle of the eighteenth century, most long fowlers were losing not only length, but also many refinements. As seen in this illustration, the raised carving has been omitted. The side plate, too, is just a flat piece of cast brass—although the early style of trigger guard, butt plate (long 5⅛" tang), and ribbed rammer pipes (four) remains. Its flat lock and round barrel are of the Dutch-Germanic type. No escutcheon plate is included.

Length: 69¾"  Tr. Guard: 10¾"  Furniture: Brass
Barrel: 54"; .68  Butt Tang: 5⅛"  Weight: 9.8 lbs.
Lock: 5½" × 1⅛"

*Author's Collection*

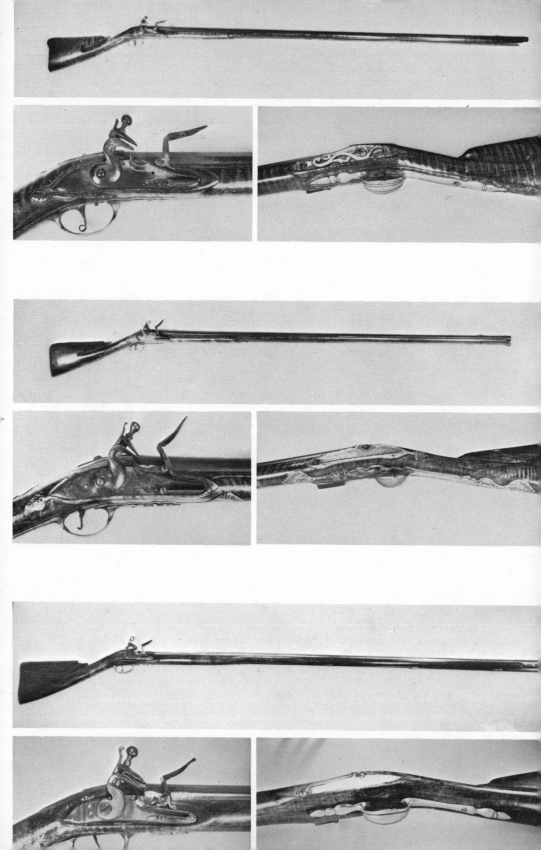

## M.58 AMERICAN CLUB BUTT FOWLER                    Circa 1700-1720

The club butt or "fish belly" stock is most often traced to New England or eastern New York State. This particular example has many early characteristics: the flat unbridled lock (old three-screw variety), semi-dragon side plate, thin simple trigger guard, and "underneath" screw for the barrel tang. Although stocked to the muzzle for hunting, it is believed that these fowling pieces saw substantial use with the American forces in the Revolution—especially among the militia and independent companies.

Length: 61¾"            Tr. Guard: 9¼"                Furniture: Brass
Barrel: 46⅜"; .72       Butt Tang: 1¼"               Weight: 10.1 lbs.
Lock: 7⅛" × 1⅜"

*Eric Vaule Collection*


## M.59 AMERICAN CLUB BUTT FOWLER                    Circa 1710-1730

Like the previous example, this "clubbed" fowling piece has an early three-screw lock, and a barrel tang screw originating underneath the stock (just forward of the trigger). A flat brass strip is nailed (small square heads) to the butt end. The side plate too is flat, with some engraving and an open center. Its oval escutcheon has a brass center pin. The marking "4" on both the lock and butt tang suggests its use as one of a group—possibly in a militia unit.

Length: 63"             Tr. Guard: 8¾"               Furniture: Brass
Barrel: 46⅞"; .72       Butt Tang: 2⅜"               Weight: 7.9 lbs.
Lock: 7" × 1¼"

*Author's Collection*


## M.60 AMERICAN CLUB BUTT FOWLER                    Circa 1740-1750

Further evolution of the American fowler is seen here. Notice the solid flat side plate, and a colonial imitation of the Brown Bess trigger guard (sling swivel hole omitted in bow). There is no butt plate or escutcheon plate. A brass tail pipe and two upper pipes hold the wooden rammer. The lock now has an outside bridle to support its frizzen, while the reinforced cock is of the early English style—reused on naval muskets in the 1750's (M.21). The barrel marking "33" indicates probable military use at some time.

Length: 66¼"            Tr. Guard: 9½"               Furniture: Brass
Barrel: 50⅜"; .72                                    Weight: 8.3 lbs.
Lock: 6⅝" × 1¼"

*Author's Collection*

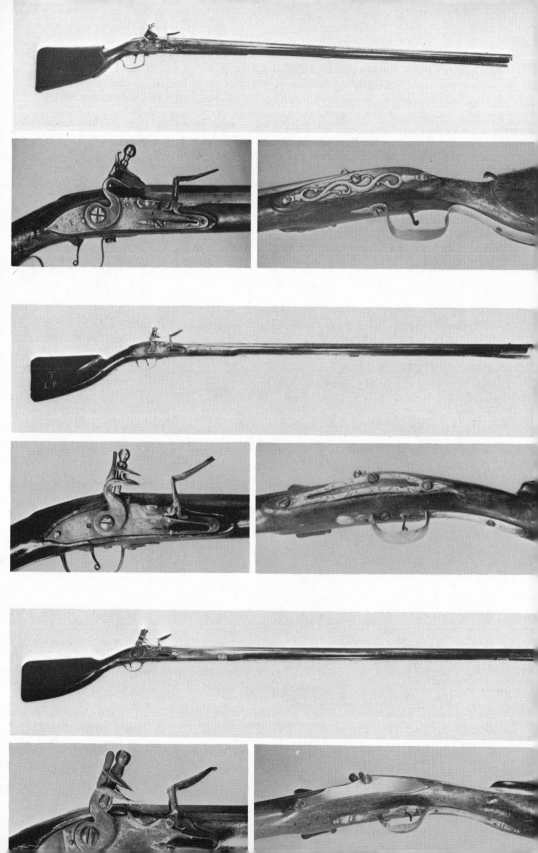

## M.61 AMERICAN "FISH BELLY" FOWLER                    Circa 1770-1785

This "fish belly" fowler has a mixture of relatively early and late characteristics. Its earlier features include: a rounded Dutch-style lock (no bridle and the frizzen spring screw comes from inside); raised carving around the fittings; a barrel tang screw originating under the stock; a "flat" along the barrel top (for 31"); and a slightly flared muzzle. Later features are the absence of a side plate and the use of four slotted keys to hold the barrel. The name J WRIGHT and two sights appear on the barrel.

Length: 59½"
Barrel: 44"; .79
Lock: 6½" × 1¼"

Tr. Guard: 11"
Butt Tang: 4¾"

Furniture: Brass
Weight: 11.1 lbs.

*Author's Collection*

## M.62 DUTCH FOWLER                    Circa 1710-1730

The Dutch fowler pictured here is typical of many traded and used in the colonies during the early 1700's. The round barrel was probably stocked to the muzzle originally, and later cut back for a socket bayonet. An early dragon-style side plate is included, as well as an embellished trigger guard (fastened with nails). The lock is heavily engraved, while the brass escutcheon plate has a raised border. The maker's name, L. TONUS, is on the lock.

Length: 60¼"
Barrel: 44½"; .68
Lock: 5⅜" × 1"

Tr. Guard: 10¼"
Butt Tang: 5½"

Furniture: Brass
Weight: 8.1 lbs.

*Joseph E. Fritzinger Collection*

## M.63 EUROPEAN MUSKET                    Circa 1700-1720

The rounded bottom of this butt is similar to early eighteenth-century English muskets, and is often referred to as a Queen Anne stock. Also of interest is the transition shown from three to two lock screws. The traditional three heads are evident in the lock plate, but only two pass through the stock. Its pinned barrel is octagonal at the breech for 10" to the first ornamental ring (a second one is 3" beyond). There is no tail pipe; the wooden rammer is held in two plain upper pipes. The nose cap is a flat strip of brass.

Length: 61½"
Barrel: 45¾"; .70
Lock: 6¼" × 1¼"

Tr. Guard: 10⅜"
Butt Tang: 3¼"

Furniture: Brass
Weight: 8.1 lbs.

*Author's Collection*

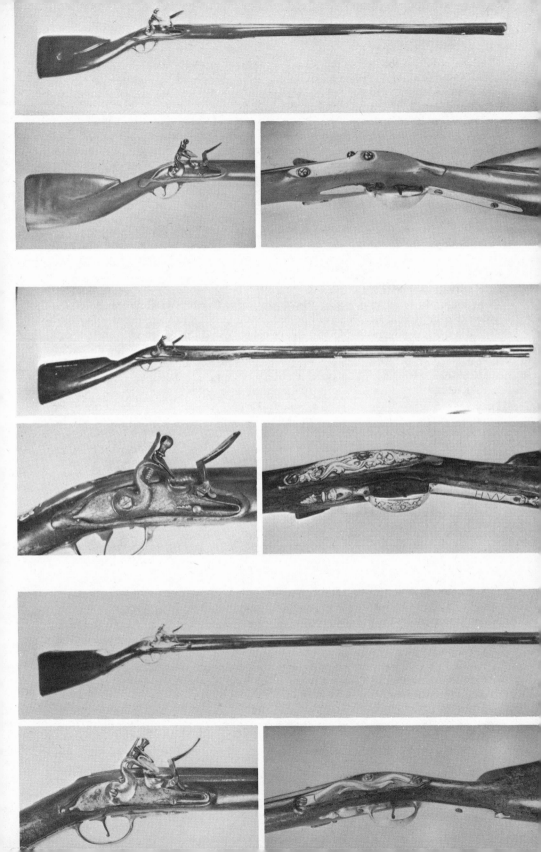

## M.64 AMERICAN FOWLER

Circa 1755-1759

The sharp drop in the butt of this fowler is similar to the style later adopted for many Pennsylvania rifles. Its side plate is inscribed LEUT. THADDEUS COOK, and the escutcheon plate is dated "1759." During the Revolutionary War, he was colonel of a Connecticut State regiment. This arm is still in the hands of the Cook family today. Its stock is of curly maple, and the top view indicates a typical long butt tang. The pinned barrel is stocked to the muzzle, with a top "flat" reaching for 44¾".

Length: 64½"                    Tr. Guard: 9½"                    Furniture: Brass
Barrel: 49¼"; .59               Butt Tang: 5⅞"                    Weight: 7.6 lbs.
Lock: 6⅛" × 1³⁄₁₆"

*Harmon Cook Leonard Collection*

## M.65 AMERICAN MILITIA MUSKET

Circa 1760-1770

This long arm is an example of the "dual purpose" gun owned by many of the eighteenth-century colonists. It served primarily as a hunting weapon, but was modified to fulfill militia requirements. Most of the colonies offered the option of a short sword or bayonet; this stock has been cut back and a stud added to qualify for the latter. The octagonal-round pinned barrel, trigger guard (brass), and flat lock (1754-style) have a French origin. Its side plate, stock, rammer pipes, and butt plate are of American design.

Length: 63"                     Tr. Guard: 11"                    Furniture: Brass
Barrel: 47¾"; .78               Butt Tang: 4¼"                    Weight: 8.6 lbs.
Lock: 6¼" × 1¼"

*Author's Collection*

## M.66 AMERICAN MILITIA MUSKET

Circa 1760-1770

Here is another example of the semimilitary musket used by so many Americans during the French and Indian War and the War for Independence. Its military connotation is apparent from the bayonet stud (top), plus a Brown Bess–style escutcheon plate. The long (46½") round pinned barrel comes from an early English arm, as does the convex lock (marked FARMER, with simple engravings of the trade-lock style). The American brass furniture includes rammer pipes bent from a flat sheet (in contrast to the usual European cast pipes).

Length: 62"                     Tr. Guard: 7½"                    Furniture: Brass
Barrel: 46½"; .75               Butt Tang: 4"                     Weight: 7.7 lbs.
Lock: 5¾" × 1"

*Author's Collection*

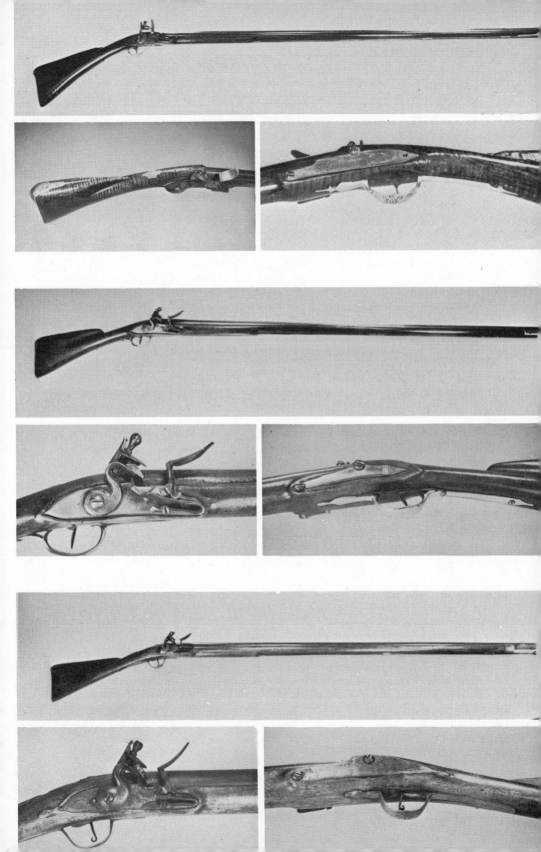

## M.67 AMERICAN MILITIA MUSKET Circa 1740-1760

This musket came from the Pennsylvania Dutch area and bears several character-istics of the section. Its rounded lock reflects Dutch influence, and the trigger guard is of a Germanic style. The popular heart figure of the region is inscribed on the escutch-eon plate, with a floral design on the butt tang. Around the edges of the lock and side plate are small stamped borders of the type found on much of their furniture. A deco-rative brass plate is nailed to the stock at the handhold position.

Length: 60″  Tr. Guard: 10½″  Furniture: Brass
Barrel: 44½″; .78  Butt Tang: 5½″  Weight: 8.1 lbs.
Lock: 5⅝″ × 1⅛″

*Joseph E. Fritzinger Collection*

## M.68 AMERICAN MILITIA MUSKET Circa 1740-1760

The stock of this arm was painted at one time with the "buttermilk-brick" red paint so often used in the early days. Its military use is evidenced by the sling swivel holes, bayonet stud, plus the markings "14" and so CAROLINA on the barrel. The convex un-bridled lock, side plate, and trigger guard are of the Dutch-German style (made of iron). Its pinned barrel is octagonal at the breech—flowing into a round form after 8½″. There is no escutcheon plate.

Length: 60½″  Tr. Guard: 13″  Furniture: Iron
Barrel: 45″; .79  Butt Tang: 7¼″  Weight: 10.2 lbs.
Lock: 6¾″ × 1⅜″

*Eric Vaule Collection*

## M.69 AMERICAN MUSKET Circa 1755-1770

This is another typical musket carried by Americans in the French and Indian War and in the Revolution. It combines styles of three or four countries. The pinned barrel (octagonal at breech for 6″) and flat lock (faceted, bridled pan) follow early French lines. Its trigger guard is a colonial copy of the Brown Bess (notice that there is no sling swivel, and two as against one rear screw). The side plate is similar to contemporary Spanish muskets (M.51), while the butt plate is fashioned in an American design. Its forward pipe is flared for an iron rammer.

Length: 60¾″  Tr. Guard: 9½″  Furniture: Brass
Barrel: 45¼″; .72  Butt Tang: 4″  Weight: 7.5 lbs.
Lock: 6¼″ × 1¼″

*Author's Collection*

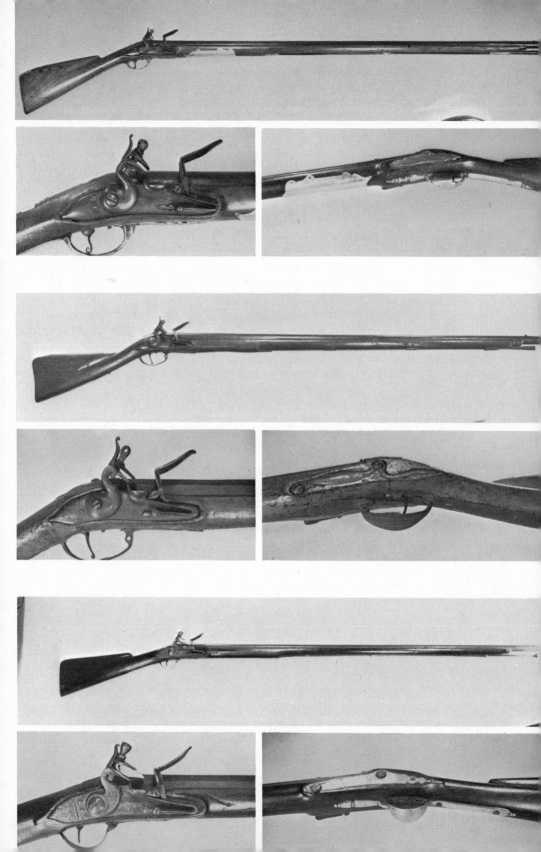

## M.70 AMERICAN MUSKET                                            Circa 1760-1776

To survive in the New World the colonists had to be a practical people. This is never more evident than in the diversity of firearms they made. Parts were constantly salvaged from older weapons regardless of their origin (just as long as they worked). The principal components of this specimen came from a 1728 French musket—although the heavy butt plate, plain iron rammer pipes (three), and stock appear to be American. Its faint barrel marking, "MB," may be a French stamp or a later Massachusetts Bay designation.

Length: 60⅛″             Tr. Guard: 12¼″             Furniture: Iron
Barrel: 44⅜″; .72        Butt Tang: 2½″              Weight 8.6 lbs.
Lock: 6⅝″ × 1⅜″

*Author's Collection*


## M.71 AMERICAN MUSKET                                            Circa 1775-1780

This musket was probably made for the American forces early in the Revolutionary War. The barrel (1702-style London proofs), lock (VERNON 1762), trigger guard, and butt plate came from an English Brown Bess. The side plate and remaining furniture seem to be American (including the curly maple stock, and a shell carving behind the barrel tang). A "US" surcharge on the barrel indicates apparent use in a Continental line regiment. There is no escutcheon plate.

Length: 58⅛″             Tr. Guard: 11⅛″            Furniture: Brass
Barrel: 43″; .78         Butt Tang: 6″               Weight: 9.1 lbs.
Lock: 7″ × 1¼″

*Foster Tallman Collection*


## M.72 AMERICAN MUSKET                                            Circa 1760-1778

This is a fine example of a long-land-pattern Brown Bess restocked for use by the colonists. Lock markings are WILSON and LONDON (plus "US"). Its trigger guard appears to be a simple American copy of the English design. No escutcheon plate is present (notice the absence of a screw in the trigger guard to secure it). Samuel Stratton of Long Island reportedly carried it in the Revolution. Its five surcharges include U.STATES behind the trigger guard and UNITED.STATES on the butt face.

Length: 62¼″             Tr. Guard: 11″              Furniture: Brass
Barrel: 46″; .77         Butt Tang: 4⅜″              Weight: 9.6 lbs.
Lock: 7″ × 1¼″

*Howard B. Greene Collection*

**100**

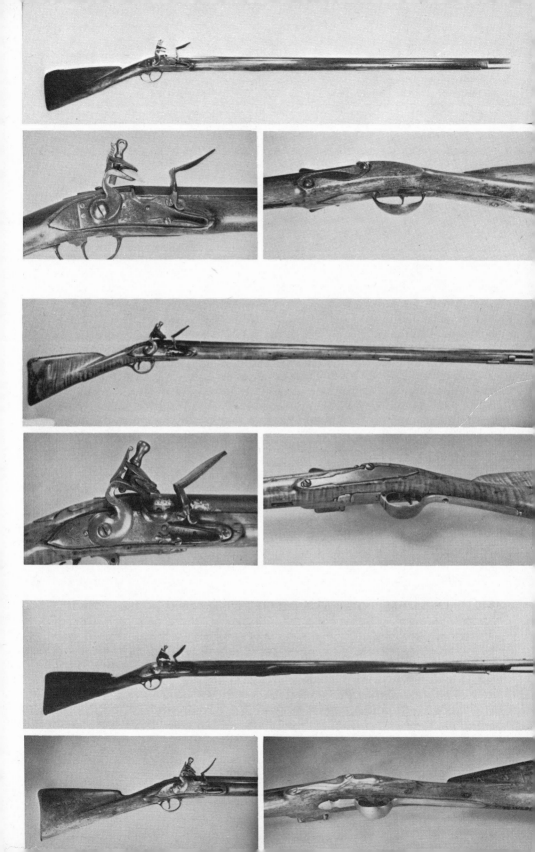

## M.73 AMERICAN MUSKET                          Circa 1770-1778

Another long-land-pattern Brown Bess furnished the metal parts for this arm. The barrel bears its original London proofs, plus "52D REGT." Its lock has the royal cipher and DUBLIN CASTLE (a British arsenal in Ireland assembling arms *ca.* 1760–1798), while the escutcheon plate is marked "R G/25" (probably Company G, Rack #25). The downward cast of the butt is indicative of its American restocking—as are the two forward rammer pipes with the flared ends. The crude letters "NR" on the stock are probably initials of an owner.

Length: 62¼″             Tr. Guard: 10⅞″           Furniture: Brass
Barrel: 46″; .77         Butt Tang: 5½″            Weight: 10.8 lbs.
Lock: 7″ × 1¼″

*Lewis H. Gordon, Jr., Collection*


## M.74 AMERICAN MUSKET                          Circa 1775-1780

The chestnut stock and five convex rammer pipes are indicative of this arm's American background. Yet, the brass furniture is typical of the British short-land pattern, while the lock and rounded barrel are Dutch. This may be a combination of odd parts or an English contract musket (from Holland) restocked in the colonies. (Note: The barrel measures 42″ with a .78-caliber bore.) An American numeral, "54," appears on the barrel. This weapon was used by Massachusetts troops in the Revolution.

Length: 58″              Tr. Guard: 11¼″           Furniture: Brass
Barrel: 42″; .78         Butt Tang: 3¾″            Weight: 9.8 lbs.
Lock: 6¾″ × 1¼″

*Author's Collection*


## M.75 AMERICAN MUSKET                          Circa 1776-1783

With the exception of an American stock, the remains of a German musket constitute most of this weapon. Since the mountings are from a pattern believed used here by German troops (see M.38), it was probably made from a captured arm. Small alterations do exist, however: the tail of the lock plate is gone, the usual POTSDAM marking is ground away, and the butt tang is shortened. The escutcheon plate is also missing. Only a stamping, "FM," remains on the barrel.

Length: 59½″             Tr. Guard: 12⅜″           Furniture: Brass
Barrel: 40⅞″; .75        Butt Tang: 3½″            Weight: 9.3 lbs.
Lock: 6¾″ × 1¼″

*Foster Tallman Collection*

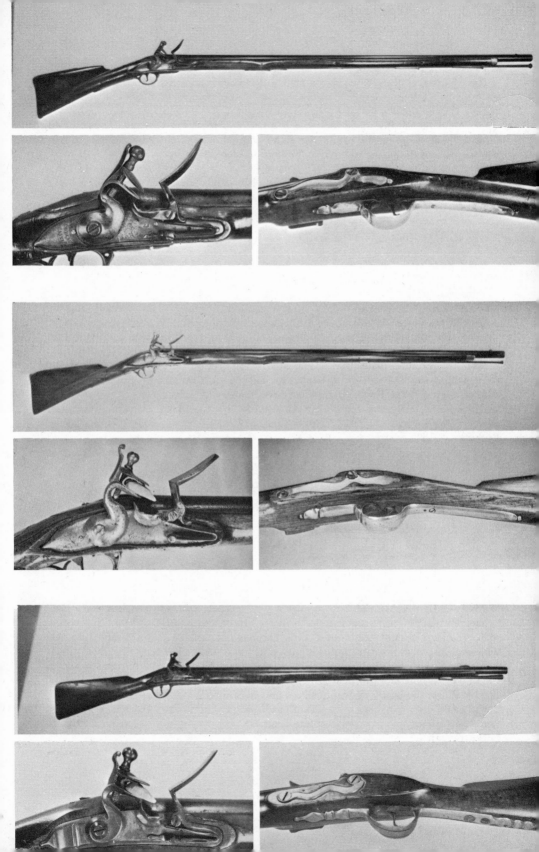

## M.76 AMERICAN MUSKET
Circa 1765-1783

This weapon appears to be a completely American-made product. With a stock of curly maple, it is apparently a colonial copy of the French 1728-1746 pattern (see M.25). Of additional interest is the simple trigger guard (with two rear supporting screws) and the locally made lock which tapers rapidly toward its tail. The rounded barrel includes a top bayonet stud. No escutcheon plate is present. Like so many American weapons of the period, there is an absence of identifying marks.

Length: 60½"                Tr. Guard: 9¾"                Furniture: Brass
Barrel: 44½"; .69           Butt Tang: 4¼"               Weight: 8.6 lbs.
Lock: 6⅝" × 1⅛"

*Gene E. Miller Collection*


## M.77 AMERICAN MUSKET
Circa 1750-1760

Robert Bradford of Haddam, Connecticut, carried this copy of the British Brown Bess under Israel Putnam during the French and Indian War. He also served at Bunker Hill, and as ensign in Cook's Connecticut regiment in the Revolution (see M.64). The thin sheet-brass furniture, undersized trigger guard, and crude barrel are typical of colonial work. Its large stock swelling just behind the tail pipe further suggests this early period. Also of interest is the English-style escutcheon plate.

Length: 59¾"                Tr. Guard: 8⅞"                Furniture: Brass
Barrel: 44¾"; .74           Butt Tang: 3¾"               Weight: 9.8 lbs.
Lock: 6¼" × 1¼"

*Author's Collection*


## M.78 AMERICAN MUSKET
Circa 1770-1780

The unusual height of this lock in relation to its length gives it a stubby proportion unlike the work of most European makers. The side plate design shows French influence, while a British trigger guard probably served as reference for the much simplified American version. Use by Continental troops is evidenced by the brand UNITED.STATES on the side of its butt face. NO 52 appears on the oval escutcheon plate, while the inscription "M.H" on the butt tang is probably an owner's initials.

Length: 60⅝"                Tr. Guard: 9⅝"                Furniture: Brass
Barrel: 45"; .79            Butt Tang: 3½"               Weight: 10.4 lbs.
Lock: 6" × 1¼"

*Hermann W. Williams, Jr., Collection*

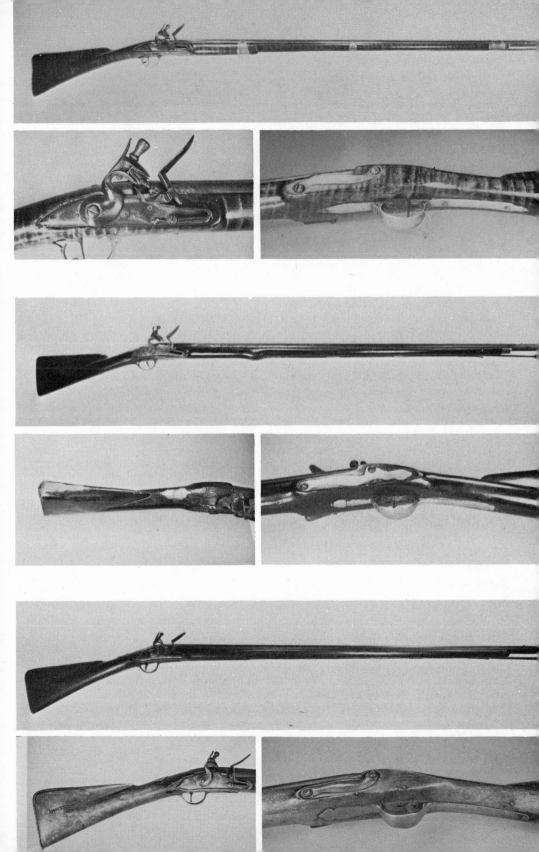

**M.79 AMERICAN MUSKET** Circa 1770-1783

Variations of the club butt stock continued to be used into the nineteenth century (mostly in New England). This piece is considered typical of some carried in the War for Independence. The curved 4″ brass piece just behind the muzzle has been found on several arms of this period (usually in eastern Massachusetts). Its long butt tang, flat cast side plate, and plain brass rammer pipes (not cast) are of colonial manufacture. The acorn motif on the trigger guard is a copy of an English design.

Length: 62⅞″            Tr. Guard: 10″            Furniture: Brass
Barrel: 46½″; .74       Butt Tang: 5½″            Weight: 8.9 lbs.
Lock: 6⅜″ × 1¼″

*Author's Collection*

**M.80 AMERICAN MUSKET** Circa 1760-1776

Except for the round barrel (faint British proofs), this long arm seems to be completely American. The trigger guard (note the early curled trigger) is a version of the popular acorn design, and the "stepped" butt tang is similar to the English style. Wrapped around the "small" of the stock is a brass sheet which was typical of early repairs. Its rounded lock bears the name ABIJAH THOMPSON. He is listed originally as a clerk of the 1st Woburn Company in Massachusetts, and then as a "Master Armorer" from 1775 to 1776.

Length: 59½″            Tr. Guard: 9⅛″            Furniture: Brass
Barrel: 44″; .77        Butt Tang: 4″             Weight: 9.0 lbs.
Lock: 7″ × 1¼″

*William H. Guthman Collection*

**M.81 AMERICAN MUSKET** Circa. 1760-1778

The British long-land pattern apparently served as the guide for this American gun. Yet the colonials again show their pragmatic approach by eliminating many of the small European refinements. For example, the finials at the ends of the side plate and trigger guard are gone—as is the point at the tail of the French-style lock. Neither sling swivels nor an escutcheon plate were provided. However, the weapon is well constructed and sturdy. Note, too, the long nose cap.

Length: 61⅛″           Tr. Guard: 9⅜″            Furniture: Brass
Barrel: 46″; .79        Butt Tang: 4½″            Weight: 9.3 lbs.
Lock: 6½″ × 1⅜″

*Author's Collection*

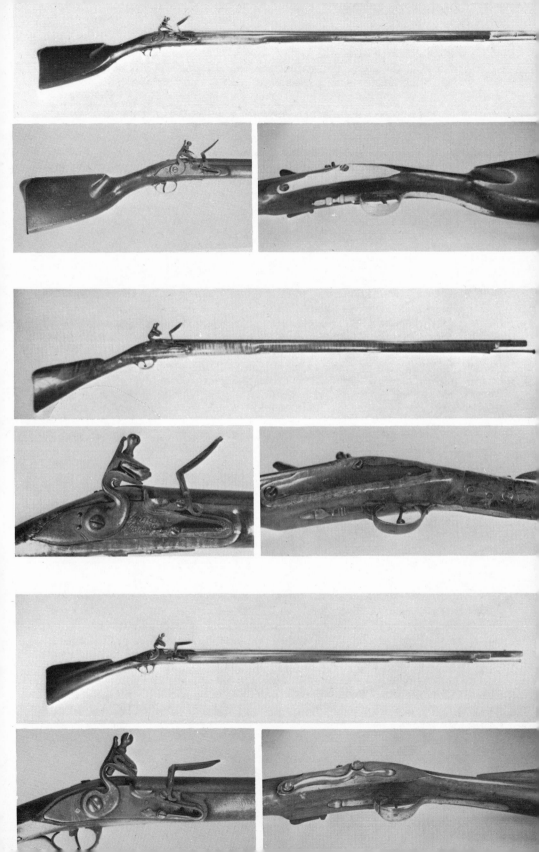

## M.82 AMERICAN MUSKET                Circa 1775-1776

Muskets such as this were produced in the colonies at the outbreak of the Revolutionary War. Being familiar with English arms, most Committees of Safety and states specified similar pinned patterns. This specimen's furniture is a smaller version of the long-land styling. Its lock is British (a crown and broad arrow still visible) and the heavy barrel has ¼" "flats" around its breech (to an ornamental ring 11¼" forward). A rear sight is also present (notched blade).

Length: 59¾"  
Barrel: 43⅞"; .71  
Lock: 7" × 1¼"

Tr. Guard: 10⅜"  
Butt Tang: 3½"

Furniture: Brass  
Weight: 10.8 lbs.

*Author's Collection*

## M.83 AMERICAN MUSKET                Circa 1775-1778

Here is another example of a colonial arm produced early in the Revolution (copying Britain's long-land pattern). Of great interest in this piece is the number of American markings. The surcharge U.STATES appears in the stock just forward of the trigger guard, with UNITED:STATES branded on the butt face. The colonial-made barrel is stamped US, C-COUNTY, and has an overlapping CP in an oval (not the postwar Pennsylvania marking). The upper 22" of the stock is a restoration.

Length: 59⅜"  
Barrel: 43¾"; .73  
Lock: 6⅞" × 1¼"

Tr. Guard: 10⅜"  
Butt Tang: 5"

Furniture: Brass  
Weight: 9.9 lbs.

*Morristown National Historical Park Collection*

## M.84 AMERICAN MUSKET                Circa 1775-1780

This state-contracted musket again uses furniture patterned after the Brown Bess. Its flat beveled lock is probably of European origin, and includes an interesting safety feature, i.e. the lug protruding into a notched section at the rear of the cock. The stock is walnut, while a tail pipe and two upper pipes (forward one flared) hold the iron rammer. Inscribed on the barrel is "SP," which is believed to have been stamped on some New Jersey arms.

Length: 59⅜"  
Barrel: 44"; .72  
Lock: 5¾" × 1¼"

Tr. Guard: 10⅜"  
Butt Tang: 4¾"

Furniture: Brass  
Weight: 9.6 lbs.

*Author's Collection*

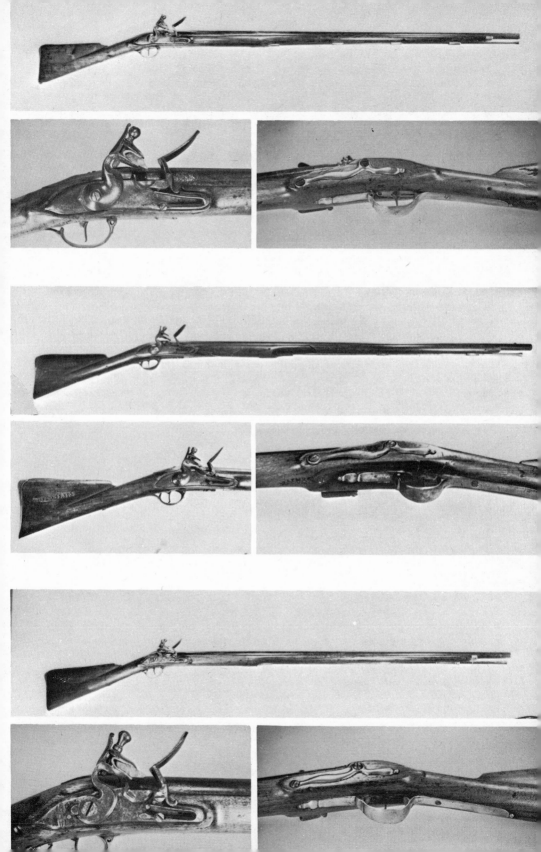

## M.85 AMERICAN MUSKET

Circa 1775-1780

Several of this particular style are known. They are thought to have been produced for Maryland during the Revolution. The lock has a rounded surface, a circular pan with bridle, plus a rather steep taper toward the tail. Its flat side plate, trigger guard (no rear finial), and butt plate follow the British short-land pattern, while a large flat screw is centered in an English-style escutcheon plate. The rammer pipes are long (4″), and formed from sheet brass. "PS" is stamped on the barrel.

Length: 57¾″
Barrel: 42″; .77
Lock: 6⅜″ × 1⅛″

Tr. Guard: 10¾″
Butt Tang: 4¼″

Furniture: Brass
Weight: 9.4 lbs.

*John C. McMurray Collection*

## M.86 AMERICAN MUSKET

Circa 1775-1780

This musket is also thought to have originated under a contract from the state of Maryland. The name on the barrel, I KING (note: "J" was written like an "I" in this period), is said to refer to John King of Talbot County. The brass furniture reflects the English style, but the flat lock is similar to many imported from Europe at this time. Four long rammer pipes are included, with a narrow nose cap. Its stock is stamped "33" behind the side plate.

Length: 57½″
Barrel: 41½″; .74
Lock: 6½″ × 1⅛″

Tr. Guard: 9⅜″
Butt Tang: 3⅜″

Furniture: Brass
Weight: 9.5 lbs.

*Valley Forge Museum Collection*

## M.87 AMERICAN MUSKET

Circa 1777-1783

Faint markings on this barrel read 6 V. REGT. SPOTSYLVANIA. Although these county designations were popular in Virginia during the 1790's, the weapon's characteristics, plus the fact that older muskets from the arsenals were used at this time, indicate its probable Revolutionary War origin. The lock is similar to the Maryland type (M.85), and the French styling on the side plate and butt tang suggest manufacture after 1777. Its barrel is thick-walled, with an off-center bore.

Length: 56¾″
Barrel: 41½″; .67
Lock: 5⅞″ × 1¼″

Tr. Guard: 10¼″
Butt Tang: 2″

Furniture: Brass
Weight: 9.3 lbs.

*Author's Collection*

110

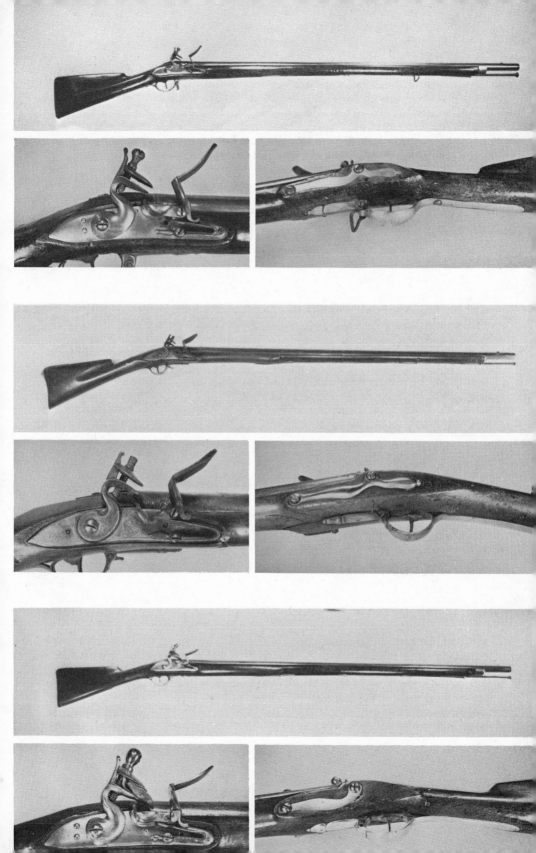

## M.88 AMERICAN MUSKET                                    Circa 1775-1780

The design of the stock in this case is definitely American, yet the contemporary British short-land pattern has again been adopted for the furniture. Note that the cock includes the rectangular top tang which became popular on English muskets in the 1770's (M.12). Its long barrel (48¼") mounts the usual top bayonet stud, while the button-headed iron rammer is held by a tail pipe and only two upper pipes (forward one flared). The brass nose cap and escutcheon plate are typical.

Length: 63¾"                    Tr. Guard: 10⅞"              Furniture: Brass
Barrel: 48¼"                    Butt Tang: 3½"               Weight: 11.1 lbs.
Lock: 7" × 1⅜₁₆"

*Thomas E. Hall Collection*


## M.89 AMERICAN FUSIL MUSKET                              Circa 1775-1777

Of principal interest in this fusil is the name ANNELY on the lock. Thomas and Edward Annely are listed as gunsmiths in New Jersey until about 1777, and made weapons for the colonial troops. In addition, the barrel has "P" stamps, which are believed by some to be Philadelphia proofs. (Note: New Jersey did buy musket parts in Pennsylvania during the Revolution.) The stock's upper end is not original.

Length: 55"                     Tr. Guard: 6⅝"              Furniture: Brass
Barrel: 39¾"; .65              Weight: 7.6 lbs.
Lock: 6⅜" × 1¼"

*R. Paul Nittolo Collection*


## M.90 AMERICAN FUSIL MUSKET                              Circa 1770-1780

This smaller-caliber (.62) fusil was probably made for an officer. The triangular brass side plate, flat butt, and downward cast of the stock are typical of colonial styling. Of interest is the trigger guard, which follows the French form at its forward end but adopts a crude arrow design in the rear. This, plus a heart shape inscribed on the escutcheon plate, and the gun being found in Pennsylvania, indicates its origin among early German settlers. Brass tacks on the butt form the letters "IA."

Length: 56½"                    Tr. Guard: 8½"              Furniture: Brass
Barrel: 41¾"; .62              Butt Tang: 4¼"               Weight: 6.6 lbs.
Lock: 5¾" × 1"

*Joe Kindig, Jr., Collection*

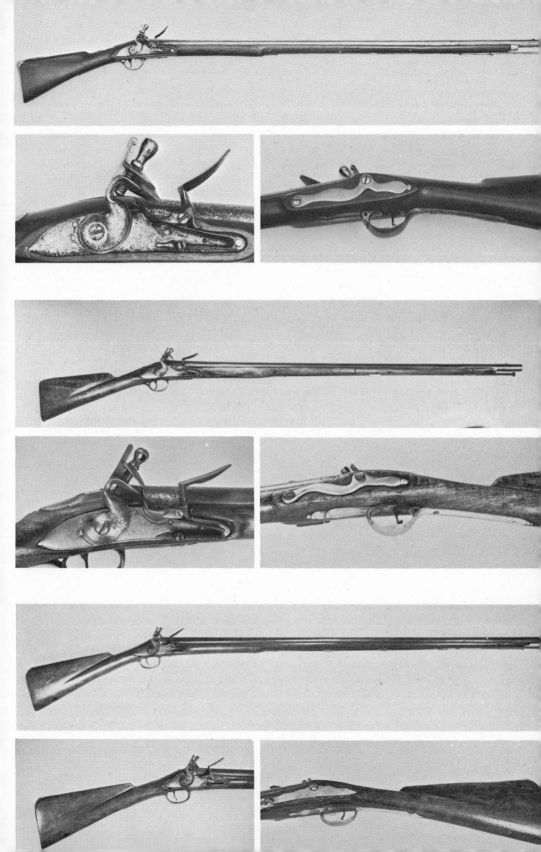

## M.91 AMERICAN FUSIL MUSKET

Circa 1776

The tail of the lock pictured here is marked VOIGHT 1776. It is believed to be the work of Henry Voight of Philadelphia, who is known to have produced arms for the Committee of Safety from 1766 to 1777. This fusil is typical of the style they favored and could be one from his contract production. A slight flare in the second of four rammer pipes (as well as the forward one) also suggests the mid-1770 period. The name J. MAGOWIN on the side of the butt probably refers to an owner.

Length: 52½"                Tr. Guard: 8¾"                Furniture: Brass
Barrel: 37¾"; .70           Butt Tang: 3⅜"               Weight: 7.3 lbs.
Lock: 6¼" × 1³⁄₁₆"

*John Bond Collection*

## M.92 ENGLISH LIGHT-INFANTRY CARBINE

Circa 1757

This carbine was apparently developed in the 1750's for use by light infantry in the rugged back country of North America. The barrel length matches the short-land pattern which was then gaining favor (42"), but the bore has been reduced to carbine size (.65). Its stock too is thinner and lighter than the regular musket, while the butt tang is shorter and the escutcheon plate oval in shape, with an arrowlike tail. Although originally carrying a brass-tipped wooden rammer as shown, many are found with iron rods. The lock is marked VERNON 1757.

Length: 57½"                Tr. Guard: 10½"               Furniture: Brass
Barrel: 42"; .65            Butt Tang: 2½"                Weight: 7.1 lbs.
Lock: 6⅛" × 1⅛"

*Author's Collection*

## M.93 ENGLISH LIGHT-INFANTRY CARBINE

Circa 1775-1785

This later version of the light-infantry weapon was probably produced during the American Revolutionary War period. Its 42" barrel and .65-caliber bore have been retained, but modifications such as the Brown Bess underwent from the 1750's to the 1770's are apparent. The side plate and trigger guard are now of the short-land pattern, a longer and flared forward pipe has been added to hold the new iron rammer, and the upper end of the cock tang is rounded. The lock includes the maker's name, INNES.

Length: 58"                 Tr. Guard: 10⅛"               Furniture: Brass
Barrel: 42"; .65            Butt Tang: 3¾"                Weight: 8.2 lbs.
Lock: 6" × 1⅛"

*Author's Collection*

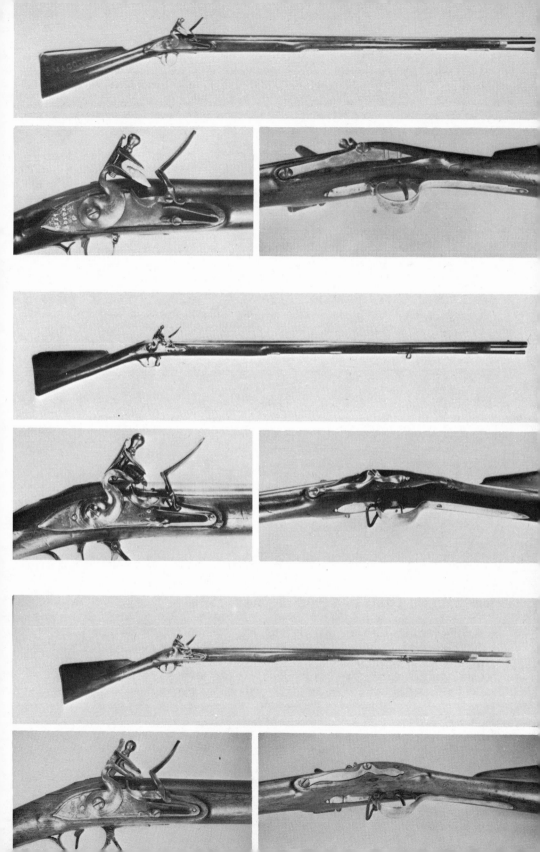

## M.94 ENGLISH CARBINE Circa 1735-1750

Prior to the 1750's, the British carbine was usually a cut-down infantry musket. This example was originally an early long-land pattern which had its barrel shortened to 34″. It is still able to fit a standard bayonet, and the forward sling swivel was remounted. A wooden rammer is secured in a tail pipe and one upper pipe. There is no nose cap. The "banana" military lock is engraved NICKSON, while the barrel bears Birmingham private proofs and the initials "TP" in a rectangular cartouche.

Length: 50⅜″
Barrel: 34″; .73
Lock: 6¾″ × 1¼″

Tr. Guard: 10¾″
Butt Tang: 4½″

Furniture: Brass
Weight: 8.8 lbs.

Author's Collection

## M.95 ENGLISH LIGHT-DRAGOON CARBINE Circa 1756-1760

A British warrant in 1756 established new light-dragoon troops and specified their first standard carbine pattern. The guiding dimensions were a total length of 51″ and a .65-caliber bore. This weapon is typical—although slightly longer than the original specifications. It is stocked to the muzzle, and mounts a side bar with a sliding ring for attachment to a shoulder strap. The furniture is a scaled-down version of the long-land pattern, with three pipes holding the wooden rammer. Its lock marking reads T HATCHER.

Length: 52½″
Barrel: 37¼″; .65
Lock: 6″ × 1″

Tr. Guard: 11″
Butt Tang: 4¾″

Furniture: Brass
Weight: 7.9 lbs.

Colonial Williamsburg Collection

## M.96 ENGLISH LIGHT-DRAGOON CARBINE (Variation) Circa 1762

This is a variation of the light-dragoon carbine (M.95 above). Chief differences include alteration for a bayonet (stock cut back, nose cap and top stud added) and inclusion of a metal rammer (with a flared forward pipe). The furniture is a smaller version of the long-land pattern. Note that a side bar was not installed, despite the notch cut for it in the side plate just forward of the rear screw. Markings include "20XR" (20th Regt.) in the stock and VERNON 1762 on the lock. The cock is not original.

Length: 52″
Barrel: 36¾″; .68
Lock: 6¼″ × 1⅛″

Tr. Guard: 11″
Butt Tang: 4¾″

Furniture: Brass
Weight: 7.4 lbs.

Morristown National Historical Park Collection

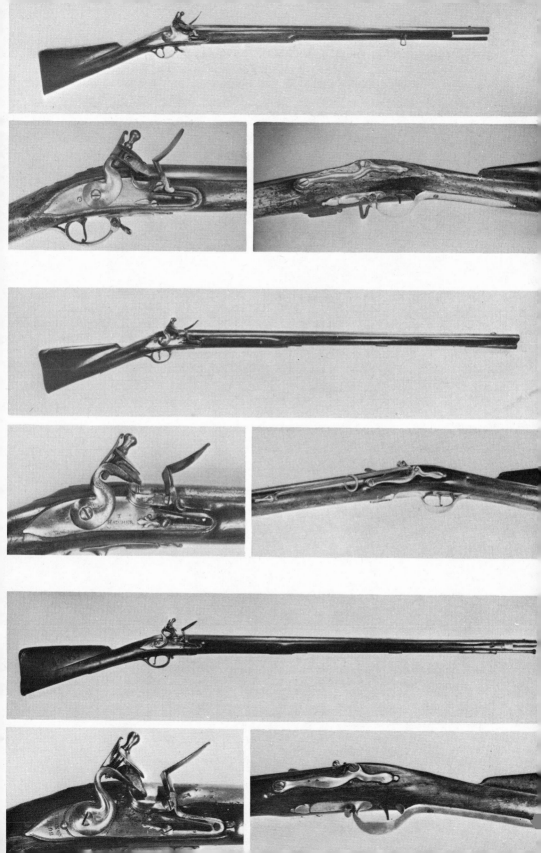

## M.97 ENGLISH LIGHT-DRAGOON CARBINE (Variation)    Circa 1750-1765

A shorter version of the light-dragoon carbine is shown here with a 31⅜″ barrel stocked to the muzzle (which is slightly flared). A simple tail pipe and two short forward pipes hold the wooden rammer, which has a brass tack in its end. A horseman's side bar and ring appear on the opposite side, while I LUDLAM (the maker) is inscribed on the face of the bridleless lock. Its brass furniture follows the long land pattern.

Length: 47⅛″            Tr. Guard: 9¼″            Furniture: Brass
Barrel: 31⅜″; .68       Butt Tang: 4¾″            Weight: 6.0 lbs
Lock: 6″ × 1⅛″

*Author's Collection*


## M.98 ENGLISH ARTILLERY CARBINE    Circa 1762

This carbine still bears faint traces of the Royal Artillery inscription on its barrel. It is very similar to the light-dragoon carbine (M.95-M.96), with a few variations: the side bar and ring are not included (with no notch in the side plate to mount one); the barrel is equipped for a bayonet (top lug); and a heavy reinforced forward pipe is present for an iron rammer. The lock bears a royal cipher and WILLETS 1762. Its escutcheon plate is marked "56."

Length: 51½″            Tr. Guard: 10⅜″           Furniture: Brass
Barrel: 36¼″; .66       Butt Tang: 4¾″            Weight: 7.1 lbs.
Lock: 6⅛″ × 1⅛″

*Warren M. Moore Collection*


## M.99 ENGLISH ELLIOTT CARBINE    Circa 1773-1785

British records of 1764 mention a new light carbine with a 28″ barrel. This apparently referred to the Elliott version, which was officially recognized in 1773. Since it was supposedly first produced in the Dublin Castle arsenal, and one of the two light-horse units in the American Revolution embarked from Ireland (the 17th), some might have seen action here. Its unique rammer has an incised ring to secure it under the nose cap. Lock markings include DUBLIN CASTLE.

Length: 44″             Tr. Guard: 8⅜″            Furniture: Brass
Barrel: 28⅜″; .65       Butt Tang: 3⅜″            Weight: 6.1 lbs.
Lock: 6″ × 1⅛″

*Lewis H. Gordon, Jr., Collection*

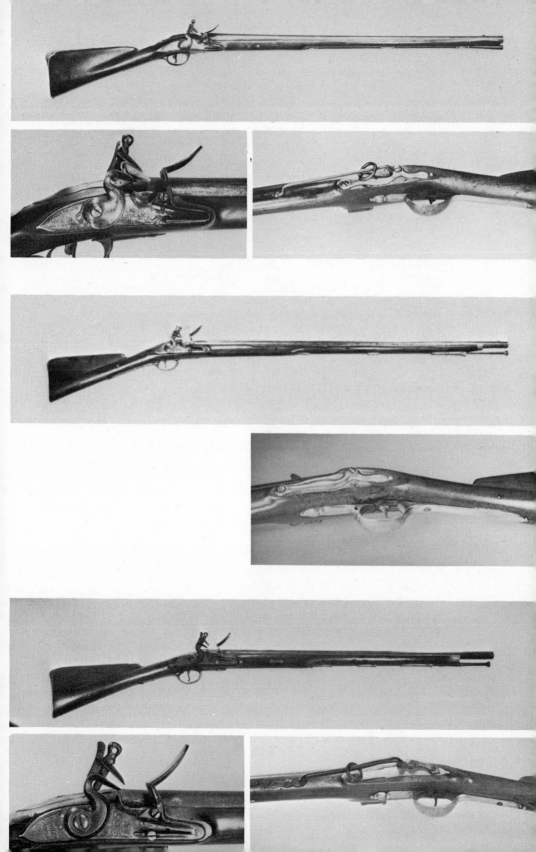

## M.100 ENGLISH CARBINE                                   Circa 1750-1780

This is one of several known carbine types which do not comply with official specifications. They may have predated the first regulation light-dragoon model (1756), been created for independent units, or hastily been fashioned during wartime shortages. The arm is a heavy naval musket of the 1750 period, with the .77-caliber barrel shortened to 26½". It includes a side bar and ring of the type used by horse troops. The original naval-style furniture (M.23) and stock proofs remain, but the only marking in metal is "MG" on the barrel.

Length: 42⅜"            Tr. Guard: 9⅝"            Furniture: Brass
Barrel: 26½"; .77        Butt Tang: 3¼"          Weight: 8.9 lbs.
Lock: 6¾ × 1⅛"

*Author's Collection*

## M.101 ENGLISH HEAVY-DRAGOON CARBINE                    Circa 1747

This model of the Brown Bess is one of the earliest standard variations with a 42" barrel. It was carried by the British heavy dragoons from the 1740's until about 1770, when regular fusils and carbines were adopted. The furniture was the same as the long-land pattern, plus a tail pipe and three equal-sized forward pipes for the wooden rammer (no nose cap). It had a full musket bore but no side bar. The barrel was also equipped for a socket bayonet. WILLETS 1747 is engraved on the lock.

Length: 58"             Tr. Guard: 11⅜"          Furniture: Brass
Barrel: 42"; .79         Butt Tang: 6"            Weight 10.0 lbs.
Lock: 6⅞" × 1¼"

*Anthony D. Darling Collection*

## M.102 AMERICAN LIGHT-INFANTRY CARBINE                  Circa 1775-1783

A British light-infantry-carbine barrel (faint London proofs) was used for this American arm. It is also interesting to notice the indentions cast into the American trigger-guard loop (which were never drilled out to mount a sling swivel), and the omission of one of the rammer pipes (three present). Aside from the barrel, no markings are visible.

Length: 57¾"            Tr. Guard: 10¾"          Furniture: Brass
Barrel: 42"; .65         Butt Tang: 5"            Weight: 6.7 lbs.
Lock: 5½" × 1"

*Lewis H. Gordon, Jr., Collection*

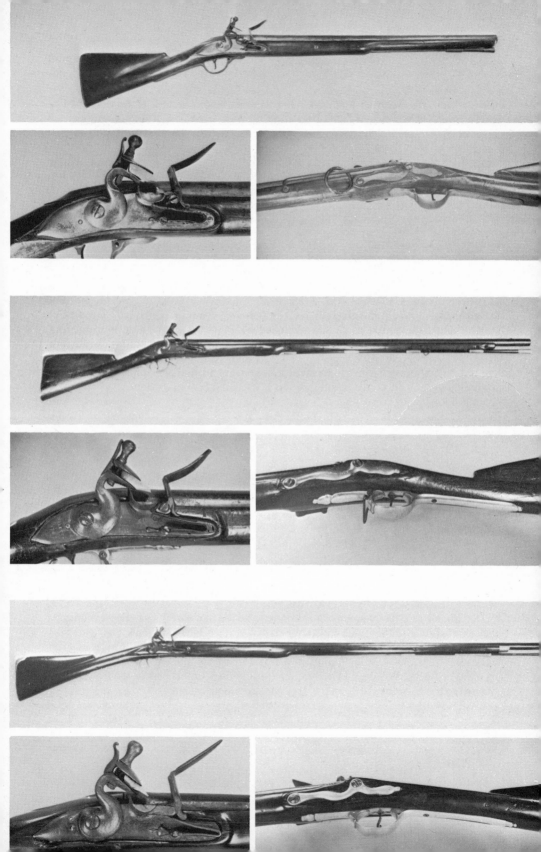

## M.103 AMERICAN CAVALRY CARBINE   Circa 1775-1783

Parts from a British long-land musket were remounted on a cherry stock to create this weapon. Its short length and the absence of a bayonet stud (brass blade sight present) indicate probable use as an American horseman's carbine. The lock is inscribed TOWER and bears a "US" surcharge of the type used in the Revolution. There is no evidence that it ever mounted a side bar, and since there is no hole in the stock for a sling swivel, it might have been carried in a "bucket."

Length: 44⅛"          Tr. Guard: 11¼"          Furniture: Brass
Barrel: 27½"; .77      Butt Tang: 5¾"           Weight: 8.1 lbs.
Lock: 7" × 1⅛"

*John K. Watson Collection*

## M.104 FRENCH CAVALRY CARBINE   Model 1766

Unlike most French infantry muskets, the horsemen's arms were usually mounted in brass. This cavalry carbine is easily identified by the short barrel, side bar and ring, double-strapped center band, and stocking to the muzzle. Note that it also carries sling swivels. The lock, side plate, trigger guard, and butt plate follow the 1766 infantry pattern (M.30). MANUFACTURE DE CHARLEVILLE appears on the lock, while "P79" on the furniture and "MY79" on the barrel indicate 1779 as the final proof date.

Length: 45"           Tr. Guard: 10¼"          Furniture: Brass
Barrel: 31"; .68      Butt Tang: 2"            Weight: 6.1 lbs.
Lock: 5½" × 1⅛"

*Author's Collection*

## M.105 FRENCH CAVALRY CARBINE   Model 1733

This Model 1733 *mousqueton de cavalerie* has a pinned barrel and brass furniture of the same pattern as the cavalry pistol of that year (see P.31). Its lock and gooseneck cock are styled after the contemporary musket. Like the later Model 1766 (M.104) its stock extends to the muzzle, and a side bar with ring are present for attachment to a shoulder belt hook. Weapons from this period made up a sizable part of the French arms shipped to the colonists during the American Revolution.

Length: 45"           Tr. Guard: 10"           Furniture: Brass
Barrel: 30¾"; .67     Butt Tang: 3¾"           Weight: 6.0 lbs.
Lock: 5¾" × 1¹⁄₁₆"

*Author's Collection*

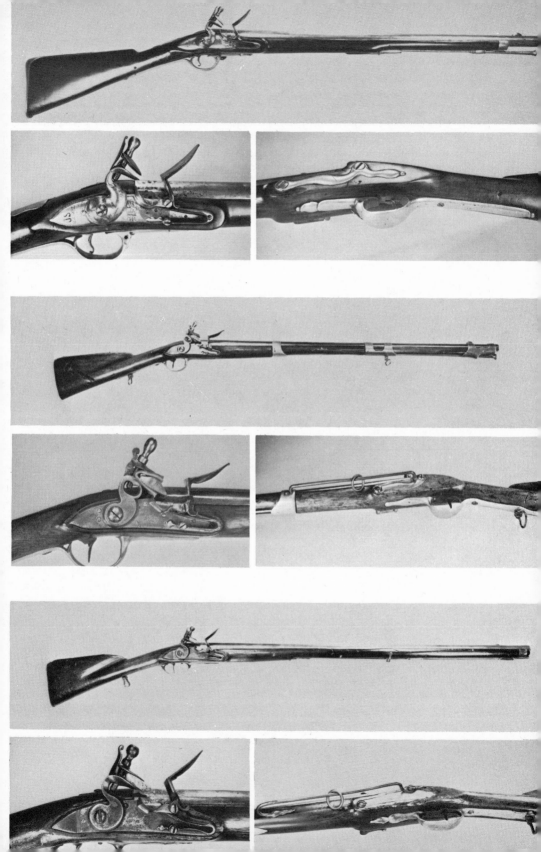

**M.106 ENGLISH MUSKETOON**  Circa 1690-1710

The term "musketoon" was loosely used during the eighteenth century. In the early 1700's, it usually meant a short, large-caliber smoothbore musket; by the 1770's it was defined as a very short blunderbuss. This example is apparently of English origin (note similarity to American Dutch-styled fowler furniture—M.54, M.55). Its heavy barrel is octagonal at the breech (for 4¼"). The muzzle flare is due to a thicker wall—not an enlargement of the .90 bore. Notice too the early ribbed rammer pipes, two ornamental barrel rings, and the trigger guard's rear finger hook.

Length: 38½"         Tr. Guard: 10¼"              Furniture: Brass
Barrel: 22"; .90      Butt Tang: 4¾"              Weight: 7.5 lbs.
Lock: 6" × 1⅛"

*Author's Collection*


**M.107 ENGLISH BLUNDERBUSS**  Circa 1700-1710

Like the contemporary muskets, this weapon has a three-screw flat dog lock of the type which persisted in England into the early 1700's. There are several other characteristics of this period: the screw from underneath holding the barrel tang; a curled trigger; and the simple round-ended trigger guard. Its flat butt is covered with a thin sheet of brass (fastened by seven square-headed nails). The flared round barrel is iron. Markings include the maker's name, HENSHAW, on the lock plate.

Length: 31"          Tr. Guard: 7½"              Furniture: Brass
Barrel: 15¼"; 1⅞"    Butt Tang: 1⅞"              Weight: 6.9 lbs.
Lock: 6⅝" × 1⅛"

*John C. McMurray Collection*


**M.108 ENGLISH BLUNDERBUSS**  Circa 1700-1720

The iron-barreled blunderbuss shown here is typical of many used by the military forces—especially the navy. In addition to a bottom barrel tang screw and flat nailed butt plate, other early features are visible: the curled trigger, octagonal-round barrel, a bridleless flashpan, and the lack of a tail pipe. Note also the side plate design, which resembles the popular dragon motif of this period. The name I COOK appears on the lock; an escutcheon plate is present.

Length: 33⅞"         Tr. Guard: 7⅜"              Furniture: Brass
Barrel: 19⅞"; 1⅜"    Butt Tang: 2½"              Weight: 8.4 lbs.
Lock: 5¾" × 1¹/₁₆"

*Lewis H. Gordon, Jr., Collection*

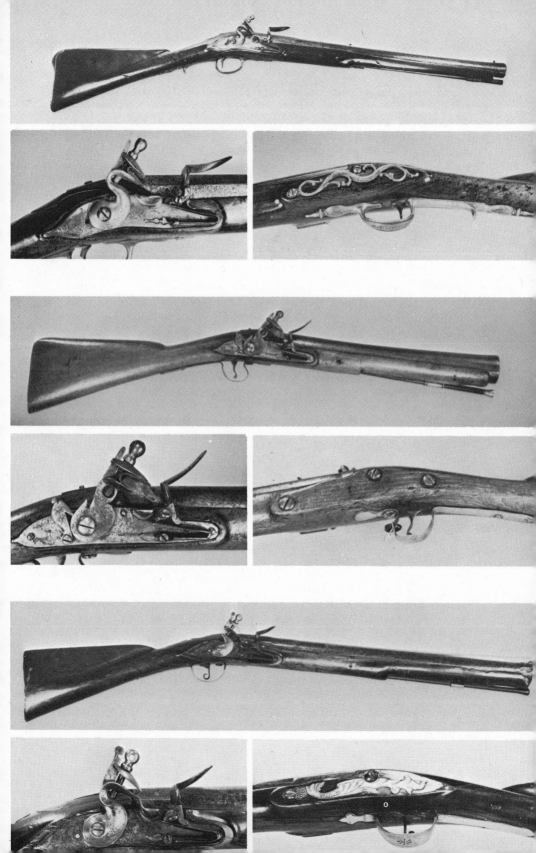

## M.109 ENGLISH BLUNDERBUSS                    Circa 1710-1720

This three-screw lock plate is evolving a tail in much the same manner as the "Queen Anne" muskets in their movement toward the Brown Bess pattern (M.2-M.7). The slightly flared iron barrel has an octagonal breech (which ends at a decorative ring after 6"), while its 16" length was the most common size through the American Revolutionary War period. The maker's name, PICKFATT, is engraved on the lock, and his initials, "CP," also appear on the barrel (in a cartouche between the 1702-style London proofs).

Length: 31⅛"          Tr. Guard: 8¾"          Furniture: Brass
Barrel: 16"; 1⁹⁄₁₆"     Butt Tang: 2¼"          Weight: 6.2 lbs.
Lock: 6" × 1"

*Lewis H. Gordon, Jr., Collection*


## M.110 ENGLISH BLUNDERBUSS                    Circa 1725-1740

This military blunderbuss is mounted with Brown Bess long-land-pattern furniture. Its massive iron barrel is octagonal at the breech and blends into a round shape after 8½". In addition to sea service, land forces probably used weapons such as this for sentry duty or fighting at close quarters. The wooden rammer is held by a tail pipe and a single forward pipe. Sling swivels and an escutcheon plate are included. The name of its manufacturer, R WATKIN, appears on the lock.

Length: 39"          Tr. Guard: 11¼"          Furniture: Brass
Barrel: 22⅞"; 2"     Butt Tang: 5¾"           Weight: 10.1 lbs.
Lock: 6¾" × 1¼"

*Author's Collection*


## M.111 ENGLISH BLUNDERBUSS                    Circa 1747-1760

The pinned brass barrel in this example has a cannon-barrel shape, i.e., the swell at the muzzle is formed more by a thicker wall than by increasing the bore size. It was a style which gained popularity during the middle and later parts of the eighteenth century. Markings on the lock establish it as a military arm. Its plate bears the crown above "GR," the government property stamp (broad arrow), plus the maker's name and date, WILLETS 1747. Notice the flat side plate of the emerging short-land pattern (M.11).

Length: 31½"          Tr. Guard: 8¼"          Furniture: Brass
Barrel: 16"; 1¼"      Butt Tang: 2⅞"          Weight 5.5 lbs.
Lock: 6⅛" × 1⅛"

*Lewis H. Gordon, Jr., Collection*

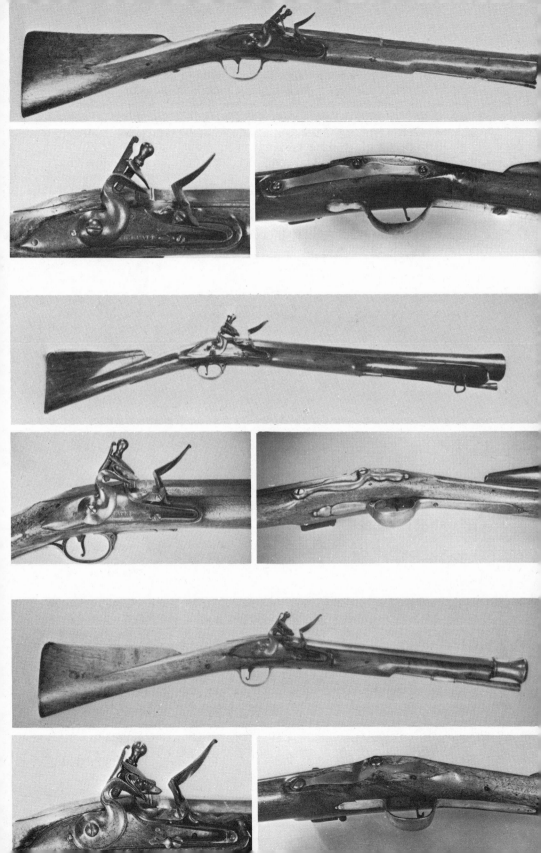

## M.112 ENGLISH BLUNDERBUSS — Circa 1750-1760

This brass-barreled weapon can probably be considered a semimilitary arm. It is short enough to be carried by a civilian in his baggage or under a cloak, and yet by its markings could signify a privately made officer's weapon. The flat side plate reflects the short-land pattern, while the trigger guard's acorn design was a mid-century favorite. Also of interest is the early flat nailed butt plate, and barrel tang screw from underneath. Its lock bears a large crown and LONDON.

Length: 27½″  Tr. Guard: 9⅞″  Furniture: Brass
Barrel: 12⅛″; 1¼″  Butt Tang: 1¼″  Weight: 4.6 lbs.
Lock: 5¾″ × 1″

*Author's Collection*

## M.113 ENGLISH BLUNDERBUSS — Circa 1760-1770

These furniture engravings indicate probable use by an officer or well-to-do individual. Fastened to the rear of the side plate is a sling swivel which appears to be original. Since there is no provision for a second one, this weapon was possibly carried on a neck strap to hang in front (under a coat), or under an arm. The brass cannon barrel is round, with two decorative rings (4¼″ and 6⅛″ from the breech). An elaborate escutcheon plate is included and the lock is marked BUCKMASTER.

Length: 31⅜″  Tr. Guard: 10⅝″  Furniture: Brass
Barrel: 16″; 1½″  Butt Tang: 2¾″  Weight: 6.0 lbs.
Lock: 5⅞″ × 1⅛″

*Lewis H. Gordon, Jr., Collection*

## M.114 AMERICAN BLUNDERBUSS — Circa 1720-1750

The unique lines and components of this weapon suggest an American product. Identifying marks are not visible, and there appear to be no salvaged parts from recognizable patterns. It is of interest, however, to see a possible Dutch-German influence in the side plate and trigger guard (see M.43). Raised stock carvings around the fittings seem to lack the flowing lines of most contemporary European work. The barrel is round, with two side "flats" at the breech (for 12¼″). An escutcheon plate is present, but no sling swivels.

Length: 40⅞″  Tr. Guard: 11″  Furniture: Brass
Barrel: 25¾″; 2″  Butt Tang: 5″  Weight: 8.1 lbs.
Lock: 5⅞″ × 1″

*Harold L. Peterson Collection*

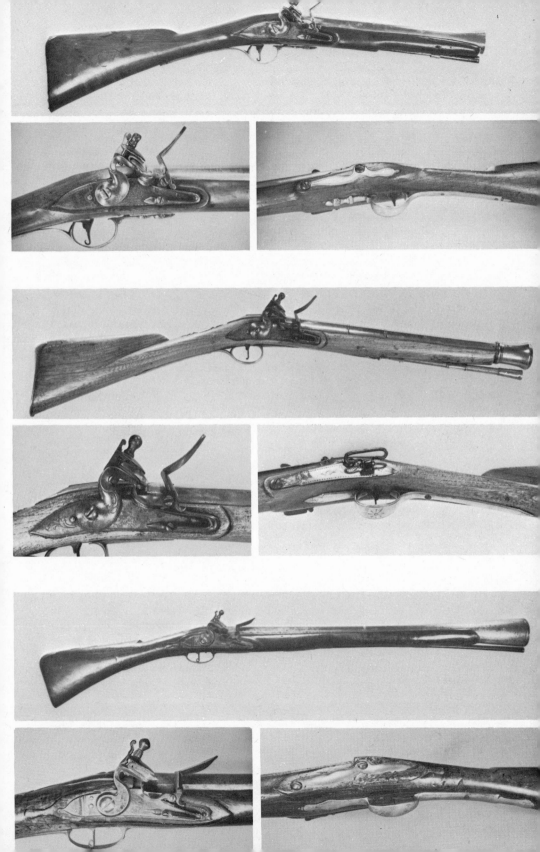

## M.115 AMERICAN BLUNDERBUSS                    Circa 1765-1783

This naval-style blunderbuss was apparently put together here in the colonies. The barrel shows the remains of early English proofs, while the lock itself is of Brown Bess parentage (marked GALTON 1762). The crude brass furniture, and the stock, however, are of American origin. Since arms of this type were continuously needed at sea, it could have been made prior to, as well as during, the Revolution. Neither a tail pipe nor an escutcheon plate were included. The barrel tang is held by a bottom screw.

Length: 37½″            Tr. Guard: 9″                 Furniture: Brass
Barrel: 21⅞″; 2″        Butt Tang: 2″                 Weight: 9.0 lbs.
Lock: 7″ × 1¼″

*Author's Collection*

## M.116 EUROPEAN BLUNDERBUSS                    Circa 1730-1750

The blunderbuss in this illustration is typical of many produced in Europe during this period. Its barrel is not round like most British and American styles, but flattened into an oval shape. Octagonal from the breech to an ornamental ring 10″ above, it is held by two pins. Although no marks are visible, the flat "banana" lock and iron fittings are very similar to those of French arms of the 1730 period (see P.31). This particular piece was probably employed for civilian or semimilitary use.

Length: 41⅛″            Tr. Guard: 10½″               Furniture: Iron
Barrel: 26″; 1¾″ × 1⅛″  Butt Tang: 5¼″                Weight: 8.0 lbs.
Lock: 6⅛″ × 1¼″

*Author's Collection*

## M.117 AMERICAN WALL GUN                       Circa 1776

The "wall gun" or "amusette" was used to fill the gap between a shoulder arm and cannon in the 1700's. It was essentially a large musket—semiportable, and yet able to throw a large ball for an extended distance. This rare example was made at James Hunter's famed Rappahannock Forge about 1776. Its barrel is rifled (twelve grooves), and round in shape. Front and rear sights are included. The swivel indicates use from a fixed position. Notice too the rifle-style patch box and trigger guard. The lock is marked RAPA FORGE.

Length: 61¼″            Tr. Guard: 11¾″               Furniture: Brass
Barrel: 44¼″; 1⅛″       Butt Tang: 3⅞″                Weight: 53.5 lbs.
Lock: 7⅞″ × 1½″

*West Point Museum Collection*

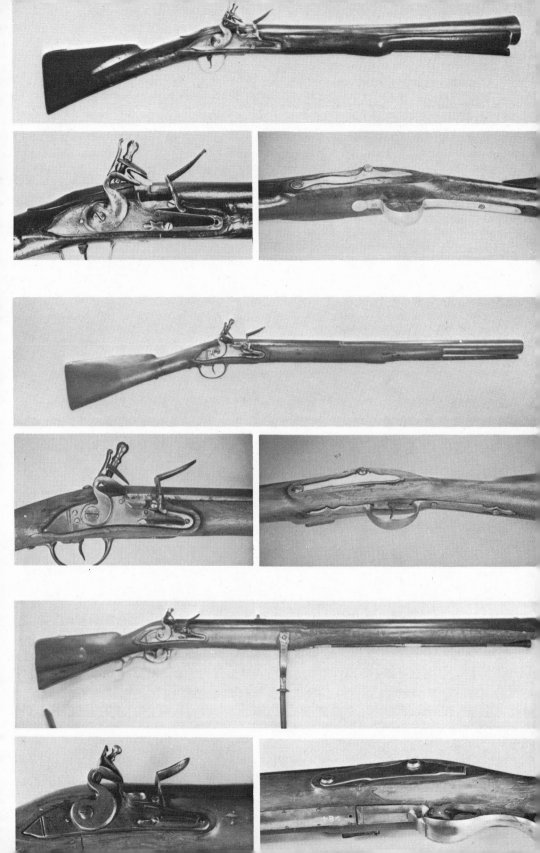

## M.118 EUROPEAN WALL GUN                           Circa 1750-1783

This wall gun is a large version of a musket, mounted on a swivel. The components appear to be of mixed parentage. Its barrel has French markings plus a "US" surcharge, and is octagonal for the entire length. The two-screw lock includes a round unbridled flashpan and a reinforced cock. Its side plate is of earlier vintage, having been originally made for a three-screw lock, while the trigger guard indicates Dutch influence (M.41). Only a front sight is mounted.

Length: 63"                     Tr. Guard: 13½"                  Furniture: Iron
Barrel: 46⅞"; .72                                               Weight: 12.7 lbs.
Lock: 7½" × 1½"

*West Point Museum Collection*


## M.119 FRENCH WALL GUN                             Circa 1730-1750

The French employed wall (or "rampart") arms, which were muskets with a larger bore size, for use mostly at fortified positions. The weapon shown here has an octagonal (full-length), smoothbore, .75-caliber barrel. The flat lock, with its faceted and bridled flashpan, the tapered trigger guard, and curved side plate are typical of French styling. A "GR" in the stock suggests onetime British possession, while a UNITED:STATES surcharge indicates American Revolutionary War use.

Length: 62⅝"                    Tr. Guard: 12¾"                  Furniture: Iron
Barrel: 47"; .75                Butt Tang: 6"                    Weight: 13.5 lbs.
Lock: 7⅛" × 1⅜"

*West Point Museum Collection*


## M.120 DUTCH WALL GUN                              Circa 1750-1780

The furniture and raised carving on this wall gun point to probable Dutch manufacture (M.40-M.41). Its flat lock has a faceted flashpan without a bridle and a frizzen with a squared top. The round barrel includes a slight flare at the muzzle. Protruding down from the upper end of the stock is an iron stud. "Hooks" of this type were often used to steady these weapons on the ramparts. The rear sight on the barrel is not original.

Length: 72¾"                    Tr. Guard: 12⅞"                  Furniture: Brass
Barrel: 55½"; .97               Butt Tang: 7⅛"                   Weight: 21.0 lbs.
Lock: 8¼" × 1¾"

*Wayne M. Daniels Collection*

132

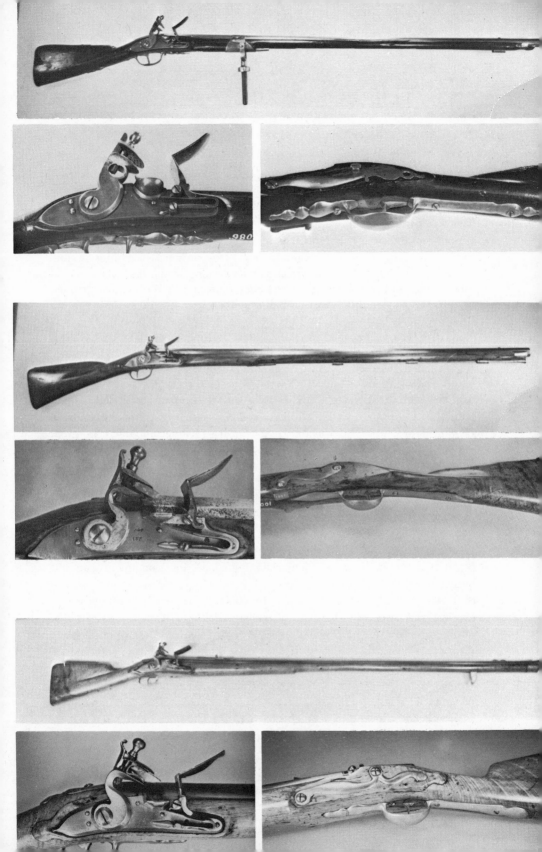

# 5 | THE LONG RIFLE

THE THEORY of cutting spiraling grooves inside the barrel of a gun seems to have evolved about 1500 in eastern Germany or Austria. The action of this "rifling" gave the ball a spin which added greatly to its distance and accuracy. By 1600 the bullet was being loaded while seated in patches of greased cloth or thin leather. This provided a tighter fit and helped loosen some of the previous powder fouling as the ball was rammed down, reduced leakage of the ignited charge around the bullet, and gripped the grooves to give the departing ball a better spin.

**THE JAEGER:** The rifled arm of Central Europe in the late 1600's is referred to in America as the Jaeger rifle (*Jaeger* means "hunter" in German). It was a short weapon, with an octagonal barrel approximating 28 inches in length and a large bore (usually .60 to .70 caliber, averaging seven grooves). The heavy stock extended to the muzzle, and traditionally included a small patch box in the butt, with a sliding wooden cover. Its furniture was mostly fashioned of brass. This was the style of arm which accompanied the great influx of Germans into Pennsylvania commencing about 1710 (Figs. R.1-R.3). From this beginning came the famous Pennsylvania rifle.

**AMERICA'S NEW LONG RIFLE:** Availability of the proper firearm could determine life or death on the colonial frontier, and gradual rifle modifications soon began to appear among the new gunsmiths in Pennsylvania. For greater accuracy, the short barrels were lengthened (to consume all of the powder charge and provide a longer aiming span); for economy of lead and lighter weight, the bore was reduced; for a flatter trajectory, a higher ratio of powder to ball evolved; and for better balance in carrying through rough country, the stock was thinned and reshaped. By 1770, the American rifle destined for use in the Revolutionary War had acquired many of its basic characteristics: a barrel length usually over 40 inches; a bore averaging .40 to .60 caliber (with seven or eight grooves); a long thin stock extending to the muzzle; a flat-style lock having a bridleless pan and gooseneck cock; an elevated handgrip on the rear of the trigger guard; raised carving around many of the fittings; and a patch box with a wooden, iron, or simple brass cover. The picturesque metal inlaid designs, double-set triggers, and sharp

"Roman nose" butt generally associated with early American rifles appeared mostly after the War for Independence.

USE DURING THE REVOLUTION: This amazing weapon, which had an accurate range of up to three hundred yards (i.e. more than three times the average musket), was actually limited to specialized service in the Continental Army. It was primarily a civilian arm, and its slow rate of fire and the inability to mount a bayonet made it impractical for use in the open field tactics of the day. However, in the hands of skirmishers and light troops operating in wooded areas, it proved to be extremely valuable.

**BRITISH RIFLES:** The British had no formal rifle units in 1775. To answer this need, they included Jaeger riflemen among the troops hired in Germany. Their arms were of the short type originally brought to Pennsylvania (R.4), and many of them reportedly used their personal hunting weapons.

Captain Patrick Ferguson of the English Army developed an ingenious and practical breech-loading rifle during this period (Figs. R.20, R.21), and equipped a small group of light infantry with it. Fortunately for the Americans, however, he failed to receive further endorsement prior to his death at the Battle of Kings Mountain in 1780.

The Pennsylvania long rifle is probably the only truly American style of firearm which saw common use in the Revolutionary War. On the following pages are examples which illustrate its early development.

**R.1 GERMAN JAEGER RIFLE**                                    Circa 1730-1740

A traditional patch box is not included in this example, although it does have the massive butt (2⅜″ across) indicative of early weapons. Raised carving is visible on the stock. Two small iron loops under the cheekpiece often held a feathered quill or other device for cleaning the flashpan and touchhole. Its flat lock is of typical Germanic design (faceted flashpan and exterior bridle). In addition to the front blade, there is a small rear sight (5¾″ from breech) with a folding second leaf.

Length: 44″                    Tr. Guard: 9″                 Furniture: Brass
Barrel: 29″; .51 (8 grooves)   Butt Tang: 3¼″               Weight: 7.8 lbs.
Lock: 5½″ × 1⅛″

*Author's Collection*


**R.2 GERMAN JAEGER RIFLE**                                    Circa 1730-1750

This rifle includes three interesting features: the long-range rear sight (supplementing the two open barrel sights); a large flare at the rear of the trigger guard; and its second, or "set" trigger, which can be adjusted by the small screw next to it. The stock includes fine early raised carving on both sides of the butt and along the fore end on each side of the rammer channel. Its nose cap is made of horn, while the wooden rammer mounts a brass tip. The barrel is octagonal for the entire length.

Length: 40½″                   Tr. Guard: 10½″              Furniture: Brass
Barrel: 25⅞″; .60 (7 grooves)  Butt Tang: 2¾″              Weight: 7.4 lbs.
Lock: 5⅞″ × 1″

*West Point Museum Collection*


**R.3 GERMAN JAEGER RIFLE**                                    Circa 1740-1760

This German-style rifle has a shorter barrel than most, but includes many typical early characteristics. Note the slanting trigger, which was believed easier to squeeze. Its stock extends to the muzzle—ending in a horn nose cap. Raised carving surrounds the patch box, barrel tang, and tail pipe. The barrel is octagonal, with a front blade and rear open sight. Its side plate is interesting too, having three screws (rear one short), and a design combining the early open style with the new scalloped motif.

Length: 38¼″                   Tr. Guard: 9¾″              Furniture: Brass
Barrel: 23½″; .60 (8 grooves)  Butt Tang: 4¼″              Weight: 7.8 lbs.
Lock: 5¼″ × 1″

*Author's Collection*

**136**

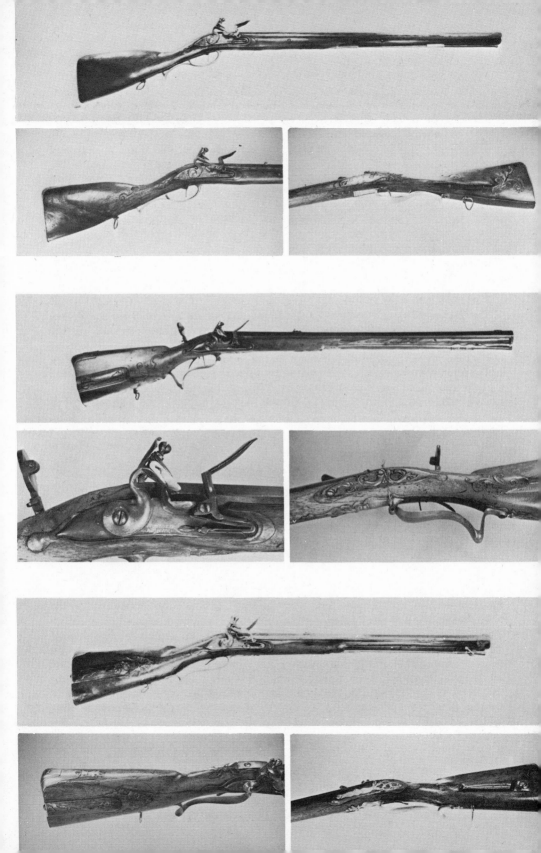

**R.4 GERMAN-DUTCH RIFLE**                                    Circa 1760-1780

Pictured here is a rifle of the type believed carried by German Jaegers during the American War for Independence. It bears the military numbers "NO 28" on the top "flat" of the octagonal barrel, and was originally found in southern Vermont. Notice its later features and impersonal military characteristics: the brief raised carving, straighter butt profile, and simple brass furniture (nose cap brass, too). An escutcheon plate is also present. The trigger guard and side plate designs indicate possible Dutch manufacture (see R.19).

Length: 43¾″                  Tr. Guard: 11″                  Furniture: Brass
Barrel: 28⅞″; .64 (7 grooves) Butt Tang: 2″                   Weight: 6.9 lbs.
Lock: 5¼″ × 1″

*John K. Watson Collection*


**R.5 AMERICAN RIFLE**                                        Circa 1730-1750

This specimen is a particularly good example of the evolution from the Jaeger into the American rifle. It still keeps many of the earlier German characteristics, yet the barrel is lengthening, a simpler style of furniture is appearing, the side plate is assuming a new triangular shape, and the carving is becoming less ornate. Little change is evident in the patch-box cover and trigger guard; its stock is still heavy and formal. "GS" and a pair of scissors in a rectangular cartouche are stamped in the slightly flared barrel.

Length: 53¾″                  Tr. Guard: 8½″                  Furniture: Brass
Barrel: 38¼″; .59            Butt Tang: 2½″                   Weight: 9.8 lbs.
Lock: 5¼″ × 1″

*Joe Kindig, Jr., Collection*


**R.6 AMERICAN RIFLE**                                        Circa 1735-1750

The common use of fancy brass patch-box covers is generally considered an American innovation. Here is an early example made of iron. The flat lock, crude carving, straighter stock profile, vertical butt plate, and high comb are all indicative of the emerging Pennsylvania style of weapon. Although many European trade locks and barrels are found on eighteenth-century American rifles, this arm is entirely a product of the colonies. The original wooden rammer, held by three plain pipes, is missing.

Length: 55½″                  Tr. Guard: 8¾″                  Furniture: Iron
Barrel: 40¼″; .57            Butt Tang: 2⅛″                   Weight: 8.4 lbs.
Lock: 6″ × 1⅛″

*Joe Kindig, Jr., Collection*

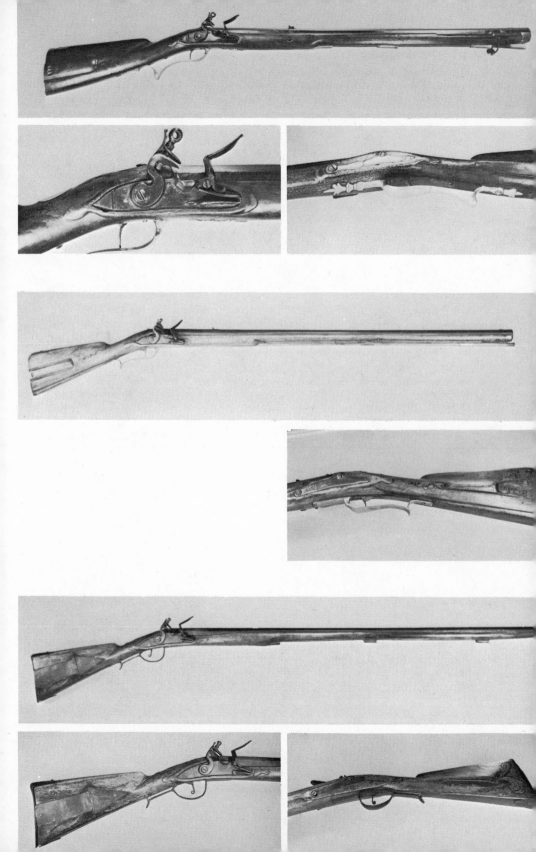

## R.7 AMERICAN "MOUNTAIN" RIFLE                    Circa 1760-1770

This is the type of early rifle often referred to as a "mountain gun." It is typical of the crude, elementary style of weapon carried for many years in the hills of the South. No raised carving is present and both the butt plate and tail pipe have been eliminated. The circular opening in the side of the butt is a "grease hole"—for holding thick grease used to rub into cloth or leather bullet patches. Its iron furniture appears to be from an early European arm, and the barrel is squared for 9" at the breech.

Length: 54½"                    Tr. Guard: 8"                    Furniture: Iron
Barrel: 39¼"; .66 (8 grooves)                                   Weight: 7.1 lbs.
Lock: 6⅛" × 1⅛"

*Author's Collection*

## R.8 AMERICAN RIFLE                                Circa 1770-1780

Many of the classic features of rifles produced just before and during the Revolution are evidenced here: the curly maple stock, which was to typify so many of the arms in the later "golden age"; a graceful comb has replaced the earlier "squared" pattern; the bottom butt line is straightened; and a triangular-shaped side plate plus a square-ended trigger guard are now established. Its butt tang is more traditional (octagonal, squared at end). Some rifles, such as this one, did not have a patch box.

Length: 62¾"                    Tr. Guard: 9"                    Furniture: Brass
Barrel: 47¼"                    Butt Tang: 2⅝"                   Weight: 7.0 lbs.
Lock: 9" × 1"

*Howard B. Greene Collection*

## R.9 AMERICAN RIFLE                                Circa 1770-1780

The simple wooden patch box, flat lock with gooseneck hammer, and square-ended trigger guard are typical of this period. It should be remembered, however, that no two of these Pennsylvania-style rifles are identical. Each was made as an individual arm, and the gunsmith himself was continually modifying his pattern. The barrel is round except for an octagonal shape at the breech (14"). The three brass pipes for the wooden rammer are octagonal, with simple raised borders at each end.

Length: 60¾"                    Tr. Guard: 8⅞"                  Furniture: Brass
Barrel: 44"½; .52                Butt Tang: 2¼"                  Weight: 8.0 lbs.
Lock: 5" × 1"

*Harmon C. Leonard Collection*

140

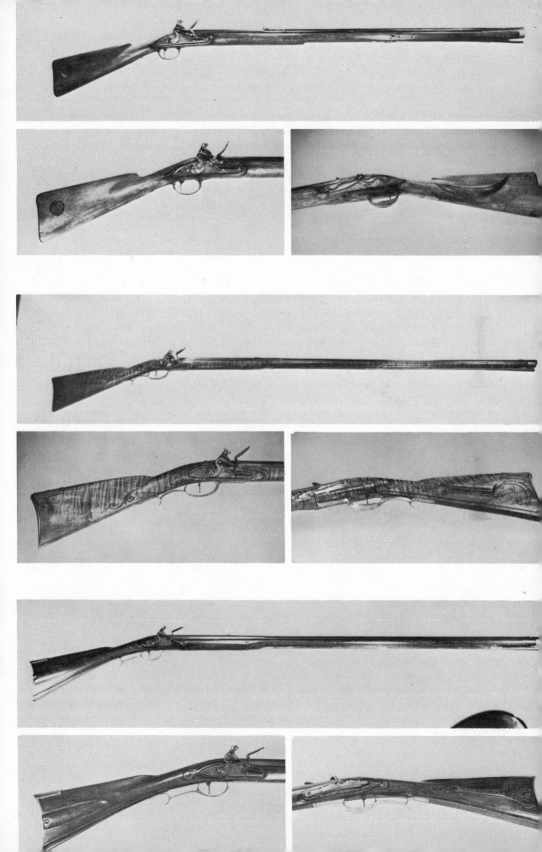

## R.10 AMERICAN RIFLE                                   Circa 1770-1780

Although the bottom edge of the butt and the line of the butt plate remain straight, the sharp drop of this stock is an early indication of the "Roman nose" pattern, which was to gain such popularity after the Revolution. Notice the typical triangular side plate, and the interesting end designs on the trigger guard. The straight American-style cheekpiece is also present (most European ones were curved). A long brass nose cap appears under the muzzle of the octagonal barrel. The striped rammer is probably not original.

Length: 53¼"                   Tr. Guard: 9⅞"              Furniture: Brass
Barrel: 38½"; .65              Butt Tang: 5¼"              Weight: 8.1 lbs.
Lock: 5¾" × 1⅛"

*Joe Kindig, Jr., Collection*

## R.11 AMERICAN RIFLE                                   Circa 1770-1780

The "stocker" of this rifle has omitted the heavy raised carving on the butt face, but did include parallel channels in the patch-box cover, an interesting scroll behind the tail pipe, and borders around most fittings. As in many of these arms existing today, the barrel rifling is not evident. Several reasons are usually given: many were bored out for later smoothbore hunting; some were made as smoothbores to fire possibly with a patched ball; and the barrels of others were simply worn smooth through generations of use.

Length: 58"                    Tr. Guard: 11"             Furniture: Brass
Barrel: 42⅜"; .66              Butt Tang: 3⅞"             Weight: 7.7 lbs.
Lock: 5¼" × 1"

*Joe Kindig, Jr., Collection*

## R.12 AMERICAN RIFLE                                       Circa 1758

This interesting weapon is marked on the butt tang MADE BY MEDAD HILLS/CT/GOSHEN, and the shield-type escutcheon plate is inscribed "4/1758/4." He was a well-known Connecticut gunmaker who was active in the Revolution. The side plate bears the name of the owner, NOAH NORTH. The bore is now smooth, but it is believed to have been originally used as a rifle. A filed notch in the breech of the round barrel, plus a front blade were used for sighting. Three brass pipes hold the wooden rammer.

Length: 67"                    Tr. Guard: 9"              Furniture: Brass
Barrel: 52"; .60               Butt Tang: 5¾"             Weight: 8.8 lbs.
Lock: 5¾" × 1"

*E. Norman Flayderman Collection*

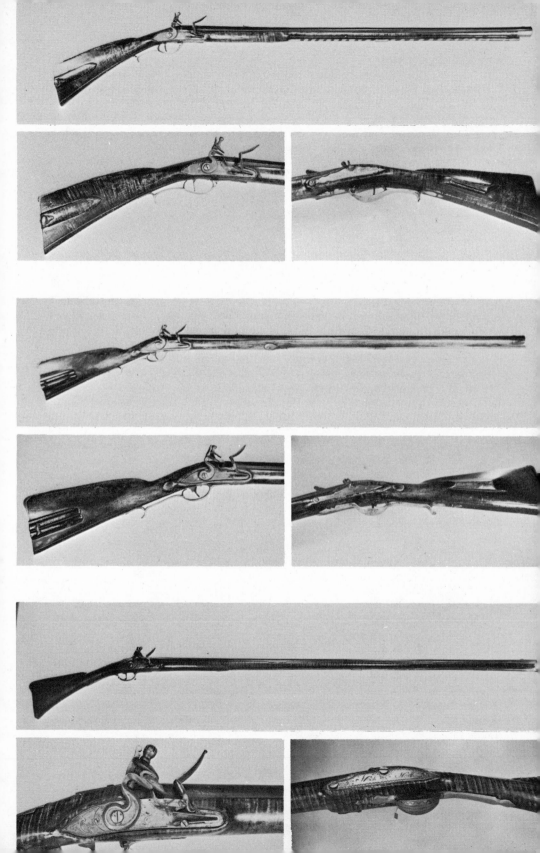

## R.13 AMERICAN RIFLE

Circa 1765-1780

The most striking feature in this example is the appearance of the brass patch-box cover, which was later to become so universal. It is of the early simple style, without piercings or elaborate decoration. The crude bird's-head shape makes it even more distinctive. Raised carvings of a floral pattern appear on the stock, plus the popular straight grooves cut along each side of the rammer channel. An early iron patch is visible around the trigger guard. The cock shown is probably not original to the lock.

Length: 54½"
Barrel: 39¾"; .52
Lock: 5⅜" × 1"

Tr. Guard: 9"
Butt Tang: 2¾"

Furniture: Brass
Weight: 8.8 lbs.

*Joe Kindig, Jr., Collection*

## R.14 AMERICAN RIFLE

Circa 1770-1785

Another version of the early brass patch box is shown here, with a rectangular lid and a rather plain forward strap. Much of the brass furniture bears the typical 1770 decorative motif, made by striking a series of single stampings. Notice too that the usual butt carvings and cheekpiece were not included, although substantial carvings are visible around the barrel tang. Its silver oval escutcheon plate is held by a center pin. The barrel is octagonal at the breech (for 14" to a "ring").

Length: 62¼"
Barrel: 47"; .50
Lock: 5" × 1"

Tr. Guard: 10¾"
Butt Tang: 3½"

Furniture: Brass
Weight: 5.5 lbs.

*Author's Collection*

## R.15 AMERICAN RIFLE

Circa 1775-1790

This patch box combines a graceful outline with a hinge along its lower edge. A simple floral design is engraved on its face—a style often used by A. Verner of Bucks County, Pennsylvania. Notice the quick taper toward the rear of the flat lock (typically American), and the big curl of the trigger. Its comb still maintains some height, and the three straight edges of the butt profile predate the later "Roman nose." The decorative tailpipe extension is also unusual.

Length: 59¾"
Barrel: 43⅝"; .51
Lock: 4⅞" × 1"

Tr. Guard: 8¾"
Butt Tang: 2⅜"

Furniture: Brass
Weight: 8.6 lbs.

*Harmon C. Leonard Collection*

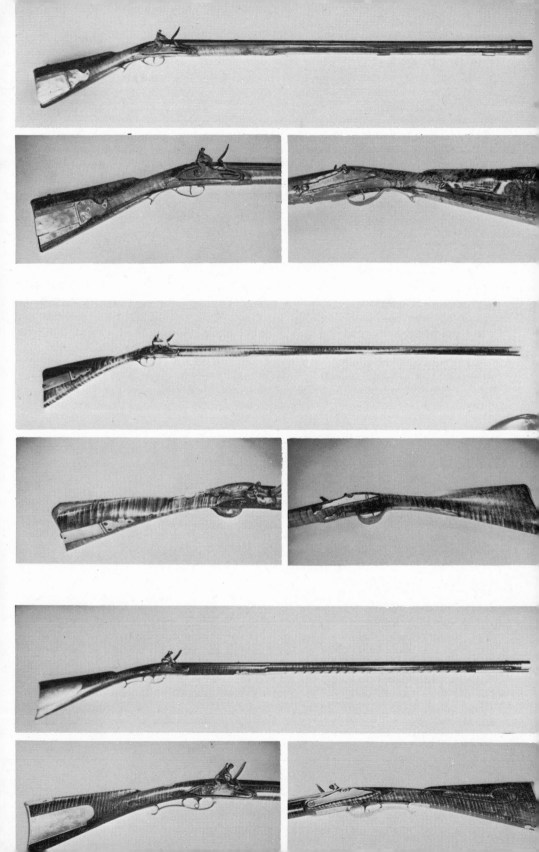

**R.16 AMERICAN RIFLE**                                      Circa 1770-1790

Few rifles prior to the War for Independence bear maker's marks. This particular specimen, however, has M. SHEETS in script on the barrel. The Sheets family are known as active Virginia rifle makers before and during the war. Contrary to the Pennsylvania tradition, this pattern has no raised cheekpiece or carving. However, the stock exhibits a typical straight outline. Its barrel is octagonal at the breech (changing to a rounded form after 16"). An early repair to the toe of the butt is visible.

Length: 64¾"                   Tr. Guard: 10½"              Furniture: Brass
Barrel: 49"; .55               Butt Tang: 4"                Weight: 8.5 lbs.
Lock: 5" × ⅞"

*Author's Collection*


**R.17 AMERICAN RIFLE**                                      Circa 1770-1785

Although most brass patch-box covers prior to 1783 were very plain, one exception was apparently the "daisy-headed" design from Lancaster County, Pennsylvania. Post-war examples were much more ornate than the one pictured here, but they all terminated at the upper end in a five- or six-petal outline of a daisy. This one is held by five screws. Its lock is a type imported by the colonies in great numbers for use on local firearms (marked KETLAND). Note the unique crosshatched area under the cheekpiece.

Length: 59½"                   Tr. Guard: 9¼"               Furniture: Brass
Barrel: 43½"; .64              Butt Tang: 2½"               Weight: 10.4 lbs.
Lock: 5⅜" × 1"

*Joe Kindig, Jr., Collection*


**R.18 ENGLISH RIFLE**                                       Circa 1775-1790

This example resembles a Pennsylvania rifle of the 1770's, but is, in reality, a British copy. It was possibly made in an attempt to study and test arms captured early in the Revolutionary War. Upon closer comparison with an American rifle (R.17 above), several differences are seen: the butt is more squared; the "small" of the stock is thicker; and the furniture is heavier. Its butt carving has been given more height by "dishing" into the surrounding wood. (Note: Ketland lock, Birmingham proofs.)

Length: 59¼"                   Tr. Guard: 8½"               Furniture: Brass
Barrel: 44"; .58               Butt Tang: 2³⁄₁₆"            Weight: 9.4 lbs.
Lock: 5½" × 1⅛"

*Harmon C. Leonard Collection*

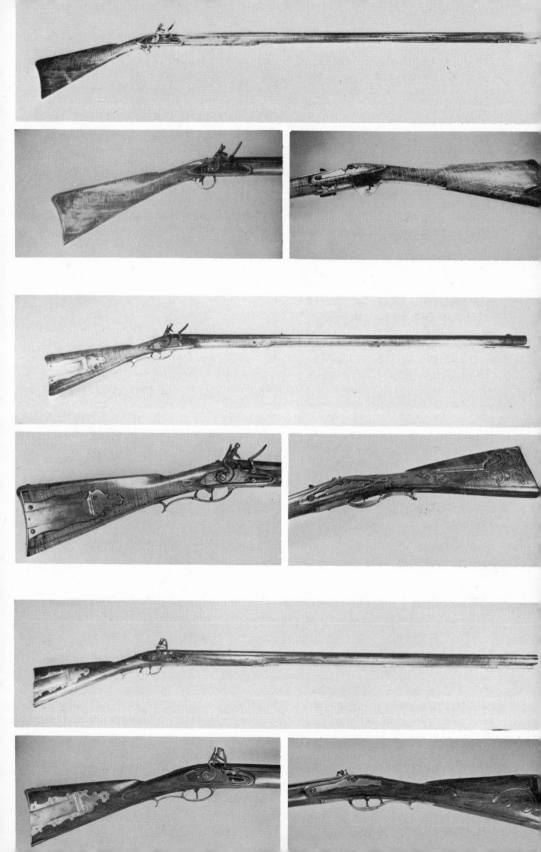

## R.19 DUTCH MILITARY RIFLE                               Circa 1775-1790

This is a Dutch military rifle. Its lock plate includes the name of the contractor, THONE/AMSTERDAM, who supplied arms to Massachusetts early in the Revolution. The round lock, brass pan, and reinforced cock are similar to those of French models that emerged in the mid-1770's (M.34). Yet, the wooden patch-box cover, wide butt, and squared butt tang are like the traditional "Jaeger" (e.g., compare the side plate and trigger-guard design with R.4). Its barrel (octagonal for 10½") bears an Amsterdam proof, while patch-box markings include "B6CN" and "6CN21."

Length: 52"                    Tr. Guard: 11½"              Furniture: Brass
Barrel: 36½"; .66 (8 grooves)  Butt Tang: 2¼"              Weight: 7.9 lbs.
Lock: 5⅞" × 1¼"

*Author's Collection*

## R.20 ENGLISH FERGUSON RIFLE                             Circa 1776-1778

This amazing weapon, developed by Captain Patrick Ferguson in the early 1770's, permitted sustained fire of five rounds per minute (as compared to the typical American rifle's two or three rounds per minute). He perfected a previous system by attaching the front end of the trigger guard to a vertical screw which passed through the barrel. Pulling the small guard handle to the side (three-quarter turn) rotated the screw down, leaving a top hole for inserting the ball and powder. The barrel is octagonal for 5½" at the breech and held by three sliding keys.

Length: 49⅝"                   Tr. Guard: 10⅝"             Furniture: Brass
Barrel: 34⅛"; .65 (8 grooves)  Butt Tang: 4¼"              Weight: 6.9 lbs.
Lock: 5⅛" × 1"

*Morristown National Historical Park Collection*

## R.21 ENGLISH FERGUSON RIFLE FUSIL                       Circa 1775-1778

Shown here is an officer's style of Ferguson's rifle—reportedly presented by him to Captain Frederic de Peyster. Its long bayonet (25½" blade) was designed for this arm and required a bottom stud. The solid nose cap of the preceding weapon is replaced here with a brass strip, but the barrel is still pinned with three keys. While the enlisted man's Ferguson (R.20 above) was made by Mathias Barker and John Whatley ("MB & IW" on barrel), this fusil is marked D. EGG/LONDON. The illustration of the barrel top is from the previous weapon (R.20).

Length: 49½"                                                Furniture: Brass
Barrel: 43"; .69

*Smithsonian Institution Collection*

148

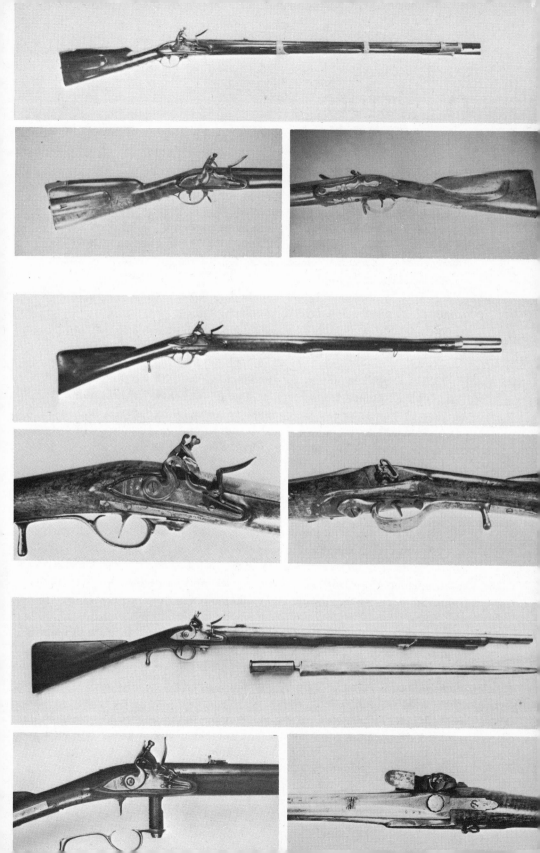

# 6 | PISTOLS

MOST ACCOUNTS of our Revolutionary War weapons give little attention to the pistol—probably because it was decidedly inaccurate except at close range, and not included in most battlefield tactics. Yet, the handgun did see considerable service as a personal weapon. It was considered normal for civilians to carry pocket pistols for protection while traveling. Among military personnel, officers, mounted troops, and seamen used them as standard arms.

They will be considered below in four groups: cavalry pistols, holster pistols, naval pistols, and civilian pistols.

## CAVALRY PISTOLS

**BRITISH:** English handguns for horsemen in the 1700's traditionally had a round barrel pinned to the stock, and mounted heavy brass furniture. By the time of the American Revolution, the early 14-inch barrel had been steadily reduced to 9 inches, and the furniture greatly simplified. The bore was either pistol (.56) or carbine (.65) size (P.6-P.14).

**FRENCH:** Prior to 1733 there were few specifications for French military pistols. The long 12-inch-barrel cavalry weapon of that year did have a pinned barrel with brass mountings. For their next official model (in 1763), however, the furniture reverted to iron (as commonly used on French infantry muskets), and barrel bands were added. By 1766, the barrel length had been reduced to 9 inches like the British. The 1777 model marked an abrupt departure from all previous types, and was later copied by the United States (after the Revolution) (P.29-P.34).

**DUTCH-GERMAN:** These arms had mostly round pinned barrels with bore diameters as large as .75 caliber. Their furniture was generally of brass and heavy in design. Many reached America from Europe through state contracts, as well as being brought by German troops (P.27-P.28; P.43-P.45).

**AMERICAN:** Prior to and during the War for Independence there was no standard American pistol. Almost every European type probably saw some

150

service with the colonial forces. Some were captured, others purchased, and many were assembled from salvaged parts. As with muskets, the majority of handguns at the start of the war were of British origin or style; toward the end of the fighting, French models were common (P.46-P.48).

## HOLSTER PISTOLS

This category includes most of the pistols carried by officers. Since regular patterns were seldom specified for commissioned ranks, they were produced by private gunmakers who stylized them (usually in pairs) for each customer. Fine metals such as silver and gold were often used in mountings, and basic designs generally followed the contemporary cavalry pistol.

## NAVAL PISTOLS

European naval handguns were quite similar to the cavalry style, with perhaps a few variations. Britain's version in the American Revolution, for example, had a 12-inch barrel, but included a flat lock with a reinforced cock like the sea service musket (M.21). The French used a regular cavalry model in the 1760's and 1770's, with brass fittings in place of iron. Most of America's action on the sea was conducted by privateers, who apparently employed whatever was available. For protection, many stocks and iron barrels were coated with black paint and had long belt hooks fastened to the side plate. (P.58-P.64).

## CIVILIAN PISTOLS

Among eighteenth-century civilians who traveled or lived in large cities, pistols were common weapons. Usually they were made to fit into pockets, and many of these small arms were also carried by military officers. Their style tended to reflect the particular country's traditional patterns. One of the most distinctive was the English Queen Anne or cannon-barrel type whose barrel unscrewed for loading (see P.1-P.5).

The following pages illustrate typical examples of handguns from this era in each of the above categories.

**P.1 ENGLISH SCREW-BARREL PISTOL**                    Circa 1750-1760

Probably the best-known civilian pistol of the 1700's was the British type known variously as the "screw-barrel," "cannon-barrel," "turnoff," or "Queen Anne" pattern. Although most were produced after Queen Anne's death, during her reign (1702-1714) two innovations occurred to the crude seventeenth-century version. First, a trigger guard was added. Second, the breech chamber and lock plate were formed as an integral part from one forging. The weapon was loaded by unscrewing the barrel (just forward of the lock) to insert the powder and ball. This one has two Birmingham proofs, with the maker's stamp, "TR" (T. Richards), between them.

Length: 12¾"                    Tr. Guard: 4¾"                    Furniture: Silver
Barrel: 5¾"; .58                                                                Weight: 1.4 lbs.
Lock: 3¾" × ¾"

*Author's Collection*

**P.2 ENGLISH SCREW-BARREL PISTOLS**                    Circa 1725-1740

These pistols have longer barrels than the preceding example, and are sometimes called "traveling" or "coach" pistols. Notice the embellishments around the grotesque mask, and the extensions along the grips (military-style). The panoply of arms on the side plate indicates that this pair was made for an officer. Their barrels have the usual stud underneath near the rear for a spanner to grip if they become difficult to unscrew. London proofs, the name of the maker, BARBAR, plus the initials "LB" are on the barrel.

Length: 13¾"                    Tr. Guard: 5"                    Furniture: Silver
Barrel: 6¼"; .60                                                                Weight: 1.6 lbs. per
Lock: 3⅜" × 1"

*Gene E. Miller Collection*

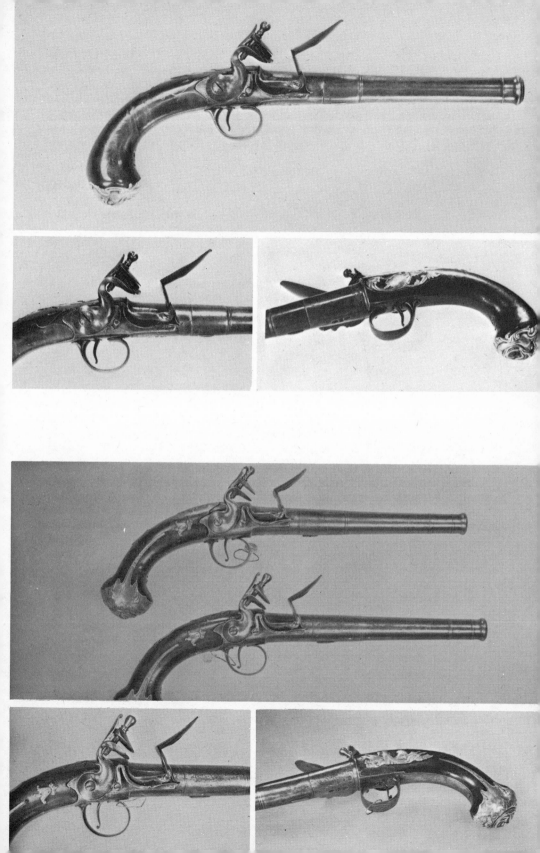

## P.3 ENGLISH SCREW-BARREL PISTOLS                   Circa 1710-1725

Another variation is illustrated here. The stock continues to the point where the screw barrel joins the chamber, and ends abruptly. Its silver furniture includes the usual grotesque mask on the butt cap, and a pierced side plate which still retains much of the early dragon design. Note the inverted frizzen spring used on most of these pistols. The lock is stamped FREEMAN (maker), while the barrel bears two London proofs and the initials "IF" between them. Its escutcheon plate is diamond-shaped with an oval center.

Length: 12¾"          Tr. Guard: 6⅝"          Furniture: Silver
Barrel: 5⅝"; .60                                    Weight: 1.4 lbs. per
Lock: 3¾" × ¾"

*Warren M. Moore Collection*

## P.4 ENGLISH SCREW-BARREL PISTOL                   Circa 1750-1770

By the middle of the eighteenth century, the cock, frizzen, and flashpan were moved from the side to the center of the chamber block. While they interfered with sighting along the barrel, the old problem of lock parts catching in pockets or on clothing was lessened. At this time the cock usually remained un-reinforced, but it was forged with its tumbler as one piece. Thus, the mainspring acted directly upon the notches cut into it. The frizzen spring operated from a recess in the top of the breech. (Markings: T. RICHARDS has been scratched over, and J. JENKINS substituted.)

Length: 12½"                                          Furniture: Silver
Barrel: 5½"; .58                                        Weight: 1.4 lbs.

*William H. Guthman Collection*

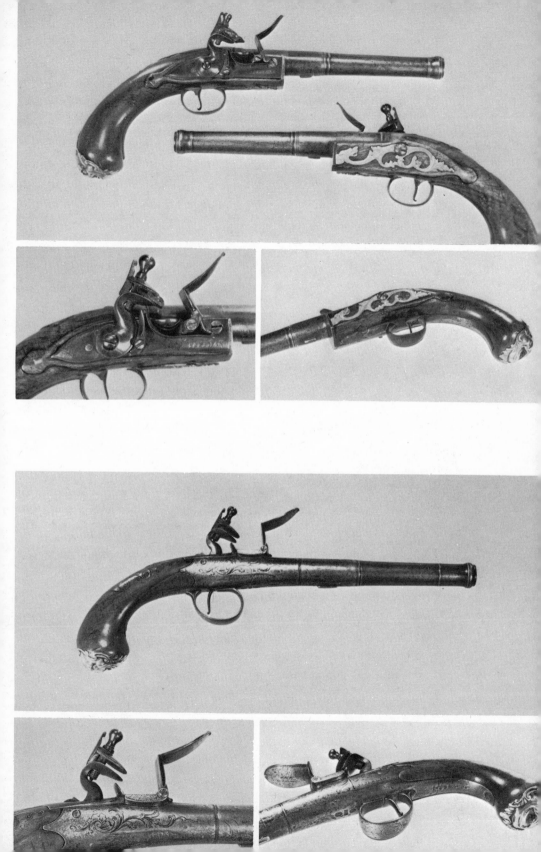

## P.5 ENGLISH SCREW-BARREL PISTOL Circa 1765-1780

By the 1770's, the chamber block has become squared, with flat sides. Also its cock has acquired a reinforcing branch under the lower jaw. The barrel is shown unscrewed to better illustrate the method of loading. It is interesting that the grotesque mask butt cap design still persists at this stage—although after 1780 most grips became squared and had no butt cap at all. The silver wire inlay in the grip was also a popular feature. Markings: T. LANE (maker), London proofs, plus the "foreigner's" mark.

Length: 8″  
Barrel: 2¼″; .44  
Lock: 3 × ¾″  

Tr. Guard: 7⅜″

Furniture: Silver  
Weight: .8 lb.

*Author's Collection*

## P.6 ENGLISH DRAGOON PISTOL Circa 1710-1725

During the first quarter of the eighteenth century, many of the British dragoon pistols had long 14″ barrels. The heavy brass butt cap (with grotesque mask design), side straps extending up the grip, plus the ribbed rammer pipes are typical of these early guns. Notice, too, the forward taper and finial of the trigger guard in its evolution toward the Brown Bess pattern of the 1720's. The tang of the cock is broken off. The lock is marked CLARKSON (maker), while its barrel has HARTFORD (under a large crown).

Length: 21″  
Barrel: 13⅞″; .60  
Lock: 5 × ⅞″  

Tr. Guard: 7⅜″

Furniture: Brass  
Weight: 2.3 lbs.

*Lewis H. Gordon, Jr., Collection*

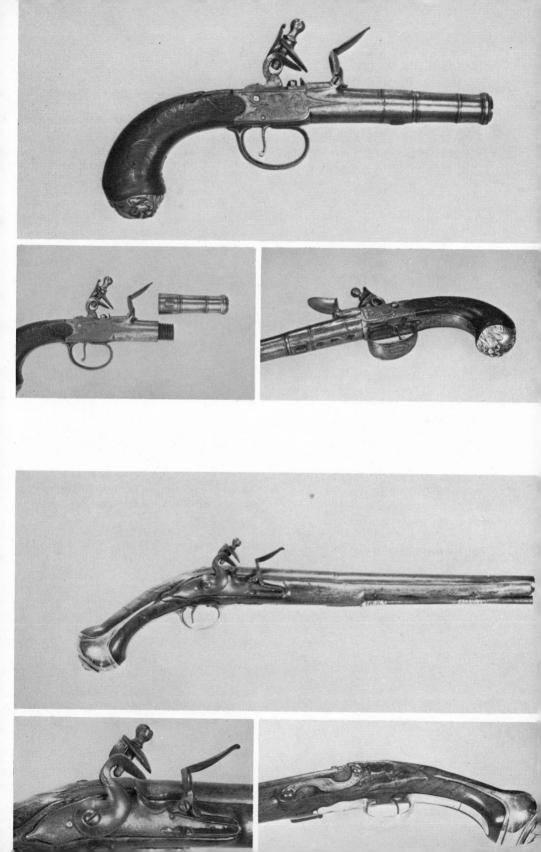

## P.7 ENGLISH DRAGOON PISTOL                    Circa 1719

This flat lock, with its reinforced cock, is another style used for British arms from 1700 to 1720. The side straps are still present on the butt cap, but the grotesque mask motif is now gone. It is also interesting to see the continuing development of the trigger guard's tapered fore end, plus the tail on the flat side plate. Markings on the lock, J. WHITE 19, denote the manufacturer and production date (1719). A crown and broad arrow are also visible just under the flashpan (signifying government property).

Length: 19″                    Tr. Guard: 6¾″                    Furniture: Brass
Barrel: 12⅛″; .68                                               Weight: 2.6 lbs.
Lock: 5½″ × 1″

*Jac Weller Collection*


## P.8 ENGLISH DRAGOON PISTOLS                    Circa 1710-1725

This side plate still bears a resemblance to the earlier dragon shape. A typical rounded iron flashpan without a bridle, plus a tang on the cock curved in the European manner are included on the rounded lock. Engraving on the furniture points to ownership by an officer. The rounded barrel (two decorative rings) is stamped with London proofs, while the lock bears the maker's name, F. SMART. Its escutcheon plate is inscribed "HC" and "4."

Length: 19⅛″                    Tr. Guard: 7¼″                    Furniture: Brass
Barrel: 12″; .66                                                Weight: 2.4 lbs.
Lock: 5⅛″ × ⅞″

*Warren M. Moore Collection*

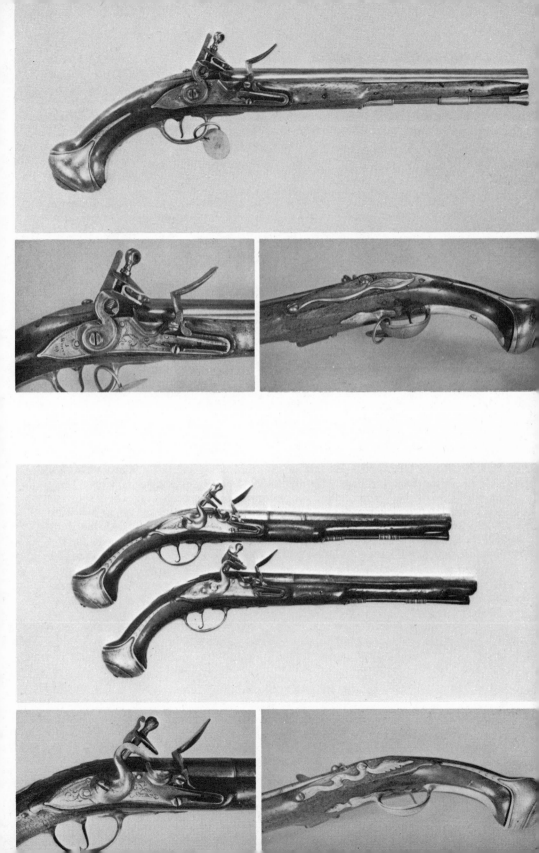

**P.9 ENGLISH DRAGOON PISTOL**                                    Circa 1725-1735

The bore of this pistol by WILSON is almost the size of a musket (.72). Its trigger guard is indicative of this formative decade, and the side plate reflects even more clearly the new long-land pattern. Also present is the typical convex lock (rounded, bridleless pan), plus a heavy brass butt cap with side straps. There are no sights on the round barrel, yet a slight flare at the muzzle is apparent. An elliptical escutcheon plate is engraved with a crude head in profile under a crown.

Length: 18¾″                     Tr. Guard: 7½″                    Furniture: Brass
Barrel: 11½″; .72                                                 Weight: 2.5 lbs.
Lock: 5⅜″ × ⅞″

*Author's Collection*

**P.10 ENGLISH DRAGOON PISTOL**                                   Circa 1725-1735

Much of the basic furniture style of the long-land-pattern musket is visible here: the rounded side plate with a tail; its trigger guard fore end and trigger bow spur (at rear); plus the two plain rammer pipes with raised edges. In this case, a short belt hook is attached to the side plate. Also of interest is the unusual butt cap with the short side lobes, which is similar to a sixteenth-century style, and was used again for the light-dragoon pistols of the 1760's (P.13). The name of the maker, R. WATKIN, is inscribed in the lock, while faint proofs are just visible on the barrel.

Length: 19¾″                     Tr. Guard: 7¾″                    Furniture: Brass
Barrel: 12¼″; .64                                                 Weight: 2.4 lbs.
Lock: 5¼″ × 1″

*Lewis H. Gordon, Jr., Collection*

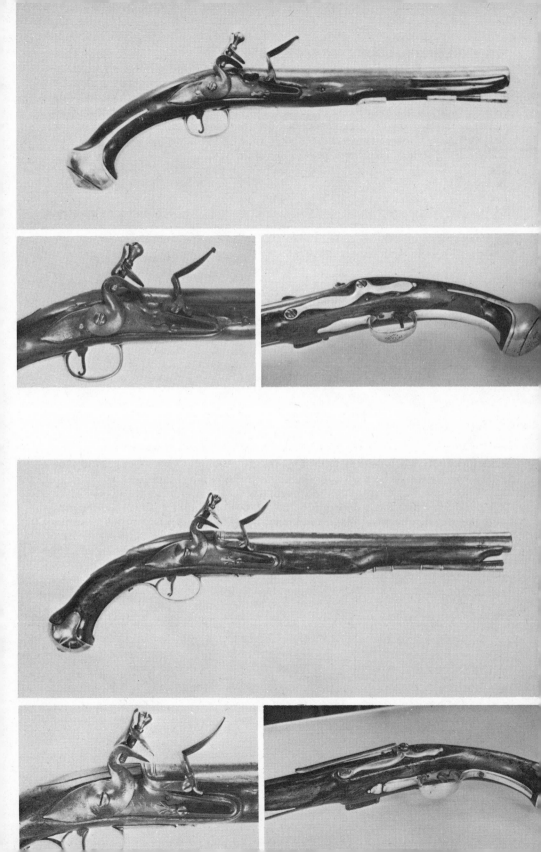

**P.11 ENGLISH DRAGOON PISTOL**                                    Circa 1744

This is an example of the standard British dragoon pistol which evolved shortly after the Brown Bess musket and continued in use for several decades. Its furniture is virtually a scaled-down version of the long-land pattern, with a simple butt cap (including side straps). Note too the raised carving around the lock, side plate, and barrel tang so similar to the long arm. Its lock is inscribed with the crown and "GR," a broad arrow, plus the maker's name IORDAN 1744 (note: early "J" was written as an "I"). The military-shield style of escutcheon plate is unmarked.

Length: 19½″                    Tr. Guard: 7¾″                    Furniture: Brass
Barrel: 12″; .56                                                    Weight: 2.9 lbs.
Lock: 5⁹⁄₁₆″ × 1″

*Author's Collection*

**P.12 ENGLISH LIGHT-DRAGOON PISTOL**                    Circa 1756-1760

The warrant establishing new light-horse troops for dragoon regiments in 1756 also specified a new 10″-barrel pistol. Although this length was officially superseded in 1759, it did see general use during the 1750's, 1760's and in the hands of special units at the time of the American War for Independence. The butt cap with straps along the grip is similar to its predecessors, yet the side plate (notice short third screw) is like a style seen on some contemporaneous fusils and carbines (M.14). The barrel continues round with no sights, and has been enlarged to carbine bore (.65).

Length: 16¾″                    Tr. Guard: 6¾″                    Furniture: Brass
Barrel: 10″; .65                                                    Weight: 2.5 lbs.
Lock: 5¼″ × 1″

*Author's Collection*

162

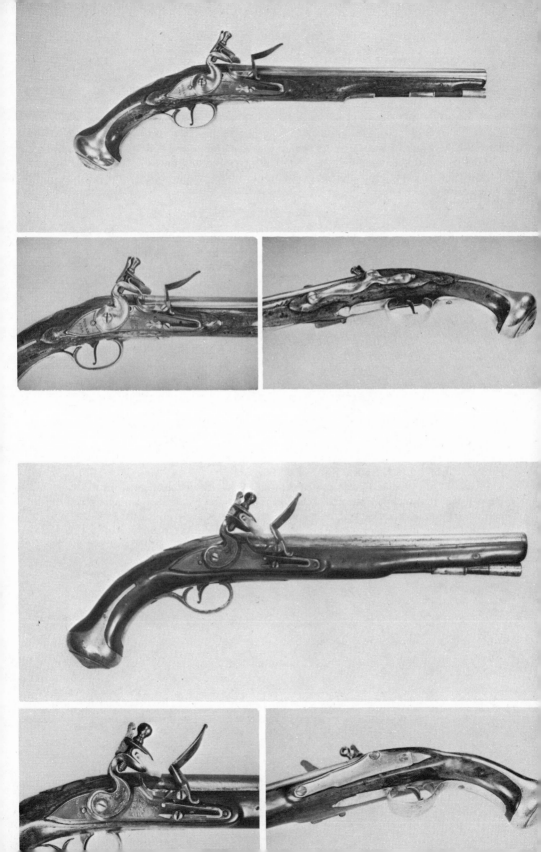

## P.13 ENGLISH LIGHT-DRAGOON PISTOL                    Circa 1760

After the use of light-dragoon units proved successful, full regiments of them were authorized in 1759. At the same time, the 10″-barrel pistol of 1756 (P.12 above) was replaced with a new 9″ version. It remained their principal handgun at the time of the American Revolution. Several characteristics of this important model can be seen: the butt cap has short lobes instead of long straps; the side plate is reshaped and flattened; its trigger guard includes a sharp forward taper and finial; the escutcheon plate is gone (company markings now on trigger bow); and only one pipe holds the wooden rammer (brass-tipped). Lock markings include VERNON 1760.

Length: 15⅜″        Tr. Guard: 6⅜″        Furniture: Brass
Barrel: 9″; .65                                         Weight: 2.1 lbs.
Lock: 5⅜″ × 1″

*Colonial Williamsburg Collection*

## P.14 ENGLISH LIGHT-DRAGOON PISTOL                 Circa 1775-1785

By the 1770's modifications had begun to appear in the light-dragoon pistol. It can be seen that the stock has been thickened in the grip and fore end. The brass furniture continues essentially unchanged, although the trigger bow is deeper. A flat lock, too, has returned. About at the end of the Revolutionary War, reinforced cocks would begin to appear. This lock plate is marked with the crown over "GR" and the name of the manufacturer, GILL.

Length: 15⅞″        Tr. Guard: 6¼″        Furniture: Brass
Barrel: 9″; .65                                         Weight: 2.6 lbs.
Lock: 5½″ × 1″

*Author's Collection*

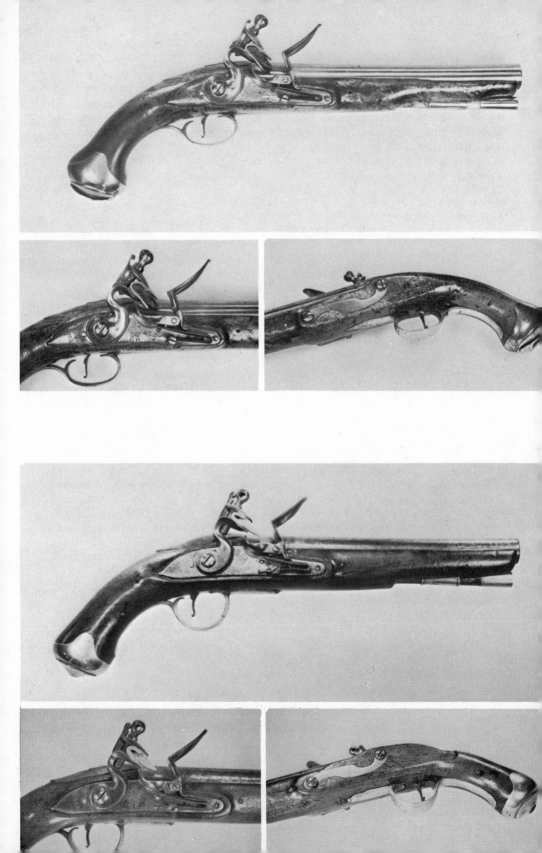

**P.15 ENGLISH HOLSTER PISTOL**                                     Circa 1720-1730

This example of an English silver-mounted holster pistol is one of a pair reportedly carried by an American officer in the War for Independence. The open side plate, three-pointed trigger-guard design, and masked butt cap (with side straps along the grips) are all typical of this early decade. Note too the raised carving around the lock, side plate, barrel tang, and tail pipe. Of added interest are the two ornamental silver bands ringing the barrel. Its horn-tipped wooden rammer is secured by two ribbed pipes, while the barrel tang is held by a bottom screw. The mark of the private maker, WILSON, is engraved on the lock.

Length: 16¾"                    Tr. Guard: 6¾"                    Furniture: Silver
Barrel: 10¼"; .68                                                Weight: 2.0 lbs.
Lock: 4⅞" × ⅞"

*Author's Collection*


**P.16 ENGLISH HOLSTER PISTOL**                                     Circa 1720-1740

This specimen is mounted in brass. The masked butt cap and three-pointed trigger-guard design are evident, as is the martial motif (which includes cannon, swords, and flags) on its open side plate. A slight flare appears at the muzzle of the round barrel, while its two rammer pipes are slightly convex (with raised edges). The wooden rammer (without a brass tip) is not original to the piece. A border in relief—including a scallop decoration at the top and shell design for the tail—surrounds an oval escutcheon plate. G JONES LONDON is inscribed on the barrel and repeated on the lock.

Length: 18⅞"                    Tr. Guard: 7⅞"                    Furniture: Brass
Barrel: 11⅞"; .73                                                Weight: 2.6 lbs.
Lock: 5⅜" × 1"

*Lewis H. Gordon, Jr., Collection*

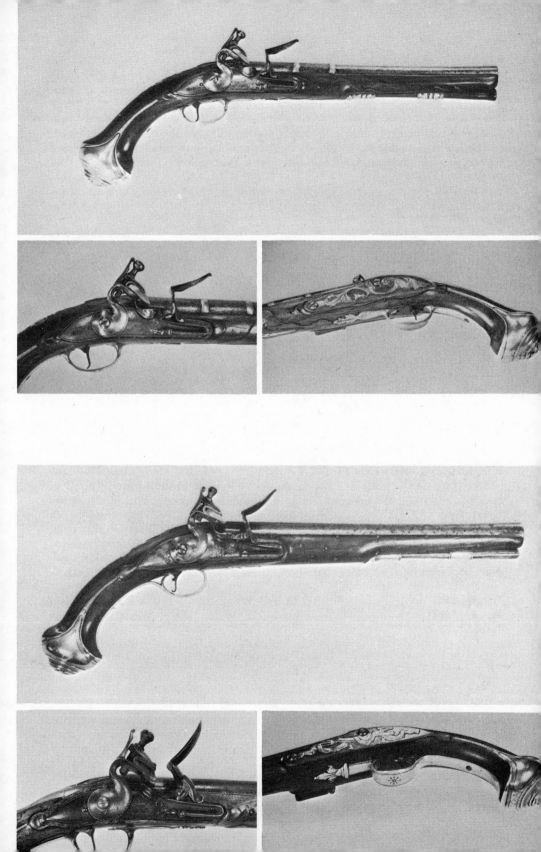

**P.17 ENGLISH HOLSTER PISTOL**                                 Circa 1735-1750

This is a style carried by many colonial officers during the French and Indian Wars and the Revolution. Its fittings are brass and include several earlier features: a three-pointed trigger-guard design, two ribbed rammer pipes, a round barrel with a "step-down" band (3⅛″ from the breech), plus a slight flare at the muzzle. Yet, the side plate now has a solid triangular shape, the barrel measures 9″, and the rounded lock has an outside bridle. Note that the "mask" on the butt cap has disappeared, although an oval escutcheon plate remains. London proofs and a faint maker's mark appear on the barrel.

Length: 15⅜″                    Tr. Guard: 7″                    Furniture: Brass
Barrel: 9″; .61                                                 Weight: 1.8 lbs.
Lock: 4¾″ × ⅞″

*Author's Collection*

**P.18 ENGLISH HOLSTER PISTOLS**                                Circa 1750-1760

Several interesting features in design and mountings are illustrated here. The silver butt cap, with its grotesque mask design, for example, is more typical of the screw-barrel pistols (P.1-P.5); a scallop decoration, which was popular in the mid-eighteenth century, is present at the forward end of the trigger guard; and its open-side-plate motif includes unusual straight lines at right angles. A horn tip appears on the wooden rammer, while the two plain pipes have raised borders. London proof marks, "IG" inside a rectangular cartouche, and GRIFFIN/LONDON are engraved in the barrel. The maker's name also appears on the lock.

Length: 13⅜″                    Tr. Guard: 6¼″                   Furniture: Silver
Barrel: 8″; .63                                                 Weight: 1.4 lbs. per
Lock: 4¾″ × ⅞″

*Warren M. Moore Collection*

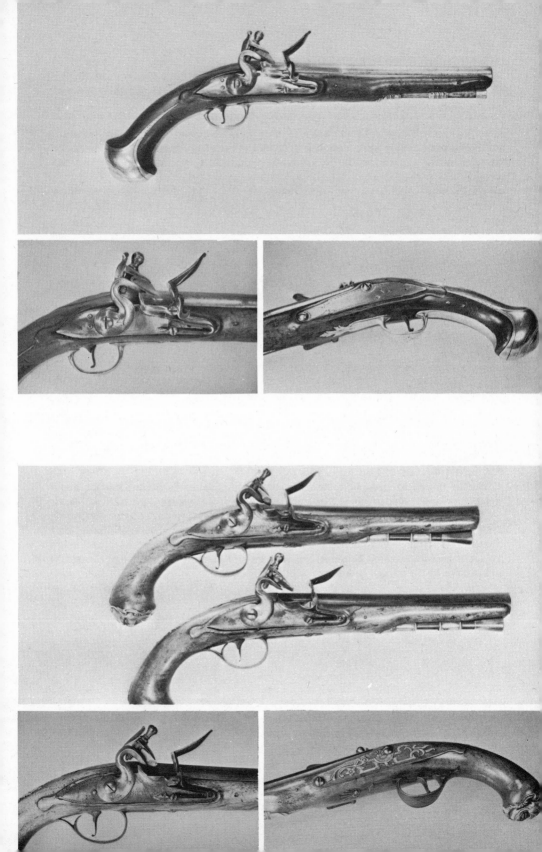

**P.19 ENGLISH HOLSTER PISTOLS**                        **Circa 1758**

These elaborately decorated weapons are fine examples of the capabilities of English silversmiths in the 1700's. Not only are the raised furniture relief and stock inlays unique, but two developments which were more typical fifteen years later are included: the barrel is held by two sliding keys, and a safety thumb catch is visible on the lock plate behind the cock. Note too that the earlier grotesque mask appears again on the butt cap, while a contemporary scallop design is present on the trigger guard. The name of the maker, BARBAR, appears on the lock, and London proofs with his initials, "IB," are stamped into the barrel. Silver hallmarks establish the 1758 date.

Length: 17¾"            Tr. Guard: 6⅞"            Furniture: Silver
Barrel: 11"; .63                                   Weight: 2.1 lbs. per
Lock: 5" × 1"

*Warren M. Moore Collection*

**P.20 ENGLISH HOLSTER PISTOLS**                        **Circa 1766**

Like the preceding example, these pistols are the product of Barbar in London (about eight years later). Aside from the absence of elaborate stock inlays, their round barrels (top flat for 3" from breech) are now 9" long (like the 1759-pattern dragoon pistol, P.13), and the side-plate design is beginning to fill in. A traditional style of masked butt cap still persists, however, including the side straps. Its wooden rammer includes a horn tip and is held by two smooth pipes. The popular scallop design, slightly embellished, is still present on the trigger guard and escutcheon plate.

Length: 15¼"            Tr. Guard: 6⅜"            Furniture: Silver
Barrel: 9"; .62                                    Weight: 1.8 lbs. per
Lock: 4¾" × ⅞"

*Warren M. Moore Collection*

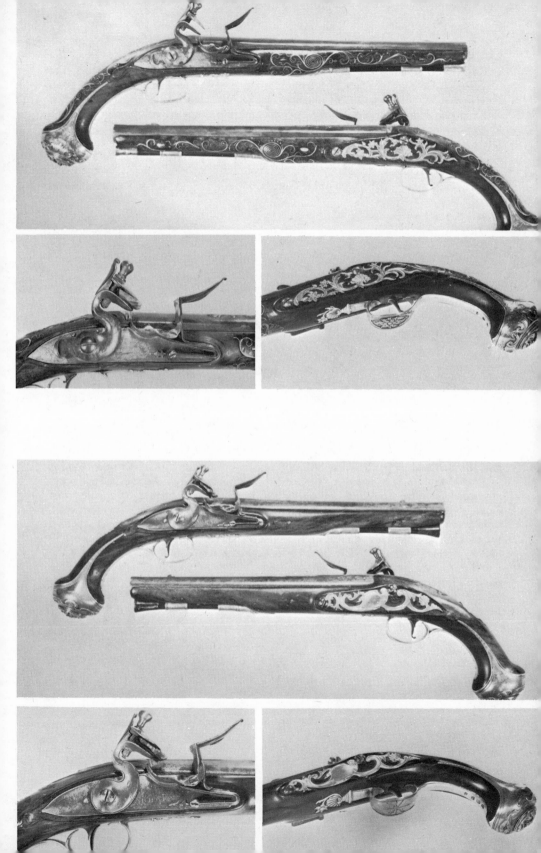

## P.21 ENGLISH HOLSTER PISTOLS                                    Circa 1774

This pair of privately made officer's pistols again combines old and new features. The brass barrels have a slight flare at the muzzles and are octagonal from the breech to an ornamental ring (3¼″ away). The re-emergence of such breech styling also occurred on contemporary blunderbusses. A butt cap mask and side straps are still present, although long since abandoned on standard military arms. Slotted keys for the barrel and a thumb safety lever on the lock were finally becoming popular. Notice too the continuance of the scallop or shell design in most of the furniture, plus the stock carving. Barrel markings are DL MOORE/LONDON.

Length: 15¼″              Tr. Guard: 6⅞″              Furniture: Silver
Barrel: 9″; .63                                       Weight: 1.8 lbs.
Lock: 5″ × ⅞″

*Warren M. Moore Collection*


## P.22 EUROPEAN POWDER TESTER                              Circa 1760-1780

A powder tester is included for the reader's information. It was a typical method of measuring the effectiveness of powder, which could vary considerably in quality even at that date. The lock, butt cap, trigger guard, and side plate are similar to contemporary pistol mountings. However, the barrel is a short vertical tubelike projection seen behind the cock. It was filled with a measured amount of powder and ignited through a touchhole by normal lock action. The force of its explosion would raise the plate across the barrel's top, which, in turn, rotated the calibrated round disk and indicated the explosion's force.

Length: 9⅜″               Tr. Guard: 4¾″              Furniture: Iron
Lock: 3″ × ⅝″                                         Weight: .9 lb.

*Colonial Williamsburg Collection*

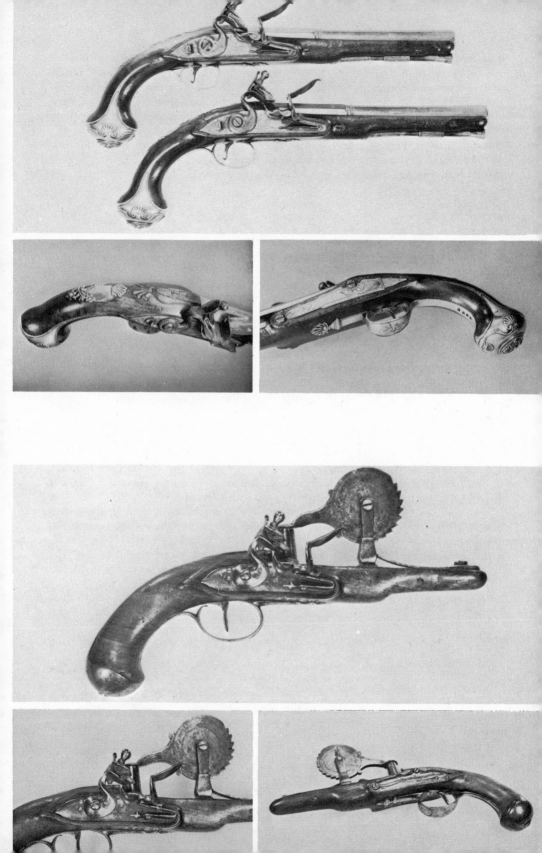

**P.23 SCOTTISH REGIMENTAL PISTOL**                    Circa 1758-1776

Scottish regiments were the only infantry units in the British Army which issued pistols to their enlisted men during the eighteenth century. They were a distinct style of hand-gun, which had been made entirely of metal since the mid-1600's. Two types were apparently carried in North America. This pattern was the more popular. It is entirely of iron, with the ram's-horn or scroll butt (and the knob of a vent pick or oiler in the center). There is no trigger bow, and its flat lock plate is cut square across the end. The lock is marked BISSELL (Isaac Bissell of Birmingham), with two private scepter proofs on the barrel, plus "RHR" (Royal Highland Regiment). The rammer is not original.

Length: 12⅞"                                            Furniture: Iron
Barrel: 7⅞"; .55                                       Weight: 1.5 lbs.


*Lewis H. Gordon, Jr., Collection*


**P.24 SCOTTISH REGIMENTAL PISTOL**                    Circa 1758-1776

This version of the Bissell style of Scottish arm is similar to the preceding one, but has embellishments in design which indicate probable ownership by a junior officer or a noncommissioned officer. The barrel is fluted for its entire length, with an ornamental ring and slight flare at the muzzle. Spiraling channels are visible on the cock screw, trigger, and vent pick knob. The oval design on the grip is typical. A belt hook is attached to the opposite side for sliding over a strap hanging under the left arm. The crude "IM" on the lock plate are probably an owner's initials. This barrel too is marked "RHR" (note: "HR" became "RHR" about 1758).

Length: 13"                                             Furniture: Iron
Barrel: 7⅞"; .55                                       Weight: 1.6 lbs.


*Author's Collection*

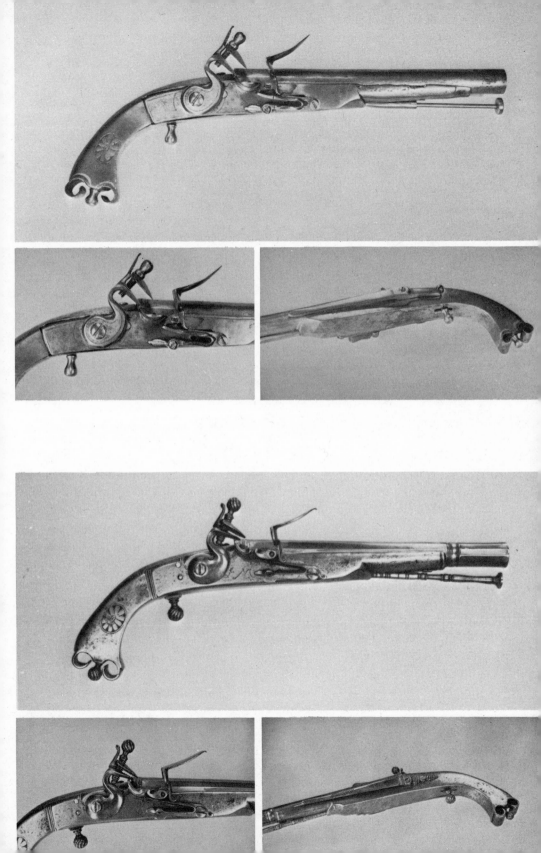

**P.25 SCOTTISH PISTOL**                                Circa 1750-1776

The brass barrel and inlaid designs seen here are indicative of the more expensive pistols carried by Scottish officers. Its barrel has a series of ⅛″ wide flutes (for 2⅞″ from the breech), followed by raised designs, an ornamental ring, and fluting again at the flared muzzle. A small stud under the muzzle helps to hold the iron rammer in place. Pierced designs at the base of the belt hook, and silver inlays on the grips add further to its decorative pattern. On the lock plate is engraved the maker's name, D. WALKER (of Dumbarton, Scotland). The initials "IM" in the ovals on the grip are probably those of the owner.

Length: 13¼″                                          Furniture: Iron
Barrel: 8½″                                           Weight: 1.9 lbs.

*George C. Woodbridge Collection*

**P.26 SCOTTISH REGIMENTAL PISTOL**                    Circa 1760-1776

Pictured here is a second style of Highland regimental pistol. The "stock," made of brasslike gun metal, terminates in a kidney-shaped butt. In many ways its construction is similar to the other pattern. Note the lock illustration with the cock at the "half-cock" position—held by a horizontal sear which pierces the plate just forward of it (there is no second notch on this tumbler). Records indicate that Scottish troops in America were ordered to discard their pistols and broadswords in 1776. However, subsequent reports of use in battle, plus their possession by Scottish settlers, would seem to indicate Revolutionary War use. These arms were usually made by John Waters (London).

Length: 11⅝″                                          Furniture: Brass
Barrel: 6⅞″; .57                                      Weight: 1.6 lbs.

*Author's Collection*

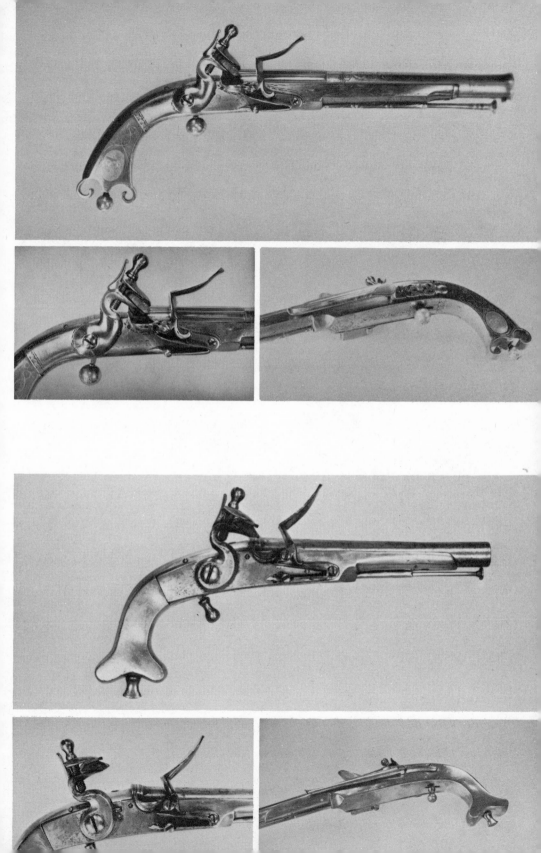

**P.27 DUTCH PISTOL**                                          Circa 1690-1710

It is hard to realize today the great number of Dutch arms which were used in our colonial era. Holland was one of the leading arms producers in Europe, and during the Revolutionary War supplied weapons to the Americans, British, and Hessians. This early pistol has the typical heavy butt cap, plus a pierced side plate. A Dutch pattern is evident in the trigger guard, while the octagonal rammer pipes reflect Germanic influence. Its interesting lock has a faceted flashpan (no bridle), squared frizzen top, and a frizzen spring screw from inside the plate. The barrel is octagonal at the breech (for 2¾″).

Length: 18⅞″              Tr. Guard: 8⅝″              Furniture: Iron
Barrel: 11⅝″; .66                                      Weight: 2.5 lbs.
Lock: 5″ × 1″

*Author's Collection*


**P.28 DUTCH DRAGOON PISTOLS**                                 Circa 1750-1770

These Dutch pistols are of the type which saw considerable use in America during the French and Indian Wars and later in the Revolution. The heavy butt cap with side straps along the grip, "tailed" side plate (three screws shown), and the lobed trigger guard are all typical. A "plump" lock with rounded pan (no bridle) and gooseneck cock is the style seen on many of their muskets (M.44-M.46). Two side flats are included at the breech of the barrel—which mounts an elliptical brass front sight. Marked on one barrel is "ED N51"; and on the other, "LC N24." There is no escutcheon plate.

Length: 20⅝″              Tr. Guard: 8½″              Furniture: Iron
Barrel: 13⅛″; .69                                     Weight: 3.1 lbs. per
Lock: 5½″ × 1″

*Gene E. Miller Collection*

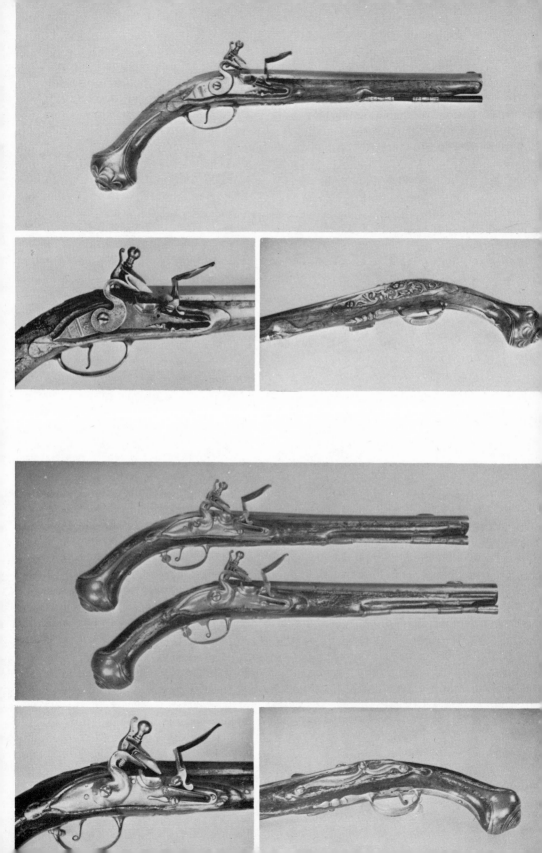

## P.29 FRENCH CAVALRY PISTOL                                    Circa 1710

This long-barreled (14¼″) iron-mounted pistol is an early French style of the eighteenth century. The tapered trigger guard and simple curved side plate so characteristic in later French patterns are already in evidence. Its barrel has an octagonal breech which ends at an ornamental ring 4¼″ forward (a second ring is 5½″ from the breech). Only one forward pipe supports the wooden rammer; there is no tail pipe nor escutcheon plate. Markings on the barrel show a crown, "3," "IS," and the date "1710"—each in a rectangular cartouche. Repairs to the stock and grip are visible.

Length: 21½″                     Tr. Guard: 9″                     Furniture: Iron
Barrel: 14¼″; .65                                                 Weight: 2.9 lbs.
Lock: 5¾″ × 1⅛″

*Morristown National Historical Park Collection*

## P.30 FRENCH CAVALRY PISTOL                              Circa 1720-1730

An apparent transition between the early style of French pistol (P.29 above) and the first standardized model (in 1733; P.31) is illustrated in this example. Note the brass furniture, 12″ octagonal-round barrel, two rammer pipes, and nose-cap strip. Also of interest is the obvious Dutch influence (see P.28) in the design of the trigger guard and butt cap (possibly produced by them under contract). The side-plate pattern is a known French type (e.g. P.39), and its lock plate is marked GROZIER on the face, with P TRONCHON 3 inside.

Length: 19½″                     Tr. Guard: 8¼″                    Furniture: Brass
Barrel: 12″; .60                                                  Weight: 2.6 lbs.
Lock: 5⅜″ × 1″

*Author's Collection*

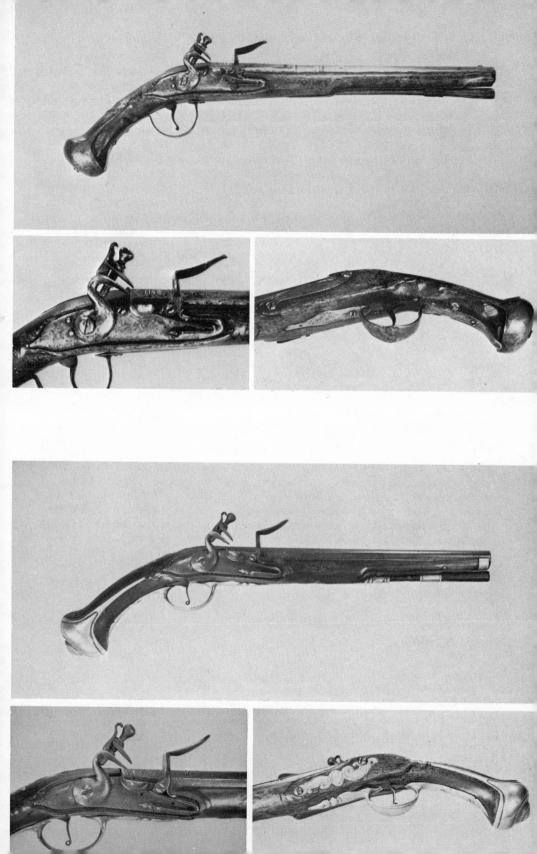

## P.31 FRENCH CAVALRY PISTOL                                    Model 1733

The Model 1733 is believed to be the first standard French cavalry pistol (first musket model: 1717). It apparently continued as such until the next official pattern appeared in 1763. The flat lock with beveled edges and a gooseneck cock is a smaller version of the infantry musket style (used from the 1720's to the 1760's). Notice too how the brass furniture has acquired a new design—including a solid triangular side plate. An elliptical sight is fixed to the barrel, which is octagonal for 4¼" at its breech. This arm was made at the Saint-Étienne Manufactory ("SE" under a crown on the lock), and the barrel bears a figure-eight-type mark (see illustration). There is no escutcheon plate.

Length: 19⅜"                     Tr. Guard: 8¼"                     Furniture: Brass
Barrel: 12"; .69                                                   Weight: 2.7 lbs.
Lock: 5⅛" × 1"

*Author's Collection*

## P.32 FRENCH CAVALRY PISTOL                                    Model 1766

Probably the most common style of handgun among the arms supplied to the colonists by France during the American Revolution was this Model 1766. Iron furniture was mounted on most for the land forces, while brass was used by the navy (see P.62). The flat lock and reinforced cock are similar to the regular musket of this year (M.30). Its "bird's-head" butt cap extends halfway up the back of the grip, while the tapered trigger guard and convex side plate follow the common style. Some of the barrels originally made for the brief 1763 pistol were cut down for use on this model. The tang here still bears an M 1763 marking. Its barrel has also lost the octagonal breech, and is round.

Length: 16¼"                     Tr. Guard: 7½"                     Furniture: Iron
Barrel: 9"; .68                                                    Weight: 2.5 lbs.
Lock: 4⅞" × 1"

*Author's Collection*

182

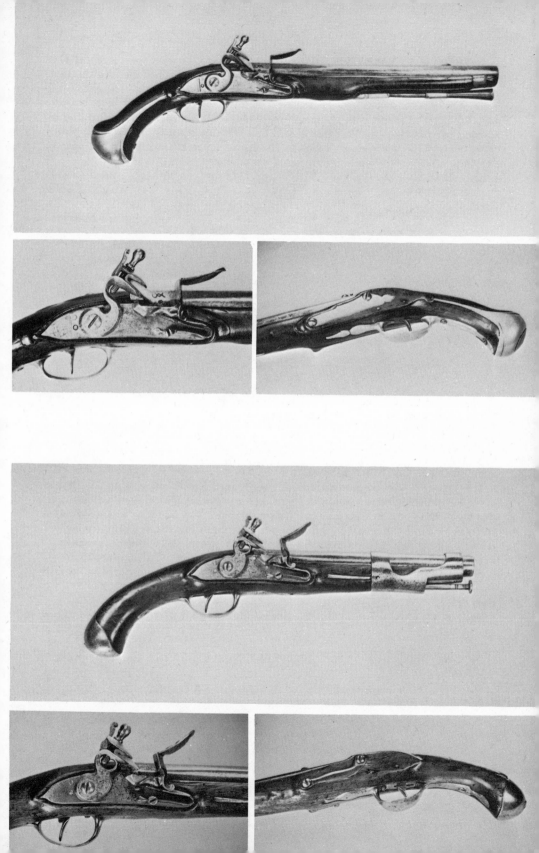

## P.33 FRENCH CAVALRY PISTOL

As with the muskets, French pistols in the early 1770's remained close to the basic pattern of the previous decade. The major change was in the lock. Notice how the earlier flat style has now become rounded on the tail. Its reinforced cock has also assumed a convex shape, with a squared upper tang. Little change is evident in the remaining parts of the arm. The lock is inscribed MANUFACTURE de ST ETIENNE, plus a crown above "IR" (inspector's initials). The barrel bears the number "76" (year of proofing), while AVRIL 76 is also stamped in the stock behind its side plate.

Length: 16⅜"  Tr. Guard: 7⅛"  Furniture: Brass (naval)
Barrel: 9⅛"; .68   Weight: 2.8 lbs.
Lock: 5" × 1"

*Author's Collection*

## P.34 FRENCH CAVALRY PISTOL

The year 1777 saw the introduction of a redesigned French infantry musket. Issued at the same time was this pistol, which was even more radical in concept. The lock and iron rammer are held in a central brass housing. From it also protrudes a tapered round barrel, with no stock fore end for support. Its cock, frizzen, and frizzen spring (inverted) are of iron, but the brass flashpan has been cast as part of the housing. CHARLEVILLE is engraved beneath the cock, and the stampings "F80" and "S80" indicate its manufacture in 1780. The barrel tang is marked "M 1777." A crude "B3" appears on the butt cap. This was the model copied by America for its first postwar pistol (the North & Cheney).

Length: 13¾"  Tr. Guard: 5⅝"  Furniture: Brass
Barrel: 7½"; .69   Weight: 2.9 lbs.

*Author's Collection*

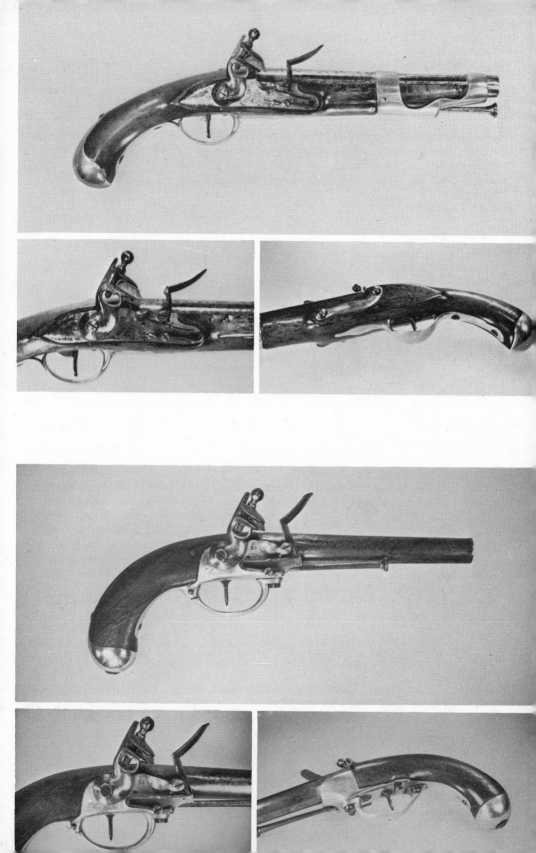

## P.35 FRENCH HOLSTER PISTOL                    Circa 1700-1720

Iron-mounted, small-caliber (.51) French pistols of this type have been found in eastern America and Canada in sufficient numbers to indicate considerable use. Its flattened style of butt cap (with thin straps extending almost to the lock), octagonal-round barrel (two ornamental rings), and convex lock plate are all similar to those of other pistols of this period (P.29). The early dragon-shaped side plate and cheap construction raise the further possibility of use as a trade arm. A tail pipe supports the wooden rammer. There is no escutcheon plate.

Length: 14⅝″                    Tr. Guard: 6⅞″                    Furniture: Iron
Barrel: 7¾″; .51                                                  Weight: 1.7 lbs.
Lock: 4½″ × ⅞″

*Author's Collection*


## P.36 FRENCH HOLSTER PISTOL                    Circa 1733-1763

The iron furniture on this weapon is a direct copy of the brass mountings for the Model 1733 cavalry pistol (P.31). Its shorter length and finer workmanship indicate use by an officer. The barrel is octagonal for 4″ before blending into a rounded shape, while two pipes hold the wooden rammer (horn tip). Raised stock carving surrounds most of the fittings, including the flat lock. It is a typical French style of the period (i.e. gooseneck cock, faceted pan with bridle), and has a frizzen spring screw which originates inside. Markings include CHEVAUX REGT (Horse Regiment) on the barrel, plus COIGNEL LE LIEUNOIS on the lock face. There is no escutcheon plate.

Length: 15⅝″                    Tr. Guard: 7⅞″                    Furniture: Iron
Barrel: 9¼″; .64                                                  Weight: 1.9 lbs.
Lock: 4⅝″ × ⅞″

*Author's Collection*

186

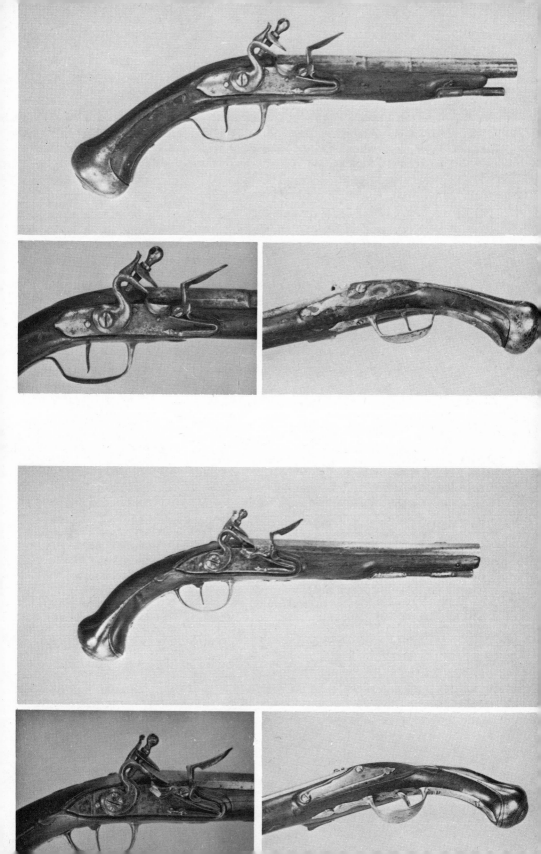

## P.37 FRENCH HOLSTER PISTOL                    Circa 1745-1760

The privately made French officer's pistol in this illustration dates from the mid-1700's. Its iron furniture is more decorative and the raised stock carvings more elaborate than those of the preceding specimen (P.36). The side plate, for example, is engraved with a panoply of flags, horns, and cannon—behind a Grecian-style helmet. Its flat lock includes a faceted iron pan without fence or bridle, and an inside frizzen spring screw. The barrel is rounded, with a "flat" on each side at the breech (2⅞"). Small channels have been cut in the stock paralleling the barrel and rammer. Identifying marks are not visible. No escutcheon plate is present.

Length: 14¾"                   Tr. Guard: 7"                   Furniture: Iron
Barrel: 8¾"; .58                                               Weight: 1.7 lbs.
Lock: 4⅜" × ⅞"

*Author's Collection*

## P.38 FRENCH HOLSTER PISTOLS                    Circa 1748

This unusual pair of officer's or gentleman's pistols exhibits fine relief work in both the mountings and the stock. A gold wash has been added to the background in most of the furniture to further highlight the designs. Notice the elaborate carvings surrounding its barrel tang, plus the pierced escutcheon plate. Both barrels are octagonal for 3¼" before becoming round. They include a "flat" along the top for the entire length, and ornamental rings at the muzzles. Thin silver plates are also fastened to the faces of the wooden rammers. Although hallmarks are not common on French arms, this pair is stamped for "1748." The lock and barrel are inscribed PUIFORCAT/PARIS.

Length: 15"                    Tr. Guard: 7½"                  Furniture: Silver
Barrel: 8⅞"; .60                                               Weight: 1.4 lbs. per
Lock: 4⅜" × ¾"

*Warren M. Moore Collection*

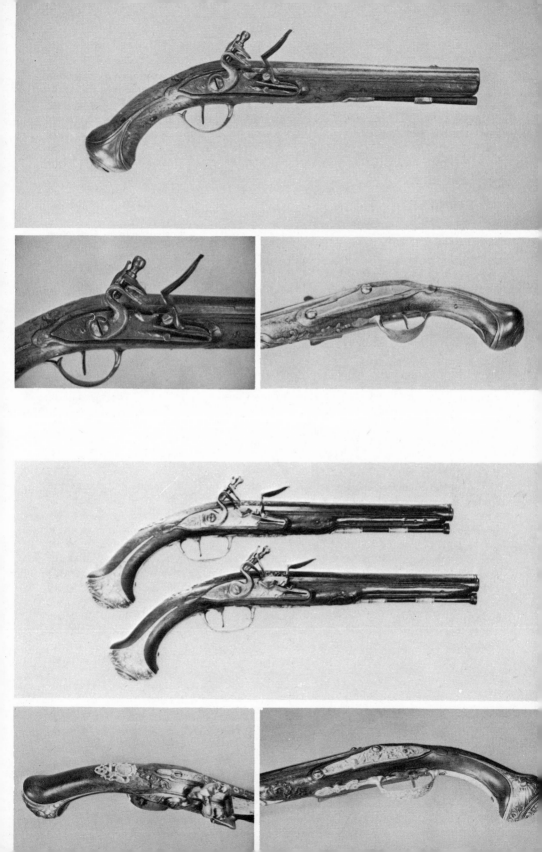

## P.39 FRENCH HOLSTER PISTOLS                    Circa 1760-1770

The bird's-head butts of these silver-mounted French officer's weapons are quite distinctive. They are, in fact, decorative modifications of the butt cap introduced on standard cavalry pistols during the 1760's (P.32). The flat locks are similar to the style prevailing during the preceding decade, and the unique side plates (with the center oval are an early French motif (P.30). All of the furniture is molded in elaborate relief design. The barrel is octagonal for 3¼" before becoming round. Markings on the barrel indicate the maker and location as ALLERY/PARIS. An oval escutcheon plate is also present.

Length: 13"                    Tr. Guard: 6½"                    Furniture: Silver
Barrel: 7½"; .57                                                 Weight: 1.3 lbs. per
Lock: 4¼" × ⅞"

*Foster Tallman Collection*

## P.40 FRENCH HOLSTER PISTOLS                    Circa 1770-1777

The official French cavalry pistols of the early 1770's (P.33) undoubtedly served as models for these officer's side arms. In this case, however, the furniture is made of silver and the large barrel band is omitted. The octagonal-round barrels are held to the stock by sliding keys (which became popular in the 1770's). The rammer is wooden, with a horn tip (note: one pipe has been moved to the rear). It is interesting to see that the contemporaneous reinforced style of cock was not included, and that the rounded lock plate has a longer and sharper taper to the tail than normal. The maker's name and address, FOULON/PARIS/RUE ST HONORE, appear on the lock, and NO 17 is engraved on both barrels.

Length: 14⅜"                    Tr. Guard: 7"                    Furniture: Silver
Barrel: 6¾"; .69                                               Weight: 1.8 lbs. per
Lock: 4½" × ⅞"

*Gene E. Miller Collection*

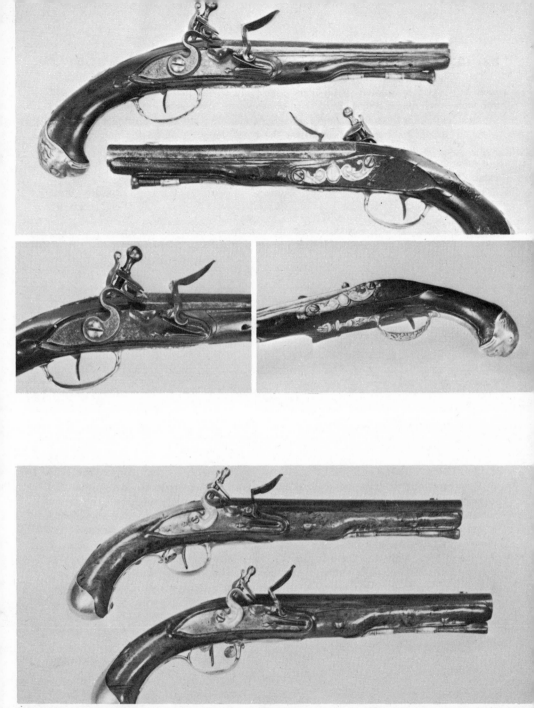

## P.41 GERMAN PISTOL                                                Circa 1710-1730

This long-barreled (13½″) German pistol has no visible military markings, and may have been used by soldiers or civilians. Engraving covers most of the brass furniture and lock—including a grotesque mask in the center of an open side plate. Raised ridges in the stock border the tail pipe and rammer channel, plus most of the fittings. Its barrel is round, except for two side "flats" near the base (for 4½″) and a top one from 2¾″ above the breech to within 2″ of the muzzle. Both pipes holding the wooden rammer are octagonal in traditional German fashion. The figure of a hen on the lock plate establishes the source of this gun as Suhl, in the county of Henneberg.

Length: 20½″                    Tr. Guard: 7⅞″                    Furniture: Brass
Barrel: 13½″; .59                                                 Weight: 2.6 lbs.
Lock: 5⅜″ × 1⅛″

*Author's Collection*


## P.42 GERMAN HOLSTER PISTOL                                        Circa 1750-1775

The flared butt on this specimen is not unusual among early German pistols. Its workmanship testifies to ownership by an officer or well-to-do gentleman. The bright furniture is iron, and the stock carvings include parallel lines bordering the pinned barrel and rammer channel. Checkering of the type visible on the grip was not very popular at this time, and may have been added later. The dark nose cap is actually a piece of horn, while the wooden rammer still retains a metal worm tip. Its barrel is octagonal for 3½″ before becoming round in shape. Lettering on the lock is not clear, but an "A" in a six-sided cartouche is stamped under the breech. A shield-shaped escutcheon plate is present.

Length: 16¼″                    Tr. Guard: 6¾″                    Furniture: Iron
Barrel: 9½″; .63                                                  Weight: 1.8 lbs.
Lock: 4½″ × 1″

*Author's Collection*

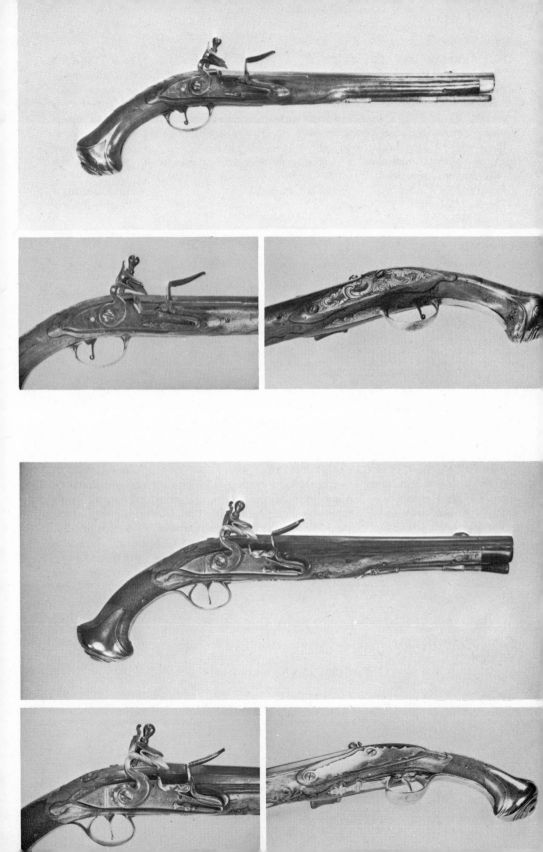

**P.43 GERMAN CAVALRY PISTOL**                           Circa 1750-1765

The lock and furniture pictured on this cavalry pistol are typical of German arms in the mid-eighteenth century. The thick trigger-guard lobes, curled trigger, wavy three-screw side plate, and octagonal rammer pipes are all similar to those on many of their muskets (M.38-M.39). Its heavy lock, with the squared cock jaws and frizzen top, is marked POTZDAMMAGAZ (Potsdam Arsenal). The raised carvings are also common to these arms. A long brass front sight is mounted on the round barrel, and the nose cap is a strip of brass about 1″ from the muzzle. An oval escutcheon plate bears the "FR" cipher (Frederick the Great).

Length: 22⅜″                    Tr. Guard: 8¾″                    Furniture: Brass
Barrel: 14⅝″; .68                                                 Weight: 3.5 lbs.
Lock: 5⅝″ × 1″

*West Point Museum Collection*


**P.44 GERMAN-DUTCH CAVALRY PISTOL**                     Circa 1760-1775

This horseman's pistol mounts a three-screw curving side plate and octagonal rammer pipes in the German style, but also includes a lobed trigger guard and flat-sided butt cap typical of many Dutch weapons—suggesting possible Low Countries manufacture. The undulating tail surface of the lock, plus the arrowhead shapes incorporated into the raised stock carvings (forward of the lock and behind the barrel tang) further emphasize Germanic influence. Its oval escutcheon plate and round barrel (12¾″) are unmarked.

Length: 20½″                    Tr. Guard: 8″                    Furniture: Brass
Barrel: 12¾″; .69                                               Weight: 3.2 lbs.
Lock: 5¾″ × 1⅛″

*Author's Collection*

194

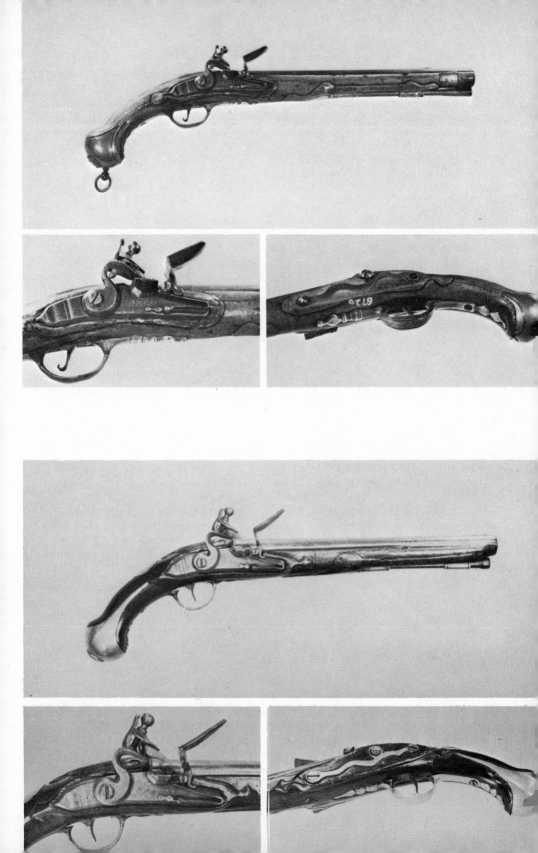

**P.45 EUROPEAN CAVALRY PISTOL**                              **Circa 1750-1770**

Here is a style of European cavalry pistol from the 1750's and 1760's. Its iron butt cap and side plate resemble those of the French 1733 model (P.31), yet the trigger guard, flat lock, and absence of a rammer channel reflect Dutch-German influences. The only marks for identification are an "O" atop the barrel, and the letters "FB" inside the lock. These characteristics seem to point toward origin in the Low Countries. Because of their availability, weapons like this probably reached America during the Revolution. Its flat lock has a faceted flashpan (no bridle) and is bordered by crude raised carving. The barrel is octagonal for 4″ at the breech.

Length: 18½″                   Tr. Guard: 8¾″                   Furniture: Iron
Barrel: 11¼″; .76                                               Weight: 2.8 lbs.
Lock: 5½″ × 1⅛″

*Author's Collection*

**P.46 AMERICAN CAVALRY PISTOL**                              **Circa 1760-1780**

This long-barreled dragoon pistol is apparently an American counterpart of the similar British model (P.11). The barrel bears English proofs, yet the triangular side plate and crude lock plus the Brown Bess–style trigger guard and butt cap all seem to be of colonial manufacture. Its American stock follows a contemporary European fashion by omitting a rammer channel. No escutcheon plate is present. The barrel is held by two pins and a flat brass band. No other marks are visible.

Length: 18¾″                   Tr. Guard: 7¼″                   Furniture: Brass
Barrel: 11¾″; .68                                              Weight: 2.5 lbs.
Lock: 5½″ × 1″

*Author's Collection*

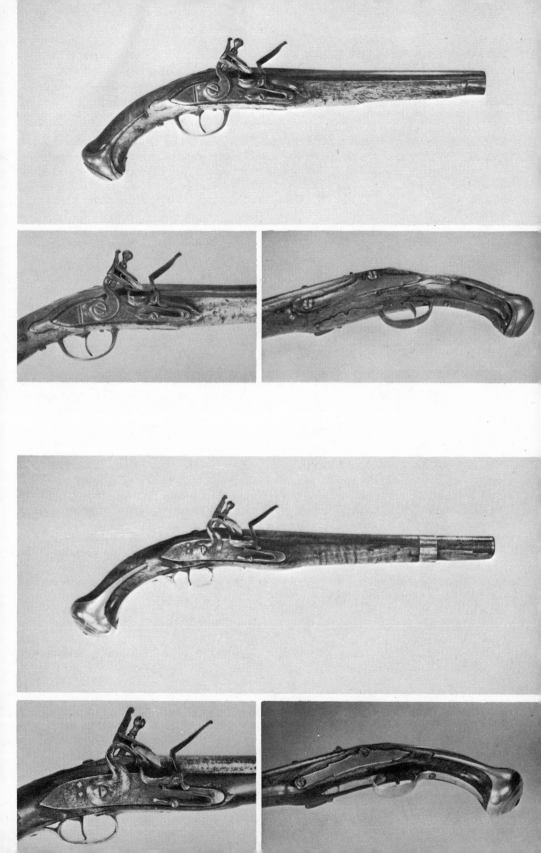

**P.47 AMERICAN CAVALRY PISTOL**                                          **Circa 1775**

Despite its mid-nineteenth-century conversion to the percussion system, and the re-placed forward end of the stock, this specimen of an American pistol is most interesting. The brass barrel is octagonal for 3¼″ from the breech to the first ornamental ring (the second one is 1½″ beyond). On the top "flat" can be seen the inscription B:TOWN PHILA, which is believed to stand for Benjamin Town of Philadelphia, who is known to have made arms for the colonial troops in 1775. The smooth butt cap with side straps, and solid side plate are uniquely American. Its shell carving and escutcheon-plate design are also distinctive. The earlier English three-pointed style appears to have been copied for the trigger guard.

Length: 17¾″                     Tr. Guard: 6⅜″                     Furniture: Brass
Barrel: 10½″; .63                                                   Weight: 2.9 lbs.
Lock: 5⅜″ × 1″

*William H. Guthman Collection*

**P.48 AMERICAN CAVALRY PISTOL**                                     **Circa 1775-1783**

This furniture and barrel appear to have come from a German dragoon pistol. Its brass mountings, for example, are almost identical to the standard Prussian arms of the period (see M.38, P.43). The flat lock has a faceted flashpan without a supporting bridle, and the top of the frizzen, plus the cock jaws, are squared. Even the two rammer pipes are octagonal in the traditional manner. Yet, the butt cap apparently had the upper ends of its side straps cut off in the process of restocking. Heavy raised carving normally found around the lock, side plate, and butt tang has also been eliminated by the Ameri-cans. This heavy pistol (over 3 lbs.) would have been a formidable weapon in anyone's hands—with or without ammunition.

Length: 20¼″                     Tr. Guard: 7¾″                     Furniture: Brass
Barrel: 12″; .65                                                    Weight: 3.3 lbs.
Lock: 5⅜″ × 1″

*Author's Collection*

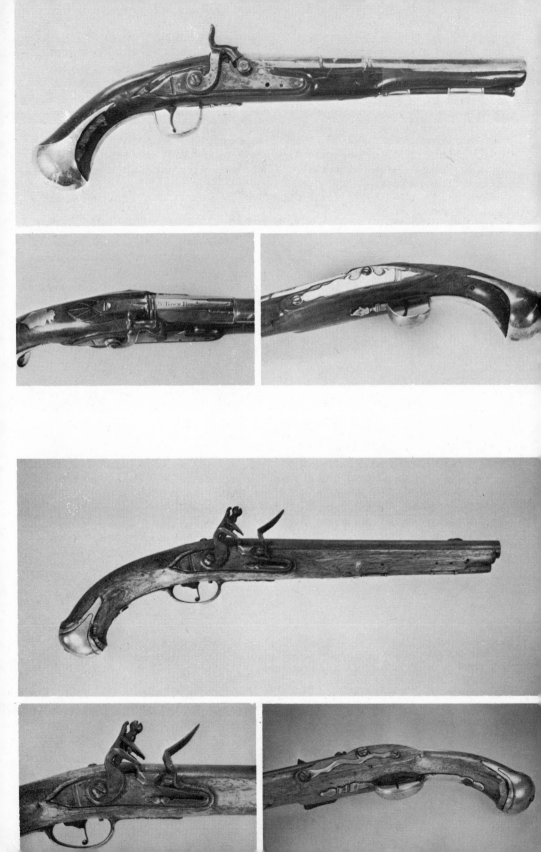

**P.49 WASHINGTON PISTOLS**                          **Circa 1770-1775**

This fine pair of silver-mo⁀⁀nted British officer's pistols is believed to have been the property of George Washi⁀ ⁀n. The elaborate butt caps include the early grotesque mask, while a panoply of arms and flags—accompanied by the lion and unicorn—appears on the open side plate. Popular shell designs are present in the raised carving behind each barrel tang, plus the trigger guard's forward end. A safety latch can also be seen to the rear of each cock. The round brass barrels have two short "flats" at the breech and flare slightly at the muzzles. They bear London proofs with the initials "RW," while the locks are engraved HAWKINS. A silver band across the back of each grip reads GEN G. WASHINGTON.

Length: 14"                    Tr. Guard: 6⅝"                    Furniture: Silver
Barrel: 8"; .66
Lock: 4⅝" × ¾"

*West Point Museum Collection*

**P.50 AMERICAN HOLSTER PISTOL**                          **Circa 1770-1783**

The lines of this arm seem out of proportion when compared with the balanced profile of most contemporary European pistols. Yet, it is not unlike many of the weapons made by the practical Americans, who seemed to prefer the least expensive functional product possible. Every component here appears to be of colonial manufacture. Its crude butt cap and trigger guard (held by two nails) are copies of earlier British styles. The rounded lock has an unsupported flashpan and a frizzen spring screwed from the inside. Its barrel is octagonal at the rear, flowing into a round surface after 3½". Cherry wood was used for the stock; there are no markings or escutcheon plate.

Length: 14"                    Tr. Guard: 6¾"                    Furniture: Brass
Barrel: 7⅜"; .56                                              Weight: 1.4 lbs.
Lock: 4⅝" × 1"

*Author's Collection*

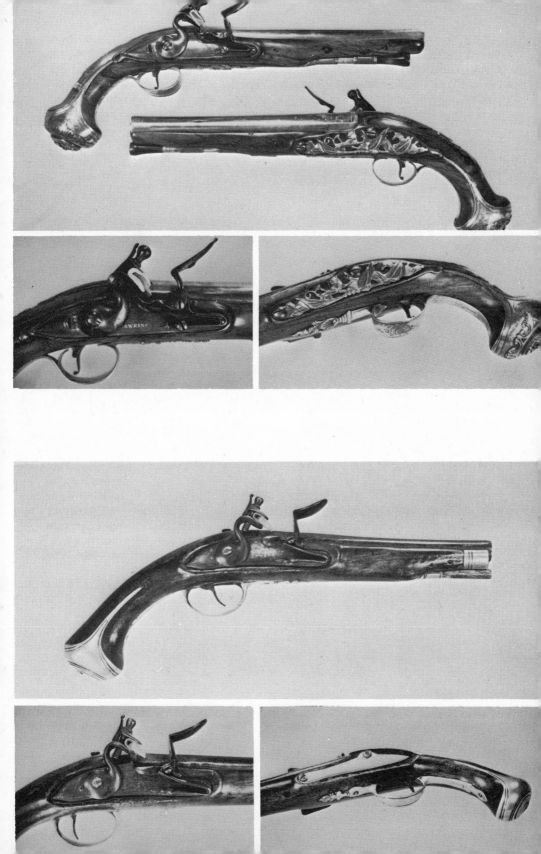

## P.51 AMERICAN HOLSTER PISTOL                    Circa 1775-1785

Aside from the LONDON-marked barrel, this appears to be an American-made arm. Its hook-type grip and flat-edged butt cap are similar to the style of some "Kentucky" pistols. Piercings in the side plate are also an interesting feature, as is the flattened front face of the trigger bow. The convex lock has an unsupported rounded pan, while a rectangular upper tang on the cock fits into the slotted base of the top jaw. Notice too the elementary arrowlike tip on the trigger guard. Its escutcheon plate is oval, and most of the brass furniture bears simple outline engraving of the style found on many colonial pieces. Other markings include a "C" on the lock plus a star under the breech.

Length: 14⅜"               Tr. Guard: 6½"                Furniture: Brass
Barrel: 9"; .58                                          Weight: 1.6 lbs.
Lock: 4⅝" × ⅞"

*Author's Collection*

## P.52 AMERICAN HOLSTER PISTOL                    Circa 1760-1780

Reflecting the pragmatic colonist's penchant for functional weapons, this one includes parts from several sources. The heavy thick-walled barrel has apparently been cut down from a shoulder arm—probably a carbine (no proofs). Its brass butt cap with a grotesque mask is typical of the early British pistol style, while the convex lock still bears the name of its English maker, BARBAR. The triangular side plate and sharp-ended trigger guard, however, seem to be of American origin. An original escutcheon plate has since been removed. No identifying marks are visible.

Length: 13"                Tr. Guard: 7"                 Furniture: Brass
Barrel: 8"; .69                                          Weight: 2.4 lbs.
Lock: 5¼" × 1"

*R. Paul Nittolo Collection*

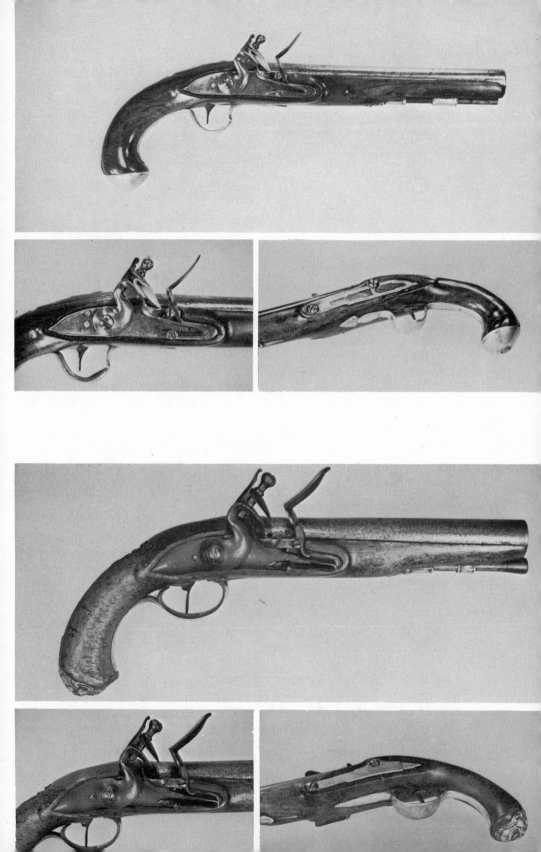

**P.53 AMERICAN HOLSTER PISTOL** Circa 1775-1785

The almost vertical grip illustrated in this specimen has been found on various American pistols into the early 1800's. The butt cap and trigger guard are of the style on contemporaneous British light-dragoon pistols (P.13), but because of symmetrical irregularities are probably American copies. Its crude convex lock is obviously of colonial origin. A simple brass pipe holds the wooden rammer, which has a pewter tip. Originally found in the Pennsylvania Dutch area, this pistol bears no marking except a small oval on the barrel with a deer in its center, plus the stamped letters "LC." Note the early curled-trigger form. A side plate was apparently never fitted to the gun.

Length: 13¾"          Tr. Guard: 5⅜"          Furniture: Brass
Barrel: 9⅛"; .70                              Weight: 2.7 lbs.
Lock: 5½" × 1"

*R. Paul Nittolo Collection*


**P.54 AMERICAN KENTUCKY PISTOL** Circa 1765-1780

Although this style of arm was normally the product of Pennsylvania rifle makers, it is commonly known today as the "Kentucky" pistol, and is the only true American type of handgun used during the Revolutionary War. Produced almost entirely as side arms for officers, their limited number was probably due to the far cheaper imports available from Europe. This particular example combines graceful lines with a fine curly maple stock. A crude colonial version of the lion head appears on its brass butt cap, while the popular English acorn design has been copied on the trigger guard. Irregular forging in the lock plus a sharp taper toward the tail testify to American manufacture.

Length: 14"          Tr. Guard: 6¾"          Furniture: Brass
Barrel: 8⅜"; .52                              Weight: 1.6 lbs.
Lock: 4⅜" × 13⁄16"

*Harmon C. Leonard Collection*

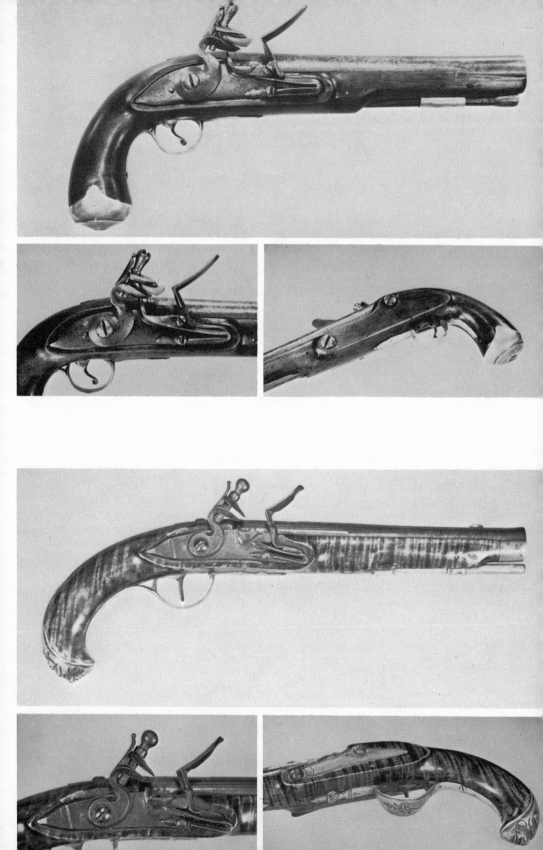

## P.55 AMERICAN "KENTUCKY" PISTOL                    Circa 1777-1785

The example shown here is believed to have been made in New England, and is marked T. HILLS on the lock. Its brass furniture and stock illustrate the flowing pattern inherent in the simple lines of so many colonial products. A bird's-head-style butt cap extends well up the back of the grip, while the tapered profile of its flat lock is repeated in the side plate on the opposite side. Notice too the elemental lobe at the end of the trigger guard. A small brass nose cap is installed at the tip of the fore end; two simple pipes hold the wooden rammer. Its barrel has a round surface and a smooth bore.

Length: 14⅞"                     Tr. Guard: 6"                    Furniture: Brass
Barrel: 8¾"; .50                                                 Weight: 1.8 lbs.
Lock: 4⅝" × ¾"

*Joe Kindig, Jr., Collection*

## P.56 AMERICAN "KENTUCKY" PISTOL                    Circa 1770-1785

This attractively striped pistol bears evidence of manufacture by a Pennsylvania rifle maker. The octagonal barrel, square-ended side plate, brass nose cap, and simple trigger guard are all typical of contemporary rifles. A large engraved cap covers the bulbous butt and extends part way along the back of the grip. Also of interest is the raised carving around the side plate and lock. Both front and rear sights are installed on the barrel, which is rifled with seven grooves. The name T HAEFFER appears in script on top of the barrel, while the oval escutcheon plate bears the letter "R."

Length: 16½"                     Tr. Guard: 5¼"                  Furniture: Brass
Barrel: 10⅜"; .48 (7 grooves)                                   Weight: 2.1 lbs.
Lock: 4⅝" × ⅞"

*Joe Kindig, Jr., Collection*

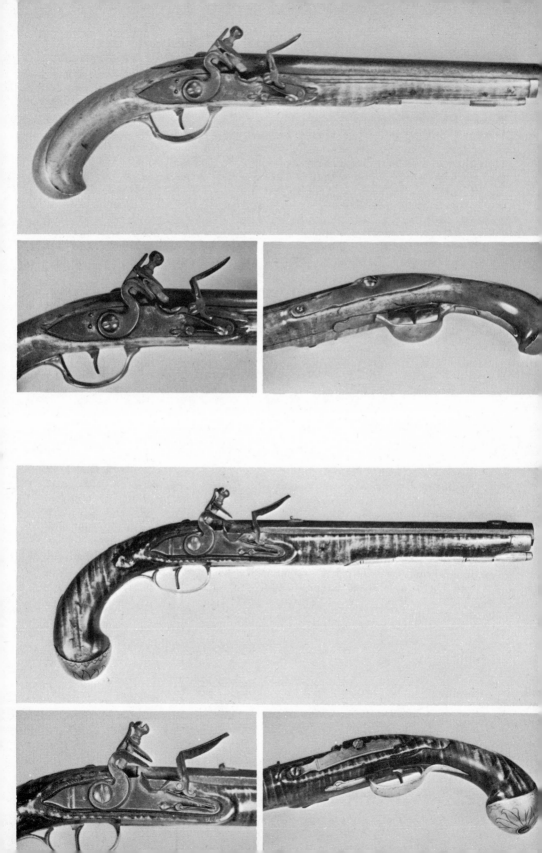

**P.57 AMERICAN "KENTUCKY" PISTOL**                     Circa 1775-1785

Here is another apparent product of Pennsylvania. The hook at the toe of the striped stock is much sharper than the others seen, and bears a rounded cap. Its flat tapered lock, with a gooseneck cock and faceted reinforced flashpan, is typical of rifles in this period. However, the pierced side plate is more like British patterns at mid-century. Octagonal in shape for its entire length, the pinned barrel is rifled (seven grooves) and mounts two open sights. Incised carving around the tail pipe and along the rammer channel are also similar to those of American rifles. On the top of the barrel is inscribed H ALBRIGHT—a well-known gunsmith in Lancaster, Pennsylvania.

Length: 16½"                 Tr. Guard: 7½"              Furniture: Brass
Barrel: 10½"; .45 (7 grooves)                            Weight: 2.1 lbs.
Lock: 4⅞" × ⅞"

*Edmund W. Budde, Jr., Collection*

**P.58 ENGLISH NAVAL PISTOL**                          Circa 1725-1740

This English pistol, made by R. Watkin, is similar to his dragoon model of the same period (see P.10), but is believed to have been produced for naval use. Its brass furniture reflects the long-land pattern, as does the unbridled lock. The butt cap has a straight upper edge—a style which was popular again near the end of the eighteenth century. Note also the belt hook attached to the side plate. Engraved on the lock plate is the maker's name, R WATKIN, while his initials, "RW," appear on the barrel between two Birmingham proofs. The barrel is round, with a slight flare at the muzzle. Its escutcheon plate is of the usual shield design.

Length: 20"                  Tr. Guard: 7⅞"              Furniture: Brass
Barrel: 12¾"; .60                                        Weight: 2.9 lbs.
Lock: 5⅜" × 1"

*Harold L. Peterson Collection*

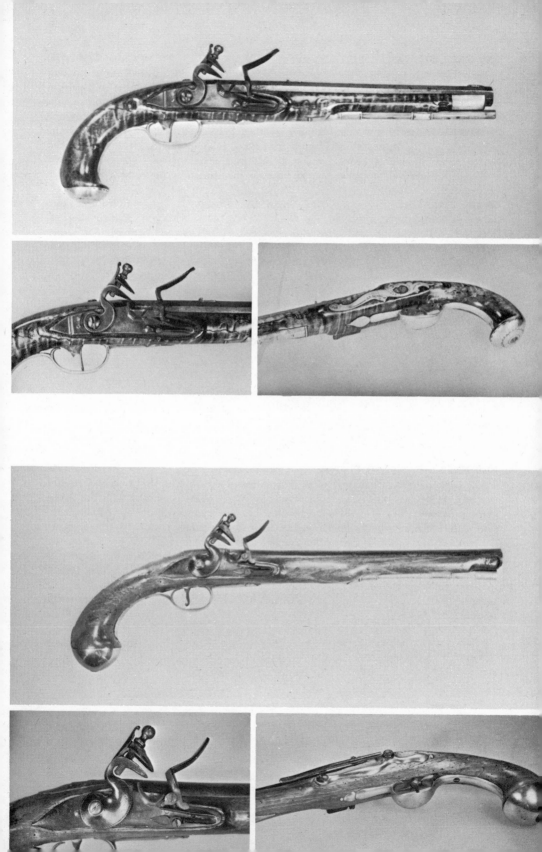

**P.59 ENGLISH NAVAL PISTOL**                              Circa 1750-1760

Here is an early version of the style of British naval pistol which would persist through the American Revolution. Notice that the flat side plate resembles the short-land pattern and includes a hole for the stud from a belt hook. Its pointed trigger guard and smooth butt cap are also typical of these sea-service weapons. There is no tail pipe; only one forward pipe holds the wooden rammer (with a brass tack in its end). Around the breech is a raised ornamental band, while the muzzle is slightly flared. Its lock is marked HEYLIN, and the barrel bears London proofs plus an inspector's stamp (a crown above "4"). Note too the spear-shaped finial of the frizzen spring, which appears on many of these naval arms.

Length: 19″                    Tr. Guard: 6½″                    Furniture: Brass
Barrel: 12″; .58                                                Weight: 2.4 lbs.
Lock: 5½″ × 1″

*Author's Collection*

**P.60 ENGLISH NAVAL PISTOL**                                  Circa 1762

The basic pattern of naval pistol used by British forces during the American Revolution is pictured here. Several modifications are noted when compared with the earlier version above (P.59). It is ½″ longer, with a heavier stock and butt cap. Although the side plate remains virtually unchanged (notice the long belt hook), its trigger guard has evolved to the Brown Bess style. The flat lock and reinforced cock popular on sea-service muskets are also repeated in this side arm (M.21). Its lock face is marked with the crown and "GR," plus the maker and date, VERNON 1762. Faint proofs remain partially visible on the round barrel. There is no escutcheon plate.

Length: 19½″                   Tr. Guard: 7¼″                   Furniture: Brass
Barrel: 12″; .61                                                Weight: 2.6 lbs.
Lock: 5⅜″ × 1″

*Author's Collection*

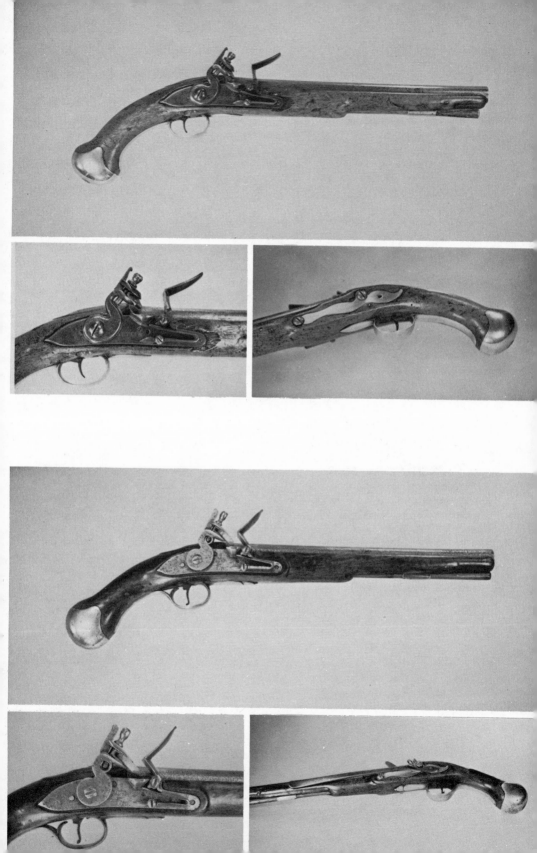

## P.61 AMERICAN NAVAL PISTOL

Circa 1740-1750

This example is a combination of early British parts restocked in America. The flat lock with a reinforced cock, rounded trigger-guard tip, and oval butt cap were all popular styles in the first quarter of the eighteenth century. In this case, the barrel has probably been shortened from an original 12" length to 9". Its side plate design resembles later English models, and was possibly added by the colonists at the time of restocking. Notice again the hole for a naval belt hook's stud. The barrel tang is fastened by the early method—a screw from underneath (head just forward of trigger). Markings include I PARR on the lock plus two Birmingham proofs on the barrel.

Length: 16⅛"            Tr. Guard: 6¼"            Furniture: Brass
Barrel: 9"; .67                                           Weight: 2.1 lbs.
Lock: 5½" × 1"

*Author's Collection*

## P.62 FRENCH NAVAL PISTOL

Model 1766

The French naval pistol of this date is almost an identical copy of their cavalry pattern (P.32). Its only real difference is brass furniture (nonrustable) in place of the usual iron fittings. Some barrels on this model were actually surplus from the short-lived preceding 1763 pistol, and although shortened to 9", still bear "M1763" on the tang. The flat lock, with the reinforced cock and faceted bridled flashpan, is similar to the contemporary musket (M.30). Its lock inscription reads MANUFACTURE de CHARLEVILLE (Royal Manufactory). The weapon has no sights, and mounts a buttonheaded iron rammer.

Length: 16"            Tr. Guard: 8"            Furniture: Brass
Barrel: 9"; .68                                       Weight: 2.7 lbs.
Lock: 5" × 1"

*Author's Collection*

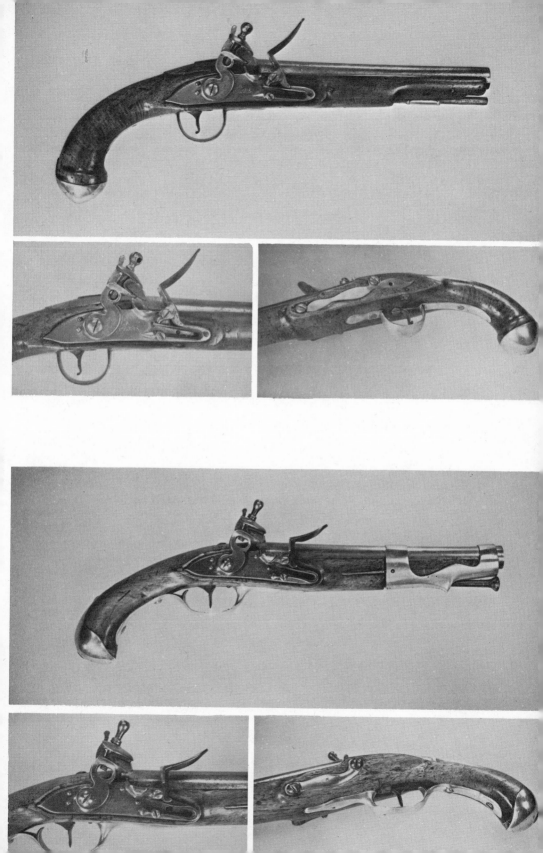

**P.63 FRENCH NAVAL PISTOL**                              Circa 1768-1780

This double-barreled silver-mounted pistol is typical of the type carried by many French naval officers in the last half of the eighteenth century. Both barrels, the lock plates, and flashpans are brass, while the furniture is of silver—molded in decorative relief. The frizzen and its spring are both held by screws from inside the lock. Raised carving in the stock surrounds most mountings, while decorative engraving appears on each of the round barrels. One lock bears the name of its maker, JEROME BLACHON; the other is inscribed with the manufactory name, ST ETIENNE. The single wooden rammer has a horn tip.

Length: 13″                    Tr. Guard: 7″                    Furniture: Silver
Barrel: 6¾″; .60                                                Weight: 1.8 lbs.
Lock: 4″ × ¾″

*Author's Collection*

**P.64 FRENCH NAVAL PISTOL**                              Circa 1775-1790

As with the previous specimen (P.63), a brass lock plate, barrel, and furniture suggest use of this short pistol by a naval officer. The side plate is typical of many French handguns, as is the thin stem at the forward end of the trigger bow (see P.63, P.37). Its barrel includes an octagonal breech (for 2½″) and a flare at the muzzle (the bore size is constant). Note, too, the bird's-head-butt cap style which was adopted for their cavalry pistols in 1763. The maker's name, LECLERC, appears on the lock plate.

Length: 11″                    Tr. Guard: 6¾″                   Furniture: Brass
Barrel: 5⅜″; .56                                                Weight: 1.4 lbs.
Lock: 3¾″ × ¾″

*Author's Collection*

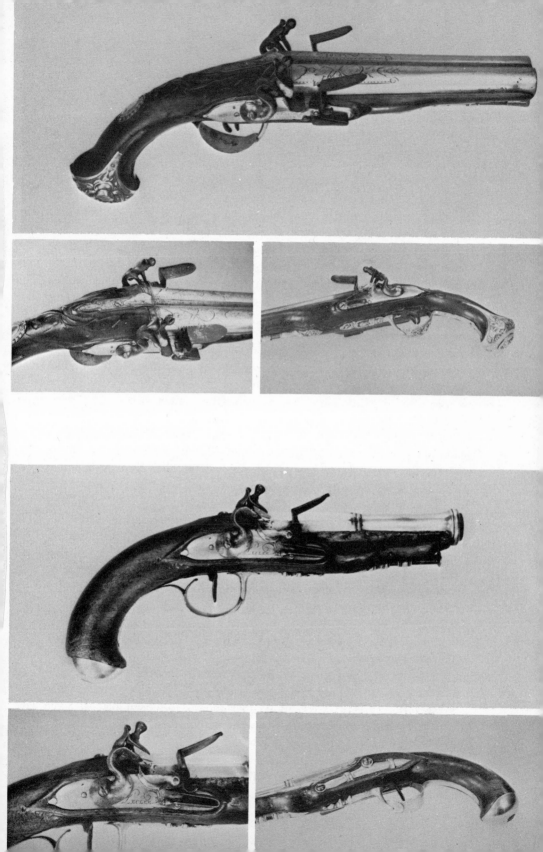

# 7 | SWORDS

THE POPULAR CONCEPTION of swordmaking in the 1700's traditionally pictures a lone craftsman bent over his forge, deftly creating each component. In reality, bladed weapon manufacture was an international business which had reached a high degree of specialization.

Solingen in Germany, for example, made most of the blades for Europe (indulging in the widespread practice of counterfeiting famous markings when advantageous). England and America received most of their blades from this source. Toledo in Spain, and Milan, Italy, were also important producers. Knowledge of ironworking was closely controlled by the guilds, and its secrets were kept under threat of death.

The local cutler would usually import the blade and hilt it himself. Large countries such as England even had swordsmiths specializing in the production of separate parts of the hilt. The one whose name appears on the weapon often did little more than assemble the components.

**ENGLISH AND FRENCH BLADES:** England tried to establish its own blade industry by inducing families from Solingen to settle in the village of Hounslow from 1620 to 1634. By the early 1700's, however, the industry had failed, not being able to compete with imports from the Continent. Another attempt was made at the village of Shotley Bridge in 1691. Although continuing to operate during the eighteenth century, ownership of the industry passed through several hands and the attempt achieved little success. France also secured most of its blades from Germany until some Solingen craftsmen were enticed to begin a manufacturing center at Klingenthal in Alsace about 1729. Even then, substantial imports continued.

**AMERICAN SWORDS:** Prior to the Revolutionary War, the Americans obtained most of their blades in Europe. Those used during the conflict came largely from existing civilian swords, colonial arsenals (left from the French and Indian Wars), local manufacture, and imports. Existing specimens indicate that blacksmiths produced many crude yet serviceable swords, while a great variety of hilts were added to standard European blades. Some American craftsmen did produce silver-hilted and other fine-quality swords, but they were limited to a small number.

**TYPES OF SWORDS USED:** Typical swords of this period are illustrated on the following pages in seven categories:

1. **MILITARY HANGER:** Usually a short, single-edged cutting sword (blade about 25 inches); carried by most infantrymen at the start of the eighteenth century. As the bayonet gained acceptance, the hanger was gradually eliminated. A British royal warrant of 1768 abolished it for all but grenadier regiments and sergeants of battalion companies (basket hilts were also kept by Highland troops). By the end of the Revolutionary War, it appears that only the sergeants retained the hanger. France stopped its use except by grenadiers and sergeants in 1764, but many of the German soldiers fighting in the colonies apparently used it. Although some of the American colonies required them in 1775, by 1783 they were mostly in the hands of sergeants (S.1–S.29).

2. **HUNTING SWORD:** A short civilian arm of the period, with a straight or slightly curved blade (mostly under 24 inches). It offered slight protection in combat, but was carried by many Americans who could not afford a military model (S.30–S.35).

3. **SHORT SABER:** The fighting style of sword worn by many officers. It had a light cut-and-thrust blade (straight or curved) of about 30 inches, with a guard on the hilt (S.36–S.67).

4. **NAVAL CUTLASS:** Technically a short saber; the blade could be straight or slightly curved (mostly with a single edge). Its guard was wide to give maximum protection in close-quarter combat (S.68–S.78).

5. **HORSEMAN'S SABER:** A heavy saber with a curved or straight blade (usually one edge) approximately 32 to 37 inches long. The hilt ranged from the full-basket style to a simple stirrup guard (S.81–S.124).

6. **SMALL SWORD:** The popular civilian pattern at the time of the Revolution, it had a narrow straight blade for thrusting, and a light hilt—which usually included a simple knuckle bow, *pas-d'âne,* and a bilobate counterguard. The small sword is considered the most common type used by American officers during the war (S.125–S.138).

7. **SILVER-HILTED SWORD:** Swords hilted in silver were popular with those officers who could afford them. This metal is found on bladed arms of all styles (S.132–S.165).

## S.1 ENGLISH HANGER

Circa 1690-1710

The British infantry hanger at the beginning of the 1700's is referred to as a simple cutting edge, with a horn grip and brass guard. This is one of several known specimens believed to be of the type. Its simple knuckle bow divides to join an oval counterguard (on the outboard side only) having raised cherub and floral patterns cast into it. A German-style running-wolf mark appears on the single-edged blade (no fullers). The arm was probably made on the Continent, and resembles many hunting swords of the period.

Length: 25¾"

Blade: 20⅜"

Hilt: Brass

Weight: 1.1 lbs.

*Harold L. Peterson Collection*

## S.2 ENGLISH HANGER

Model 1742

Infantry swords of this pattern are called Model 1742 because they are shown in illustrations of that date prepared for the Duke of Cumberland (*Representation of Cloathing of His Majesty's Forces*). It was probably in use for some years prior to that time. Several variations are known. This type has a brass hilt cast in two pieces (grip plus pommel; knuckle bow plus counterguard). A simple knuckle bow spreads into a heart-shaped counterguard with a raised border and center ridge. Its curved single-edged blade bears marks of Germanic origin.

Length: 29"

Blade: 23¼" × 1¹⁄₁₆"

Hilt: Brass

Weight: 1.1 lbs.

*Author's Collection*

## S.3 ENGLISH HANGER

Model 1742 (Variation)

Since the colonel of each regiment was given an allowance to purchase equipment for his men, many variations occurred in the weapons. This particular Model 1742 has the usual cast brass hilt, with spiraled grip and ball-shaped pommel, but the knuckle bow has an additional branch beginning on each side at its mid-point and extending outward to the flat heart-shaped counterguard. Its blade is in the popular slightly curved single-edged cutting style. A single fuller at the back begins at the hilt and ends 3¾" from the tip.

Length: 32⅛"

Blade: 26¼" × 1¼"

Hilt: Brass

Weight: 1.7 lbs.

*Author's Collection*

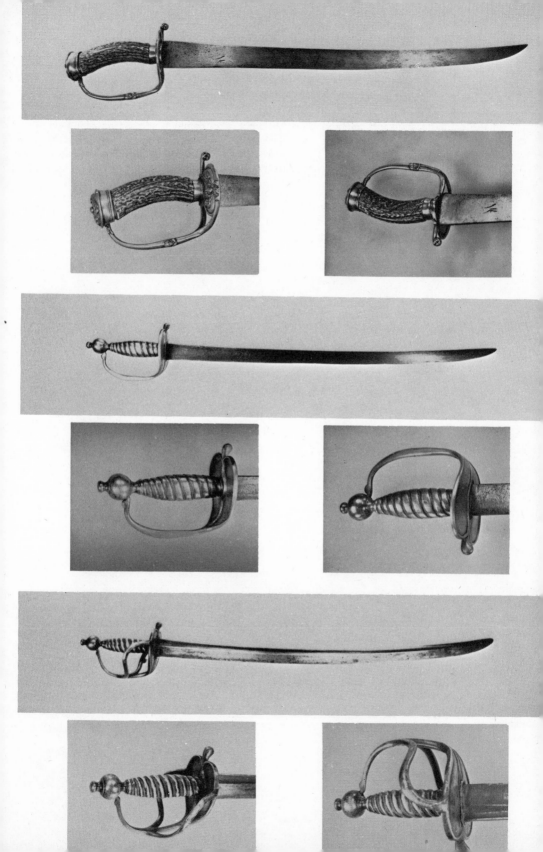

**S.4 ENGLISH HANGER**                                          Model 1742 (Variation)

These short infantry swords were used by colonial and British forces during the French and Indian Wars. Many were left in American hands and appeared again at the start of the Revolution. They gradually lost out to the bayonet, however, and remained mostly in the hands of sergeants on both sides by 1783. This common version has a longer blade and a wooden grip wrapped with twisted brass wire. Practically all of this style known today have lost the wire. (This one was rewrapped). The letters "SH" within a running-fox figure indicate an English blade (probably Shotley Bridge).

Length: 33⅜"                                                    Hilt: Brass
Blade: 27⅞" × 1¼"                                               Weight: 1.8 lbs.

*Lewis H. Gordon, Jr., Collection*


**S.5 ENGLISH HANGER**                                          Circa 1740-1765

This heavy-hilted, long-bladed sword has a counterguard which resembles the "1742" pattern and a known history of use in America during the Revolution. The large "RA" engraved beneath the counterguard is believed to designate the Royal Artillery. The almost vertical spiral on the brass grip, the ovoid pommel, and heavy double-fullered blade are very similar to German styling (see S.20), and were possibly manufactured in Germany. Its two fullers measure ¼" × 23" and ½" × 10".

Length: 35½"                                                    Hilt: Brass
Blade: 29½" × 1½"                                               Weight: 2.0 lbs.

*Author's Collection*


**S.6 ENGLISH HANGER**                                          Model 1751

The exact date of origin for this style is not known; the "1751" designation is based upon its first appearance in paintings of troops done that year by David Morier for the British government. Illustrated here is a common version, which saw substantial service in North America. The cast brass grip has a ball pommel and capstan rivet. Its knuckle bow includes two branches, which form a half-basket hilt. Notice the slightly dished heart-shaped counterguard (no raised border). The Shotley Bridge—marked blade has a single fuller (¼" × 19¼").

Length: 30¼"                                                    Hilt: Brass
Blade: 24⅞" × 1⅜"                                               Weight: 1.8 lbs.

*Harold L. Peterson Collection*

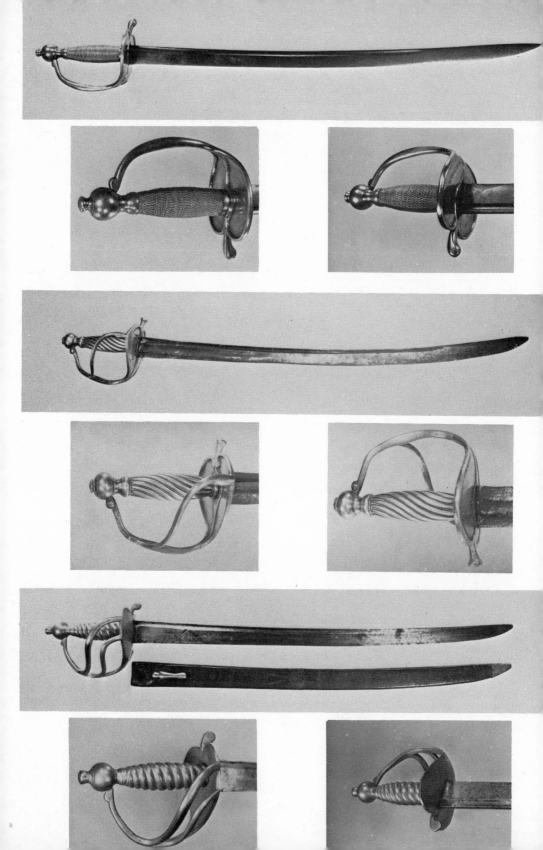

## S.7 ENGLISH HANGER                                    Model 1751 (Variation)

One of the principal variations of these early hangers was to cast the brass grips into a distinctive shape for a particular regiment. This specimen, for example, has a raised instead of a channeled spiral on its grip, a crude lion-headed pommel, and one instead of two branches. Notice too that the counterguard has abruptly narrowed where it joins the knuckle bow, while the earlier raised border has been reinstated. The blade is again single-edged, with a slight curve. A ¼″ fuller at the back runs for 20″.

Length: 32″                                              Hilt: Brass
Blade: 26½″ × 1⅟₁₆″                                      Weight: 1.5 lbs.

*Author's Collection*


## S.8 ENGLISH HANGER                                    Model 1751 (Variation)

This version of the "1751" hanger varies in several ways from the more typical pattern (S.6); its hilt has horizontal ridges on the grip and lacks side branches, while the single-edged blade is straight instead of curved (one fuller at the back; ¼″ × 19″). A typical British marking, "2/48," is engraved under the usual dished counterguard. Its ball pommel and capstan rivet are in keeping with the more common styling.

Length: 28¾″                                             Hilt: Brass
Blade: 23¼″ × 1⅛″                                        Weight: 1.3 lbs.

*Author's Collection*


## S.9 ENGLISH HANGER                                    Model 1751 (Variation)

Another interesting practice was to cast a regimental device into the brass grip. Shown to the right is a fine example bearing the famous insignia of the Royal Welsh Fusiliers. Although a regular heart-shaped counterguard is visible (with a raised border added to the underside), the usual branches are not present. Other specimens of the "1751" indicate that the men often removed these branches. This sword, however, is one of several, all of which were cast as shown. The blade has one edge and no fuller.

Length: 30¾″                                             Hilt: Brass
Blade: 24¾″                                              Weight: 1.8 lbs.

*Colonial Williamsburg Collection*

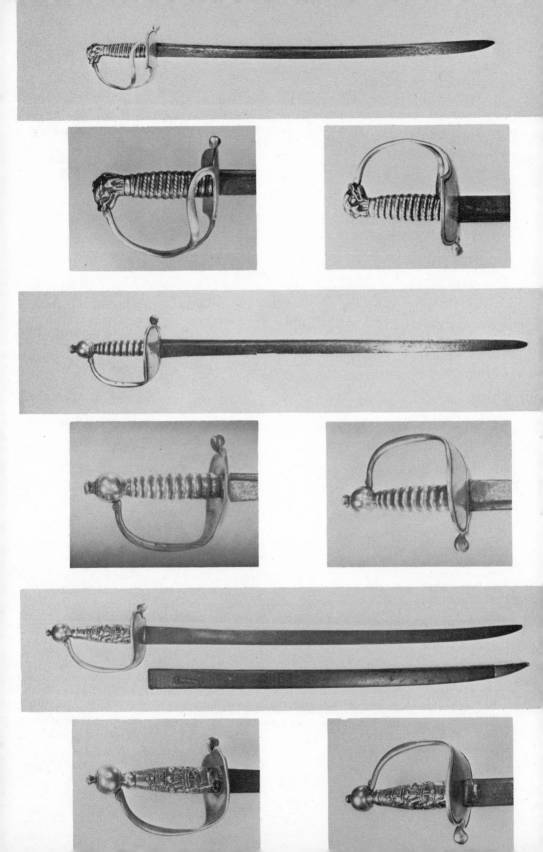

## S.10 ENGLISH HANGER                                    Circa 1740-1760

Semi-basket hilt hangers incorporating an S design are shown in illustrations of some grenadier and battalion companies of the period. This example is iron-hilted, with an open heart-shaped counterguard covered by a leather pad. Leather also covers the grip—which has a spiraled brass wire binding plus a ¼" Turk's-head ferrule at each end. A running fox with an "H" in the center (English marking; "H" probably for the maker, Harvey) appears on the typical single-edged blade. Its fuller measures 20¾" × ¼".

Length: 34⅛"                                             Hilt: Iron
Blade: 27⅞" × 1¼"                                        Weight: 2.0 lbs.

*Author's Collection*


## S.11 SCOTTISH BROADSWORD                               Circa 1725-1740

While the British soldier was equipped with a brass hanger, the traditional arm of Highland regiments was the basket-hilted broadsword. This grip is a wooden center with a tight outer wrapping of twisted iron wire. Its blade has two edges and is inscribed ANDRE M on one side and FERARA on the other (probably a forgery—after the famous sixteenth-century Italian swordsmith). It also bears a running-wolf engraving with the letters "SS." A lobe on the hilt is marked "D/5"—an indication of its military use.

Length: 39"                                              Hilt: Iron
Blade: 33" × 1⅛"                                         Weight: 1.8 lbs.

*Author's Collection*


## S.12 SCOTTISH BACKSWORD                                Circa 1760-1776

Here is the backsword style (one edge) usually associated with the famed Black Watch (42nd) Regiment and other Scottish troops during the French and Indian War and again in 1776. Although they were officially ordered to discard swords in America at the latter date, it is probable that many saw service with both sides during the Revolution. The wooden grip originally had either a leather or wire covering. Earlier in the century, most Scotch hilts terminated in slots cut into the pommel, but by this period many were attached to a circular ring. Its straight blade is marked "GR" and DRURY (the maker).

Length: 35¾"                                             Hilt: Iron
Blade: 29½" × 1⅛"                                        Weight: 2.3 lbs.

*Lewis H. Gordon, Jr., Collection*

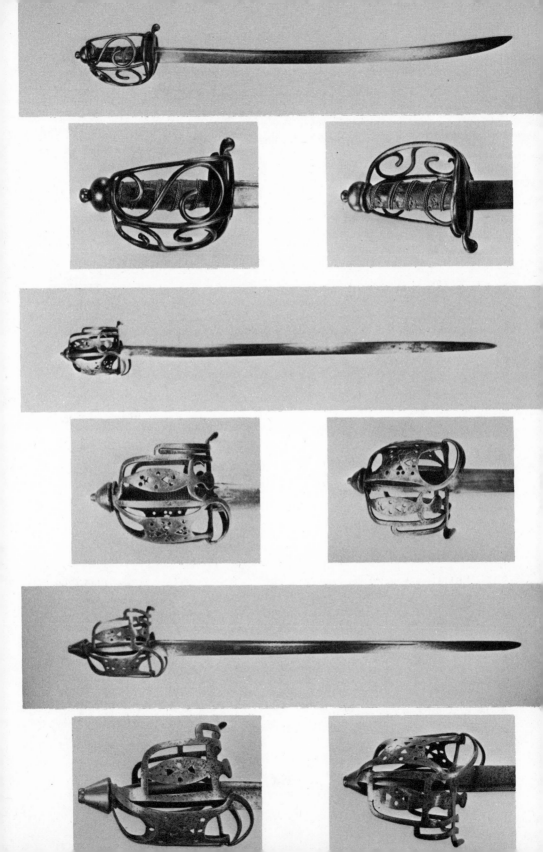

**S.13 GERMAN HANGER** Circa 1743

This simple semi-basket hilt (with thumb ring) is typical of many used in Europe during the first half of the eighteenth century. Its wooden grip is wrapped in twisted brass wire, and includes two ferrules (each ¼″). The curved blade is single-edged, with a ⅜″-wide fuller 18″ long. Inscribed on one side is a crown over a lion, plus FOR GOTT UND DAS VATTERLAND 1743. The other face bears a crown above a cipher, plus a panoply of flags. Note the early screws attaching the hilt to the pommel.

Length: 28½″                                                                Hilt: Iron
Blade: 22¾″ × 1⅜″                                              Weight: 1.8 lbs.

*Valley Forge Museum Collection*

**S.14 GERMAN HANGER** Circa 1735-1750

A circular knuckle bow, bulbous quillon, and flared counterguard (on the outboard side) are typical of early German hunting swords and many of their military hangers. The raised cipher on this guard, including an ax and hammer, is believed to indicate use by "pioneer" companies. Its grips are wrapped with twisted copper wire, plus a ½″ bottom ferrule, and an oval cap pommel having a capstan rivet. There is no fuller in the blade; contemporaneous designs are engraved on its faces, i.e. a sun, moon, and stars.

Length: 28⅜″                                                              Hilt: Brass
Blade: 22⅞″ × 1¼″                                              Weight: 1.3 lbs.

*Author's Collection*

**S.15 GERMAN HANGER** Circa 1745-1760

The hanger in this case has an unusual hilt. Its brass grip is completely smooth, with a crude lion's-head pommel (and a capstan rivet). An exposed thumb ring is attached to the inboard side. About 1½″ below the pommel, a transverse branch leaves the knuckle bow and flares into a broad panel (creating a semi-basket hilt). Its smooth grip and straight two-edged blade are indicative of a style later adopted by Jaeger troops (riflemen). A crowned lion appears in relief on the guard; under the hilt is engraved: "7:C N: O: 33."

Length: 33″                                                               Hilt: Brass
Blade: 27⅝″ × 1⅛″                                             Weight: 1.8 lbs.

*Author's Collection*

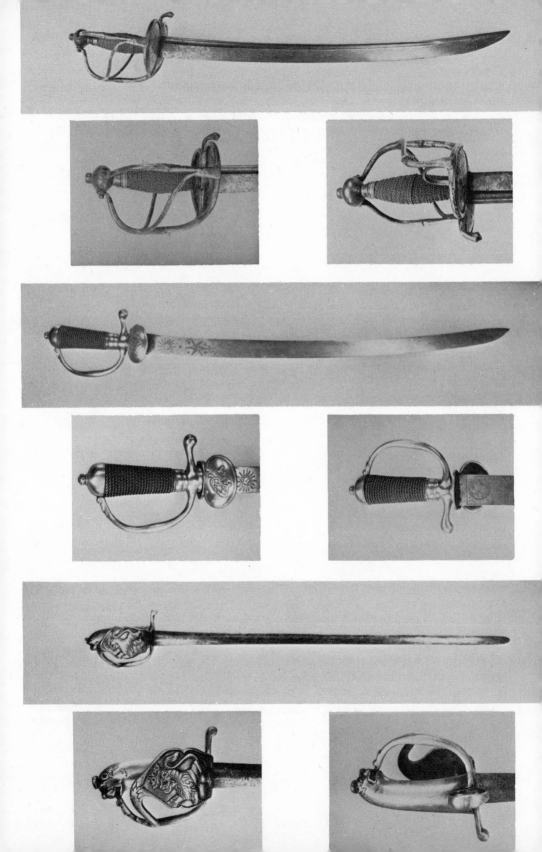

## S.16 GERMAN HANGER                                   Circa 1740-1760

Brass-hilted hangers of this pattern are virtually the same as many English Model 1742's (which were mostly made in Germany; see S.2). This particular example bears the "FR" cipher under a crown (Frederick II or Frederick the Great). The hilt's brass grip has an accelerating spiral, with an urn-shaped pommel. Notice the heart-shaped counterguard, whose raised edges slope into two lower wells on either side of the grip. Its blade has a single fuller (⅜″ × 19¼″). The scabbard illustrates the German practice of covering most of the brass tip.

Length: 30¾″                                            Hilt: Brass
Blade: 24¾″ × 1¼″                                       Weight: 1.8 lbs.

*Author's Collection*

## S.17 GERMAN HANGER                                   Circa 1740-1760

The swords issued troops coming to America in 1776 were apparently a motley mixture of modern and obsolete styles. This type was among them. The thumb ring on the inboard side was not universal, but the heart-shaped counterguard with its sunken panels, and the bulbous ovoid pommel were quite common. There is a single cutting edge on the curved blade (no fuller). Guard markings include NO 9:28. Many found today have the inboard side of the counterguard cut off—probably an effort to ease leg chafing.

Length: 27⅞″                                            Hilt: Brass
Blade: 22″ × 1⅛″                                        Weight: 1.8 lbs.

*Author's Collection*

## S.18 GERMAN HANGER                                   Circa 1760-1786

Similarities of the German hanger with Britain's "1742" pattern are again demonstrated here (see S.2). In this case, however, there are three principal differences: the spirals in the grip are steeper, appearing only on the outboard side (the inboard side is smooth); the knuckle bow and quillon are much flatter and thinner than previously; and the single-edged blade has a wide fuller (½″ × 19″). Frederick the Great's cipher on blades of this model indicate its use during his reign (1740-1786). Stampings in the brass hilt include "KC" in a rectangular cartouche.

Length: 31¾″                                            Hilt: Brass
Blade: 25¾″ × 1¼″                                       Weight: 1.5 lbs.

*Author's Collection*

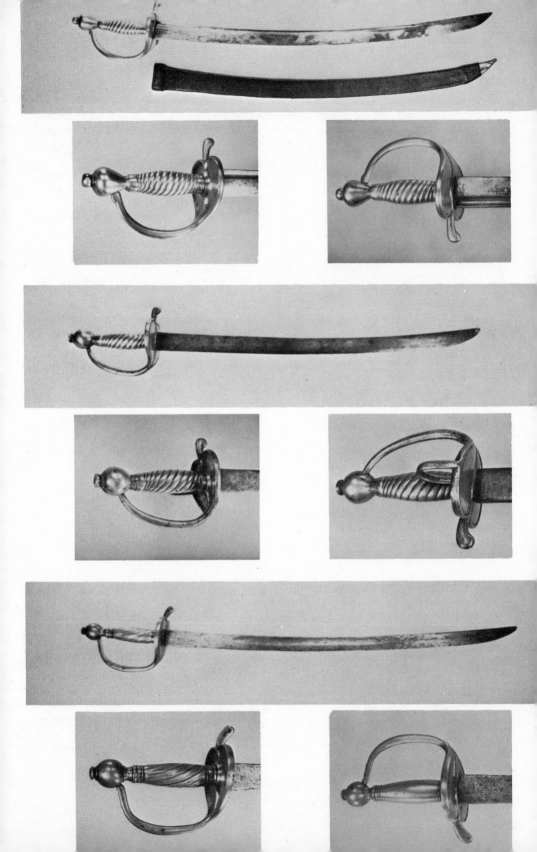

## S.19 GERMAN HANGER

Circa 1775-1800

This style of iron-hilted sword appears to have been introduced about the time of the American Revolution, and continued in use through the end of the century. Its curving wooden grip has carved parallel ribs, while the iron backstrap rises from a ⅜" ferrule to the flat pommel (where a diamond-shaped nut secures the top of the tang). The wide blade (1⅜") includes a shallow fuller (1¼" across), which extends almost to the point (25½"). It is engraved on each face with a floral spray and the characteristic crown above a script cipher.

Length: 31¼"
Blade: 26" × 1¾"

Hilt: Iron
Weight: 1.3 lbs.

*Author's Collection*

## S.20 GERMAN HANGER

Circa 1740-1765

Swords like this one were apparently also produced in Germany for Britain (see S.5). Notice the same gradual spiraling ridges on the grip, flattened pommel, and the big blade. Its hilt, however, includes a cupped style of counterguard that flows into an outboard vertical branch—which, with the knuckle bow and a transverse branch, creates a semi-basket hilt. The rounded quillon is typical of that of many German swords. Two fullers are present on the single-edged blade (⅜" × 23½", ½" × 10⅜"), while the popular sun, moon, stars, and wind are engraved on its faces.

Length: 35¼"
Blade: 30" × 1½"

Hilt: Brass
Weight: 2.1 lbs.

*Author's Collection*

## S.21 FRENCH HANGER

Circa 1720-1750

Prior to about 1750, swords of this type were carried by French grenadiers and line companies. Some had cast-brass grips, but most of them used wood wrapped with brass wire (as this was originally). Its hilt is typical of the contemporary small sword—including the oval pommel (with capstan rivet), thin knuckle bow, and dished bilobate counterguard. In this case, raised figures have been cast into brass. The straight, double-edged blade has a fleur-de-lis on each convex face, plus a central fuller (¼" wide) extending for 5⅜".

Length: 33⅜"
Blade: 27" × 1¹⁄₁₆"

Hilt: Brass
Weight: 1.1 lbs.

*Author's Collection*

230

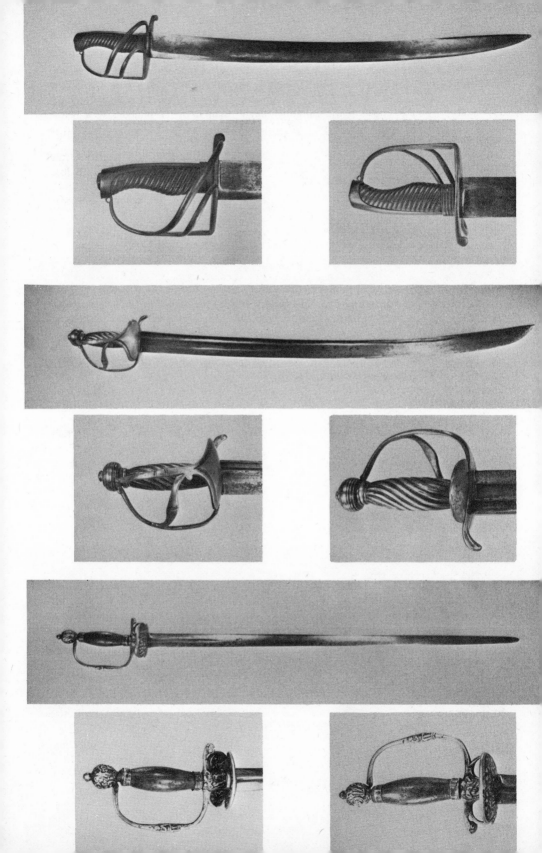

## S.22 FRENCH HANGER                                      Circa 1750-1767

About mid-century, infantry arms similar to this one began to replace the weaker small-sword style. It resembles sword styling of the previous century with a spiraling metal grip, ball pommel, and bilobate counterguard. The quillon ends in a flattened oval finial. A double-edged blade (slightly longer than normal) includes a ⅜″-wide fuller in the center, which measures 25⅛″. Engravings on its faces show a sun, plus a sword-wielding figure.

Length: 34⅞″                                                Hilt: Iron
Blade: 29 × 1¼″                                          Weight: 1.8 lbs.

*Author's Collection*

## S.23 FRENCH GRENADIER HANGER                    Circa 1747-1767

This is believed to be one of the wide variety of patterns used by French grenadiers during the period. Its semi-basket iron hilt includes a leather-covered grip. The backstrap is nailed at its base and extends up to form a flat-headed pommel (with a large capstan rivet). A thumb ring is mounted inboard on the counterguard; the opposite side has a high cupped shape. The single-edged blade includes two fullers (⅛″ × 9¼″, ¼″ × 27″), while a false edge extends for 18½″.

Length: 34″                                                 Hilt: Iron
Blade: 27¾″ × 1¼″                                       Weight: 1.3 lbs.

*Author's Collection*

## S.24 FRENCH GRENADIER HANGER                         Model 1767

A French ordinance in 1767 gave specific dimensions for a new grenadier *briquet*. Its brass hilt was usually cast in two parts as shown here (the grip with pommel, the knuckle bow with counterguard). Horizontal ribbing is included on the grip, and a simulated backstrap terminates in a bird's-head pommel. The thin rectangular guard includes reverse langets, plus a rounded finial on the quillon. Like the British and German hangers, this blade is slightly curved, with a single cutting edge. Its lone fuller measures 19¼″ in length.

Length: 30¼″                                                Hilt: Brass
Blade: 25″ × 1½″                                        Weight: 1.5 lbs.

*Author's Collection*

232

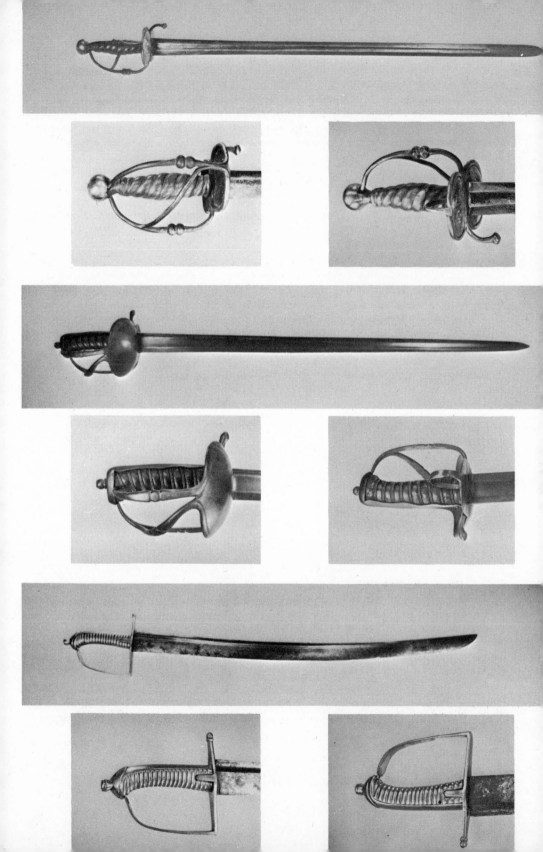

## S.25 AMERICAN HANGER Circa 1775-1780

Several of these crude infantry swords are known. Their simplicity of construction suggests probable manufacture under pressure at the beginning of the Revolutionary War. This particular blade is straight and double-edged. Its markings include a crown above a two-headed eagle (in an oval), plus the words VIVAT and SOLINGEN (Germany). Smooth leather covers the grip, which mounts ¼" ferrules. The elementary knuckle bow is flattened at the top end to serve as a pommel, and attached to a circular dished counterguard by an outside screw.

Length: 31"                                                  Hilt: Iron
Blade: 26⅞" × 1¼"                                     Weight: 1.3 lbs.

*Harold L. Peterson Collection*

## S.26 AMERICAN HANGER Circa 1775-1780

The basic construction of this weapon is similar to that of the preceding example (S.25), yet it incorporates several differences. To provide ridges a rope was wrapped around the wooden grip before covering it with leather. A high ¾" ferrule binds it at the top, where the flattened end of the knuckle bow extends over the edge by ⅛" on all sides. A screw secures the other end of the knuckle bow to the oval counterguard. Its double-edged straight blade is short (18½"), and bears a Solingen style mark.

Length: 23"                                                  Hilt: Iron
Blade: 18½" × 1⅛"                                     Weight: .8 lb.

*Author's Collection*

## S.27 AMERICAN HANGER Circa 1775-1780

The extremely unsophisticated work on the blade and guard of this piece indicate another blacksmith's product. Yet, its simple, turned wooden grip adds a measure of balance and proportion lacking in many. The knuckle bow consists of a rounded iron bar flattened at each end, first to cap the grip, and then to provide a miniature counterguard—with a turned-down outboard side to create a shell guard. Its slightly curved single-edged blade includes an uneven fuller (⅛" × 16½"), plus a 3" false edge. This sword was found in New Hampshire.

Length: 26⅝"                                                 Hilt: Iron
Blade: 22" × 1"                                          Weight: .8 lb.

*Author's Collection*

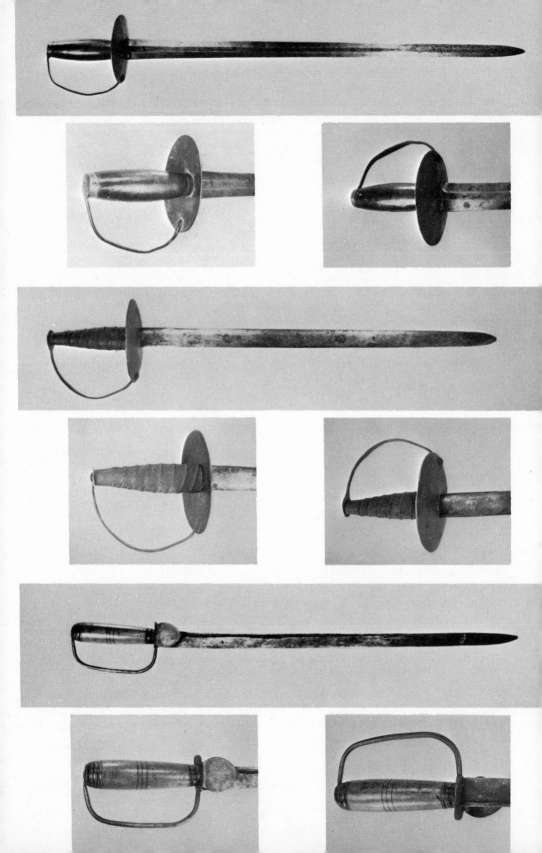

## S.28 AMERICAN HANGER                                     Circa 1777-1783

The hilt in this illustration closely resembles the French 1767 *briquet* (S.24). Because of its lack of embellishment, however, it is assumed to be an American copy. Since the French model was created after the end of the French and Indian War (1763), and French aid did not begin arriving in quantity until 1777, this piece is dated during the later war years. A smooth backstrap forms a bird's-head pommel with capstan rivet. The knuckle bow and quillon are made of flat brass, while the single-edged curved blade is a style imported in great numbers (fuller: ¼″ × 19″).

Length: 30″                                                 Hilt: Brass
Blade: 25⅝″ × 1¼″                                           Weight: 1.0 lb.

*Author's Collection*

## S.29 AMERICAN HANGER                                     Circa 1775-1785

Because of the heavy guard and uneven fuller, this specimen is assumed to be completely of American manufacture. The wooden grip is leather-covered and originally included brass wire in the grooves. Its heavy knuckle bow is an integral part of the pommel—terminating in a down-turned flattened finial. The blade was fashioned for a real fighting man. It measures 1⅜″ at the hilt, with a single cutting edge. Rather elementary renderings of the popular moon, sun, wind, and stars motif are still visible on both faces.

Length: 30⅝″                                                Hilt: Brass
Blade: 25½″ × 1⅜″                                           Weight: 1.5 lbs.

*Author's Collection*

## S.30 EUROPEAN HUNTING SWORD                              Circa 1700

Short swords were popular among civilians as a side arm while hunting, both here and in Europe. Being available, many were carried by American officers during the Revolutionary War. Their practical fighting qualities, however, provided little beyond an indication of rank. This early version has a relatively short (19½″) single-edged blade (no fullers), with German-style heads wearing crowns stamped into both faces. Long ferrules (1⅜″) secure the horn grip. Its brass knuckle bow and counterguard are cast as a single piece.

Length: 24⅞″                                                Hilt: Brass
Blade: 19½″ × 1¼″                                           Weight: 1.0 lb.

*Author's Collection*

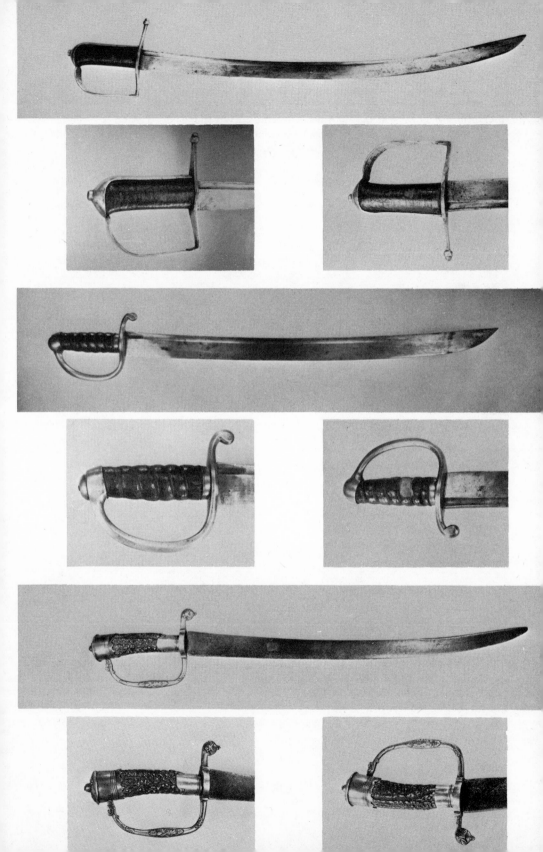

## S.31 HUNTING SWORD                                   Circa 1730-1750

The horn grip with a brass shell guard is typical of many of these hunting arms. In this sword, the slanted knuckle bow is anchored at the top in a rounded cap pommel; it continues as a single brass casting to include the shell guard and simple quillon. The horn grip is held by a ⅜" base ferrule, while the curved single-edged blade is a shorter version (22") of the type on most contemporaneous infantry hangers. A ⅜"-wide fuller begins at the hilt and ends 3" from the tip.

Length: 26¾"                                          Hilt: Brass
Blade: 22" × 1¼"                                      Weight: 1.0 lb.

*Author's Collection*


## S.32 HUNTING SWORD                                   Circa 1740-1760

This shell guard, unlike the almost horizontal style in the preceding example (S.31), has been bent into a position virtually parallel to the blade. The fish skin covering its grip is nailed at the seam, with oval brass tacks added to each face—probably to provide decoration and reduce hand slippage. Two fullers (⅛" × 12½", ⅜" × 14") are present on the single-edged straight blade, which also has a 4" false edge. Faint designs on its faces indicate a German origin.

Length: 26⅝"                                          Hilt: Brass
Blade: 21¾" × 1"                                      Weight: .9 lb.

*Author's Collection*


## S.33 FRENCH HUNTING SWORD                            Circa 1750-1760

Another pattern of hunting sword is illustrated here. The quillons remain straight (although the animal-head finials face in opposite directions), while the horn grip bends at an angle. It has a flat pommel, and a ⅜" ferrule at the bottom. The popular shell guard in this case is in the shape of a bird. Its interesting blade has double fullers (⅛" each); they commence 6½" below the hilt and stop ½" from the tip. Engraving on the face includes a crowned crest containing three fleurs-de-lis, plus a mounted horseman with a saber.

Length: 28"                                           Hilt: Brass
Blade: 21½" × 1¼"                                     Weight: 1.3 lbs.

*Author's Collection*

238

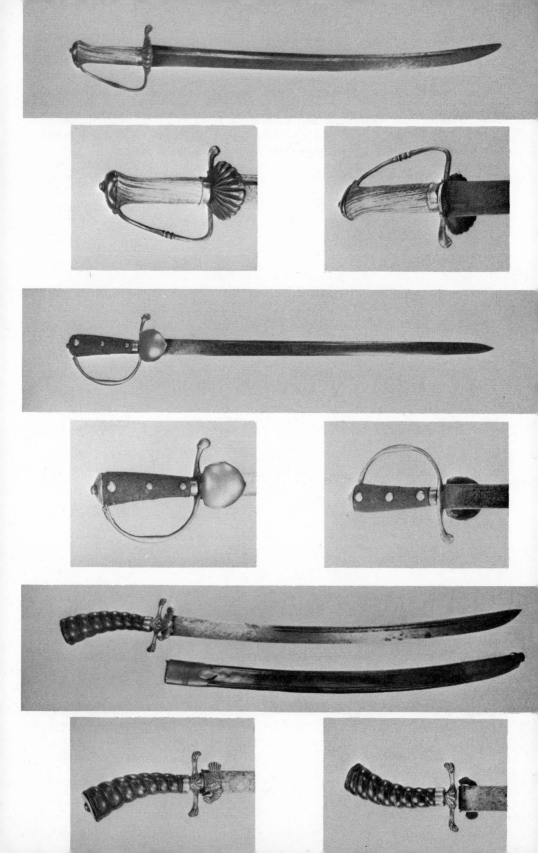

## S.34 AMERICAN HUNTING SWORD                    Circa 1760-1780

The simple hilt on this blade suggests an American origin. It consists of a leather-covered wooden center, with narrow copper strips spiraled through the channels. A cap pommel (with capstan rivet) appears at one end, while a ¼″ ferrule encloses its base. The S-shaped quillons are flat; its blade is of European manufacture. Being straight with a single edge, it has a wide fuller centered in its face, beginning 4″ from the hilt and ending ¼″ above the point. A 3½″ false edge is also included.

Length: 26⅝″                                               Hilt: Iron
Blade: 21½″ × 1⅛″                                          Weight: .6 lb.

*Author's Collection*


## S.35 ENGLISH SHORT SWORD                       Circa 1775-1785

Among the swords worn by American officers was a short-bladed style as shown here. They are classified in various ways, e.g. officers' hangers, hunting swords, cuttoes, or short swords. Most of them include silver-mounted hilts (S.140-S.143), but this specimen has one cast in bronze (one piece). Its quillons end in disk finials, which extend in opposite directions. The blade is typical—with a single edge and two fullers. A small fuller (¼″) begins at the hilt and runs to the upper end of a 9″ false edge; the central one (½″) measures 15⅜″.

Length: 29⅝″                                               Hilt: Bronze
Blade: 24⅞″                                                Weight: 1.1 lbs.

*Author's Collection*


## S.36 AMERICAN SHORT SABER                       Circa 1720-1740

Officers of the 1700's wore a great variety of swords. There was less control over their selection, and the majority were privately purchased from independent cutlers. The short saber was one of the most popular styles, especially during the second half of the century. Both American and British versions included pommels shaped like animal heads (lion heads most numerous). An early colonial example is illustrated here. The head is crudely chiseled from a block of solid brass; most of its lines are not raised, but incised into the metal. Its grip is wrapped with brass wire.

Length: 35″                                                Hilt: Brass-Iron
Blade: 29¼″ × 1¼″                                          Weight: 1.4 lbs.

*Author's Collection*

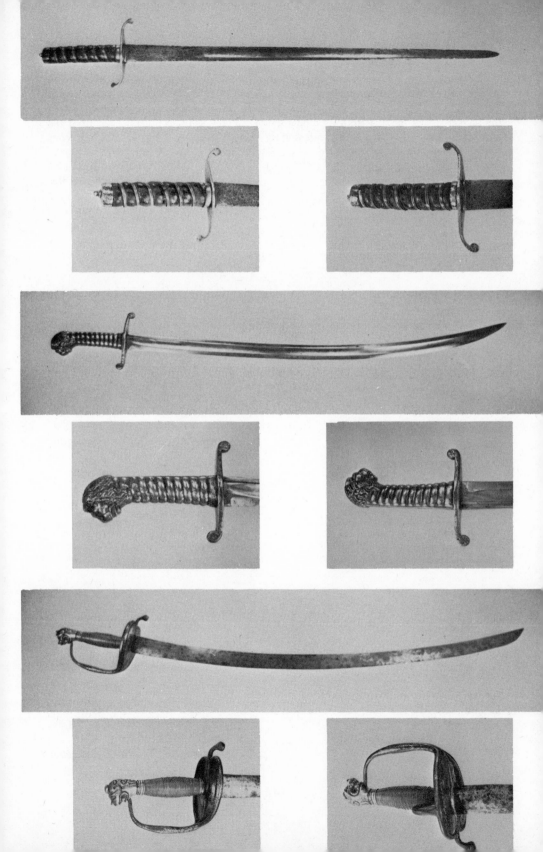

## S.37 EUROPEAN SHORT SABER                    Circa 1735-1745

This semi-basket hilt and blade appear to be European-made. Its wooden grip (prob-ably wrapped with wire originally) and lion pommel are of a German-Swiss pattern of the time. Like the small swords of this period, the counterguard is bilobate (with the pierced panel missing from its inboard side). Three shallow fullers reach from the hilt for 3⅛″ along the blade. Although slightly curved, it has two edges extending from the point to within 5⅝″ of the guard.

Length: 34¾″                                           Hilt: Iron
Blade: 28⅜″ × 1″                                    Weight: 1.1 lbs.

*Joseph E. Fritzinger Collection*

## S.38 AMERICAN SHORT SABER                    Circa 1770-1780

All components of this sword appear to be of American manufacture. The elementary lion head was made from one piece of brass, and the large links in the chain have been formed individually. A brass strip is spiraled around the wooden grip, which has a ½″ ferrule at its base. The counterguard is simply a flat piece of brass with four pierced openings. Colonial stamped designs are present on the flat single-edged blade (no fuller).

Length: 33⅛″                                           Hilt: Brass
Blade: 27½″ × 1⁵⁄₁₆″                               Weight: 1.5 lbs.

*Author's Collection*

## S.39 SHORT SABER                              Circa 1770-1780

This pattern is similar to many silver-mounted swords of the period. Yet, the hilt is made of steel (including the lion-head pommel). Its grip is wrapped in fish skin and bound with a flat silver strip. The heavy short blade has a ¼″-wide fuller at the back (18⅛″ long), with a central fuller beginning 1⅜″ below the guard (⅝″ × 24½″). Its only marking, /X/, is repeated on the flat edge of the blade plus the throat of the scabbard. While the style is English, the heavy blade and grotesque lion head also suggest possible American workmanship.

Length: 32¾″                                           Hilt: Steel
Blade: 26⅛″ × 1⅜″                                  Weight: 1.3 lbs.

*Author's Collection*

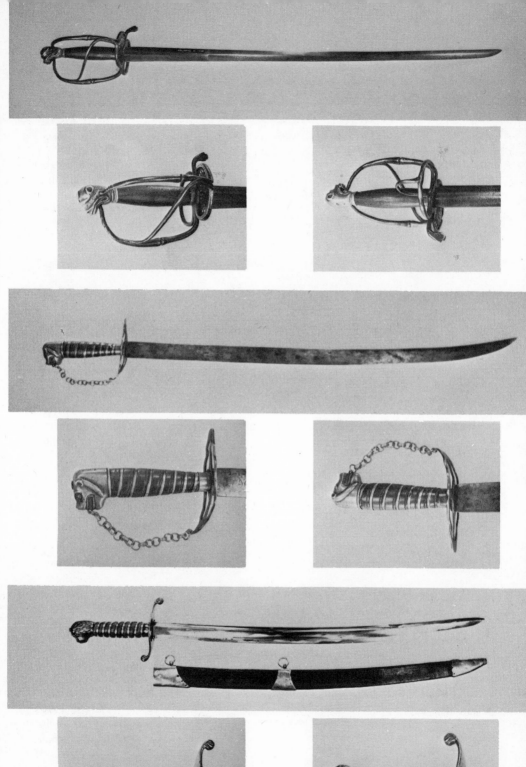

**S.40 ENGLISH SHORT SABER**   Circa 1770-1780

Lion-headed sabers similar to this were popular with both British and American officers during the Revolution. Its ribbed ebony grip has a thin copper spiral binding with a ⅝″ ferrule at the base. The flat knuckle bow includes channeled decorative lines on its outer face, and divides as it crosses the blade (notice supporting bars) to end in a rounded quillon. The brass hilt appears to have been gilded originally. Two fullers can be seen in the curved single-edged blade (¼″ × 17¾″, ½″ × 24½″).

Length: 31⅛″   Hilt: Brass
Blade: 25½″ × 1″   Weight: 1.1 lbs.

*Author's Collection*


**S.41 AMERICAN SHORT SABER**   Circa 1770-1780

The heavy lines of this hilt and the uneven fuller in the blade indicate probable American colonial origin. Its lion pommel and attached backstrap were originally cast in two halves (center seam), while the round stirrup hilt ends in a bulbous quillon which is similar to those of German styling (see S.14). A ½″ ferrule appears at the base of the grip (wood with leather covering). The blade is straight, with one edge and a single fuller (⅝″ × 23¾″).

Length: 35⅞″   Hilt: Brass
Blade: 29¾″ × 1¼″   Weight: 2.0 lbs.

*Author's Collection*


**S.42 AMERICAN SHORT SABER**   Circa 1770-1780

This horse-head pommel and grip are cut from a single piece of ivory. A ⅛″ brass strip is spiraled around the grip, which has an iron ferrule at the base (½″ high). Its flat S-shaped counterguard is pierced, with two supporting bars on each side. The curved single-edged blade is of the three-fuller style imported in such great quantities from Europe. The fullers begin 2¾″ beneath the guard and extend for 22¼″ (top one only 18″). No marks are visible.

Length: 35⅜″   Hilt: Iron
Blade: 29½″ × 1¼″   Weight: 1.4 lbs.

*Author's Collection*

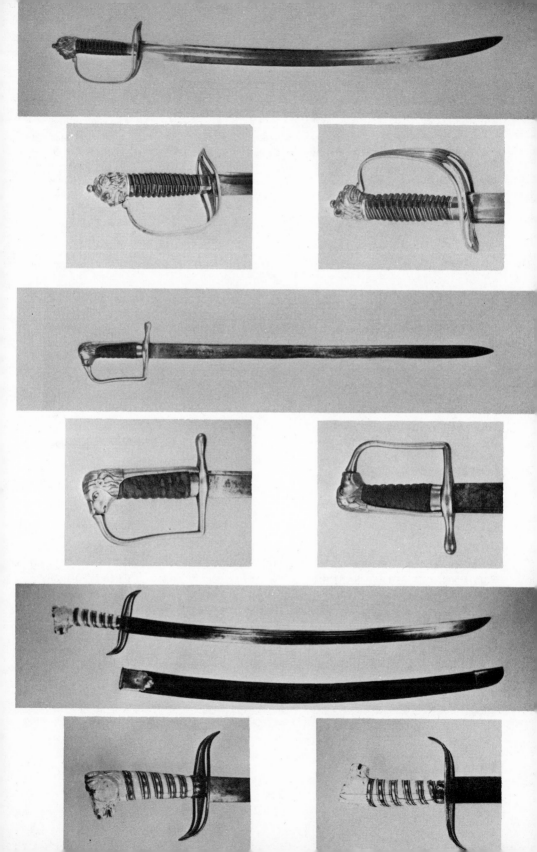

### S.43 AMERICAN SHORT SABER — Circa 1760-1779

The short saber pictured here is believed to have belonged to Israel Putnam, who led Connecticut troops and later joined Roger's Rangers during the French and Indian Wars. He then served as a major general in the Continental Army of the Revolution. Although one branch is missing, and the guard partially deformed, this American-hilted specimen is obviously a fighting-man's weapon. The grip is of wood, with a bronze guard. Its flat single-edged blade includes three fullers (each ⅛" wide). Early traces of bluing remain near the hilt.

Length: 36⅝"  
Blade: 30¾" × 1¼"

Hilt: Bronze  
Weight: 2.0 lbs.

*Dr. John K. Lattimer Collection*

### S.44 AMERICAN SHORT SABER — Circa 1770-1780

This American hilt has a lion head and backstrap apparently formed from one piece of brass. The vertically ribbed grip is of ivory (¼" base ferrule). Its simple guard is cut from flat brass, and divides on either side of the blade to meet again in a blunt-ended quillon. The blade itself bears earlier Spanish markings: VIVA ESPANA, plus a shield and panoply of arms. It has a single cutting edge, a 6½" false edge, and two fullers (¼" × 16½", 1⅛" × 29½").

Length: 37⅝"  
Blade: 31⅛" × 1⅜"

Hilt: Brass  
Weight: 1.3 lbs.

*Author's Collection*

### S.45 ENGLISH SHORT SABER — Circa 1750-1759

The straight-bladed sword at the right is reported to have been carried by an Ensign Fraser at Quebec in 1759. It still includes the red velvet hilt liner and sword knot (for attachment around the wrist). The semi-basket hilt's knuckle bow has three curving branches on the outboard side and two inboard. Its counterguard is bilobate in shape. Fish skin covers the grip (a Turk's-head ferrule at each end), which is topped with a ball-shaped pommel with a capstan rivet. The two-edged straight blade tapers to a centered point (one fuller).

Length: 36½"  
Blade: 30½" × 1⅛"

Hilt: Brass  
Weight: 1.5 lbs.

*Christie Collection*

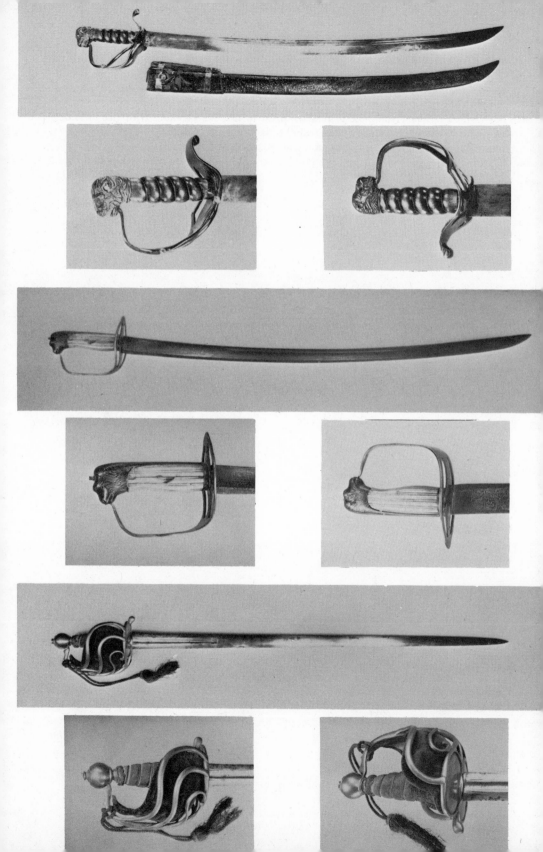

## S.46 ENGLISH SHORT SABER                    Circa 1750-1765

This is another typical British officer's sword of the French and Indian Wars period. Its iron-mounted hilt includes three outboard branches, with a heart-shaped counterguard. Notice that its two halves are open, and were originally covered with a leather liner which has survived. The grip is wrapped in fish skin—bound with two spiraling twisted brass wires. Its single-edged straight blade has two fullers ($\frac{1}{4}'' \times 22''$, $\frac{1}{2}'' \times 29''$) plus a 7¾" false edge. A capstan rivet tops the large ovoid pommel.

Length: 35⅝"                                                          Hilt: Iron
Blade: 29⅝" × 1⅛"                                         Weight: 1.4 lbs.

*Author's Collection*

## S.47 ENGLISH SHORT SWORD                    Circa 1775-1780

Swords of this style were popular with both British and American officers in the Revolutionary War. The back of the blade is marked G HARVEY BIRMM, while its face is inscribed with a crown above the "GR" cipher, plus the royal coat of arms. Its horn grip includes a flat spiraling brass strip in the channels. The knuckle bow spreads near the base to add a reinforced outer branch on each side of the grip. Included on the curved single-edged blade are a 8¾" false edge and two fullers ($\frac{1}{4}'' \times 16\frac{5}{8}''$, $\frac{3}{8}'' \times 23''$).

Length: 31¼"                                                          Hilt: Iron
Blade: 25⅛" × 1¼"                                          Weight: 1.0 lb.

*Author's Collection*

## S.48 ENGLISH SHORT SABER                    Circa 1770-1785

Many British officers carried a sword of this type during the fighting in North America. It eventually became the model for the official pattern adopted in 1796 (although later versions include raised decorations on the pommel, and often a hinged inboard "wing" for the counterguard). The hilt was usually steel, gilt, or silver—depending upon the buttons of the regiment's uniform. This specimen has a faceted urn-shaped pommel, with a slightly dished bilobate counterguard. Its brass hilt was probably gilded originally.

Length: 37¼"                                                        Hilt: Brass
Blade: 31½" × 1"                                          Weight: 1.5 lbs.

*Author's Collection*

248

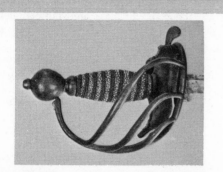

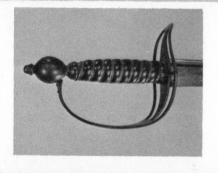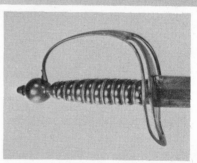

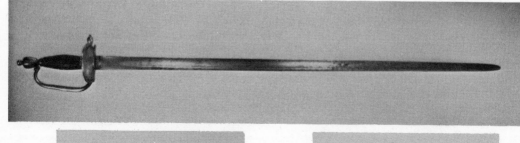

## S.49 ENGLISH SHORT SABER                    Circa 1775-1790

The iron knuckle bow in this illustration divides gracefully near its base to permit a lateral branch to form an oval outboard extension to the counterguard—a styling also common among naval officers. The quillon ends in a simple teardrop finial. A wide copper strip combines with two iron wires to cover the grip, which has an ovoid pommel and capstan rivet. Two fullers characteristically appear on the straight single-edged blade ($\frac{1}{8}'' \times 18\frac{1}{2}''$, $\frac{1}{4}'' \times 25\frac{3}{4}''$). A false edge measures 6".

Length: 33½"                                    Hilt: Iron
Blade: 27⅜" × ⅞"                                Weight: 1.1 lbs.

*Author's Collection*


## S.50 GERMAN SHORT SABER                     Circa 1740-1770

This brass-hilted officer's sword is very similar to the British infantry hanger styling of the period (S.4). It has a wooden center for the grip—wrapped in twisted brass wire. The simple knuckle bow spreads into a heart-shaped counterguard, with high ridges around each side. Its flat blunt quillon is typically Germanic. The straight blade has one edge and two fullers ($\frac{1}{8}'' \times 15\frac{1}{4}''$, $\frac{1}{2}'' \times 26\frac{1}{4}''$), plus an 11" false edge. One face bears a crown above an eagle; the other has a sunlike symbol. Two double-cross stamps appear on the guard.

Length: 38⅜"                                    Hilt: Brass
Blade: 32½" × 1¼"                               Weight: 1.8 lbs.

*Author's Collection*


## S.51 GERMAN SHORT SABER                     Circa 1765-1780

The heavy brass guard and wire wrapping evident in these pictures are typical of swords believed carried by German officers in the American Revolution. The urn-shaped pommel is faceted and mounts a large capstan rivet. Rapidly disappearing *pas-d'âne* are also visible just above the slightly dished bilobate counterguard. Its double-edged blade tapers in a straight line toward a centered point. The long stud for a frog attachment is visible on the throat of the brass-mounted leather scabbard.

Length: 40"                                     Hilt: Brass
Blade: 32¾" × 1⅜"                              Weight: 2.0 lbs.

*Author's Collection*

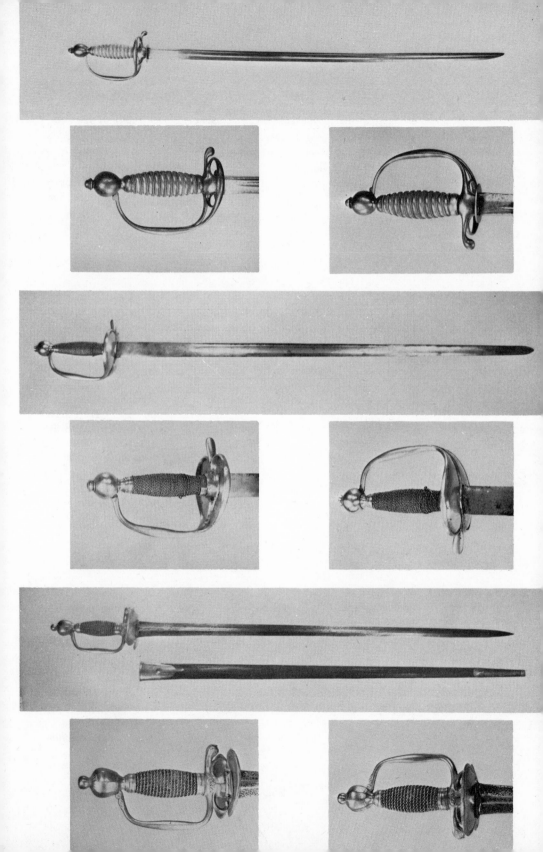

## S.52 DUTCH SHORT SABER

Circa 1774

Both faces of this blade bear Dutch markings, plus the date "1774." It is single-edged, and includes a ½" fuller (23" long). The brass stirrup guard is thin and flat, terminating in a ⅜"-wide disk finial, while the backstrap is integral with a flat cap pommel. The grip is wooden; its parallel ribs are filled with brass wire. Most edges of the hilt have a stamped border design of the kind used on numerous contemporaneous swords. Since many arms were ordered by the colonies from Holland during the mid-1770's, they probably included some of this style.

Length: 33⅝"  Hilt: Brass
Blade: 28½" × 1½"  Weight: 1.4 lbs.

*Author's Collection*

## S.53 EUROPEAN SHORT SABER

Circa 1775-1790

This hilt pattern was popular in France and other European countries during the last quarter of the eighteenth century. Its vertically ribbed grip is ebony, with an iron backstrap and flat cap pommel. The stirrup-hilt guard includes a shell design at the end of the quillon, and a langet extending down over the blade from underneath the counterguard (one side broken off). The single-edged curved blade is engraved with a sun, bird, and floral motif in Germanic styling. Two fullers begin at the hilt (⅛" × 19", ½" × 25").

Length: 30⅝"  Hilt: Iron
Blade: 25½" × 1"  Weight: .8 lb.

*Author's Collection*

## S.54 AMERICAN SHORT SABER

Circa 1740-1760

The very simplicity of this early American sword bespeaks its colonial origin. A smooth wooden grip ends in a square tapered pommel, which has notches cut into it as a simple design. The thin knuckle bow curves into a small base around the grip, with a double-ended elliptical counterguard just beneath. Its diamond-shaped double-edged blade tapers unevenly toward the tip. Probably the product of a local blacksmith, this specimen was found in Pennsylvania.

Length: 35⅛"  Hilt: Iron
Blade: 29¾" × 1"  Weight: .9 lb.

*Author's Collection*

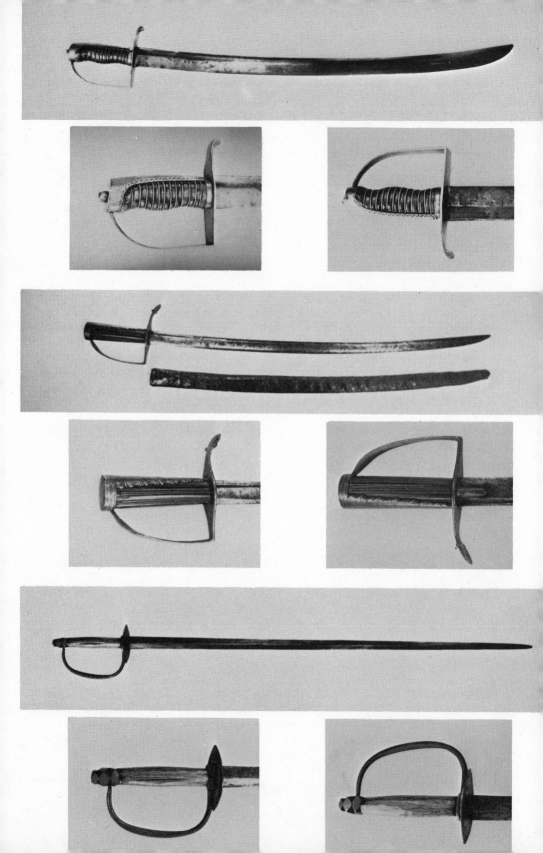

## S.55 AMERICAN SHORT SABER · Circa 1775-1783

Mounted on a blade which is probably European, this hilt is in a style common to many made in America for officer's swords. Its wooden grip includes a spiraling channel and two ½" ferrules. A plain urn-shaped pommel secures the upper end of a brass stirrup guard, while a lateral branch has been added next to the grip as a counterguard. Its single-edged cut-and-thrust blade has a fuller at the back (¼" × 20½"). A false edge measures 5½".

Length: 32¼"                                   Hilt: Brass
Blade: 26⅝" × 1¼"                              Weight: 1.2 lbs.

*Author's Collection*


## S.56 AMERICAN SHORT SABER · Circa 1775-1783

This blade is almost identical to the European one in the preceding illustration. Its hilt, however, is another of the styles produced by the colonists. The brass pommel is close to a baluster shape, while the guard appears to have been cut from a flat sheet of brass and formed into a simple curve (to end in a flattened disk finial bearing a small private mark on one face). The single fuller in the curved blade extends for 21" from the hilt. A false edge is 5¼" long.

Length: 32⅝"                                   Hilt: Brass
Blade: 26¾" × 1¼"                              Weight: 1.2 lbs.

*Author's Collection*


## S.57 AMERICAN SHORT SABER · Circa 1775-1780

Another crude version of American sword-making is illustrated here. The grip is a rectangular piece of wood, with a letter "H" (probably an owner's initial) cut into the outboard face. A flat iron strap forms its guard. It is widened at the upper end to cap the grip, and adds about ¼" in width as a token counterguard opposite the blade. Its curved single-edged blade includes three fullers (⅛" each); they originate 6¼" below the hilt and extend for 16¼". It has good balance as a fighting weapon.

Length: 34¼"                                   Hilt: Iron
Blade: 29⅞" × 1½"                              Weight: 1.3 lbs.

*Author's Collection*

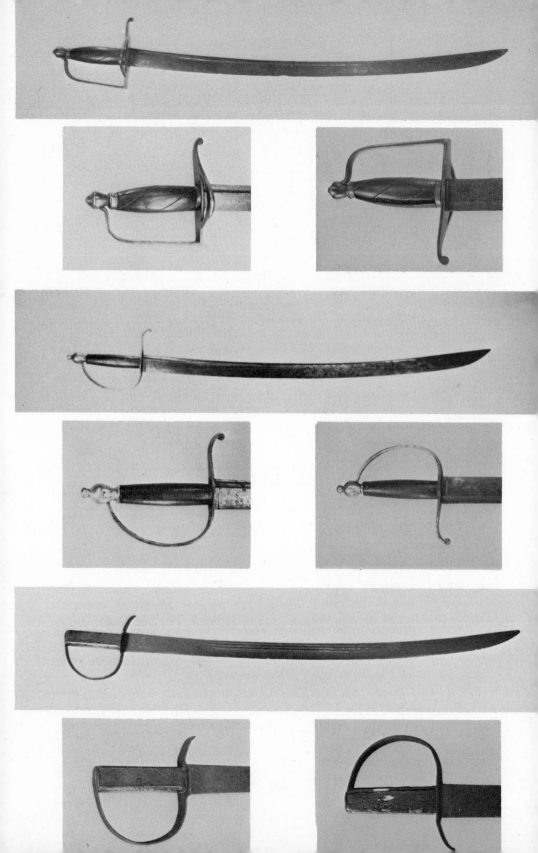

## S.58 AMERICAN SHORT SABER                          Circa 1775-1783

The single-fullered blade found on this sword is another common type apparently imported by the colonists and mounted with a variety of American hilts. Its turned wooden grip has a ⅛″ ferrule at the base (since lost), plus a heavy ⅜″ upper one to which the knuckle bow is fastened. A flat piece of brass, formed into the common stirrup shape, comprises the guard. The curved blade has one edge and one fuller (19¾″ long). Its leather scabbard mounts plain brass fittings which include both a stud and mounting ring at the throat.

Length: 31½″                                        Hilt: Brass
Blade: 26½″ × 1¼″                                   Weight: 1.3 lbs.

*Author's Collection*


## S.59 AMERICAN SHORT SABER                          Circa 1775-1783

Although this hilt is distinctly American in design, it has an imported blade almost identical to the one in the preceding example (S.58). The round ivory grip includes parallel ribbing, and a ¼″ bottom ferrule. Its flattened ball pommel has a large capstan rivet, while the vertical channel visible in the outboard face of the grip might have been cut to mount a decorative piece of metal or to act as a sweat gutter. The scabbard's throat mounting includes a tail, which extends into the leather and reappears 2″ below as a bent-over tip.

Length: 32⅛″                                        Hilt: Brass
Blade: 26″ × 1¼″                                    Weight: 1.3 lbs.

*Author's Collection*


## S.60 AMERICAN SHORT SABER                          Circa 1775-1783

Variations in the blade and its fuller suggest that this weapon might be of complete American manufacture. Parallel ribs are cut into the ivory grip, which mounts a ⅜″ ferrule at each end. The unique capstan rivet gives it a distinctive elongated appearance. Formed from flat brass, the stirrup guard terminates in a disk finial at the end of the quillon. A narrow (⅛″) fuller appears at the back of the single-edged blade (23⅜″ length). As in most cases, no identifying marks are visible.

Length: 33⅞″                                        Hilt: Brass
Blade: 28⅜″                                         Weight: 1.3 lbs.

*Warren M. Moore Collection*

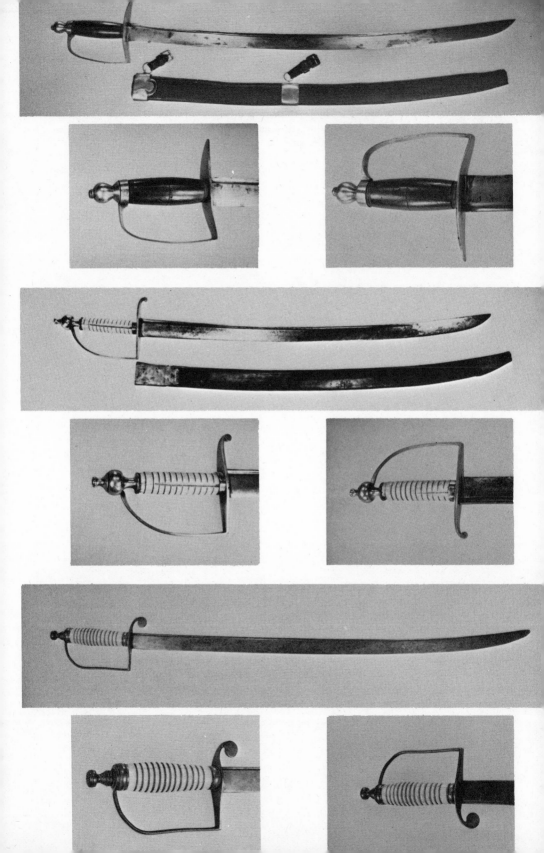

## S.61 AMERICAN SHORT SABER                                   Circa 1775-1783

This unique colonial sword has a hilt completely of brass. The faceted grip includes two ⅜" ferrules, and is topped by a large ovoid pommel. Its knuckle bow divides as it bends toward the blade into three branches. They, in turn, merge into a down-turned quillon at the far side of the grip. Crude sun, moon, and star engravings appear on the blade—apparently in an effort to imitate the popular European style. Also interesting are the two equal fullers on the single-edged blade (⅛" × 17½")—both beginning 6" below the hilt.

Length: 36⅝"                                                   Hilt: Brass
Blade: 31⅜" × 1⅜"                                              Weight: 2.0 lbs.

*Author's Collection*

## S.62 AMERICAN SHORT SABER                                   Circa 1775-1783

The brass hilt in this illustration has a flat knuckle bow, which spreads as it descends to include a wheellike counterguard with thin spokes projecting in toward the blade. A ball pommel and capstan rivet are mounted at the upper end of the wooden grip. Its curved American blade is flat, with a single edge.

Length: 35⅛"                                                   Hilt: Brass
Blade: 28⅞"                                                    Weight: 1.9 lbs.

*William H. Guthman Collection*

## S.63 FRENCH SHORT SABER                                     Circa 1730

This French infantry sword of the 1730 period has markings that suggest subsequent use by an American militia unit. The engraved letters "D.M. No. 38" appear on the inboard side of the guard just below the grip, while "I.C." is inscribed on the lower side of the counterguard. Its grip is wood, wrapped in twisted wire (⅜" ferrules). Unlike the typical contemporary infantry hanger (S.21), this has a straight single-edged blade with one fuller (½" × 21⅜"). A fleur-de-lis is stamped on both faces.

Length: 33⅞"                                                   Hilt: Brass
Blade: 28¼" × 1⅛"                                              Weight: .8 lb.

*Author's Collection*

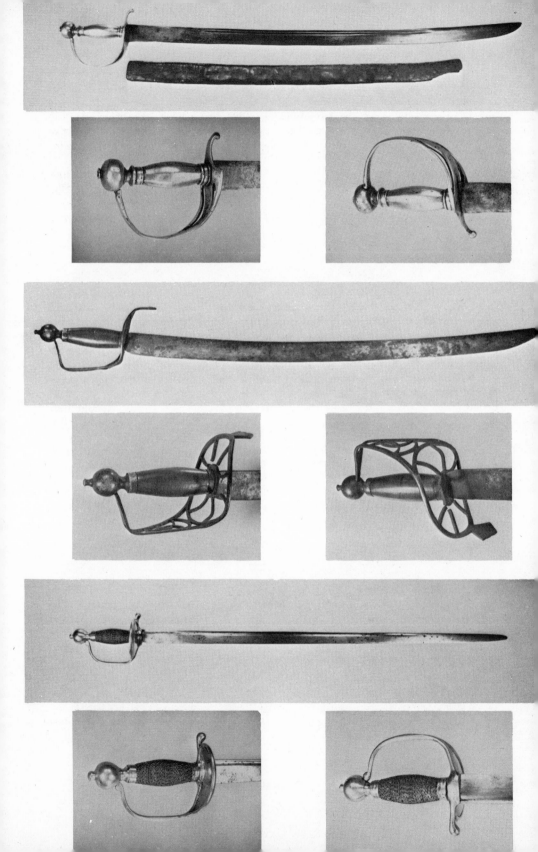

## S.64 AMERICAN SHORT SABER · Circa 1770-1780

It appears that this entire sword originated in America. The flat single-edged blade has imperfections in the metal and is marked with three connected crosses. An S-shaped counterguard includes a thumb ring attached to its inboard side. Spiraling channels in the ivory grip still have the wire binding, while an opening just below the cap pommel indicates that the guard originally extended to form a complete knuckle bow. The finished end of the present upturned quillon, however, suggests that the missing section was lost at an early date.

Length: 34⅛″  
Blade: 28⅞″ × 1⅛″

Hilt: Brass  
Weight: 1.1 lbs.

*Author's Collection*

## S.65 AMERICAN SHORT SABER · Circa 1775-1778

Swords with grips which swell in profile near their base were popular near the end of the 1700's, but this example is considered to be of Revolutionary War vintage. Its wooden ribbed grip is quite narrow, and mounts a bottom ¼″ ferrule plus a cap-type pommel. The flat iron stirrup guard is typical of many colonial examples. Although patterned after the European style, this single-edged blade has an uneven fuller, which points to possible American manufacture. A crude script engraving on one face appears to read C FT VALLEY FORG.

Length: 33⅜″  
Blade: 27¾″ × 1¼″

Hilt: Iron  
Weight: 1.1 lbs.

*Author's Collection*

## S.66 AMERICAN SHORT SABER · Circa 1775-1783

Another version with a ribbed grip and flat iron guard is shown in this illustration. The single-edged blade is virtually straight for most of its length, and suddenly begins curving a short distance from the point. Two fullers extend from the hilt for 21″. Notice that the scabbard has shrunk with age—as is common with many original leather pieces. A flat stud is mounted near the neck.

Length: 32½″  
Blade: 27¾″ × 1⅛″

Hilt: Iron  
Weight: 1.5 lbs.

*Author's Collection*

260

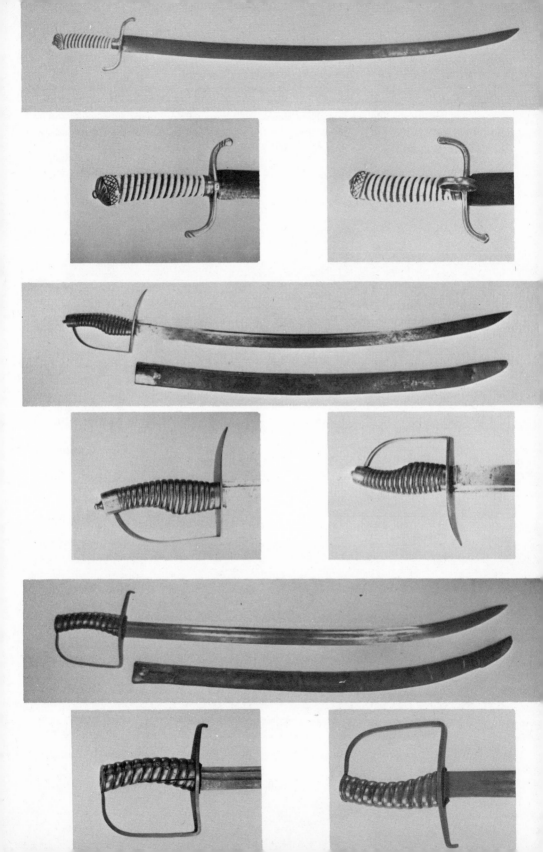

## S.67 AMERICAN SHORT SABER
Circa 1775-1783

A stirrup-type hilt is again present on this sword. Its ivory grip has a ⅜″ ferrule at the base, and a cap pommel. The elliptical counterguard was apparently cut from a flat piece of brass; it has three decorative piercings opposite each side of the blade, including crude stamped decorative borders. Note the wavy edge on its outboard side, while the inboard surface is smooth (probably to decrease wear on the pants). Its American blade (uneven fuller; iron imperfections) has a single edge and one fuller (¼″ × 17½″).

Length: 30¾″                                                     Hilt: Brass
Blade: 26″ × 1¼″                                                 Weight: 1.0 lb.

*Author's Collection*


## S.68 EUROPEAN CUTLASS
Circa 1744

The naval cutlass is essentially a short cutting sword, normally with a wide guard for protection in close fighting. This one is dated "1744" on the blade (plus a running-wolf mark), but is characteristic of types used earlier. Its hilt has a wide shell guard on the outboard side, which reduces in size and bends over to form an inboard thumb ring. Notice too that one of the quillons curves upward like a knuckle bow—only to end in a backward curl just before the ball pommel. Its grips are wire-wrapped, and the blade has one fuller (⅛″ × 20½″).

Length: 32⅜″                                                     Hilt: Iron
Blade: 27⅛″ × 1⅛″                                                Weight: 1.3 lbs.

*Author's Collection*


## S.69 AMERICAN CUTLASS
Circa 1750-1780

This specimen still includes the early shell guard (S.68 above), but illustrates the evolutionary trend underway, i.e. the loss of its thumb ring on the inboard side, plus the establishment of a true knuckle bow (secured at each end). The faceted hilt is ivory, and the quillon ends in a simple down-turned iron lobe. Its heavy blade measures 1½″ wide at the hilt, with a ½″ fuller beginning under the guard (18″ long). A 6″ false edge is also present. No marks are visible.

Length: 28½″                                                     Hilt: Iron
Blade: 24″ × 1½″                                                 Weight: 1.4 lbs.

*Harold L. Peterson Collection*

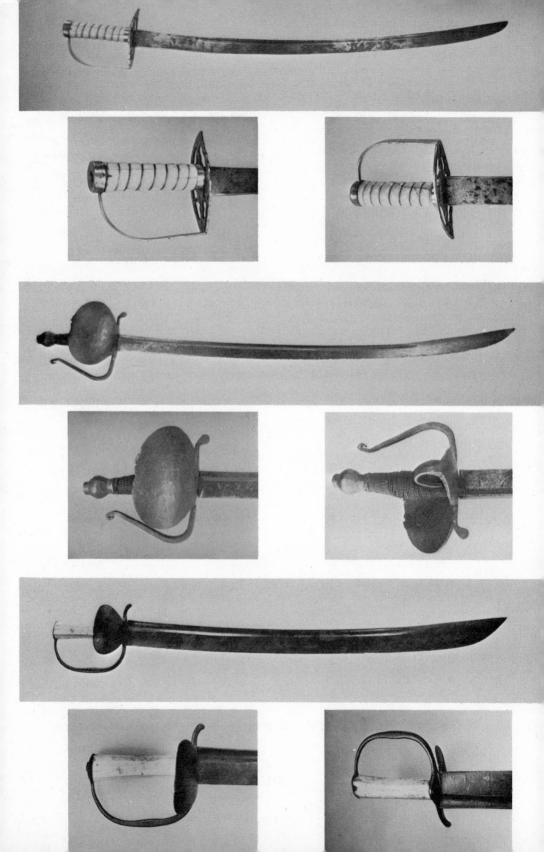

**S.70 AMERICAN CUTLASS**                                    Circa 1750-1780

A shell guard is not present on this cutlass. The plain wooden grip is protected by a heavy guard. There is a ¾" ferrule at its base, and a rounded cap pommel topped by a wide capstan rivet. Its iron knuckle bow swells in width to form the counterguard (having two piercings outboard of the grip), while the crude blade is double-edged, with a median ridge. As in most cases, there are no identifying marks.

Length: 29⅝"                                              Hilt: Iron
Blade: 23" × 1⅛"                                          Weight: 1.6 lbs.

*Author's Collection*


**S.71 ENGLISH CUTLASS**                                     Circa 1765-1785

By the time of the American Revolution, British cutlasses were following a standard design. As shown here, the straight blade had a single cutting edge and a ¼" fuller at the back (21" long). Its grip was a smooth cylinder of lapped iron (note: similar styles with corrugated grips are usually considered postwar). The distinctive knuckle bow is fastened flat to the top of the grip, and about one-third of the distance to the blade flares out into a wide elliptical shape; it then narrows before spreading into another to form the counterguard.

Length: 33½"                                              Hilt: Iron
Blade: 29" × 1¼"                                          Weight: 1.8 lbs.

*Author's Collection*


**S.72 AMERICAN CUTLASS**                                    Circa 1775-1783

Many of the American cutlasses from the Revolution are copies of the British pattern. They can usually be identified by the crude workmanship. This one, for example, has a rough vertical seam where the iron grip is lapped. The knuckle bow too is of thinner iron, and remains flat instead of being "dished" for the counterguard (i.e. easier to make). Many of the colonial cutlasses used English blades. Traces of the black paint used to protect it from rusting are still visible.

Length: 33½"                                              Hilt: Iron
Blade: 28¾" × 1⅛"                                         Weight: 1.6 lbs.

*Author's Collection*

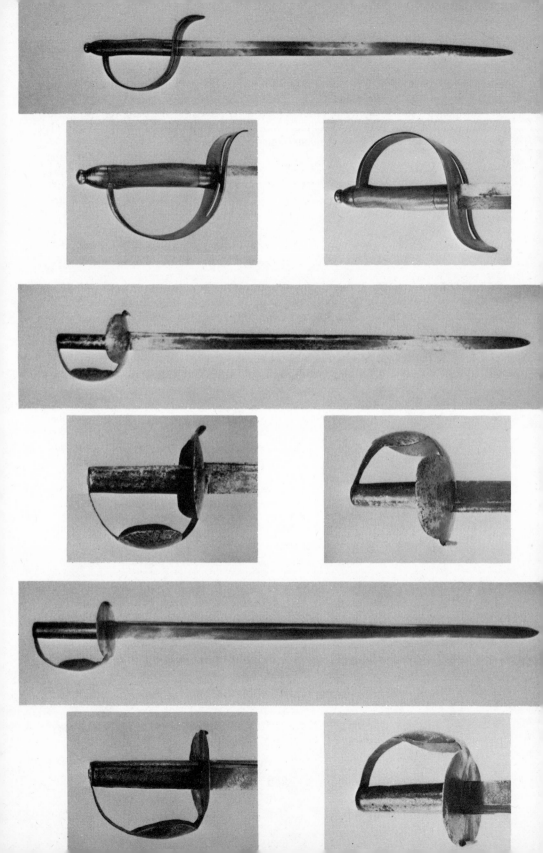

**S.73 AMERICAN CUTLASS**                                    Circa 1775-1783

This interesting variation is believed to be American. It maintains the straight single-edged blade (one fuller, ¼″ × 22¼″), but adds some typical Yankee individuality to the hilt. The grip is of wood—"turned" to create parallel ribbing of varying diameters. A flat cap pommel has been added, and a ½″ ferrule is present at the base. Its iron guard includes the popular two large elliptical lobes, while the wide (1½″) quillon bends down from the leading edge of the counterguard in a short curl.

Length: 32¾″                                                Hilt: Iron
Blade: 28⅛″ × 1¼″                                           Weight: 1.4 lbs.

*Hermann W. Williams, Jr., Collection*


**S.74 AMERICAN CUTLASS**                                    Circa 1775-1783

A curved blade was used for this cutlass (one fuller at the back, ¼″ × 24⅜″). Its pattern is similar to the one followed by Rose for his later cutlasses during the American war with Tripoli. The grip is of smooth wood, with the top end of the knuckle bow formed into a brief cap pommel. The two elliptical lobes again appear on its guard. Variations in the hilt and blade indicate manufacture in the colonies. Crude markings on the grip include IXIX and a broad arrow (if original, it suggests onetime possession by British forces).

Length: 32¾″                                                Hilt: Iron
Blade: 27¼″ × 1⅜″                                           Weight: 1.5 lbs.

*Author's Collection*


**S.75 AMERICAN CUTLASS**                                    Circa 1775-1783

Illustrated here is another variation of the cutlasses probably carried by American and European privateers (or regular merchantmen) during the 1770's. Its octagonal ivory grip has a crude design stained into the surface (seen on several swords of this period). The simple hilt includes an elliptical counterguard, plus a thin knuckle bow. Each face of the blade bears European markings (a moon and three stars), while a single fuller (¼″ × 20½″) appears at the back. A false edge measures 6″.

Length: 31″                                                 Hilt: Iron
Blade: 26¾″ × 1¼″                                           Weight: 1.1 lbs.

*Author's Collection*

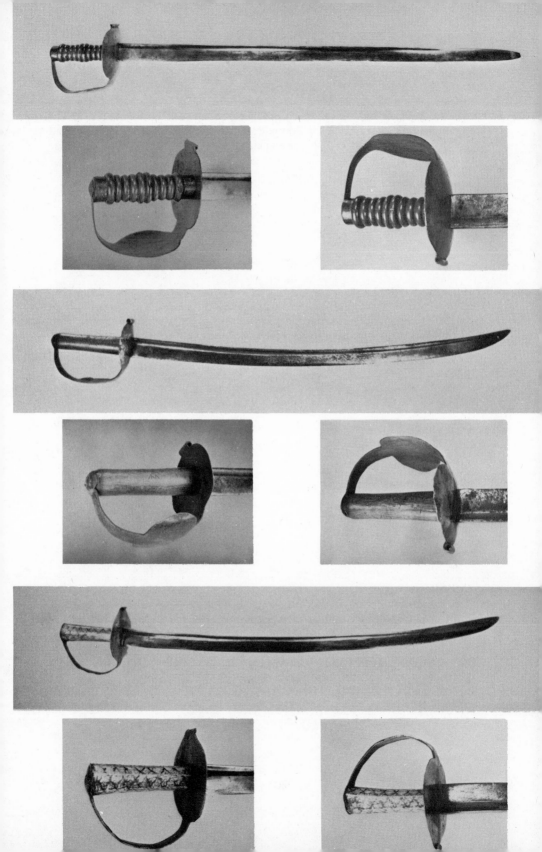

**S.76 AMERICAN CUTLASS**                                    Circa 1775-1783

The wooden grip of this piece has a series of slow spirals cut into its surface, plus a ¼" ferrule at each end. The thin guard is secured to the top of the grip with a round metal washer just under the flattened end of the blade's tang; at the base of the grip, it flares on the outboard side to create a half-elliptical shape for the counterguard. The quillon ends in a crude down-turned teardrop finial, and traces of the original black paint coating still remain on the hilt. The uneven blade is slightly curved—with one edge and no fuller.

Length: 30½"                                                 Hilt: Iron
Blade: 25¾" × 1¼"                                            Weight: 1.1 lbs.

*Author's Collection*


**S.77 AMERICAN CUTLASS**                                    Circa 1750-1780

Elementary cutlass styles such as this were apparently produced in America from the mid-1700's through the War for Independence. The grip is a wooden cylinder, with the guard cut from a sheet of iron. It is secured to the top of the grip as a rudimentary pommel, and near the bottom spreads into a flat elliptical counterguard. The curved, single-edged blade includes one fuller (¼" × 20"). Its face bears a unique fleur-de-lis stamp (three-pointed design on top of large center lobe). This work is typical of Richard Gridley (Sharon, Massachusetts, 1776-1777).

Length: 30½"                                                 Hilt: Iron
Blade: 26½" × 1¼"                                            Weight: 1.0 lb.

*Author's Collection*


**S.78 AMERICAN CUTLASS**                                    Circa 1760-1780

Another example of an early cutlass which includes little beyond the barest essentials for fighting is pictured here. Compared with the previous illustration (S.77), it has a "reverse" heart-shaped counterguard mounted on a rough single-edged colonial blade (with a slight curve). The initials "SD" (probably the maker) in a heart-shaped cartouche are clearly stamped on its inboard face, just below the hilt. A 3" false edge and short clipped point are present; there is no fuller.

Length: 30⅛"                                                 Hilt: Iron
Blade: 26⅛" × 1⅛"                                            Weight: 1.1 lbs.

*Author's Collection*

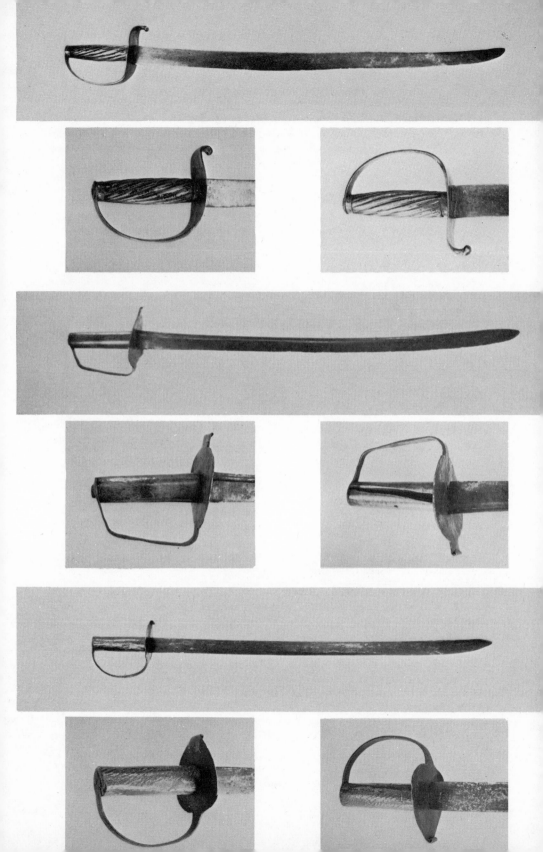

## S.79 ENGLISH NAVAL OFFICER'S SWORD          Circa 1770-1785

By the decade of the 1770's, a British naval officer's dress was becoming standardized. The sword, however, was still a matter of personal preference, and his choice ranged from the contemporaneous hunting pattern to the small sword. This interesting example is a recognized English infantry style (see S.47), but includes an anchor engraved on the front of the pommel (and a brass instead of an iron hilt). Fish skin covers the channeled grip (the original wire wrapping is gone). Its single-edged blade has two fullers (¼″ × 18¼″, ⅜″ × 24¼″).

Length: 31¾″                                                       Hilt: Brass
Blade: 26″ × 1⅛″                                          Weight: 1.0 lb.

*Author's Collection*


## S.80 ENGLISH NAVAL OFFICER'S SWORD          Circa 1780-1800

This interesting sword combines the popular lion-head pommel with definite naval markings. The pierced design of a fouled anchor has been included in the bottom half of the flat knuckle bow, and in the outboard side of the counterguard (just opposite the blade). Its ivory grip has close parallel ribs, while the hilt itself is gilded. The curved blade has one cutting edge and two fullers (¼″ × 19″, ⅜″ × 26⅛″). A false edge extends for 8″.

Length: 33″                                                        Hilt: Brass
Blade: 27″ × 1⅛″                                         Weight: 1.4 lbs.

*E. Norman Flayderman Collection*


## S.81 ENGLISH HORSEMAN SABER          Circa 1690-1720

Records indicate that as early as 1702 Queen Anne sent equipment for four hundred horsemen to America (including pistols, carbines, and swords). Subsequent information confirms the presence of heavy cavalry sabers here in the colonies during the early eighteenth century. This example has a basket-style hilt formed by three iron shell guards which extend branches to the ovoid pommel, as was common in the mid-seventeenth century. Its hilt is wrapped in twisted iron wire, with two Turk's-head ferrules. The two-edged blade tapers to a center point; its German markings include EN: ALEMANIA and EN:R LOVE:GOEL:EH.

Length: 38½″                                                      Hilt: Iron
Blade: 32¾″ × 1½″                                        Weight: 1.9 lbs.

*Author's Collection*

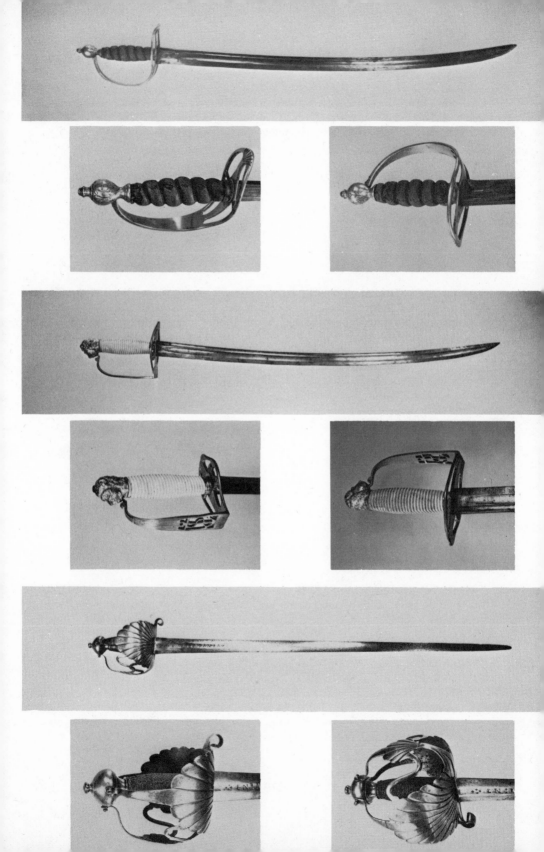

**S.82 ENGLISH HORSEMAN SABER**                              Circa 1735-1750

This style of basket hilt was used by British horsemen in the first half of the 1700's. Its guard is made of iron, and attaches to a collar just beneath an ovoid pommel. The grip is leather-covered, with a spiraling copper wire binding, and a Turk's-head ferrule at each end. The single-edged straight blade includes two fullers ($\frac{1}{4}'' \times 25''$, $\frac{1}{2}'' \times 31''$). Its markings show a "GR" script cipher under a crown on each face.

Length: 41"                                                    Hilt: Iron
Blade: 35⅜" × 1¼"                                        Weight: 2.3 lbs.

*Author's Collection*

**S.83 ENGLISH HORSEMAN SABER**                              Circa 1740-1750

The basket-hilted saber in steadily modified versions continued as the principal British dragoon sword well into the eighteenth century. This grip still retains the original fish skin covering (with spiraling wire in the grooves). Notice the large oval opening in the inboard side of the guard. It is typical of these hilts, and believed by some to have permitted holding the horse reins with the sword hand. The straight single-edged blade has two fullers ($\frac{3}{8}'' \times 25\frac{1}{4}''$, $\frac{3}{4}'' \times 33\frac{7}{8}''$). Markings include "GR," IRWIN (the maker), and a broad arrow (on pommel).

Length: 40¼"                                                   Hilt: Iron
Blade: 34½"

*Edmund W. Budde, Jr., Collection*

**S.84 ENGLISH HORSEMAN SABER**                              Circa 1740-1750

Although the blade of this sword bears a French-style fleur-de-lis, the almost enclosed hilt is a pattern thought to have been used by British dragoons in the 1740's. Three transverse branches appear on each side to join the solid sections of the guard. Its wooden grip is wrapped in fish skin, and the original inside leather liner remains. The blade has a single edge, with one fuller ($\frac{1}{4}'' \times 25''$).

Length: 39¼"                                                   Hilt: Iron
Blade: 33¾"

*Edmund W. Budde, Jr., Collection*

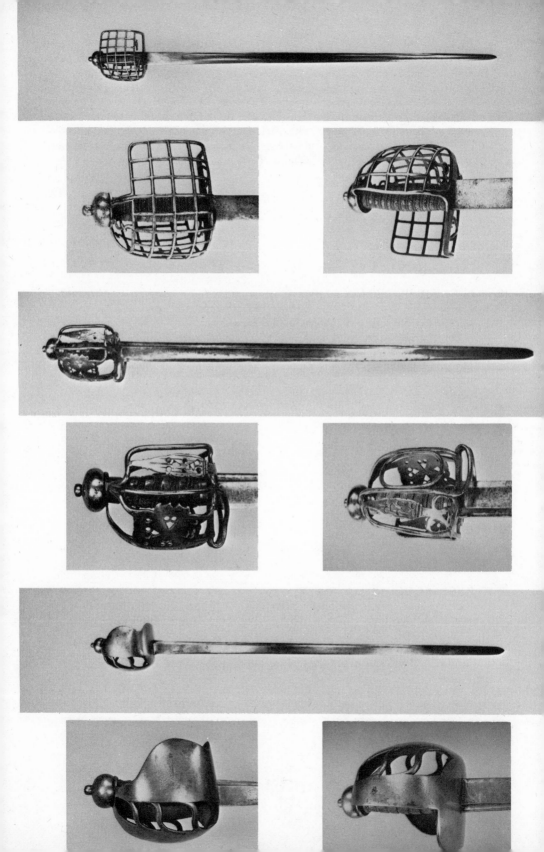

## S.85 ENGLISH HORSEMAN SABER                                          Circa 1745-1765

This interesting example is topped by an early type of conical pommel, which was still in use at the time (mostly on Scotch backswords; see S.12). The guard, with its three lateral branches, does not extend inboard past the knuckle bow, and remains a "half-basket." Its spiraled wooden grip has lost the original leather covering, while a "half-moon" opening appears opposite each face of the blade in the flat counterguard. The single-edged straight blade has the typical 36" length of the period, plus two fullers (¼" × 26½", ½" × 34¾"). A false edge measures 7".

Length: 42½"                                                          Hilt: Iron
Blade: 36" × 1¼"                                                      Weight: 2.3 lbs.

*Author's Collection*


## S.86 ENGLISH HORSEMAN SABER                                          Circa 1750

Basket hilts with "S" designs were used for both infantry and horseman swords at this time (see S.10). The hilt seen here is made of brass, with a 34" single-edged blade. Its wooden grip is covered with leather and a spiraling wire binding. A single fuller begins at the hilt and terminates 8" from the tip. The false edge is 9½" long. A British broad arrow (denoting government property) plus a German maker's mark appear on the blade.

Length: 40¼"                                                          Hilt: Brass
Blade: 34" × 1¾"                                                      Weight: 2.8 lbs.

*Colonial Williamsburg Collection*


## S.87 ENGLISH HORSEMAN SABER                                          Circa 1760-1770

The arm pictured here is typical of a basket-hilt pattern popular with British dragoons just prior to the Revolution. Notice the tall pommel (faceted in this case), and the straight single-edged blade which usually reached for 34"-36". Fish skin covers the grip, with decorative wire in its spiraling grooves. Inscribed on the blade is a crown over the "GR" cipher, plus GILL (the maker) in script on a ⅞" *ricasso*.

Length: 41½"                                                          Hilt: Iron
Blade: 34" × 1¼"                                                      Weight: 2.4 lbs.

*Author's Collection*

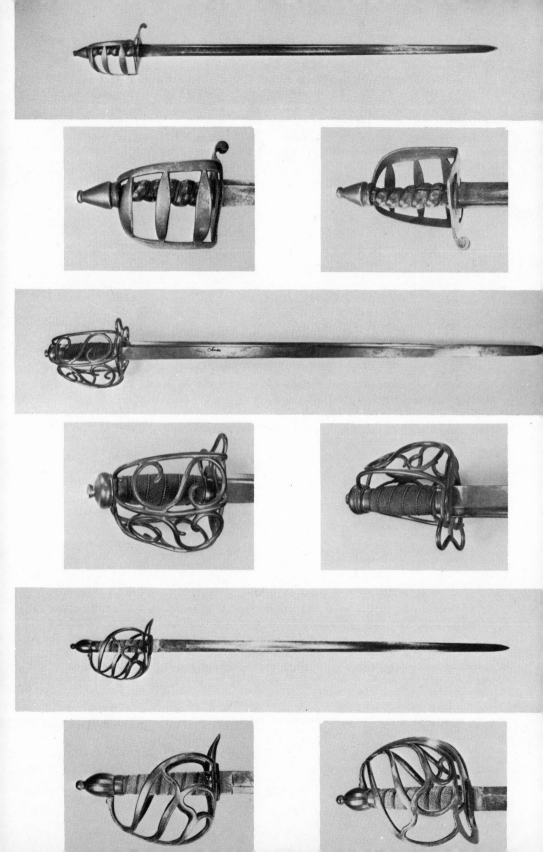

## S.88 ENGLISH HORSEMAN SABER

Circa 1765-1785

This half-basket style is thought to typify the arm carried by many British dragoons in the late 1760's and 1770's. The towering pommel and pierced counterguard remain from previous patterns. Yet, the hilt has been shortened and lightened to include only two lateral branches (on the outboard side only). Its grip is covered in fish skin, with a ⅜" base ferrule. The straight, single-edged blade remains 36" long, including two fullers (³⁄₁₆" × 27", ⅜" × 35"). It is stamped GILL and bears a viewer's mark (a crown above "9").

Length: 42¾"                                                        Hilt: Iron
Blade: 36" × 1¼"                                              Weight: 2.1 lbs.

*Author's Collection*


## S.89 ENGLISH HORSEMAN OFFICER'S SABER

Circa 1740-1760

This British officer's dragoon sword includes fluting and pierced designs in the unique semi-basket hilt. A ⅜" ferrule is present at each end of the grip (covered with fish skin and a binding silver strip). The knuckle bow originates at a ring under the ovoid pommel and adds three branches on the outboard side (plus a short one inboard), while a circular counterguard has supporting spokes radiating to its outer circumference. The straight blade, with a single cutting edge, includes a short 6" fuller; it is marked ANDRIA FARARA (a common forgery).

Length: 37½"                                                        Hilt: Iron
Blade: 31½" × 1¼"                                           Weight: 1.8 lbs.

*Author's Collection*


## S.90 ENGLISH LIGHT HORSEMAN SABER

Circa 1756-1765

In 1756, light-horse troops were added to the British dragoon regiments. Among their new arms was specified a short cutting sword, having a 34" blade (straight or curved), plus any style of hilt—as long as it was light and without a basket. This example, with a curved blade just under 34" and two transverse branches on the guard, is thought to be one of these early light-dragoon sidearms. The wire-wrapped grip and heart-shaped counterguard resemble the earlier "1742" hanger (S.4). Its flat blade (clipped point) is marked "GR" (with a crown) and DRURY.

Length: 39¼"                                                        Hilt: Brass
Blade: 33¼" × 1⅛"                                           Weight: 1.8 lbs.

*Author's Collection*

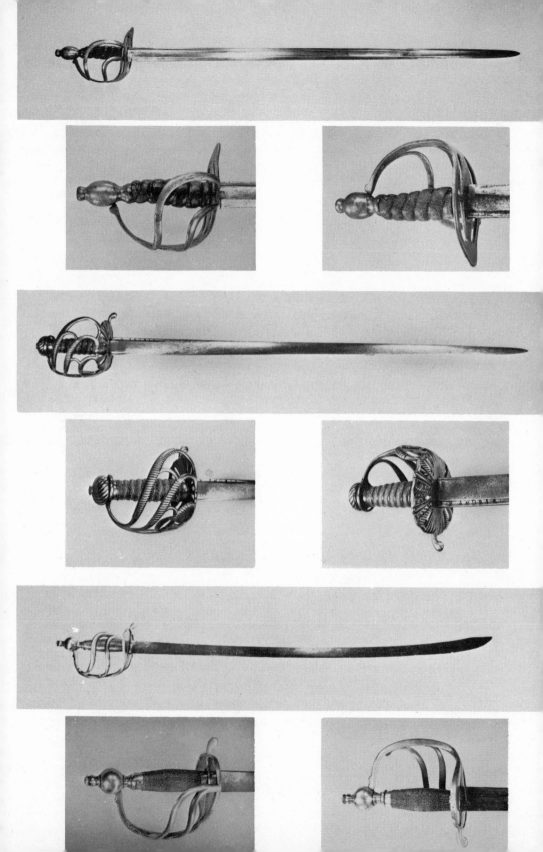

## S.91 ENGLISH LIGHT HORSEMAN SABER                    Circa 1759-1770

When the initial test of light dragoons (begun in 1756) proved successful, they were formed into complete regiments in 1759. The blade for their swords was officially lengthened at that time to 37" (no standard hilt). This light saber is believed to be one of them. The earlier high pommel and semi-basket guard have been reduced to a flat top on the grip, with only vestigial branches at the bottom of the knuckle bow. The traditional counterguard's two piercings on each side opposite the blade remain, while the 37" blade has no fuller.

Length: 42¼"                                                   Hilt: Iron
Blade: 37"                                                     Weight: 1.9 lbs.

*Christie Collection*

## S.92 ENGLISH LIGHT HORSEMAN SABER                    Circa 1765-1785

The simple stirrup hilt illustrated here is believed to be the last stage in the evolution of British horseman blades prior to the American Revolution. Its leather-covered grip has an iron backstrap, which continues on to form a semi-bird's-head pommel. The hilt includes langets both above and below the counterguard; its quillon ends in a ⅝"-wide down-turned finial. The flat, single-edged blade curves slightly toward a clipped point. There is no fuller. This hilt design apparently continued in use into the 1790's.

Length: 41¼"                                                   Hilt: Iron
Blade: 36⅛" × 1¼"                                              Weight: 2.1 lbs.

*Author's Collection*

## S.93 EUROPEAN HORSEMAN SABER                          Circa 1700-1740

Iron-mounted semi-basket hilts of this type were popular on the European continent during the seventeenth and early eighteenth centuries. Lateral and transverse wrapping by twisted wire covers the wooden hilt, with braided Turk's-head ferrules at each end. The modified urn pommel includes a capstan rivet, while its bilobate counterguard has a reduced inboard lobe—mounting a thumb ring (the pierced center panel is missing). Its single-edged blade has a fuller at the back (⅜" × 26½") and an 8" false edge.

Length: 40⅛"                                                   Hilt: Iron
Blade: 34⅝" × 1¼"                                              Weight: 1.9 lbs.

*Author's Collection*

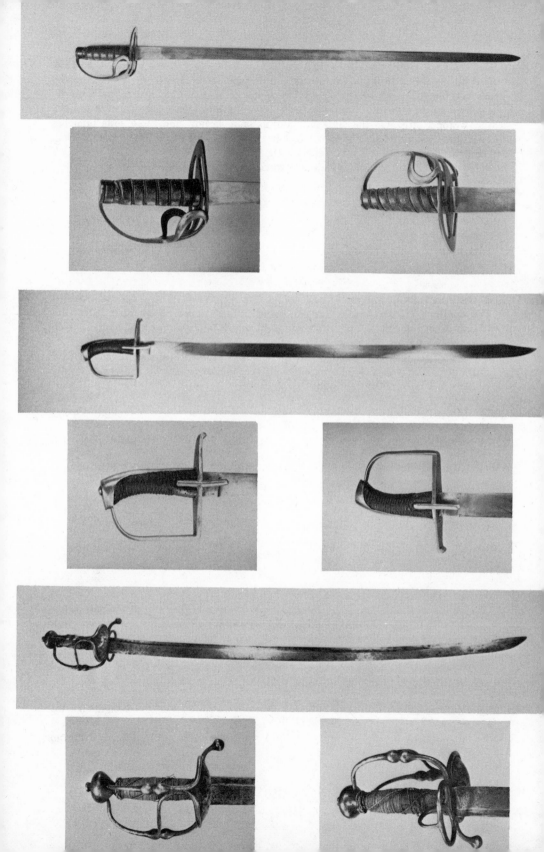

## S.94 GERMAN HORSEMAN SABER

Circa 1735-1790

It is believed that heavy-hilted sabers of this type were carried in America by the Brunswick Dragoons (dismounted) accompanying General Burgoyne, and probably by other German units here. A crude brass lion-head pommel and capstan rivet top the leather-wrapped grip. On the outboard side, its knuckle bow and three wide branches form a half-basket, while an extended inboard loop supports a large thumb ring. Its straight double-edged blade (shorter than normal; see S.95, S.96) tapers to a centered point. The scabbard is leather-covered wood with brass bindings.

Length: 40½″                                      Hilt: Brass
Blade: 33¾″ × 1⅛″                                 Weight: 3.3 lbs.

*West Point Museum Collection*


## S.95 GERMAN HORSEMAN SABER

Circa 1735-1797

The variations of this German dragoon sword from the previous example (S.94) are the bird's-head pommel, a longer two-edged blade (37″), plus removal of the thumb ring and inboard part of the guard (usually by the trooper to prevent chafing). Its closely ribbed grip, typical blunt-ended quillon, and crossed branches remain similar. The straight blade is slightly convex on each face; markings include its arsenal stamp, POTZDAM (in a rectangular cartouche).

Length: 43½″                                      Hilt: Brass
Blade: 37″ × 1⅜″                                  Weight: 2.4 lbs.

*Author's Collection*


## S.96 GERMAN HORSEMAN SABER

Circa 1732-1797

This additional variation of a German horseman sword has a heavy dome-shaped pommel (with a capstan rivet) and a wide guard which includes a crowned eagle (Prussian) cast into it. The flat counterguard itself is bilobate in shape, with a thumb ring on the inboard side. Its typical Germanic quillon was bent down after manufacture. The blade is the usual two-edged type—having slightly convex faces. A POTZDAM stamp in a rectangular cartouche is present, plus a crude eagle under a crown.

Length: 43¼″                                      Hilt: Brass
Blade: 36¼″ × 1⅜″                                 Weight: 3.1 lbs.

*Author's Collection*

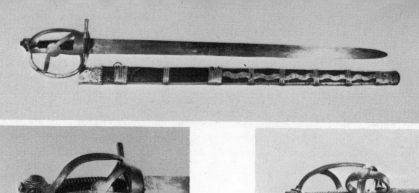

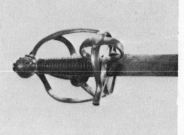

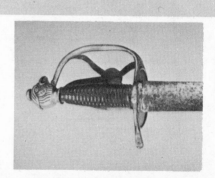

**S.97 HORSEMAN SABER**                                    Circa 1770-1780

The tall hilt on this saber again illustrates the popular stirrup guard of the Revolutionary War period. Its wooden grip is covered with leather and has decorative wire bindings in the ribbed grooves. An iron backstrap terminates in a cap, which is covered by the upper end of the knuckle bow. Under the flat counterguard protrudes a small langet on each side. The slightly curved single-edged blade was apparently broken in the center and brazed together at an early date. It has one fuller (¼″ × 24¾″).

Length: 41″                                              Hilt: Iron
Blade: 35″ × 1⅜″                                         Weight: 1.8 lbs.

*Author's Collection*

**S.98 AMERICAN HORSEMAN SABER**                          Circa 1770-1780

Most American sabers are actually colonial hilts mounted on blades imported from abroad. This example includes a "turned" wooden grip, with an interesting brass pommel which has only a rudimentary suggestion of an animal head. Its flat knuckle bow spreads to add two outer branches around the hilt, and narrows again to form a broad-pointed quillon. The upper 14½″ of the curved single-edged blade was originally blued (European-made). Three parallel fullers (each ⅛″ wide) begin about 7¼″ under the hilt and extend for 21″ (top one only 16¼″). Its false edge is 8½″.

Length: 38½″                                             Hilt: Brass
Blade: 33″ × 1½″                                         Weight: 1.7 lbs.

*Valley Forge Museum Collection*

**S.99 AMERICAN HORSEMAN SABER**                          Circa 1765-1780

The elementary lion head on this sword is an early style found primarily in New England. Details in the face and nose of the cast brass pommel have been added by engraving and small punched dots. Its smooth grip is curly maple, while the flat knuckle bow widens just below its mid-point to form a wide counterguard with pierced openings. The blade is single-edged and curved; three parallel fullers begin 6¾″ below the guard. The top one terminates at the upper end of a 9″ false edge; the others extend for 23″.

Length: 39½″                                             Hilt: Brass
Blade: 33¾″ × 1½″                                        Weight: 1.6 lbs.

*Harold L. Peterson Collection*

282

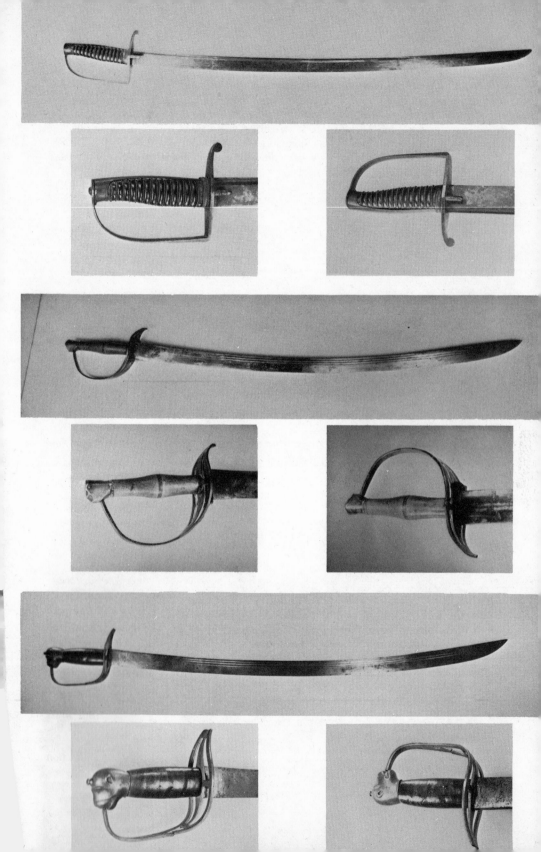

### S.100 AMERICAN HORSEMAN SABER                                  Circa 1780-1785

Although the eagle was not adopted as a national symbol until the early 1780's, an eagle head, as well as the lion, dog, dove, hawk, phoenix, etc. (the lion head was the most popular), was being used at the outbreak of the Revolution. Except for the crude eagle pommel on this weapon, it resembles many other sabers made during the war. The 33″ three-fuller blade was a common imported style (e.g. S.98, S.104, S.109). The pierced openings in the knuckle bow plus the looped edges on the counterguard suggest production about 1780.

Length: 39⅛″                                                       Hilt: Brass
Blade: 33″ × 1⅜″                                                    Weight: 1.9 lbs.

*Author's Collection*

### S.101 AMERICAN HORSEMAN SABER                                  Circa 1760-1780

The brass hilt on this light-cavalry pattern was apparently cast in one piece. Details of the lion's face and name have been engraved into the surface, while crude reverse langets are indicated on the flat sides of the grip. The long (35¼″) curved blade has a single edge plus a 7″ false edge and two fullers (⅛″ × 16¼″, ¾″ × 30″). Engravings on each face of the European blade include the sun, moon, stars, a floral motif, and a cross—with the popular phrase "Cox mi Ley y Cox mi Rey."

Length: 40½″                                                       Hilt: Brass
Blade: 35¼″ × 1¼″                                                   Weight: 1.5 lbs.

*Author's Collection*

### S.102 AMERICAN HORSEMAN SABER                                  Circa 1765-1780

This American hilt is mounted on a 36″ single-edged straight blade of the type used for British dragoon swords in the mid-1700's (see S.85). The wooden grip has deep channels cut into it, and ¼″ ferrules at each end. A tall ovoid pommel mounts a uniquely ridged capstan rivet. Its brass knuckle bow spawns two lateral branches on the outboard side for a semi-basket style, and widens to form a typical counterguard having two piercings opposite each blade face. There are a false edge (5½″) and two fullers (⅛″ × 26″, ½″ × 35″) present.

Length: 42½″                                                       Hilt: Brass
Blade: 36″ × 1⅜″                                                    Weight: 2.1 lbs.

*Author's Collection*

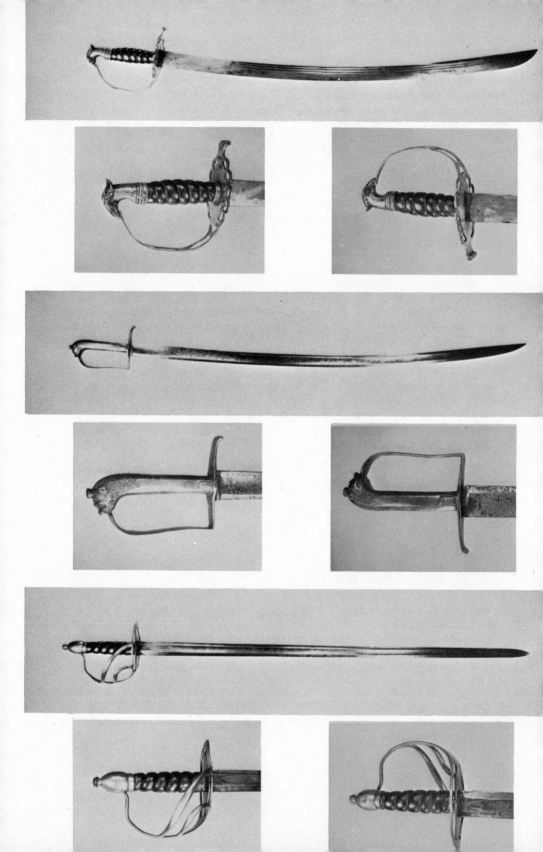

## S.103 AMERICAN HORSEMAN SABER                    Circa 1775-1783

The ribbed wooden grip shown here has ¼″ ferrules at its ends, plus a diminutive ball pommel with a capstan rivet. The flat brass knuckle bow widens just above its midpoint to form two transverse branches outboard, and continues on to spread into a wider counterguard having double pierced openings on both sides. A large teardrop shape cut through the bottom of the knuckle bow presents an interesting pattern in the photographs. Another of the 33″-long, three-fuller, imported blades completes this American-hilted weapon.

Length: 38″                                        Hilt: Brass
Blade: 33″ × 1⅜″                                    Weight: 1.7 lbs.

*Paul J. Doniger Collection*


## S.104 AMERICAN HORSEMAN SABER                    Circa 1770-1783

This hilt is plainer than most, but still sturdy and serviceable. The smooth walnut grip is secured in two ferrules (top, ⅜″; bottom, ½″), while the vase-style pommel includes a tapering capstan rivet. The brass knuckle bow with two branches provides limited hand space, and the quillon narrows to end in an abrupt right-angle finial. Its blade is again of the three-fuller imported pattern. Notice that both a stud and a carrying ring are present on the throat of the scabbard.

Length: 39¼″                                        Hilt: Brass
Blade: 33″ × 1⅜″                                    Weight: 1.9 lbs.

*R. Paul Nittolo Collection*


## S.105 AMERICAN HORSEMAN SABER                    Circa 1770-1783

The attractive ivory grip with raised spirals shown at the right has a baluster-shaped pommel. Its brass guard is like that of many American swords of this period. Two outer branches connect the knuckle bow and counterguard (which again includes two pierced openings on each side of the hilt). Its flat, single-edged curved blade is another of the three-fuller type (each ⅛″ wide). They begin about 6″ under the hilt; the top one ends after 18¾″, but the two lower ones continue for 22½″. No markings are present.

Length: 39½″                                        Hilt: Brass
Blade: 33⅛″ × 1⅜″                                   Weight: 1.8 lbs.

*Hermann W. Williams, Jr., Collection*

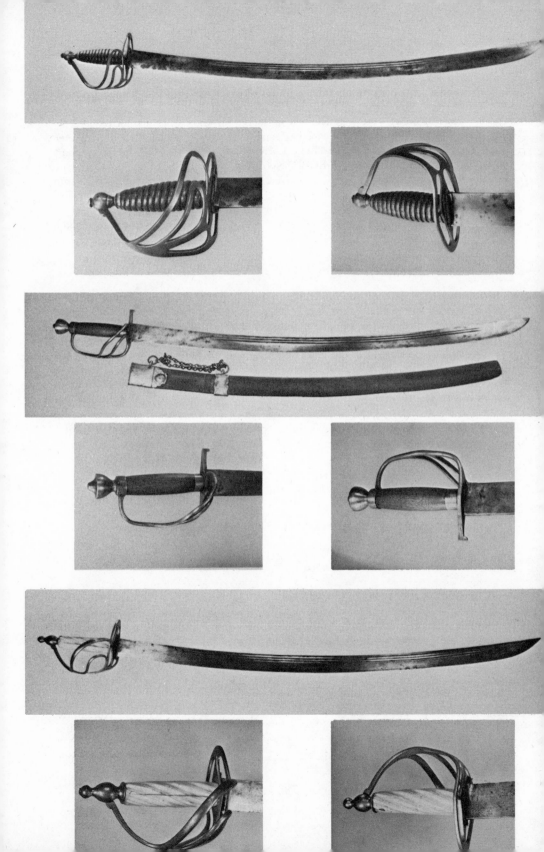

## S.106 AMERICAN HORSEMAN SABER

Circa 1775-1783

American simplicity is again evident in this iron-hilted light-dragoon sword. The smooth wooden grip projects up from a ½″ ferrule to a graceful ball-shaped pommel. A curving single-edged European blade includes two fullers (⅛″ × 16⅝″, ¾″ × 29″). Popular Spanish phrases are engraved on its faces: NO ME SAQUES SIN RAZON and NO ME EN BAINES SIN HONOR. This weapon is reported to have belonged to Major Peter Jaquett of the Delaware line (1776-1783). Early light-dragoon markings are also present on the back of the knuckle bow: 3 RG LD NO35 3-T.

Length: 41⅜″

Blade: 34¾″ × 1¼″

Hilt: Iron

Weight 1.8 lbs.

*Author's Collection*

## S.107 AMERICAN HORSEMAN SABER

Circa 1760-1783

This all-brass hilt with its cast grip, ball pommel, semi-basket guard, and heart-shaped counterguard is very similar to some English and German types. It possibly originated in one of these countries. The long, flat, single-edged blade, however, is typical of many produced by the colonists in America. There are no fullers and no identifying marks.

Length: 40⅛″

Blade: 33⅜″ × 1½″

Hilt: Brass

Weight: 2.1 lbs.

*Author's Collection*

## S.108 AMERICAN HORSEMAN SABER

Circa 1775-1780

The weight (3.3 lbs.) of this crudely fashioned weapon indicates its probable use in a militia or short-lived enlisted company which required little time in the field. Its hilt and ovoid pommel are turned from a solid piece of brass. The counterguard is an elliptical flat sheet, connected to the rest of the guard by pins at the edge. Small holes indicate that the original guard also had branches on the inboard side. The long sweeping single-edged blade has a rough uneven fuller (28½″) on the outboard side only. A false edge measures 7½″.

Length: 42½″

Blade: 36¼″ × 1⅜″

Hilt: Brass

Weight: 3.3 lbs.

*Author's Collection*

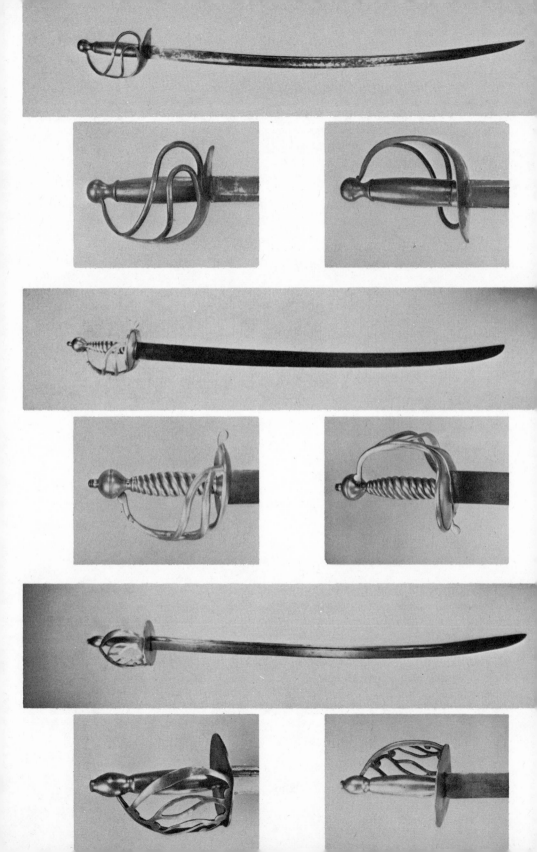

**S.109 AMERICAN HORSEMAN SABER**            Circa 1775-1780

The familiar 33″ single-edged blade with three parallel fullers (European) was again used in making this specimen. Its colonial hilt has a base of wood wrapped with spiraling string and then covered with leather. Decorative brass wire appears in the channels. A brass backstrap rises from a ½″ ferrule to form an elementary bird's-head pommel with a capstan rivet. The thin knuckle bow spawns two diagonal branches for the guard—which ends in a down-turned finial (¼″ wide). Note that its leather scabbard includes crude carrying rings.

Length: 38¼″                                      Hilt: Brass
Blade: 33″ × 1⅜″                              Weight: 1.8 lbs.

*Author's Collection*

**S.110 AMERICAN HORSEMAN SABER**            Circa 1775-1783

Both the unusual hilt and heavy cutting blade on this arm probably originated in the colonies. A horn grip bends back slowly toward a ball-shaped pommel, which has a median ridge and capstan rivet. The flat knuckle bow is narrow until midway in its curve, where it spreads to form a wide counterguard with a lateral branch (strengthened by one supporting bar). There is one fuller (½″ × 25¾″, uneven); the false edge is 5½″ long. Note the oval stud on the throat of the scabbard for attachment to a frog.

Length: 36¼″                                      Hilt: Brass
Blade: 30⅝″ × 1½″                           Weight: 2.1 lbs.

*Harold L. Peterson Collection*

**S.111 AMERICAN HORSEMAN SABER**            Circa 1775-1783

The shaped wooden grip in this case has small channels cut into its ridges to hold decorative pieces of wire. A plain backstrap begins at the ¼″ base ferrule and forms a simple bird's-head pommel with a low capstan rivet. The guard was apparently cut from a flat sheet of brass. It expands at the bottom of the knuckle bow and is pierced twice to form branchlike strips on the outboard side. The familiar 33″ three-fullered cutting blade from Europe is again used here. There are no markings.

Length: 38″                                          Hilt: Brass
Blade: 33″ × 1⅜″                              Weight: 2.0 lbs.

*Author's Collection*

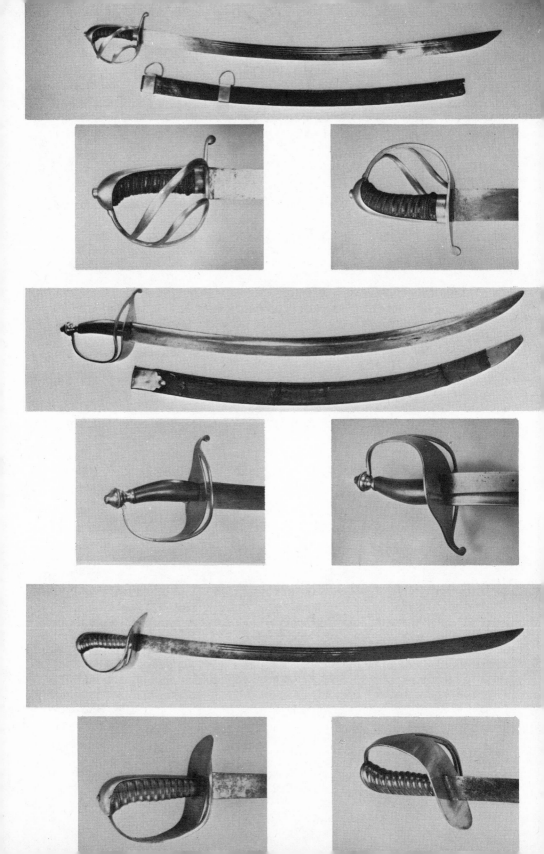

## S.112 AMERICAN HORSEMAN SABER

Circa 1775-1780

The bulbous wooden grip seen here is typical of many American swords. Its base has a ⅛" ferrule, and the upper end a ½" one—to which a rectangular knuckle bow is attached. The pommel is mushroom-shaped, with a small capstan rivet. The stirrup guard includes two openings in its outboard side to simulate a lateral branch opposite the grip. Its blade is another of the 33", triple-fullered, single-edged pattern. The original bluing, which extended for 15" from the hilt, is still visible.

Length: 38½"  
Blade: 33" × 1⅜"

Hilt: Brass  
Weight: 1.5 lbs.

*Harold L. Peterson Collection*

## S.113 AMERICAN HORSEMAN SABER

Circa 1775-1783

This hilt again illustrates a simple yet distinctive style by colonial craftsmen. Its channeled wooden grip rises from a ⅜" bottom ferrule into an ovoid cap pommel. A flat knuckle bow widens as it descends to form a counterguard with double pierced openings on each side. Its long, curved, single-edged blade includes two fullers (¼" × 23", ½" × 31").

Length: 42⅛"  
Blade: 36" × 1⅜"

Hilt: Iron  
Weight: 2.0 lbs.

*Author's Collection*

## S.114 AMERICAN HORSEMAN SABER

Circa 1775-1783

Several of these sabers exist in collections today. Each of them, as in this case, has the letter "H" stamped into the back of its knuckle bow. The leather-wrapped grip includes an iron binding wire in its spiraling channels, plus a ¼" ferrule at each end. The guard appears to have been cut from a flat sheet of iron and bent into a stirrup shape. It has two pierced slots on each side of the grip. A slightly curved single-edged blade displays an uneven fuller (⅜" × 30") and enough imperfections in the ironwork to indicate American manufacture.

Length: 41½"  
Blade: 36⅜"

·Hilt: Iron  
Weight: 1.9 lbs.

*Bergen County (N.J.) Historical Society Collection*

292

### S.115 AMERICAN HORSEMAN SABER
Circa 1775-1795

The upper part of this blade is inscribed 4 REGT VIRGA CAVALRY ESSEX. The use of markings by county designation was popular in Virginia during the 1790's (see M.87). Yet, the majority of arms they used appear to have been leftovers from the Revolution. This classic stirrup-hilt example typifies a pattern common with colonial horsemen. The style was copied toward the end of the century by makers such as Starr, but small variations had occurred by that time—including the extension of a lip beyond the pommel's top edge.

Length: 38¼″      Hilt: Iron
Blade: 32¾″ × 1⅜″      Weight: 2.1 lbs.

*Author's Collection*


### S.116 AMERICAN HORSEMAN SABER
Circa 1775-1783

The large hilt and heavy blade of this saber establish it as a real fighting weapon. Its grip is leather-covered, with a twisted wire in the spiraling grooves. Two ⅜″ ferrules are present, while the ball-shaped pommel anchors a flat brass guard which spreads on the outboard side to spawn two horizontal branches. The single-edged blade has a wide fuller (1″ × 26¾″) beginning ⅛″ under the counterguard.

Length: 40″      Hilt: Brass
Blade: 33″ × 1½″      Weight: 2.5 lbs.

*Author's Collection*


### S.117 AMERICAN HORSEMAN SABER
Circa 1778-1790

Among the French arms acquired in the middle and later years of the American Revolution were swords and components imported by Virginia. Although the high pommel and pierced guard on this arm are more typical of early styling, the French blade indicates its assembly during or after 1778. The flat, single-edged curved blade is inscribed on one side with DRAGOON OF VIRGINIA, a flaming bomb, a floral design, and a cross above "R." The other face includes VICTORY OR DEATH (under an inverted crown) and a panoply of arms. The name of France's swordmaking center KLINGENTHAL appears on the back of the blade.

Length: 42½″      Hilt: Iron
Blade: 36″ × 1¼″      Weight: 2.1 lbs.

*Harold L. Peterson Collection*

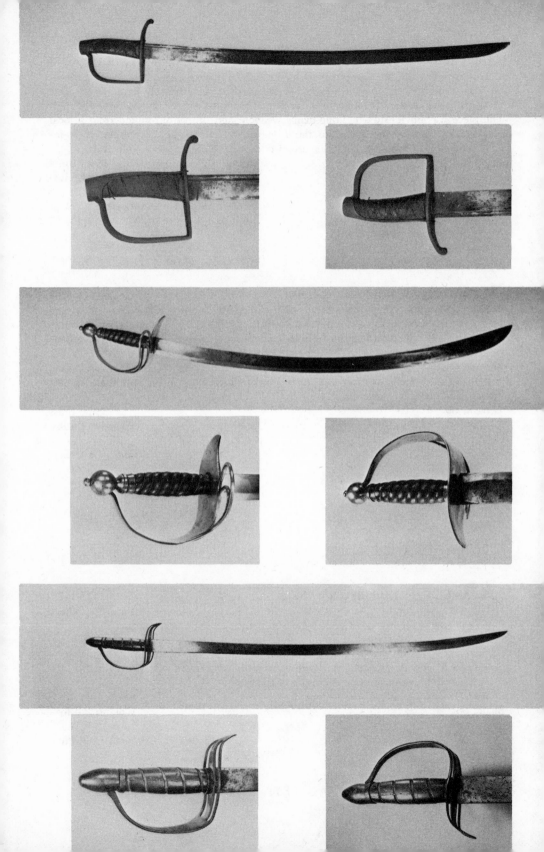

## S.118 AMERICAN HORSEMAN SABER                    Circa 1778-1783

This sword is the incongruous combination of a French brass hilt of the type used on their 1767 infantry *briquet* (see S.24) mounted on an extremely long (38½″) and crudely forged blade. Its rough finish and uneven taper suggest an American source. The piece was obviously a fighting-man's weapon, and probably resulted from a local blacksmith's blade being added to the French hilt during the Revolution. It is included here to illustrate the colonists' use of odd parts to create serviceable arms.

Length: 43⅝″                                            Hilt: Brass
Blade: 38½″ × 1⅛″                                    Weight: 1.8 lbs.

*Author's Collection*


## S.119 AMERICAN HORSEMAN SABER                    Circa 1775-1780

A typical hunting sword hilt of the mid-eighteenth century was combined with a long military-length blade to form this sword. Its grip is of horn, with the cap pommel including a capstan rivet. The simple brass knuckle bow, its shell guard, and the teardrop quillon are cast as one piece. The flat single-edged cutting blade is of a length (34¼″) and weight used by horse troops of the period; it is also light enough to have been carried on foot. Contemporary European marks—a crescent moon and three stars—are inscribed on each face.

Length: 39″                                              Hilt: Brass
Blade: 34¼″ × 1⅛″                                    Weight: 1.4 lbs.

*Author's Collection*


## S.120 AMERICAN HORSEMAN SABER                    Circa 1775-1776

This cavalry saber is signed POTTER on the blade. It is believed to stand for James Potter, an American sword cutler of New York City, who was active during the Revolutionary War. Its sweeping flat, single-edged blade is of the style so often seen on colonial-made arms of the period. A false edge measures 9⅛″. The leather-covered grip includes a ⅜″ ferrule at each end, with a large ovoid pommel. Its stirrup guard has the popular double openings on each side of the grip.

Length: 42⅜″                                            Hilt: Iron
Blade: 35⅜″                                            Weight: 3.0 lbs.

*William H. Guthman Collection*

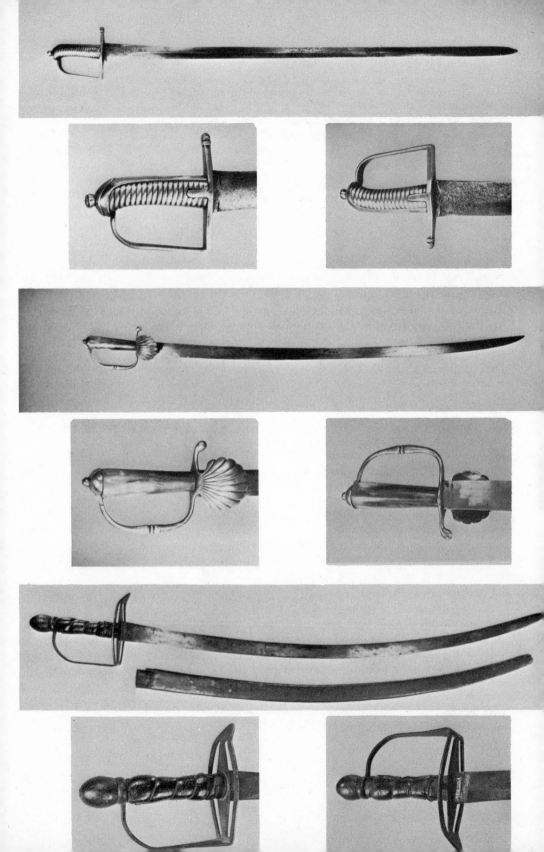

## S.121 AMERICAN HORSEMAN SABER                    Circa 1775-1783

Much of this wooden grip has been worn away, but it still portrays a type of long horseman saber produced for colonial troops over blacksmith forges. The flat cap pommel is fastened to the wide sweeping guard, which finally terminates in a down-turned blunted quillon. Its single-edged 37″ blade includes a shallow fuller which originates 2″ below the hilt and extends for 32″. The false edge is 7½″ long. No marks are visible.

Length: 42¾″                                          Hilt: Iron
Blade: 37″ × 1¼″                                      Weight: 2.0 lbs.

*Author's Collection*


## S.122 AMERICAN SABER                              Circa 1775-1783

This wooden grip has a spiraling brass wire set into the crest of the carved ribs. The ferrules are each ⅜″ high, and the ball pommel includes decorative ridges. The slightly curved, single-edged blade with its clipped point is in a style used on British light-dragoon swords. It is marked with the name HARVEY (an English cutler) inside the figure of a running fox.

Length: 36¾″                                          Hilt: Brass
Blade: 30½″ × 1⅜″                                     Weight: 2.0 lbs.

*Author's Collection*


## S.123 AMERICAN HORSEMAN SABER                     Circa 1779-1783

The interesting hilt illustrated here has an ivory grip with narrow ribbing, set in a ½″ base and ⅝″ top ferrules. Its flattened guard sweeps down under the hilt in a constant curve, ending in a broad-ended quillon. Note the unusual pierced heart design forward of the blade. The four openings cut in the knuckle bow reach up past its midpoint. This is usually indicative of swords produced late in the Revolution or during the 1780's. The blade is typical of colonial wartime manufacture: single-edged, curved, and flat-sided (no fuller).

Length: 39¾″                                          Hilt: Iron
Blade: 34⅝″ × 1¼″                                     Weight: 1.9 lbs.

*Hermann W. Williams, Jr., Collection*

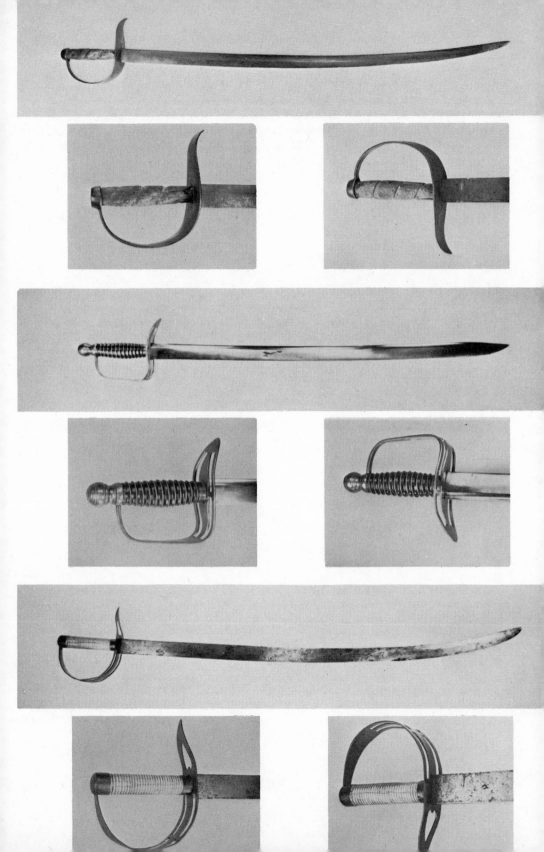

## S.124 AMERICAN HORSEMAN SABER                    Circa 1775-1783

The high-domed pommel on this sword was probably designed from earlier British dragoon sabers (S.87–S.88). But the remainder of the weapon illustrates many American characteristics: its wooden grip has no leather covering (only decorative brass wire spiraled along its ridges); the flat stirrup guard shows two pierced openings opposite each side of the blade (ending in a rounded quillon); the long, flat, single-edged curving blade has no fullers, yet does include a clipped point. Its only marking is "VIII" cut into the blade's top edge.

Length: 41″                                            Hilt: Brass
Blade: 34¾″ × 1⅜″                                      Weight: 2.5 lbs.

*Author's Collection*


## S.125 EUROPEAN SMALL SWORD                         Circa 1700

The "small sword" is essentially a thin blade, designed for thrust and dexterity. It was the popular eighteenth-century civilian style, and the most common British officers' side arm prior to 1750. A majority of American officers carried them during the Revolution since, as the contemporary civilian pattern, they were available. This early example has a pommel, oval in profile, but squared in cross section. Notice its hexagonal knuckle bow, plus the large and unequal *pas-d'âne* (through which two fingers were reportedly thrust). Its flat counterguard is bilobate.

Length: 40¼″                                           Hilt: Brass
Blade: 33⅜″ × ⅞″                                       Weight: .9 lb.

*Author's Collection*


## S.126 EUROPEAN SMALL SWORD                         Circa 1740-1750

An early variation in the small sword was the colichemarde blade. It is wide just below the hilt for about 8″, and then narrows suddenly to a thin profile which tapers to the point. This allows greater strength near the guard for receiving an opponent's blow—without sacrificing lightness near the tip. The blade here is hexagonal in cross section, with engraved panels on its faces. Notice that the *pas-d'âne* in the fine steel hilt are losing their roundness as they begin to reduce in size. The colichemarde continued in use as late as 1780.

Length: 38¾″                                           Hilt: Steel
Blade: 32½″ × 1″                                        Weight: 1.0 lb.

*Author's Collection*

300

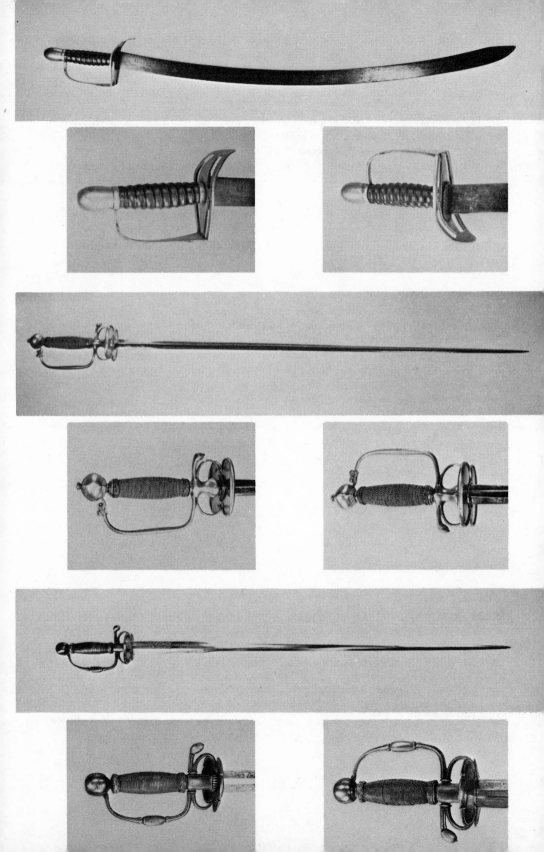

**S.127 EUROPEAN SMALL SWORD**  Circa 1720-1740

During this period, the *pas-d'âne* began to reduce in size; the knuckle bow lost some of its squared shape; its teardrop finial on the quillon ceased to project beyond the edge of the bilobate counterguard; and raised decoration appeared on the hilt. Its ball-style pommel is also beginning to grow taller into a more ovoid shape. The two-edged blade illustrated is a modified colichemarde style (see S.126), with three narrow fullers extending for 9¾" below the hilt.

Length: 39⅜"  Hilt: Brass
Blade: 33" × 1"  Weight: 1.3 lbs.

*Author's Collection*

**S.128 SMALL SWORD**  Circa 1750-1770

Small swords with plain hilts such as this one were worn by many American officers during the French and Indian Wars and the Revolution. As the prevailing pattern of side arm they were already available, without requiring further investment for a true military style. Brass wire covers the grip, while the pommel has assumed a modified urn shape. Its dished counterguard is smaller, and bilobate in shape. The *pas-d'âne* are also reduced in size (although one is still larger than the other). The hilt is brass, with traces of an original silver finish. Its blade is triangular.

Length: 37⅜"  Hilt: Brass (Silvered)
Blade: 31¾" × 1⅛"  Weight: .9 lb.

*Author's Collection*

**S.129 EUROPEAN SMALL SWORD**  Circa 1760-1770

About 1760, some small swords began to acquire the boat-shaped counterguard illustrated at the right. Notice that it also includes a second quillon (under the knuckle bow), and that the *pas-d'âne* by this stage was only vestigial. Spiraled channels on most parts of the hilt (gadrooning) was another popular style of this period. The triangular straight blade has concave surfaces on the two outboard sides, and two narrow deep fullers in the center of the wide inboard face.

Length: 35½"  Hilt: Bronze
Blade: 29⅝" × 1"  Weight: .9 lb.

*Author's Collection*

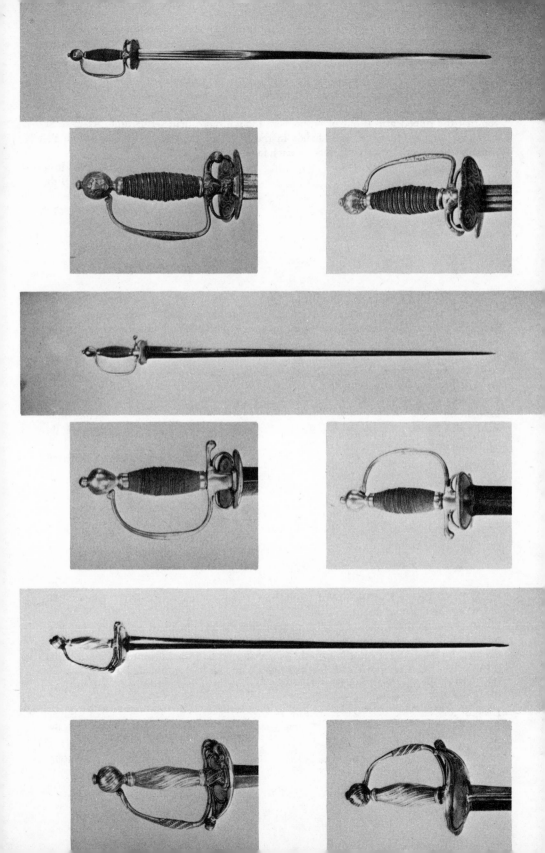

## S.130 AMERICAN SMALL SWORD                Circa 1760-1780

It usually took a decade or more for European sword patterns to be accepted in the colonies. This American-made arm still has a modified urn pommel, fairly sizable *pas-d'âne,* and bilobate counterguard—which were popular in Europe years earlier. Notice too that the ribbed grip is out of proportion, though more than serviceable. As in most cases, its quillon's teardrop finial bends in the outboard direction. The blade is three-sided, with a slightly concave surface on each face.

Length: 33¾″                                       Hilt: Iron
Blade: 27⅛″                                  Weight: .9 lb.

*Warren M. Moore Collection*

## S.131 EUROPEAN SMALL SWORD              Circa 1770-1785

By the 1770's, the counterguard on some small swords had begun to assume an elliptical outline. The second quillon remains under the knuckle bow, and the *pas-d'âne* have almost flattened into extinction. Decorative pierced steel as seen in the ovoid pommel and guard were also fashionable. The "sword knot" shown was more common prior to 1725, but continued through this period. It was meant to fasten around the owner's wrist to prevent his dropping the weapon when in use. The scabbard is wrapped in parchment.

Length: 38¾″                                     Hilt: Steel
Blade: 32⅛″                                 Weight: .9 lb.

*Warren M. Moore Collection*

## S.132 ENGLISH SILVER SMALL SWORD           Circa 1726

During the first two decades of the 1700's, British small swords reverted to the plain-hilt style seen in these photographs. This specific weapon is hallmarked "1726," but is a good example of the simplicity developed during the preceding decade, and later adopted by many American silversmiths in the second half of the century (see S. 136, S.137). The hilt is wrapped with braided silver wire, while the knuckle bow still retains the squared profile. Note too that the *pas-d'âne* are already beginning to flatten. The blade is triangular, with concave faces.

Length: 35⅝″                                    Hilt: Silver
Blade: 29″ × 1″                               Weight .8 lb.

*Author's Collection*

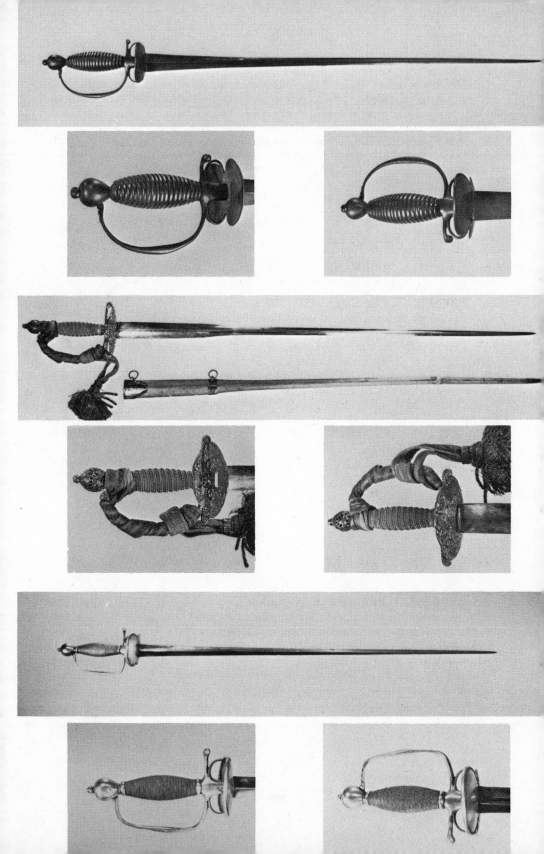

**S.133 EUROPEAN SILVER SMALL SWORD**                    **Circa 1750-1760**

The decorative use of "gadrooning" (channeled ridges) came into style about mid-century. This silver-hilted example demonstrates the degree to which it was carried. Washington wore a French sword of this style during the Braddock expedition in 1755 (S.150). The grip is wrapped in braided silver wire, while the counterguard is bilobate in shape. Its *pas-d'âne* are small, but still large enough for the fingers. The triangular blade includes a fuller in the center of the wide inboard face; the two smaller faces are concave.

Length: 40″                                              Hilt: Silver
Blade: 33⅛″ × 1¼″                                        Weight: .9 lb.

*Author's Collection*


**S.134 FRENCH SILVER SMALL SWORD**                     **Circa 1740-1760**

The technique of using pierced decorations in the hilt seems to have gained favor about 1730, and continued to appear in the evolving patterns until the 1780's. This French example has its grip wound in silver braid, a pierced oval pommel and capstan rivet, plus raised decorations on the two flat sides of the thin knuckle bow. Its colichemarde blade is engraved with the popular French phrases NE ME TIREZ PAS SANS RAISONS and NE ME REMETTEZ POINT SANS HONNEUR. Each of the three faces is concave; a center fuller appears on the wide inboard surface.

Length: 39⅛″                                             Hilt: Silver
Blade: 32½″ × 1¼″                                        Weight: .7 lb.

*Author's Collection*


**S.135 ENGLISH SILVER SMALL SWORD**                    **Circa 1755**

This elaborate "boat-guard" weapon is hallmarked "1755" by George Fayle of London. Its rococo decoration is an indication of the elaborate hilts produced in Europe—which seem to have found little favor in America prior to the Revolutionary War. The pommel is a modified urn shape, while the two quillons have opposite curving finials. Notice too that the *pas-d'âne* are almost completely flattened. Its narrow triangular blade is typical of the later 1780 period. The pierced sword carrier fits over the waist belt; its chains hold the scabbard.

Length: 38⅝″                                             Hilt: Silver
Blade: 32″ × ⅝″                                          Weight: 1.0 lb.

*Lewis H. Gordon, Jr., Collection*

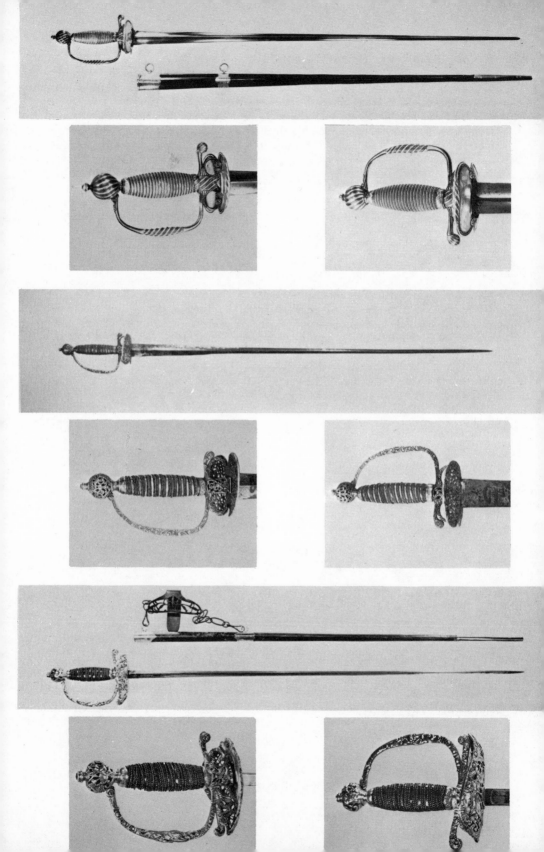

**S.136 AMERICAN SILVER SMALL SWORD**                    Circa 1750-1755

Simple but well-proportioned silver-hilted swords were being produced by American craftsmen as early as 1690. Contrary to the English practice, few of them were marked. This one bears the touch mark (on the inboard side of the knuckle bow, and the quillon) of Timothy Bontecou, Jr., of New Haven, Connecticut (1723–1789). It also has the name of an owner engraved on a shell of the bilobate counterguard: DAVID DAY 1755. The triangular blade includes floral patterns near the hilt, and is of the colichemarde pattern.

Length: 34″                                             Hilt: Silver
Blade: 27¾″ × 1″                                        Weight: .8 lb.

*Hermann W. Williams, Jr., Collection*

**S.137 AMERICAN SILVER SMALL SWORD**                    Circa 1745-1755

This specimen is another good example of the small-sword styling in the colonies prior to the Revolution. Silver-mounted side arms were worn by many officers (primarily as dress swords) during the war. Its maker's name, HURD (Jacob Hurd, Boston, 1702–1758), is visible (in an elliptical cartouche) on the upper face of the inboard counterguard. The grip is wrapped in silver wire. Floral designs of gold inlay appear on the triangular blade just under the guard. It tapers evenly toward the tip, and adds a center fuller on the inboard side 4″ from the hilt.

Length: 35″                                             Hilt: Silver
Blade: 28⅞″ × 1″                                        Weight: .8 lb.

*Dr. John K. Lattimer Collection*

**S.138 AMERICAN SILVER SMALL SWORD**                    Circa 1765-1770

The boat-guard pattern as shown on this small sword reached its greatest popularity with the colonists after 1760. The name of the swordsmith, J OTIS (Jonathan Otis, Newport, Rhode Island, and Middletown, Connecticut), appears on the outboard face of the knuckle bow next to the round pommel. Notice that like the European guards (S.129, S.135) there are double quillons, while the *pas-d'âne* are reduced in size. Its colichemarde triangular blade has blued and gilded designs near the hilt.

Length: 32¾″                                            Hilt: Silver
Blade: 25½″ × 1¾″                                       Weight: 1.1 lbs.

*Hermann W. Williams, Jr., Collection*

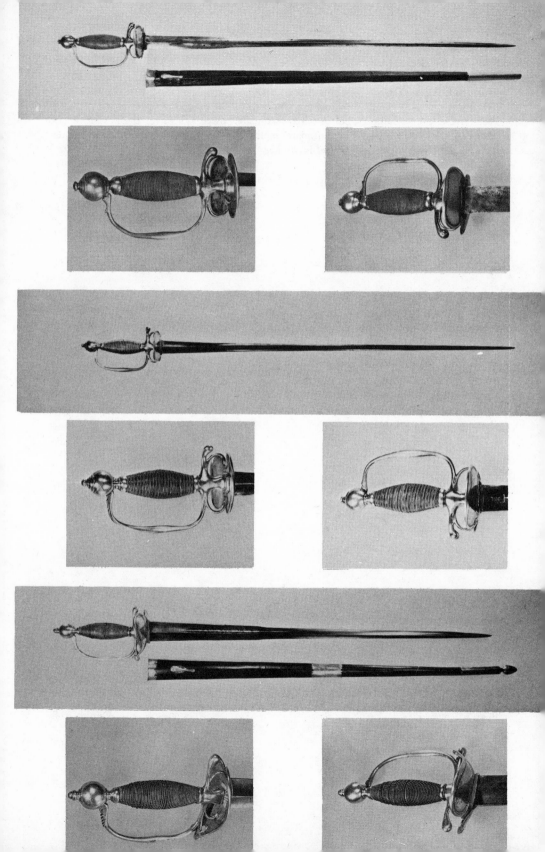

## S.139 ENGLISH SILVER HANGER                         Circa 1690-1710

This is a silver-hilted hanger of a type believed to have been worn by British foot and naval officers about 1700 (see S.1). Its style of touch mark (in the knuckle bow) indicates probable manufacture on the Continent. The smooth grip is horn, with a ¼″ base ferrule, plus a cap pommel. A narrow knuckle bow divides near the bottom to provide a supporting branch for the outboard shell guard. Its quillon turns down into a disk finial, while the single-edged curved blade has two central fullers (⅜″ × 19½″, ⅛″ × 20″).

Length: 29¼″                                              Hilt: Silver
Blade: 24½″ × 1″                                          Weight: 1.0 lb.

*Author's Collection*


## S.140 ENGLISH SILVER HUNTING SWORD                   Circa 1742

The popularity of silver carried over into hunting swords too. This British piece includes grotesque masks in relief on virtually every metal part of the hilt. The shell guard, for example, includes heads of a jester, eagle, dog, and stag in the border around a wild central face. Its grip is a combination of alternate panels of light and dark horn. The blade is straight, with a single edge and two fullers (¼″ × 16″, ½″ × 21½″). An English hallmark on the knuckle bow establishes its date as 1742.

Length: 27¾″                                              Hilt: Silver
Blade: 22″ × ⅛″                                          Weight: .9 lb.

*Author's Collection*


## S.141 FRENCH SILVER HUNTING SWORD                    Circa 1767

The almost flat pommel (with capstan rivet) is a typical pattern among silver-hilted hunting swords. It includes a raised grotesque face, with a punched dot design behind it. At the other end of the channeled ebony grip is a ¼″ ferrule, and small S-shaped quillons (each of their finials bears decorative ridges). Its blade has two fullers (1⁄16 × 9½″, ⅜″ × 13¾″). The French touch marks are 1767. These short-bladed arms served principally as symbols of rank for American officers.

Length: 23¼″                                              Hilt: Silver
Blade: 17½″ × 1″                                          Weight: .6 lb.

*Author's Collection*

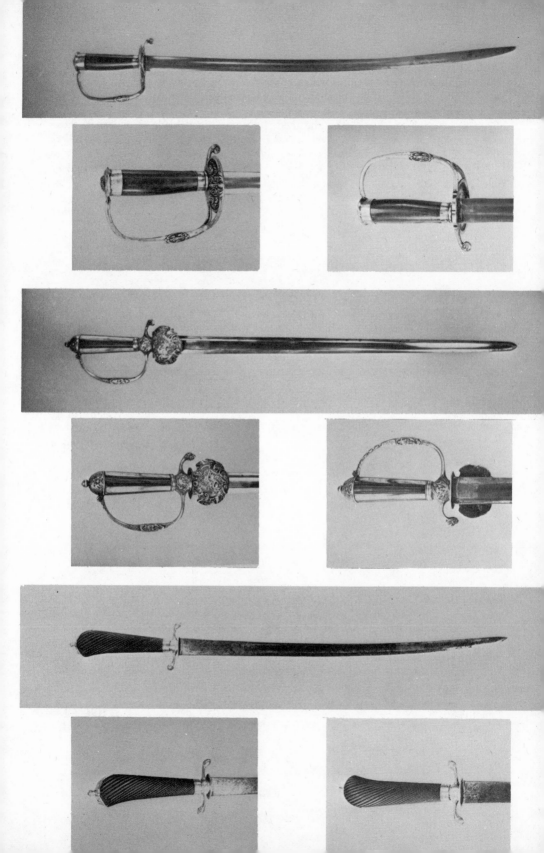

## S.142 ENGLISH SILVER HUNTING SWORD Circa 1765-1780

This hilt has a semi-flat pommel with a grotesque face raised on its surface. The spiral-fluted grip is ivory which has been tinted green (commonly done). Raised decorations are also present on the S-shaped quillons. Notice too the caplike cover at the base of the hilt to fit over the scabbard when sheathed. Its single-edged blade is typical of those used on many of these British silver-mounted hunting swords. There are two fullers (⅛″ × 17″, ¼″ × 23″). No hallmarks are visible.

Length: 30″
Blade: 24½″ × 1″

Hilt: Silver
Weight: 1.1 lbs.

*Author's Collection*

## S.143 AMERICAN SILVER HUNTING SWORD Circa 1760-1780

The black ebony grip of this sword includes a ½″-high base ferrule and a braided silver wire in the channels. A simulated pommel has been carved at the top, with a flat silver button mounted in the center. The S-shaped silver guard is rather plain; it bears the initials "RH" in the face of each finial. The straight single-edged imported-type blade has two fullers (1/16″ × 15½″, ⅜″ × 20¼″). A false edge extends back 5⅛″ from the tip.

Length: 29¾″
Blade: 24⅛″ × 1″

Hilt: Silver
Weight: .8 lb.

*Dr. John K. Lattimer Collection*

## S.144 AMERICAN SILVER HUNTING SWORD Circa 1770-1783

A silver bottom ferrule (½″) and a flat-cap pommel secure the ends of this spiraled ivory grip. One finial of the flat curved quillons is connected to the pommel by an open-link chain. The interesting aspect of this weapon, however, is the "US" surcharge visible on the blade. Since this marking was normally affixed to arms issued by the Congress, it is unusual to see one on a silver-hilted sword (most privately purchased). If authentic, it may be a remounted blade. There are two fullers (⅛″ × 12¼″, ¾″ × 21″). The quillon bears "WB" in a rectangular cartouche.

Length: 30¼″
Blade: 25½″

Hilt: Silver
Weight: 1.1 lbs.

*Edmund W. Budde, Jr., Collection*

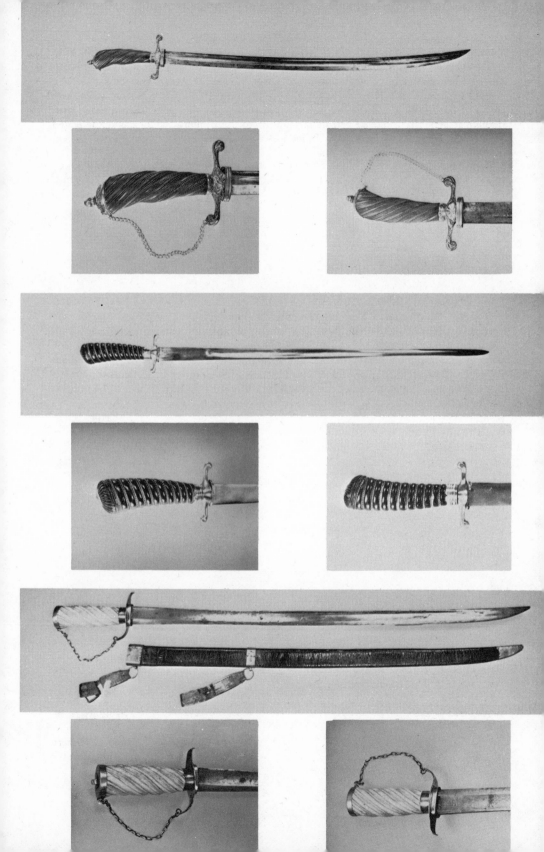

## S.145 AMERICAN SILVER HUNTING SWORD — Circa 1750-1775

The elementary hunting sword pattern in this illustration is marked C CHOUSO (in a sunken cartouche on both upper and lower quillon faces). He is believed to have resided in New York's Hudson Valley during the mid-1700's. Its grip consists of two pieces of horn fastened to the tang by two rivets. The flat-cap pommel also has a rivet through it. A high (¾″) base ferrule is soldered to the quillons, while the single-edged slightly curved blade has a shallow fuller (½″ wide), reaching from the hilt to the end of a 4″ false edge.

Length: 32¼″  
Blade: 27¼″ × 1⅛″  

Hilt: Silver  
Weight: 1.2 lbs.

*Harold L. Peterson Collection*

## S.146 ENGLISH SILVER HUNTING SWORD — Circa 1750-1780

Lion-headed specimens like this one were popular side arms with colonial officers during the French and Indian Wars and the Revolution. Its spiral-grooved grip again illustrates the contemporary practice of tinting ivory (green). The guard has a raised panoply of arms for a center design and an animal head at the end of each quillon. Its silver chain acts in place of a knuckle bow, while the familiar curved cutting blade is again evident (two fullers: ⅛″ × 17½″, ⅜″ × 24¾″). Hallmarks on the quillon are faint, but include "W.K" in a rectangular cartouche.

Length: 32½″  
Blade: 26½″ × 1″  

Hilt: Silver  
Weight: 1.0 lb.

*Author's Collection*

## S.147 SILVER HUNTING SWORD — Circa 1765-1780

This unique hilt includes a lion head as a carved upper end of the ivory grip (tinted green). Only a capstan rivet projects above it. The silver base ferrule (¼″) and simple guard (with opposite pointing finials) follow more conventional styling. Its short straight blade has one edge; a wide fuller begins under a ⅛″ *ricasso*, and after 6¼″ forms two smaller fullers which continue for 14½″. No marks are visible.

Length: 27¾″  
Blade: 22⅛″ × ⅞″  

Hilt: Silver  
Weight: .7 lb.

*Gene E. Miller Collection*

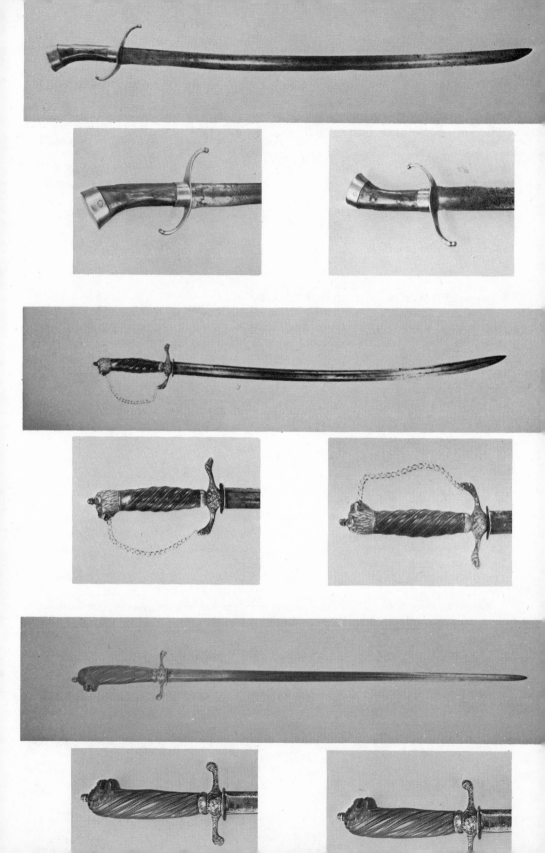

### S.148 WASHINGTON SILVER HUNTING SWORD          Circa 1750-1770

This sword is believed to have been owned by George Washington prior to and early in the American Revolution. It was reportedly given to him by his brother, John Augustine Washington, who received it back at a later date. It is typical of the popular colonial style—the ribbed ivory hilt has a ¼″ base ferrule and a silver lion-head pommel. The S-shaped quillons are connected by a chain from one finial to a ring in the lion's mouth. Its blade is of the hunting-sword pattern—single-edged, slightly curved, plus two fullers (³⁄₁₆″ × 24¼″, ⅜″ × 29⅛″).

Length: 35½″                                                          Hilt: Silver
Blade: 29¾″ × 1″                                                 Weight: 1.0 lb.

*Dr. John K. Lattimer Collection*

### S.149 WASHINGTON SILVER HUNTING SWORD          Circa 1775

What is considered the principal service sword worn by General Washington during the Revolutionary War is illustrated here. Its green-tinted ivory grip is wound with silver wire and has a flat silver pommel. Note the animal-head finials on the S-shaped quillons, plus the typical two-fuller blade. Silver bands on the leather scabbard are marked J BAILEY/FISH KILL (American maker).

Length: 36″                          Blade: 30″                          Hilt: Silver

*The Smithsonian Institution Collection*

### S.150 WASHINGTON SWORDS                                   (left to right)

*a. Small Sword:* believed worn on the Braddock expedition in 1755; hallmarks indicate a French origin and later importation into England (1753–1754); silver wire is missing from the wooden grip (see S.133).

Length: 36½″                          Blade: 30″                          Hilt: Silver

*b. Mourning Sword:* typical of plain swords worn for funerals and mourning periods. Its blade is triangular.

Length: 41½″                          Blade: 35″                          Hilt: Silver

*c. State ("Dress") Sword:* thought to have been worn when resigning his commission in 1783, and when inaugurated President in 1789. Circa 1756; blade triangular.

Length: 40″                          Blade: 33½″                          Hilt: Silver

*The Mount Vernon Ladies' Association Collection*

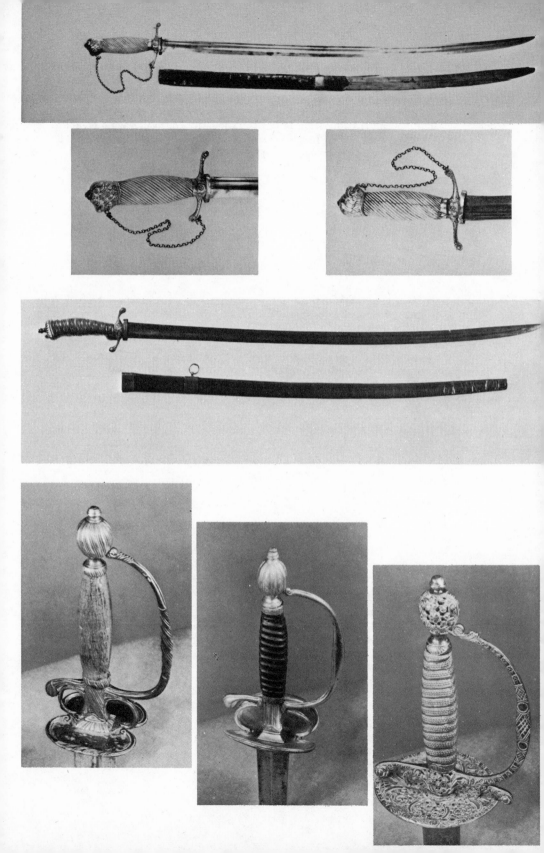

## S.151 ENGLISH SILVER HUNTING SWORD                    Circa 1770-1780

An ivory grip, wound with a flat silver band and two bordering twisted wires, is another style seen on British hilts of this era. At the center of the brief guard is a pierced circular design (note: its present quillons are not original to the piece), while a chain connects the upturned finial with a ring in the lion's mouth. The blade again conforms to the single-edged cutting style. Its two fullers measure ⅛″ × 16¾″, and ⅜″ × 24″. English hallmarks on the pommel include "FT" in a rectangular cartouche.

Length: 31⅛″                                              Hilt: Silver
Blade: 25⅛″ × 1″                                          Weight .8 lb.

*Author's Collection*


## S.152 SILVER HUNTING SWORD                            Circa 1765-1780

Although the guard technically qualifies this arm as a hunting sword (no fixed knuckle bow), the size and weight of both its blade and hilt are equivalent to that of many short sabers. The grip has a silver band and wire around an ivory center (see S.151). Shell fluting is visible on the guard. Notice too the oversized lion-head pommel and double strands of chain. Its eighteenth-century links are formed in "figure 8's," with the upper and lower halves at right angles. No markings are visible. Swords of this type were worn by American foot officers and some British naval officers.

Length: 33½″                                              Hilt: Silver
Blade: 27″ × 1¼″                                          Weight: 1.1 lbs.

*Author's Collection*


## S.153 AMERICAN SILVER HUNTING SWORD                   Circa 1765-1775

This American-style hunting sword is another with a long blade (27″). Its ivory hilt has a spiraling silver wire, while a chain connects the mouth of its rudimentary lion pommel with an upturned quillon. At the base of the hilt is a cap overhanging the blade to fit as a cover for the scabbard when sheathed. The markings "IWG" on the quillon probably stand for John Ward Gilman, a well-known New Hampshire silversmith of the period. The single-edged, curved blade has one fuller (¼″ × 20½″).

Length: 32¾″                                              Hilt: Silver
Blade: 27 × 1½″                                           Weight: 1.1 lbs.

*Hermann W. Williams, Jr., Collection*

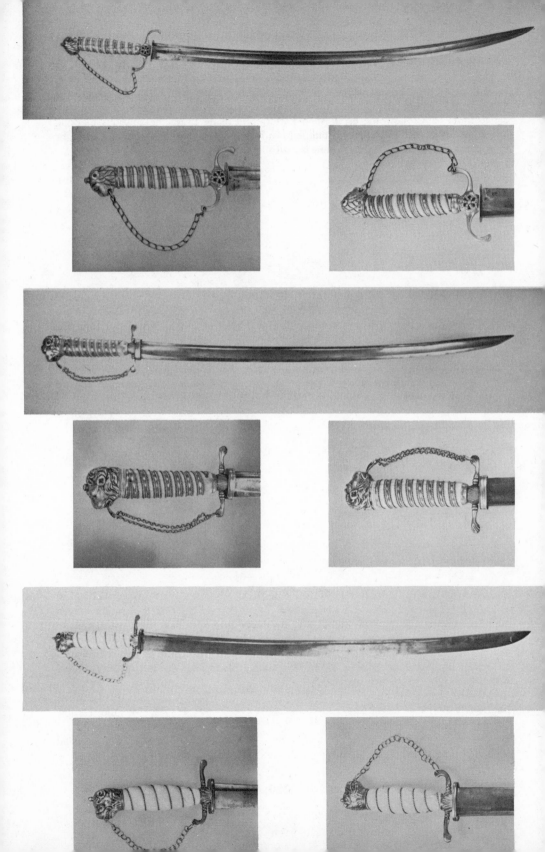

## S.154 AMERICAN SILVER HUNTING SWORD    Circa 1765-1775

The tapering grip of green-tinted ivory was a style used on American silver hilts prior to and during the Revolutionary War. It probably had silver wire originally tracing the grooves. The lion-head pommel, S-shaped quillons (with bird heads as finials), and connecting chain follow the established pattern. Its blade bears the spurious marking ANDRE FARARA (with interspersed stamped heads—usually a German practice). Straight lines parallel the engraving, but there is no fuller.

Length: 32¼″                           Hilt: Silver
Blade: 25¾″                           Weight: 1.1 lbs.

*Edmund W. Budde, Jr., Collection*


## S.155 AMERICAN SILVER HUNTING SWORD    Circa 1772

Just as the lion was the favorite animal-head pommel, the dog head was one of the rarest. This fine example is the product of David Hall of Philadelphia, and from the work lavished upon it, was probably his personal weapon. The scabbard throat is inscribed DAVID HALL PHILAD., with a date scratched above it: 3–9–72. On the opposite side are his initials, "DH" (script within an oval). The chain connecting the pommel with the guard has links which increase in size at the center and diminish toward each end. Every link is also stamped "DH."

Length: 31″                           Hilt: Silver
Blade: 25″ × 1″                       Weight: 1.0 lb.

*Dr. John K. Lattimer Collection*


## S.156 AMERICAN SILVER HUNTING SWORD    Circa 1770-1780

The elliptical counterguard with pierced openings seen in this illustration was a popular American pattern in the 1770's. An ivory grip (¼″ base ferrule) mounts a "full-nosed" lion-head pommel—which connects with the guard by an open-link silver chain. The blade is single-edged and curved; its fuller (¼″) is at the back and measures 19″ in length (the false edge is 4½″). This simple blade, like the hilt, is probably of American origin. No marks are visible.

Length: 29″                           Hilt: Silver
Blade: 23¼″ × 1⅛″                     Weight: 1.1 lbs.

*Hermann W. Williams, Jr., Collection*

320

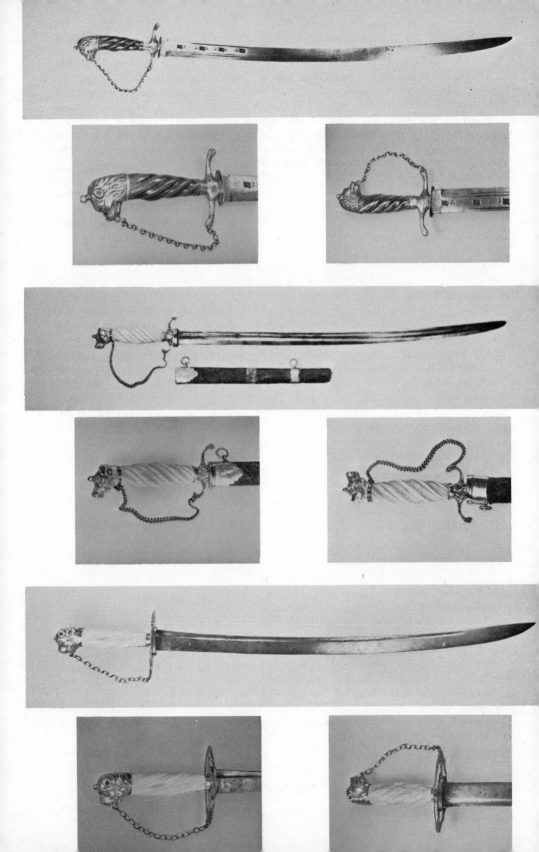

## S.157 AMERICAN SILVER HUNTING SWORD                    Circa 1770-1780

This fine dog-headed specimen was Ethan Allen's dress sword. It was made by Ephraim Brasher of New York (1744-1810) who often, as in this case, inserted tiny jewels in the dog's eyes. The pierced elliptical counterguard has a decorative serrated edge on the outboard side, but a smooth inboard surface (edged with an inlaid iron strip to prevent wear and tarnish stains to the pants). Its grip is ivory, and the silver pommel has a thin gold wash. The curved blade is of the contemporary two-fuller style; it still bears an early British crown above a "GR" cipher.

Length: 32⅞"                                                              Hilt: Silver
Blade: 27" × 1¼"                                                    Weight: 1.3 lbs.

*Dr. John K. Lattimer Collection*

## S.158 AMERICAN SILVER HORSEMAN SABER                  Circa 1770-1783

The lion pommel in this example was made by the usual practice of taking two hollow shell-like halves and soldering them together along a middle seam. The elliptical counterguard, with its diamond-shaped center and radiating spoke construction, is also interesting. Most of the hilt follows a popular practice of having a layer of silver applied over a copper base ("Sheffield" coating). The imported three-fuller curved blade still shows traces of its original bluing (usually applied only to the top 14"-15").

Length: 39⅜"                                                             Hilt: Silver
Blade: 33¾" × 1⅜"                                                   Weight: 1.5 lbs.

*Author's Collection*

## S.159 AMERICAN SILVER SHORT SABER                          Circa 1780

In the late 1770's and early 1780's, the formal knuckle bow began to find more favor on American silver swords. This one has an ebony grip wrapped with a silver band and seated in a ¼" base ferrule. The flat guard includes decorative openings around the grip and about one-third of the distance up the knuckle bow (note: by the mid-1780's they commonly extended up past the middle point). A maker's touch, "WR" (in a rectangular cartouche), is visible on the hilt. The name A STORY on the scabbard's throat was probably an owner's. Its blade has two fullers (⅛" × 17½", ⅜" × 25").

Length: 31⅞"                                                             Hilt: Silver
Blade: 26"                                                              Weight: 1.4 lbs.

*Edmund W. Budde, Jr., Collection*

322

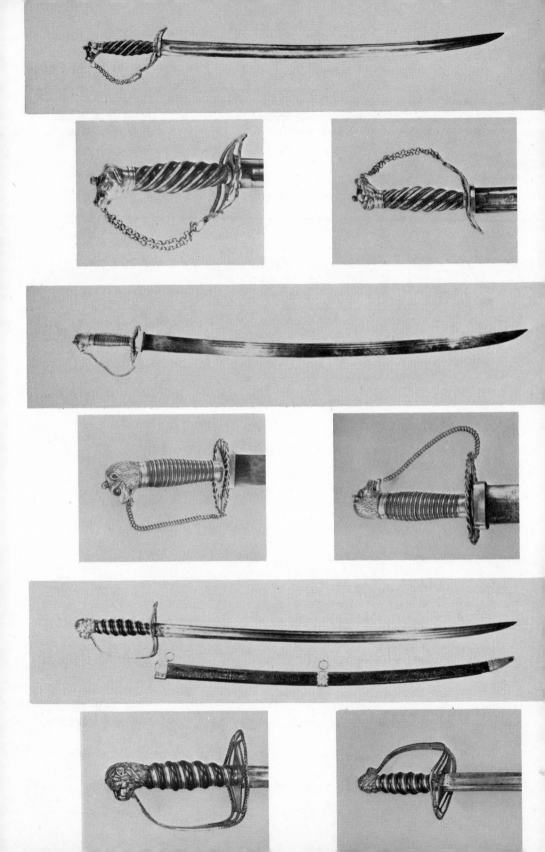

## S.160 ENGLISH SILVER SHORT SWORD                    Circa 1777-1778

Here is a good illustration of the open-guard design which became popular during the Revolutionary War and through the 1780's. This one is hallmarked 1777-1778. The spiraled ivory grip is tinted green, while its silver lion head is much more finished than the usual American product. The blade appears to have been shortened at some time (and given a clipped point). This was often done to prevent undue hindrance when worn in the field. The blue and gold blade decoration became more stylish in the decade following the war.

Length: 29⅜″                                          Hilt: Silver
Blade: 23⅝″ × 1½″                                     Weight: 1.0 lb.

*Author's Collection*


## S.161 AMERICAN SILVER SHORT SABER                   Circa 1778-1783

Further open-work design is pictured in this counterguard and knuckle bow. Like most of the lion heads, this backstrap and bird's-head pommel have been formed by joining two shell-like halves along a median seam. The silver wire–wrapped grip has a ½″ ferrule at the bottom. Its wide, single-fullered (½″ × 20¾″) blade is of a military weight—and probably of American origin. The remains of crudely engraved sun, moon, and star shapes are still to be seen. A false edge measures 7½″. There are no hallmarks.

Length: 32⅜″                                          Hilt: Silver
Blade: 27½″ × 1⅜″                                     Weight: .8 lb.

*Author's Collection*


## S.162 AMERICAN SILVER HUNTING SWORD                 Circa 1775-1780

Eagle-head pommels were being made during the 1770's, and some early styles are illustrated here. They reached their great era of acceptance in the following decades, however, after the eagle became the national symbol (about 1782). This primitive version has a thin silver foil applied over an iron base. It is also interesting to note that the handmade links of the chain guard increase in size toward the center. The single-edged curved blade includes a thin fuller at the back (⅛″ × 20¾″). Its false edge is 5½″ long.

Length: 31½″                                          Hilt: Silver
Blade: 26½″ × 1¼″                                     Weight: 1.4 lbs.

*Hermann W. Williams, Jr., Collection*

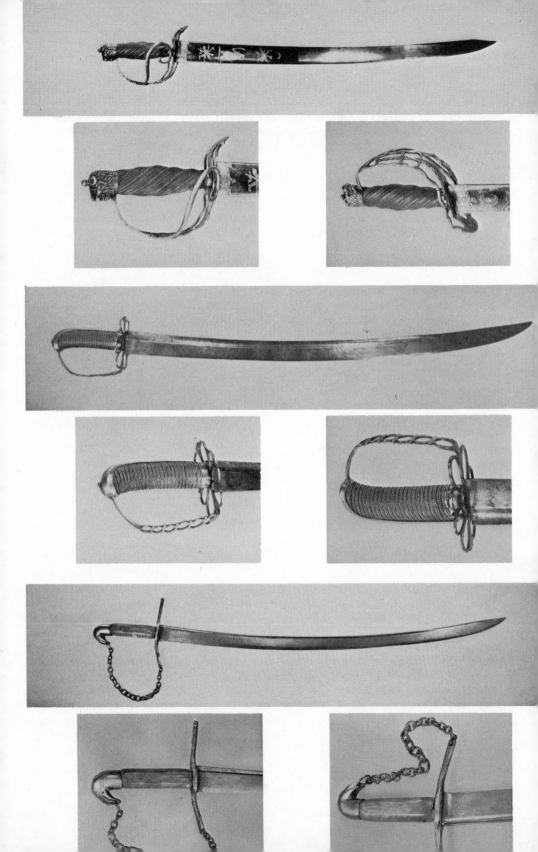

## S.163 AMERICAN SILVER HUNTING SWORD Circa 1775-1780

The blade of this sword is apparently one of the three-fuller style imported in such large quantities by the colonists. It was probably cut in length for use on the lighter hilt. Another early type of eagle pommel is included, along with simple eagle finials on each end of the S-shaped quillons. The silver finish appears to have been applied over a brass or iron base. Its vertically ribbed ivory grip has a ⅛" bottom ferrule. As seen in the photograph, the upper half of the blade was originally blued (in the accepted style of the day).

Length: 31⅝"  Hilt: Silver
Blade: 26⅝" × 1⅜"  Weight: 1.5 lbs.

*Hermann W. Williams, Jr., Collection*


## S.164 AMERICAN SILVER HUNTING SWORD Circa 1780-1785

More refined eagle heads began to appear during the last years of the Revolutionary War. Collectors tend to classify them as being of the "Baltimore" or "Philadelphia" eagle styles. This rounded profile, lacking any tufts of feathers (and looking more like a pigeon), is from the "Baltimore" school. The grip is of wood, with twisted silver wire in its channels. Notice that the ends of the quillons also have rudimentary eagle features. The single-edged, two-fuller blade is like the European type on similar side arms (S.146). No hallmarks are visible.

Length: 32⅜"  Hilt: Silver
Blade: 26⅛" × 1⅛"  Weight: 1.1 lbs.

*Author's Collection*


## S.165 AMERICAN SILVER HUNTING SWORD Circa 1780-1785

The large full beak, long head, and rear tuft of feathers on this eagle pommel are indicative of the "Philadelphia" pattern. Its spiraled ivory grip has two ferrules (¼" at base, ½" at top). As in the previous example (S. 164), the finials of the S-shaped quillons repeat the eagle-head motif. Its curved two-fuller (¼" × 18½", ⅜" × 27") cutting blade is of the contemporary style (false edge 10" long). No touch marks or engravings are visible. The original chain guard is missing.

Length: 34⅜"  Hilt: Silver
Blade: 27⅞" × 1⅛"  Weight: 1.1 lbs.

*Warren M. Moore Collection*

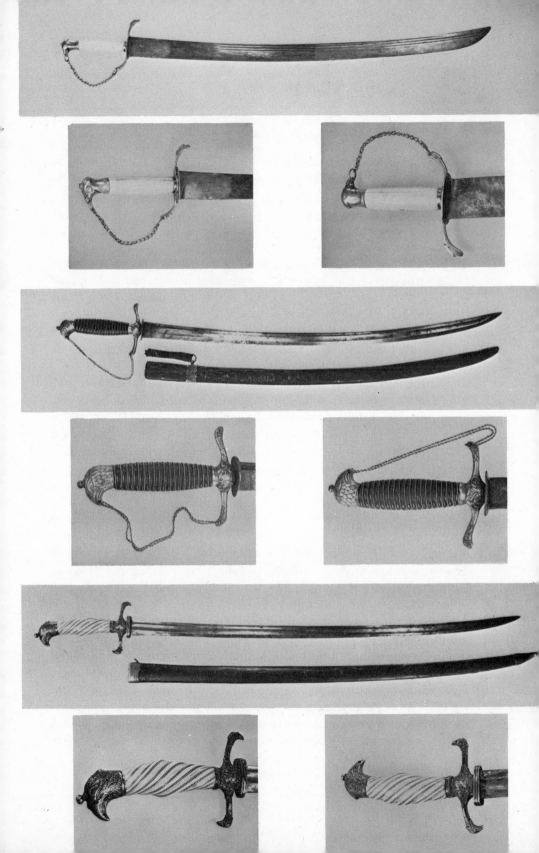

# 8 | POLEARMS

ALTHOUGH THE LONG INFANTRY pike officially ceased as the basic weapon of war about 1700, polearms persisted in limited use until the nineteenth century. During the colonial and American Revolutionary War era, they served mostly as symbols of rank. Three fundamental types will be considered here: the halberd, spontoon, and trench spear ("pike").

**THE HALBERD:** This weapon was the combination of a battle-ax-type blade with a spear point above it, mounted on a six- to seven-foot shaft ("haft"). A "butt point" or cone of metal covered the other end. It had been developed for warfare in the fourteenth century, but by the 1700's was surviving mostly as a designation of rank for infantry sergeants. Court and municipal officials also used them in civil ceremonies, as did many night watchmen on their lonely rounds.

Contemporary military theory held that a sergeant should be free to give full attention to his men in the line of battle, and not be encumbered with the involved musket-firing procedure. Issuing him the broad-bladed halberd on a tall haft was intended to provide a weapon of sorts, while making him easily identifiable to his men. The sharpened edges on many of them testify to actual use at close quarters.

Unfortunately, they were not practical in the heavily wooded areas of North America. British warrants of 1768–1769 specified fusils or carbines for grenadier sergeants, but still required sergeants of battalion companies to carry halberds (PA.1). In spite of this, the ageless ability of fighting men to adapt to local conditions (despite official orders) seems to have won out. This weapon saw limited use with the British Army during the American Revolution—except on garrison duty. It was officially abolished for English troops in 1791.

American forces used the halberd for sergeants at the beginning of the Revolutionary War, but like their opponents, soon dropped them in favor of the bayonet-equipped fusil. The British halberd was quite standardized in design (PA.1), but the colonists created a great variety (PA.4–PA.18).

French and German halberds were closer to the seventeenth-century partisan in shape, i.e., a spear point with symmetrical branches on each side at the base. As in most armies, they were carried by sergeants. Although French grenadier sergeants were allowed muskets and bayonets as early as 1703,

**328**

it wasn't until 1758 that line sergeants were officially permitted to dispense with the polearm (briefly reinstated from 1764 to 1766). Evidence indicates that they were used here during the French and Indian War (PA.22, PA. 23), and reused by some Americans in the Revolution.

It is believed that some halberds were carried by the Germans during our War for Independence. Their spear point tended to be shorter and wider than the standard French style. Another distinctive feature was that their base socket often had a faceted surface, as against the French socket's rounded shape (PA.24, PA.25).

**THE SPONTOON (ALSO ESPONTOON OR HALF-PIKE):** The spontoon of the 1770's was essentially an officer's spear. As the halberd served the sergeant, the spontoon was a badge of rank and semi-weapon for the commissioned officer. It usually consisted of a spear-type head, plus a base pierced with a crossbar or "toggle" (mounted on a long haft by two riveted or nailed straps).

An English warrant in 1743 specifically directed all foot officers to carry one. Yet, General Braddock saw fit to order them left behind during his 1755 expedition into the wilderness. As with the halberd, most English officers in the field seem to have abandoned them in favor of the fusil and bayonet during the American Revolution. The spontoon was discontinued as an official weapon in 1786.

Contrary to British practice, this arm was standard equipment for commissioned officers in the American Army throughout the war. An order to line troops in January 1778 at Valley Forge specified the haft as 6½ feet in length, 1¼ inches thick at the largest part, plus a 1-foot-long iron point (head). It can be assumed, however, that there were many departures from these dimensions, especially among the militia (PA.26–PA.42).

The French spontoon usually had a leaf-shaped blade above a rounded socket. Although an ordinance in 1758 abolished the arm, it was officially reinstated in 1764 before final abandonment in 1766.

German spontoons were of two basic styles. One included a broad blade with an atrophied decorative base (PA.44, PA.45), while the other was shaped in a symmetrically curved design, with decorative piercings through it (PA.46–PA.48). They measured roughly 7½ feet.

**THE PIKE (OR TRENCH SPEAR):** Substantial numbers of American troops were equipped with spears or pikes (8 to 12 feet long) early in the Revolution. Although the shortage of muskets and bayonets was the primary reason for it, many strongly believed in their effectiveness against British bayonet attacks on fortified positions. Substantial numbers of these "trench spears" were recovered at camp sites used from 1775 to 1777 (PA.50–PA.53).

## PA.1 ENGLISH INFANTRY HALBERD — Circa 1740-1780

This was the standard British sergeant's halberd during most of the French and Indian Wars and the Revolution. Its spear point is sharpened on each edge, and unscrews at the joint just above the broad cross-blade. There is a slight ridge down its center. The beak and blade were cut from a flat sheet of iron; they pass through a slot in the base and are held by friction. Neither edge is sharpened. The head measures 14″ to the ring; its straps are 15″ long.

*Author's Collection*

## PA.2 EUROPEAN HALBERD — Circa 1750-1770

Illustrated here is a generic style used in Europe and often copied by the Americans (see PA.17). Both the spear point and cross-blade are one integral piece of iron. Each has a slight median ridge, which intersects in the center, and no edges are sharpened. Three raised rings circle the round base. Its straps are fastened to the haft by six nails on each side. (Note: Long straps also served as protection against an attacker cutting through the wooden haft below the iron head.) The base is engraved R.II.M.B. NO 1. Head and base measure 15½″; the straps are 20¾″.

*Author's Collection*

## PA.3 ENGLISH ARTILLERY HALBERD — Circa 1740-1760

It is believed that this halberd is the type carried in the Royal Artillery during the mid-1700's. Its four-sided top spike measures 13¼″ in length. The sweeping curves of the blade and beak are not sharpened; this indicates that their principal function was as a symbol of rank. They are fastened to a round collar, which has the main shaft pass through its center. Large pierced designs as seen here are unusual for most European halberds of this period. The head (including the base) is 18¼″ long. Each strap (four rivets) extends for 12½″.

*Harold L. Peterson Collection*

330

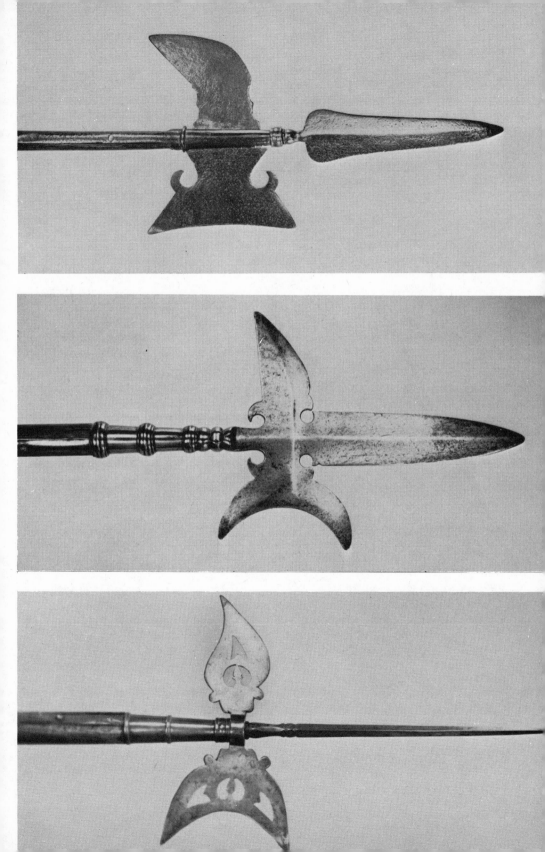

**PA.4 AMERICAN HALBERD**                                    Circa 1690-1710

The extremely crude design and craftsmanship of this American halberd is an indication of the early work by local blacksmiths. The spear point and base were apparently forged in one piece. Then the base was wrapped around the haft, and a beak and blade were added to the sides. The 31½″ straps were also attached separately (four rivets each). None of the edges has been sharpened. The head and base are 16″ long. A small V-shaped mark is stamped into the reverse side.

*Author's Collection*

**PA.5 AMERICAN HALBERD**                                    Circa 1700-1725

The long thin spear point with squared shoulders is indicative of the early date of this example. It is interesting also to note that the haft is octagonal, and held by four straps (each 23″ long). The cross-blade passes through a vertical slot in the squared metal shaft of the head, and is held by a rivet. Its head measures 25″ above the base ring. This particular arm came from Pennsylvania.

*Harold L. Peterson Collection*

**PA.6 AMERICAN HALBERD**                                    Circa 1700-1725

Here is another early halberd from Pennsylvania. The long thin spear point is again evident (sharpened on both edges), while the "petal" pierced designs are of a style still seen on furniture in that area. Notice too the blade's straight profile. It was common on halberds a century prior to this one, and apparently found some favor with the colonists during the early 1700's. The straps have been shortened at some time (total length shown 18½″).

*Joseph E. Fritzinger Collection*

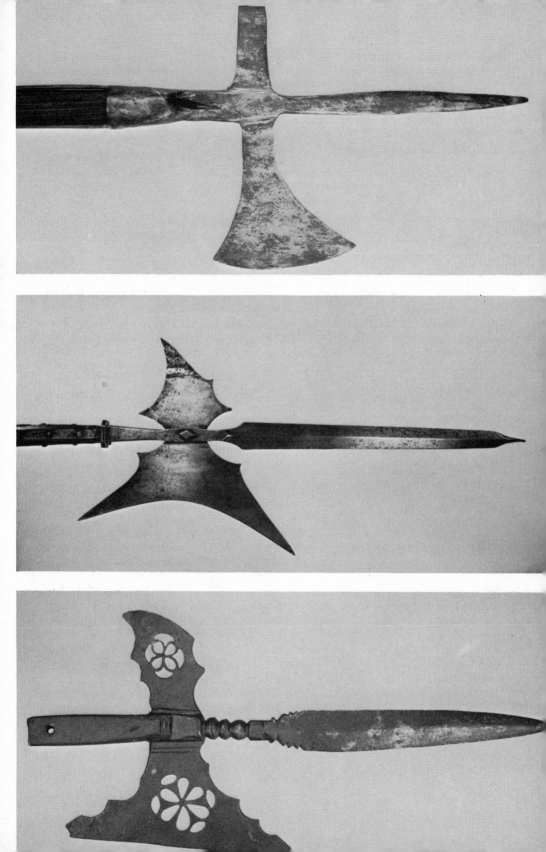

**PA.7 AMERICAN-EUROPEAN HALBERD**                     Circa 1710-1730

This example also illustrates a straight-edged blade. Yet, the spear point is beginning to follow the trend of the eighteenth century by growing wider. It has a middle ridge, plus an abrupt angle at the bottom corners. The beak and blade pass through a vertical slot in the octagonal shaft of the head (fastened by two rivets). Two straps measuring 21¾″ are each held by seven nails. Its head is 15⅝″ long. The haft appears to be original; it has a diameter of 1¼″ and a length of 81½″ below the head ring.

*Author's Collection*

**PA.8 AMERCAN HALBERD**                     Circa 1710-1730

The spear point and cross-blade are united by an alternate method in this case. They were notched to fit together in a locking joint and secured with a large rivet. The head was attached to the haft by driving the naillike tang (seen at its base) into the wood. A slight median ridge exists on the spear point and the beak. Its very simple yet functional design is another indication of the practical colonist of this era. The head is 13″ long (plus the 3¼″ tang).

*Harold L. Peterson Collection*

**PA.9 AMERICAN HALBERD**                     Circa 1710-1730

Another way of combining halberd components is illustrated to the right. The spear point, blade, and beak were apparently all forged together. Two heavy straps were then riveted to each side, bent outward to fit over the top of the haft, and secured to the wood in the usual manner. The two edges on the convex spear point plus the blade have been sharpened, indicating use as a weapon as well as a badge of rank. Its head is 11½″ long; the straps along the wood are 24½″.

*Author's Collection*

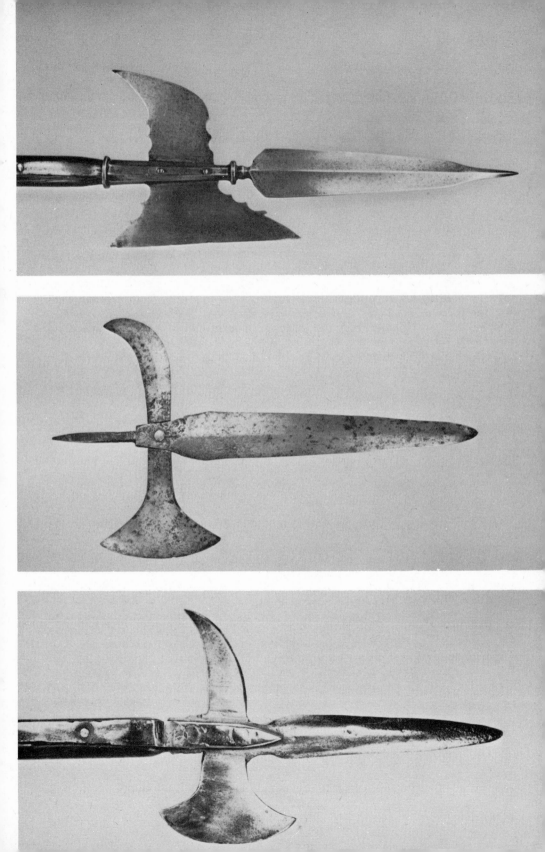

**PA.10 AMERICAN HALBERD**                                    Circa 1720-1740

These parts have been forged and joined to form a single piece—with graceful lines spreading into a socket for the haft (held by one rivet—no straps). As in the preceding example (PA.9), its blade shape has the ends curving inward, exposing a sharp cutting edge. The spear point is also extremely sharp on each side, and the knifelike inside edge on the beak was probably intended to cut reins or saddle straps of horsemen. Notice the narrow silhouette of the spear point, which was so typical in these early halberds. Total height is 21⅝".

*Author's Collection*

**PA.11 AMERICAN HALBERD**                                            Circa 1745

The construction of this head is also very elementary. All components have been forged and jointed into a single unit, which splits at its base to form two straps along the haft. The spear point and base are both square in cross section. A date, "1745," is crudely inscribed on the face. Its head is 12¾" long and the straps extend for 9¾".

*Edmund W. Budde, Jr., Collection*

**PA.12 AMERICAN HALBERD**                                    Circa 1720-1740

The spikelike spear point again suggests that this halberd is from the early 1700's. As in previous examples, its principal parts have been forged as a single unit. It flares into a crude socket at the bottom of the base, with straps continuing from each side. The spear point is diamond-shaped (cross section), while the concave edge of the blade has been sharpened. Total length of the head is 10⅝". The side straps were shortened at some time.

*Author's Collection*

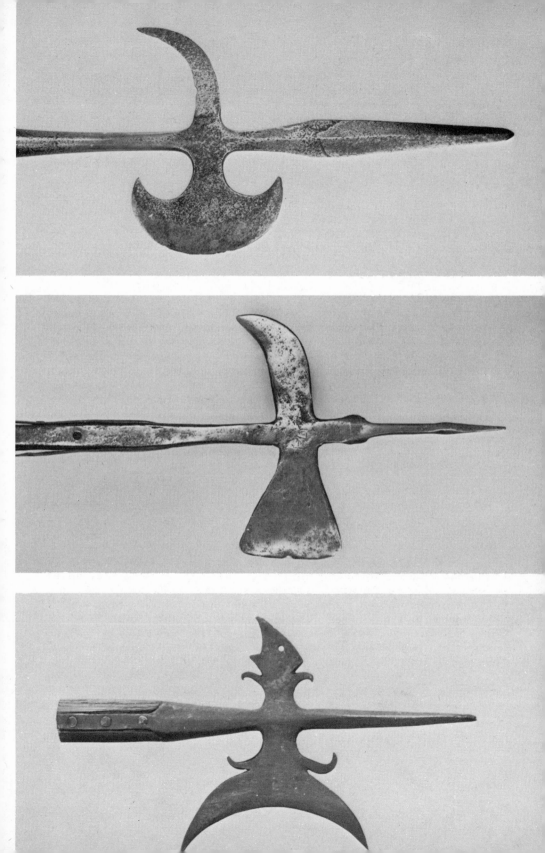

**PA.13 AMERICAN HALBERD**                              Circa 1739

This is an early version of the style which was to be popular around mid-century (PA.14-PA.16). The flat spear point mounted on a slender metal shaft, straight edges outlining the beak, and concave blade profile are all characteristic of this pattern. The typical piercings, e.g., round holes, squares, crosses, include the date of manufacture ("1739") in this case. It was originally found in Connecticut.

*C. O. v. Kienbusch Collection*

**PA.14 AMERICAN HALBERD**                              Circa 1750-1760

Here is an illustration of the style shown immediately above (PA.13), but in a later stage of development. The workmanship is much more precise and finished—its profile more graceful, and pleasing to the eye. Notice, for example, the slender and delicate shaping where the blade and beak pierce the shaft, as contrasted with the earlier specimen. No edges are sharpened for use as a weapon. Its head is 18″ high (including base rings), while the straps extend for 16½″ (five nails on each side). The haft (69″ from the head, 1¼″ diameter, 4⅛″ butt point) appears to be original.

*Author's Collection*

**PA.15 AMERICAN HALBERD**                              Circa 1750-1760

This version of the "flat-pierced" style has a slight taper to the spear point, and a wider cross-blade where it passes through the thin head shaft. The larger scallops in the design, plus the "turned" base, are also interesting. The initials "T:E" are visible on its face. The head and base measure 19″, while the straps extend for 16½″ (six rivets each). Its haft seems original, and measures 71¼″ to the base of the head (diameter ⅞″ at top, 1⅛″ at butt).

*Harold L. Peterson Collection*

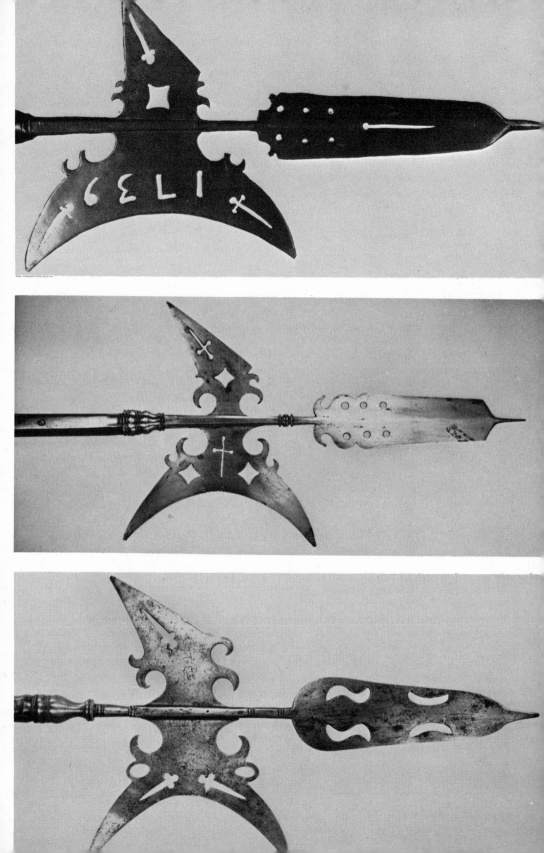

**PA.16 AMERICAN HALBERD**                                    Circa 1750-1760

The halberd in this case has a spear point without the usual sharp tang at its tip —plus two lateral extensions which are reminiscent of the early partisan design. The beak and blade were cut from a single flat sheet, and have no sharp edges. They fit through a vertical slot in the metal shaft of the head (held by friction). The frailty of these "flat-pierced" halberds indicates their use more as symbols than as weapons. The head and base measure 15".

*Hermann W. Williams, Jr., Collection*


**PA.17 AMERICAN HALBERD**                                    Circa 1750-1760

The American halberd shown here is a copy of a popular European style (see PA.2). All components are forged into a single piece, which includes a socket in its base (there are no side straps). A slight median ridge runs the length of the spear point. While most concave-shaped blades on these halberds have their tips in a vertical line, the upper end of this one overhangs the other. Its head and base are 13⅜" long.

*Edmund W. Budde, Jr., Collection*


**PA.18 AMERICAN HALBERD**                                    Circa 1750-1770

The tang-like tip is again present on this spear point. Notice too that only the suggestion of lateral extensions remains at its bottom corners. The unique part of this piece, however, is the forming of the blade and beak to include outlines of bird heads on each side. Because the eagle was not recognized as our national emblem until near the end of the Revolution, it is believed that these simply had a decorative function. The base was made by roughly lapping metal around the haft to form a socket (there are no straps). Its head and base are 15⅜" high.

*Edmund W. Budde, Jr., Collection*

340

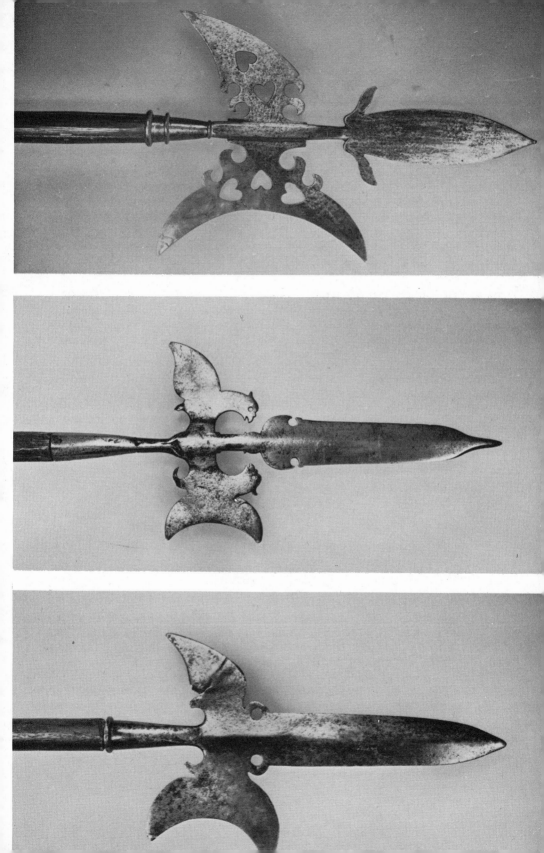

## PA.19 "TRADE" HALBERD HEAD                    Circa 1750-1770

Despite periodic attacks on outlying settlements, there was a great deal of trade constantly carried on with Indians in colonial times. Among the most popular barter goods (besides firearms) were iron tools and hand weapons. Copies of the white man's halberd heads were included in these items. The majority were manufactured abroad and shipped to North America. This specimen combines the spike-shaped beak (seen on many trade tomahawks) with a long barbed spear point (for fishing?). It totals 20" in length.

*John C. McMurray Collection*

## PA.20 "TRADE" HALBERD HEAD                    Circa 1750-1770

This is also believed to be a halberd head for the Indian trade. It is cast in one piece, with a round socket for easy installation on a haft. (Note: Some were mounted on short handles for use as tomahawks.) Its wide spear point is similar to the style popular just before the War for Independence. The entire head measures 12".

*R. Paul Nittolo Collection*

## PA.21 "TRADE" HALBERD HEAD                    Circa 1760-1780

The trade halberd head in this case was made flat, with a circular socket fastened to its base. The spear point, blade, and inside beak edge have all been sharpened. This is of a size which could have been mounted on either a long or short haft. The spear point and metal shaft each have a slight median ridge. It is 12" long.

*Author's Collection*

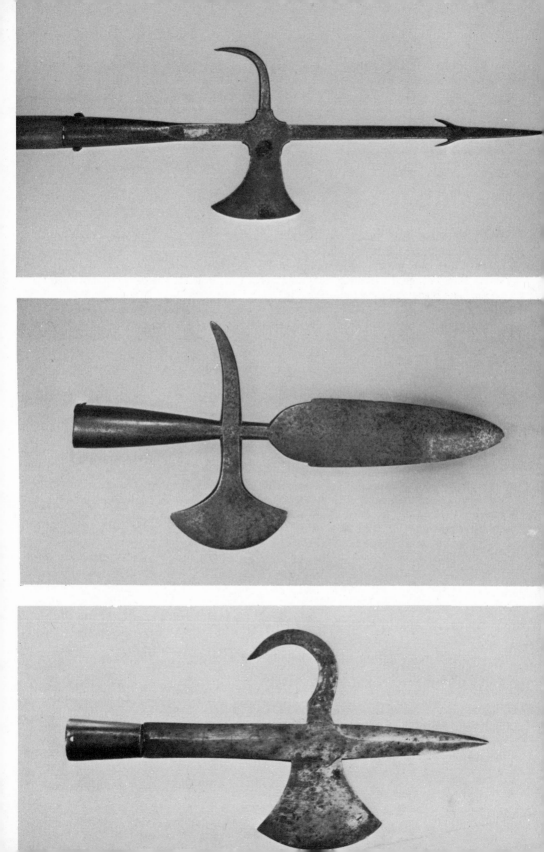

## PA.22 FRENCH HALBERD  Circa 1710-1730

The French halberd (carried by their sergeants) had little resemblance to the English pattern, and was closer to the earlier "partisan." Its spear point had lateral extensions on both sides at the bottom. This example includes a high median ridge extending down to the base. Notice also how the middle extension on each side has a wavy outline instead of a straight taper. This characteristic appears to continue in later French polearms. Its full height is 11".

*Colonial Williamsburg Collection*


## PA.23 FRENCH HALBERD  Circa 1720-1740

The central ridge has been reduced considerably in this later specimen. A wider flange has also appeared on the base just above the rounded socket. Its outline, however, shows little change (in contrast to PA.22 above). The name I BON——— is inscribed on the face. Blade and socket measure 13⅛".

*Wayne M. Daniels Collection*


## PA.24 GERMAN HALBERD  Circa 1760-1780

The German halberd was quite similar to the French type. There are some differences, however: this spear point is shorter and wider, the median ridge does not extend down as far, and the base is often octagonal (instead of the round style). Typical markings on its face show a crown above a script cipher. Its head and base are 13½"; the straps extend for 19¾" (six rivets each). The haft, which appears to be original, is 75½" long below the base (1¼" diameter).

*Author's Collection*


## PA.25 GERMAN HALBERD  Circa 1760-1780

This halberd is very much like the German specimen just above (PA.24). In this case, the engraving shows a crown above a leaping horse—which was the insignia for Brunswick troops. The heads of both of these German halberds unscrew at the bottom of the blade. Note too that this base is round instead of the more usual octagonal shape. Its head and base measure 13¼", while the straps are 8⅜" long.

*William H. Guthman Collection*

**PA.26 FRENCH SPONTOON**                                    Circa 1740-1766

The leaf-shaped spear point of this typical French spontoon has a high center ridge extending along its full length. The toggle piercing the base is at right angles to the blade face, and two side straps (three nail holes each) extend from beneath its 8¾" head.

*Author's Collection*

**PA.27 AMERICAN SPONTOON**                                  Circa 1700-1730

The rough work of an early blacksmith is seen in this piece. Its uneven flat blade was forged separately, before attachment to the ornamental ring and base. The pierced design is typical of many early polearms. Both edges are sharpened. Total length is 11½".

*Author's Collection*

**PA.28 AMERICAN SPONTOON**                                       Circa 1739

This leaf-shaped spontoon is pierced with its date of manufacture, "1739," and the religious inscription "IHS." This re-emphasizes the strong undertones of religion which entered into colonial life, and the wars with France. The spear point has a median ridge for its entire length. Base and blade are 14⅛" long.

*Author's Collection*

**PA.29 AMERICAN SPONTOON**                                  Circa 1740-1760

Although out of alignment, the curved design on the base of this spontoon was a brave attempt—probably with the crudest of facilities—to add a touch of elegance to a rather plain weapon. Its spear point has squared corners at the bottom edges, which usually indicates an early period. The head and base measure 11¼", while the straps end after 8½".

*Hermann W. Williams, Jr., Collection*

346

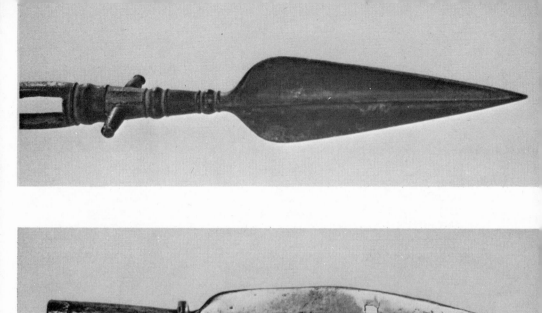

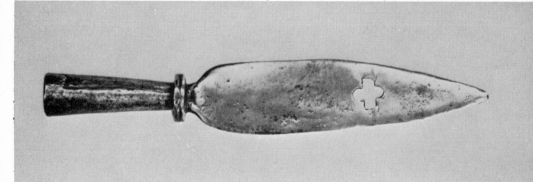

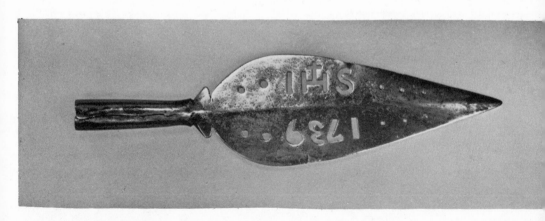

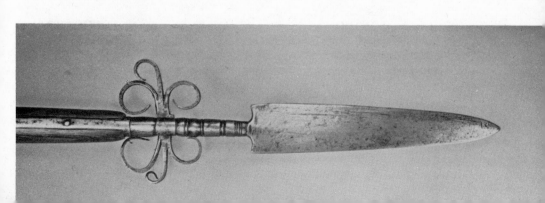

**PA.30 AMERICAN SPONTOON**                              Circa 1740-1760

This long thin blade, with right angles at the bottom corners, again typifies an early spontoon. A median ridge extends the length of the blade, and its edges have been sharpened for use as a weapon. The socket base has a sliding ring, apparently to help secure it tightly to the haft. Total length is 15¼". This particular example came from Connecticut.

*Author's Collection*

**PA.31 AMERICAN SPONTOON**                              Circa 1750-1760

The thin tip of this halberd is a type seen on many polearms in the mid-1700's. Of additional interest are the lateral projections, which have been shaped like bird heads and wings. A slight median ridge appears on the blade, while three ornamental rings circle the rounded base. Its straps were shortened at one time; the head and base are 13⅜" long.

*Colonial Williamsburg Collection*

**PA.32 AMERICAN SPONTOON**                              Circa 1760-1770

Believed to have been made in northern Pennsylvania, this pierced spontoon (with its spear point cut from a flat sheet of iron) shows a marked similarity to some of the German polearms of the Revolutionary War period (PA.48). A short turned shaft joins the blade to the cylindrical cap mounted on the haft. The total length is 10⅞".

*Harold L. Peterson Collection*

**PA.33 AMERICAN SPONTOON**                              Circa 1760-1780

Here is an American copy of the standard British infantry spontoon of the mid-1700's (PA.36). The blade is also similar to the spear point on their halberd (PA.1). It includes the characteristic bulbous lower end of the blade, plus a simple crossbar. A short cap over the end of the haft leads directly into two side straps.

*Lewis H. Gordon, Jr., Collection*

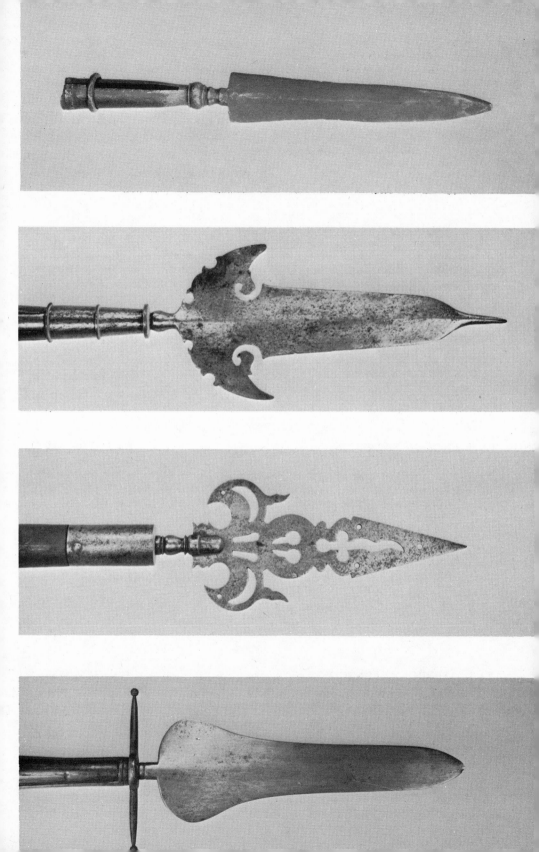

**PA.34 AMERICAN SPONTOON**                          Circa 1760-1780

Apparently the English pattern served again as the model for this spontoon. As can be seen, however, the crosspiece was omitted. Its head is 8⅛″ long; the short straps end after 3¼″.

*Foster Tallman Collection*


**PA.35 AMERICAN SPONTOON**                          Circa 1775-1780

British influence is also apparent in the expanded bottom of this blade, although the blade's angle of meeting with the upper edges is more abrupt. The crossbar (with rounded finials) follows the German practice of having each curve in an opposite direction. A median ridge extends for the full length of the spear point. The head and neck are 15¾″; its straps measure 18¼″.

*Author's Collection*


**PA.36 ENGLISH SPONTOON**                          Circa 1750-1786

This is the standard British spontoon of the Revolutionary War period, and the apparent pattern for the preceding three American examples (PA.33-PA.35). Notice its thinner proportions and finer workmanship. The blade (sharpened edges; unscrews at crossbar) is 9½″ long, while the base measures 4¼″ and the straps 10⅜″.

*Author's Collection*


**PA.37 AMERICAN SPONTOON**                          Circa 1775-1780

The shape of this piece is very similar to the British sergeant's pike at the end of the eighteenth century. Yet, the fact that similar blades and crossbars are found on other Revolutionary War polearms, plus the crude American workmanship, indicate that it could easily be a product of the 1770's. The head extends for 16¼″ to the lowest band; its straps are 9½″ long (four rivets each).

*Author's Collection*

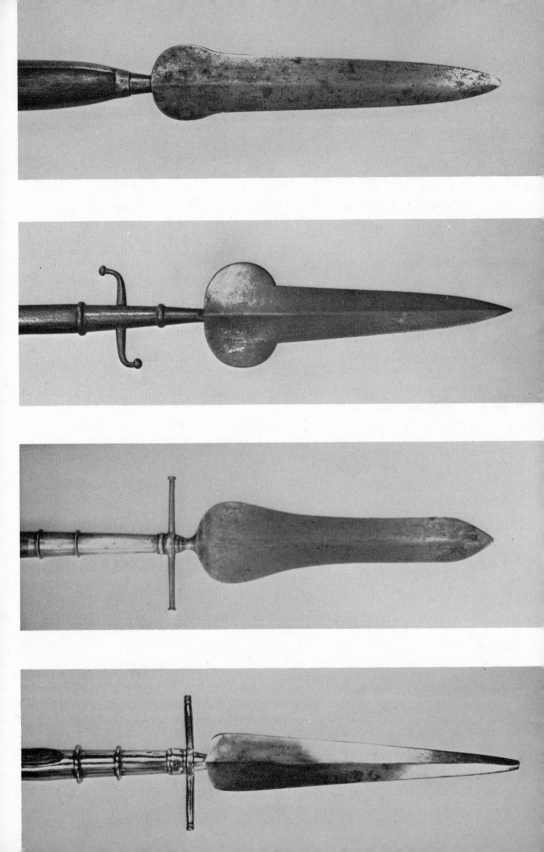

**PA.38 AMERICAN SPONTOON**                                    Circa 1775-1776

The plain spontoon in this illustration is marked PRAHL on one of the straps—undoubtedly for Lewis Prahl of Philadelphia, who had pike and sword contracts at the start of the Revolution. Its head and base are 11″ high. Three nails hold each strap (9¾″).

*Hermann W. Williams, Jr., Collection*


**PA.39 AMERICAN SPONTOON**                                    Circa 1775-1780

Although crude to the eye, this is a real fighting-man's weapon. All blade edges are sharpened. The spear point itself is divided into two branches to secure the crosspiece. These, in turn, terminate on a base which again splits to hold a haft between two 3″ straps. Its total length measures 13½″.

*Harold L. Peterson Collection*


**PA.40 AMERICAN SPONTOON**                                    Circa 1775-1780

Well made for its purpose, the oversized crossbar and lack of continuity in this spontoon's lines emphasize the colonist's stress on utility instead of design. The spear point unscrews from the base (allowing the crossbar to be removed). Its bottom ring is 10⅞″ from the tip, while the straps are 10⅜″ long.

*Author's Collection*


**PA.41 AMERICAN SPONTOON**                                    Circa 1775-1780

A leaf shape was used for this simple spear point, which unscrews just above the crossbar. The crossbar, in turn, has a hole through its middle collar to admit the center shaft of the head. Its tips curve in opposite directions within the horizontal plane. The head and base are 12″ in length (the head alone, 8½″); two straps extend for another 13¼″ (three nails in each).

*Author's Collection*

352

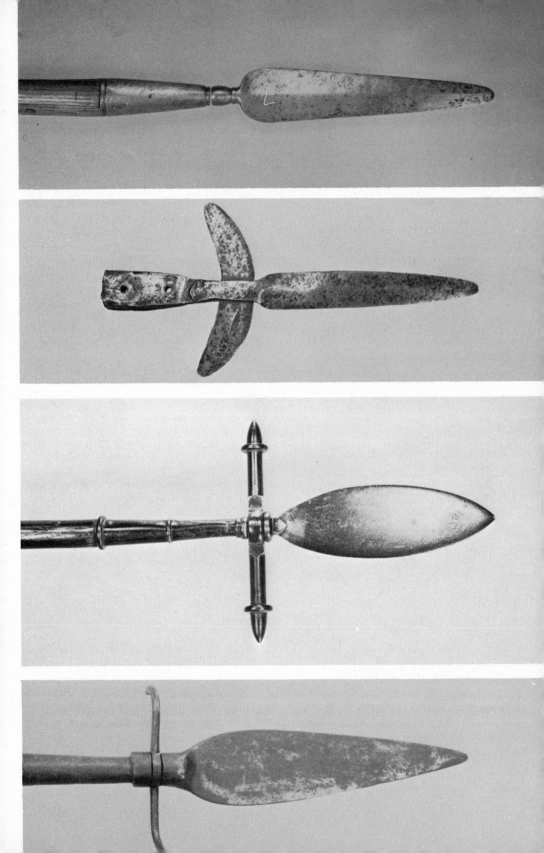

**PA.42 AMERICAN SPONTOON**                                    Circa 1775-1780

Notice here how the squared bottom corners of the earlier blades have evolved to a wider angle, giving a more tapered appearance to its metal neck. Both edges have been sharpened. The socket still has the original single rivet through it. Total length is 14″.

*Author's Collection*

**PA.43 AMERICAN SPONTOON**                                    Circa 1775-1783

Utilizing all items at hand to create weapons, the Americans apparently converted the blade (9⅝″) from an early plug bayonet into this spontoon head. A wooden base covers the blade's tang (threaded), while a metal collar secured it to the haft. Overall length is 14⅛″.

*Author's Collection*

**PA.44 GERMAN SPONTOON**                                      Circa 1750-1770

A broad blade with a narrowed decorative bottom, tips of the crossbar curling in opposite directions, and a mounting socket are indicative of many German spontoons believed used here during the Revolution. In this case, it has a simple pierced design in the blade, plus side straps (19″). The base and head total 16″.

*Anthony D. Darling Collection*

**PA.45 GERMAN SPONTOON**                                      Circa 1750-1770

This variation of the German spontoon has no pierced designs, nor side straps. The inscription, however, is quite typical. A crown appears above a cipher and the leaping-horse figure used by Brunswick troops (see PA.25). The panoply of arms and flags underneath is a common eighteenth-century style of military motif.

*Author's Collection*

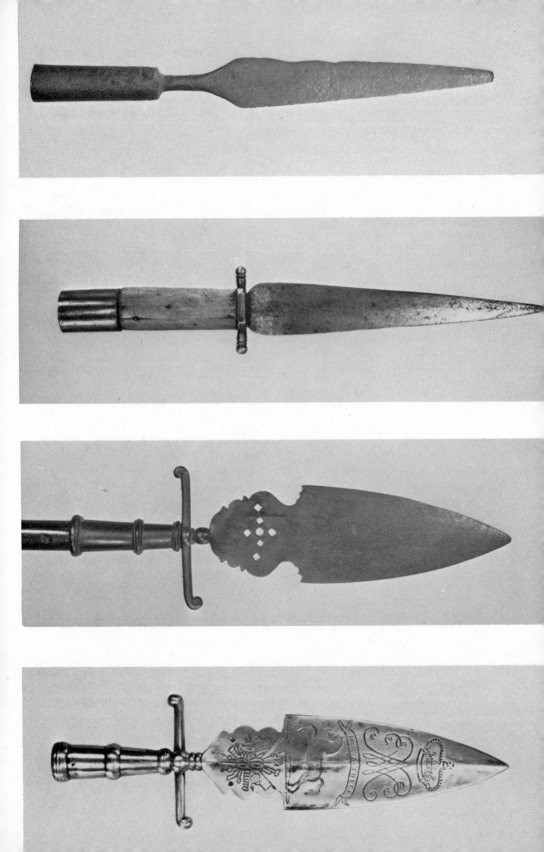

**PA.46 GERMAN SPONTOON**                                    **Circa 1760-1780**

Several of this spontoon design are known; they are believed to be Germanic. Its lower outline and piercings resemble previous examples (PA.44, PA.45), while the spear point is of the style on their halberds (PA.24, PA.25). The crossbar has been eliminated and the base is not faceted. The entire head is 15″; its two straps extend for 12¾″ (four rivets each).

*Author's Collection*

**PA.47 GERMAN SPONTOON**                                    **Circa 1760-1780**

Similarity to the spontoon in the preceding illustration (PA.46) is apparent here. The spear point retains its slight median ridge, ending in an expanded bottom design, and the rounded socket bears three raised rings (with center ridges). Its head and socket together measure 15¾″; the two straps are 20⅜″ (six rivets each). "R V 1K3" is crudely engraved on one strap.

*Author's Collection*

**PA.48 GERMAN SPONTOON**                                    **Circa 1760-1780**

This is another style of spontoon believed carried by some of the German troops during the Revolutionary War. The spear point has a wide flat median ridge and distinctive pierced shapes. Its base is octagonal, as are so many parts of German arms. The head and base are 11¾″ high; the straps are 15½″.

*Valley Forge Museum Collection*

**PA.49 GERMAN LINSTOCK**                                    **Circa 1740-1760**

The majority of artillery linstocks were simply two bent iron arms on a pole, holding a smoldering "match rope" for igniting cannon. More elaborate styles such as this one with a center fighting blade were also used. This head is 16½″ high; most hafts varied from 2′ to 6′.

*Author's Collection*

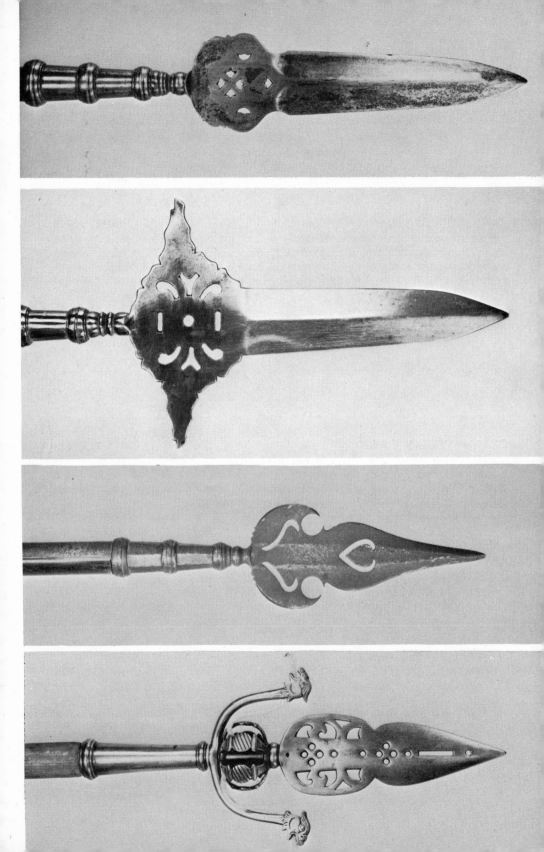

**PA.50 AMERICAN PIKE**                                      Circa 1775-1778

The crude tang for driving into the top of a wooden shaft is visible at the base of this blade. A middle ridge runs the full length, with a slightly concave surface on each side. Its outer edges have been sharpened. Total length is 16¾" (including the 4" tang).

*Author's Collection*

**PA.51 AMERICAN PIKE**                                      Circa 1775-1778

This example is more substantial than many of the other trench spears. Its sharp blade (convex on each face) is attached to a narrow iron shaft which, in turn, is seated at the juncture of two broad (1½" wide) straps for attachment to a haft. The head is 14¾" long; its straps extend for 12¾" (three rivets each).

*Author's Collection*

**PA.52 AMERICAN PIKE**                                      Circa 1775-1778

This "ox-tongue" style is similar to European polearms used in the 1600's and again in France during the French Revolution. Several of these crude blades were found in upper New York State, and are believed to have been carried during our War for Independence. It totals 26" in length. There are no side straps.

*Harold L. Peterson Collection*

**PA.53 AMERICAN PIKE**                                      Circa 1775-1776

The spear point in this case splits at its base to form two long side straps for mounting. It was excavated in the New York City area, and is thought to be one of the trench spears issued to Washington's men in 1776. The blade is 9" long; the straps are 15".

*Author's Collection*

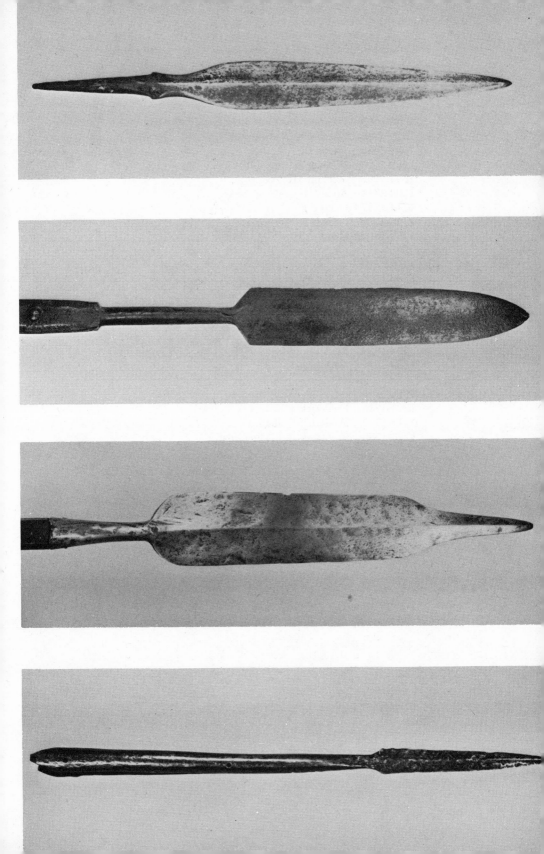

# PRINCIPAL EUROPEAN RULERS 1600–1800

## ENGLAND

| | |
|---|---|
| 1603-1625 | James I |
| 1625-1649 | Charles I |
| 1649-1660 | Commonwealth (Oliver Cromwell) |
| 1660-1685 | Charles II |
| 1685-1688 | James II |
| 1689-1694 | William III and Mary II |
| 1694-1702 | William III |
| 1702-1714 | Anne |
| 1714-1727 | George I |
| 1727-1760 | George II |
| 1760-1820 | George III |

## FRANCE

| | |
|---|---|
| 1589-1610 | Henry IV |
| 1610-1643 | Louis XIII |
| 1643-1715 | Louis XIV |
| 1715-1774 | Louis XV |
| 1774-1792 | Louis XVI |
| 1792-1804 | First Republic |
| 1804-1814 | Napoleon I |

## PRUSSIA

| | |
|---|---|
| 1701-1713 | Frederick I |
| 1713-1740 | Frederick William I |
| 1740-1786 | Frederick II ("The Great") |

## SPAIN

| | |
|---|---|
| 1598-1621 | Philip III |
| 1621-1665 | Philip IV |
| 1665-1700 | Charles II |
| 1700-1746 | Philip V |
| 1746-1759 | Ferdinand VI |
| 1759-1788 | Charles III |
| 1788-1808 | Charles IV |

| 1607 | Jamestown, Virginia, settled |
| 1620 | Plymouth, Massachusetts, settled |
| 1642-1646 | *Civil War* in England |
| 1689-1697 | *King William's War* (Europe's War of the League of Augsburg) |
| 1702-1713 | *Queen Anne's War* (Europe's War of the Spanish Succession) |
| 1744-1748 | *King George's War* (Europe's War of the Austrian Succession) |
| | 1745: 6/16 Colonists capture Louisburg |
| 1754-1763 | *French and Indian War* (Europe's *Seven Years' War*) |
| | 1755: 7/9 Braddock's defeat |
| | 9/8 Battle of Lake George |
| | 1757: 8/9 Ft. William Henry captured |
| | 1758: 7/8 Abercrombie repulsed at Ft. Ticonderoga |
| | 7/26 Amherst and Wolfe capture Louisburg |
| | 11/25 Forbes captures Ft. Pitt |
| | 1759: 7/26 Amherst captures Ft. Ticonderoga |
| | 9/13 Wolfe captures Quebec |
| 1763-1765 | *Pontiac's Uprising* |
| 1775-1783 | *American War for Independence* |
| | 1775: 4/19 Lexington-Concord raid |
| | 6/17 Battle of Bunker Hill |
| | 12/31 Attack on Quebec |
| | 1776: 3/17 British evacuate Boston, Mass. |
| | 6/28 British attack Charleston, S.C. |
| | 7/4 Declaration of Independence adopted |
| | 8/27 Battle of Long Island |
| | 9/15 British occupy New York City |
| | 10/28 Battle of White Plains, N.Y. |
| | 12/26 Battle of Trenton, N.J. |
| | 1777: 1/3 Battle of Princeton, N.J. |
| | 8/16 Battle of Bennington, Vt. |
| | 9/11 Battle of Brandywine, Pa. |
| | 10/4 Battle of Germantown, Pa. |
| | 10/17 Burgoyne surrenders at Saratoga, N.Y. |
| | 1778: 2/6 France enters war |
| | 6/28 Battle of Monmouth, N.J. |
| | 12/29 British capture Savannah, Ga. |
| | 1779: 7/16 Storming of Stony Point, N.Y. |
| | 10/9 Assault on Savannah fails |
| | 1780: 5/12 British capture Charleston, S.C. |
| | 8/16 Battle of Camden, S.C. |
| | 10/7 Battle of Kings Mountain, N.C. |
| | 1781: 1/17 Battle of Cowpens, N.C. |
| | 3/15 Battle of Guilford Court House, N.C. |
| | 10/17 Cornwallis surrenders at Yorktown, Va. |
| | 1783: 9/3 Treaty of Paris |

# MEASUREMENT DEFINITIONS

Following are brief descriptions of the weapon measurements used in the arms descriptions.

BARREL: (First Figure) the length from the muzzle to the end of the breech— its tang is not included; (Second Figure) the *actual* bore diameter (inches) measured in the barrel's final ⅜ inch, i.e., not necessarily the original or official size. For rifles, the distance between "lands" is recorded.

BLADE: (First Figure) the straight distance between the point and its contact with the hilt; (Second Figure) the width of the blade at the hilt.

BUTT TANG: A horizontal measurement from the tang's tip to a point opposite the upper butt plate's rearmost extension.

FULLER: (First Figure) the average width; (Second Figure) the full length measured in a straight line.

LOCK: (First Figure) the length of the lock plate; (Second Figure) height of the lock plate as measured at a point between the cock and flashpan.

TOTAL LENGTH: A straight-line distance between the two outermost points.

TRIGGER GUARD: The distance along the stock between the guard's two ends.

In planning the book, much consideration was given to the choice between describing a few weapons in detail, or presenting many specimens with their major points included. The latter approach was selected to best provide the reader with the important "feel" of an arm's pattern evolution. Because of this, some features visible in the photographs are not included in the text, and points basic to a given style may be mentioned once in the course of several examples illustrated.

# GLOSSARY OF TERMS

## Used in This Volume

BACKSTRAP:   A strip of metal along the back of a sword grip or pistol grip.

BACKSWORD:   A long sword with a single cutting edge.

BARREL:   The metal tube of a firearm through which a bullet passes.

BLUNDERBUSS:   A short, large-caliber shoulder firearm with a flared muzzle.

BORE:   The interior diameter of a firearm barrel.

BREECH:   The rear end of a barrel (opposite the muzzle).

BRIDLE:   A supporting strap on a lock—usually (inside) to brace the tumbler; (outside) to strengthen the frizzen screw.

BROADSWORD:   A long sword with a double-edged blade.

BUTT PLATE TANG:   The upper extension of the butt plate—reaching along the top of the stock comb.

CARBINE:   A short, light shoulder firearm usually for mounted troops; in the eighteenth century also a small-bore musket for light troops.

COCK:   The pivoting arm on a lock, which holds the flint in its upper jaws.

COMB:   The thin "shoulder" along the top of the stock butt.

COUNTERGUARD:   Part of the sword hilt—between the grip and blade.

CUTLASS:   A naval short saber, usually with a wide guard.

ESCUTCHEON PLATE:   A shaped metal piece on the "small" of the stock.

FERRULE:   A supporting or binding base at either end of the sword grip.

FINIAL:   An ornamental end, usually on sword quillons or trigger guards.

FLASHPAN:   A pan outside the barrel's touchhole, holding the priming powder.

FLINTLOCK:   A method of firearm ignition which strikes flint against steel.

FRIZZEN (BATTERY):   The pivoting steel piece struck by the flint to produce sparks.

FULLER:   A groove cut into the face of a sword to improve balance and reduce weight.

FURNITURE:   Metal fittings on a firearm (not barrel, lock, or rammer).

FUSIL ("Fusee"):   A light, small-bore musket carried by officers (eighteenth century); earlier, a flint musket as against a matchlock.

GRIP:   The part of a sword hilt normally held by the hand.

HAFT:   The shaft or handle of a polearm, tomahawk, etc. (when longer than blade).

HALBERD:   A polearm used by infantry sergeants.

HANGER:   A short cutting-sword carried mostly by foot soldiers.

HEAD:   The upper part of a polearm mounted above the base.

HILT:   The grip, pommel, mountings, and guard of a sword.

HOLSTER PISTOL:   A military-style pistol usually carried by officers.

HUNTING SWORD:   A short civilian sword originally used as a side arm while hunting.

INBOARD-OUTBOARD:   Inboard—the side of a sword against the body when worn on the left side; outboard—the side away from the body.

KNUCKLE BOW:   The part of the sword guard designed to protect the knuckles.

LOCK PLATE:   The external iron plate upon which most of the lock parts are mounted.

363

MATCHLOCK: An early ignition system using a slow-burning "match" cord to ignite the priming powder.

MIQUELET LOCK: An early form of Spanish flintlock (used into the nineteenth century in Africa).

MUSKET: A military smoothbore large-caliber shoulder firearm (standard infantry musket) used in the eighteenth century.

MUSKETOON: Early eighteenth century—a short large-caliber smoothbore musket; by the 1770's, a very short blunderbuss.

MUZZLE: The mouth or open end of a barrel (from which the bullet leaves).

PAS-D'ANE: The two rings on the hilt of a small sword (one on each side of its *ricasso*).

PIKE: A long military spear.

PISTOL: A small firearm which can be fired with one hand.

POMMEL: The upper end of a hilt—furthermost from the blade.

PROOF MARKS: Devices stamped on weapons to indicate completion of specific proofing tests.

QUILLON: The end of a sword guard—after it passes the grip.

RAMMER: A wooden or metal rod for ramming a charge down the barrel.

RICASSO: A squared area under the hilt on the sword blade; and the lower stem of small sword blades (between the counterguard and the grip).

RIFLE: A shoulder firearm with grooves cut inside the barrel.

SERPENTINE: An S-shaped metal cock holding the lighted match for a matchlock.

SHORT SABER: A light cut-and-thrust sword worn by many officers.

SIDE PLATE: A metal piece supporting the lock screws on the side of the stock opposite the lock.

SMALL SWORD: A civilian sword with a thin straight blade.

SNAPHAUNCE: An early form of flintlock ignition, having a separate battery and pan cover.

SPONTOON: An officer's spearlike polearm.

STOCK: The wooden part of a firearm.

TANG: A thin extension of a piece; e.g., the part of a sword blade through the grip, or the top extension of a barrel breech plug.

WALL GUN ("RAMPART GUN"): A large smoothbore or rifled shoulder arm for use from a fixed position.

WHEEL LOCK: An early ignition system using sparks from a wheel revolving against an iron pyrites or flint.

# BIBLIOGRAPHY

This list does not include all of the sources used in preparing this volume. It is intended to present the major references, and to indicate the range of material studied.

## I. TEXTS

*Acts and Laws of His Majesty's Province of the Massachusetts-Bay in New England.* Boston, 1726.

ALLEN, GARDNER, *A Naval History of the American Revolution* (Vols. I, II). Russell & Russell, Inc., New York, 1962.

ARMY, DEPT. OF, *American Military History 1607-1953.* U.S. Government Printing Office, Washington, D.C., 1956.

AYLWARD, J. D., *The Small Sword in England.* Hutchinson & Co., Ltd., London, 1960.

BARNES, MAJOR R. MONEY, *A History of the Regiments and Uniforms of the British Army.* Seeley Service & Co., London, 1962.

BERNARDO, C. JOSEPH, and BACON, EUGENE H., *American Military Policy; Its Development since 1775.* The Stackpole Co., Harrisburg, Pa., 1961.

BLACKMORE, HOWARD L., *British Military Firearms.* Arco Publishing Co., Inc., New York, 1962.

———, *Firearms.* E. P. Dutton & Co., Inc., New York, 1964.

BLAIR, CLAUDE, *European and American Arms.* Crown Publishers, Inc., New York, 1962.

BLAND, HUMPHREY, *A Treatise of Military Discipline.* London, 1746.

BOOTHROYD, GEOFFREY, *Guns Through the Ages.* Sterling Publishing Co., New York, 1962.

BOSANQUET, CAPT. HENRY T. A., *The Naval Officer's Sword.* London, 1955.

BOSTON, NOEL, *Old Guns and Pistols.* Ernest Benn, Ltd., London, 1958.

BOUDRIOT, JEAN, *Armes à Feu Françaises.* Paris, 1961.

BOWMAN, HANK W., *Antique Guns.* Fawcett Publications, Inc., Greenwich, Conn., 1953.

———, *Famous Guns from Famous Collections.* Fawcett Publications, Inc., Greenwich, Conn., 1957.

CALVER, WILLIAM LOUIS, and BOLTON, REGINALD PELHAM, *History Written with a Pick and Shovel.* New-York Historical Society, New York, 1950.

CAREY, A. MERWYN, *American Firearms Makers.* Thomas Y. Crowell Co., New York, 1953.

———, *English, Irish, and Scottish Firearms Makers.* Thomas Y. Crowell Co., New York, 1954.

*Catalog of the United States Cartridge Company's Collection of Firearms.* Lowell Mass., 1947.

CHAPELLE, HOWARD I., *The History of the American Sailing Navy.* Bonanza Books, New York, 1949.

DEWATTEVILLE, COL. H., *The British Soldier.* G. P. Putnam's Sons, New York, 1954.

DILLON, JOHN G. W., *The Kentucky Rifle.* Ludlum & Beebe, New York, 1946.

FOULKES, CHARLES, *Arms and Armament*. George G. Harrap & Co., London, 1945.

FULLER, COL. J. F. C., *British Light Infantry in the Eighteenth Century*. Hutchinson and Co., London, 1925.

GARDNER, COL. ROBERT E., *Small Arms Makers*. Crown Publishers, Inc., New York, 1963.

GEORGE, JOHN NIGEL, *English Guns and Rifles*. The Stackpole Co., Harrisburg, Pa., 1947.

————, *English Pistols and Revolvers*. Arco Publishing Co., Inc., New York, 1962.

GLENDENNING, IAN, *British Pistols and Guns 1640–1840*. Cassell & Co., Ltd., London, 1951.

GLUCKMAN, ARCADI, *United States Muskets, Rifles and Carbines*. The Stackpole Co., Harrisburg, Pa., 1959.

GLUCKMAN, ARCADI, and SATTERLEE, L. D., *American Gun Makers*. The Stackpole Co., Harrisburg, Pa., 1953.

GRANCSAY, STEPHEN V., *Arms and Armor*. Allentown Art Museum, Allentown, Pa., 1964.

GROSE, FRANCIS, *Military Antiquities, a History of the English Army* (Vols. I, II). London, 1801.

GYNGELL, DUDLEY S. HAWTREY, *Armourers Marks*. Thorsons Publishers, Ltd., London, 1959.

HELD, ROBERT, *The Age of Firearms*. Harper & Brothers, New York, 1957.

HICKS, MAJOR JAMES E., *French Military Weapons 1717–1938*. N. Flayderman & Co., New Milford, Conn., 1964.

HINDE, CAPT., *The Discipline of the Light Horse*. London, 1778.

JACKSON, C., *A Complete System of the Military Art*. Dublin, 1780.

JACKSON, HERBERT, JR., and WHITELAW, CHARLES E., *European Hand Firearms of the Sixteenth, Seventeenth, and Eighteenth Centuries*, 2nd ed. The Holland Press, London, 1959.

KAUFFMAN, HENRY J., *Early American Gunsmiths 1650–1850*. The Stackpole Co., Harrisburg, Pa., 1952.

————, *The Gunsmith*. Century House, Watkins Glen, N.Y., 1959.

KINDIG, JOE, JR., *Thoughts on the Kentucky Rifle in Its Golden Age*. Trimmer Printing, Inc., York, Pa., 1960.

KOLLER, LARRY, *The Fireside Book of Guns*. Simon & Schuster, New York, 1959.

LAVIN, JAMES D., *A History of Spanish Firearms*. Arco Publishing Co., Inc., New York, 1965.

LAWSON, CECIL C. P., *A History of the Uniforms of the British Army* (Vols. I-III). Norman Military Publications, London, 1940, 1942, 1961.

LENK, TORSTEN, *The Flintlock: Its Origin and Development*. The Holland Press, Ltd., London, 1965.

LEWIS, BERKELEY R., *Small Arms and Ammunition in the United States Service, 1776–1865*. Smithsonian Institution, Washington, 1956.

LEZINS, MARTIN, *Das Chrenfleid des Soldaten*. A. G. Ullstein, Berlin, 1936.

McDONALD, CAPT. ALEXANDER, *Letter Book 1775–1779*. New-York Historical Society, New York, 1882.

MILLIS, WALTER, *Arms and Men*. New American Library, New York, 1958.

MOORE, WARREN, *Guns: The Development of Firearms, Air Guns and Cartridges*. Grosset & Dunlap, Inc., New York, 1963.

**366**

MOUNT VERNON LADIES' ASSOCIATION, *General Washington's Military Equipment*. Mount Vernon, Va., 1963.

MYRUS, DON, *Collectors' Guns*. Maco Publishing Co., Inc., New York, 1961.

NEAL, W. KEITH, *Spanish Guns and Pistols*. G. Bell & Sons, Ltd., London, 1955.

PETERSON, HAROLD L., *American Indian Tomahawks*. Museum of the American Indian, New York, 1965.

————, *American Silver Mounted Swords 1700–1815*. Corcoran Gallery of Art, Washington, D.C., 1955.

————, *Arms and Armor in Colonial America*. The Stackpole Co., Harrisburg, Pa., 1956.

————, *Encyclopedia of Firearms*. E. P. Dutton & Co., Inc., New York, 1964.

————, *The American Sword 1775–1945*. The River House, New Hope, Pa., 1954.

————, *The Treasury of the Gun*. Golden Press, New York, 1962.

RICKETTS, HOWARD, *Firearms*. G. P. Putnam's Sons, New York, 1962.

ROGERS, COL. H. C. B., *The Mounted Troops of the British Army, 1066–1945*. Seeley Service & Co., Ltd., London, 1959.

————, *Weapons of the British Soldier*. Seeley Service & Co., Ltd., London, 1960.

RUSSELL, CARL P., *Guns on the Early Frontiers*. University of California Press, Los Angeles, 1957.

SAWYER, CHARLES WINTHROP, *Firearms in American History*. Boston, 1910.

SAXE, FIELD MARSHAL COUNT, *Reveries on Memories upon the Art of War* (translation). London, 1757.

SHIELDS, JOSEPH W., JR., *From Flintlock to M1*. Coward-McCann, Inc., New York, 1954.

SHY, JOHN, *Toward Lexington: The Role of the British Army in the Coming American Revolution*. Princeton University Press, Princeton, N.J., 1965.

SIMES, THOMAS, *The Military Medley*. London, 1768.

STOCKEL, JOHAN F., *Haandskydevaabens Bedommelse*. Copenhagen, 1943.

STONE, GEORGE CAMERONE, *A Glossary of the Construction, Decoration and Use of Arms and Armor*. Jack Brussel, New York, 1961.

TALLMADGE, SAMUEL, *et al.*, *Orderly Books of the 4th N. Y. Regt. 1778–1780, 2nd N. Y. Regt. 1780–1783*. University of the State of New York, Albany, 1932.

UPPER CANADA HISTORICAL ARMS SOCIETY, *The Military Arms of Canada*. Museum Restoration Service, West Hill, Ontario, 1963.

VANRENSSELAER, STEPHEN, *American Firearms*. Century House, Watkins Glen, N.Y., 1947.

VONKRAFFT, LT. JOHN C. P., *Journal 1776–1784*. New-York Historical Society, New York, 1882.

WARD, CHRISTOPHER, *The War of the Revolution* (Vols. I-II). The Macmillan Co., New York, 1952.

WILKINSON, FREDERICK, *Small Arms*. Ward Lock & Co., Ltd., London, 1965.

WRIGHT, COL. JOHN WOMACK, *Some Notes on the Continental Army*. National Temple Hill Association, Vails Gate, N.Y., 1963.

WRIGHT, LOUIS B., *The Atlantic Frontier Colonial Civilization*. Cornell University Press, Ithaca, N.Y., 1959.

WYLER, SEYMOUR B., *The Book of Old Silver*. Crown Publishers, New York, 1937.

## II. PERIODICALS

"American Pole Arms or Shafted Weapons," *Bulletin of the Fort Ticonderoga Museum*, Vol. V, July 1939.

BAXTER, CAPT. D. R., "The Pocket Pistol," *Guns Review*, Jan. 1964.

BLACKMORE, HOWARD L., "The British Rifle in America," *The American Rifleman*, June 1963.

BURNSIDE, GRAHAM, "Arms of the American Revolution," *Shooting Times*, Sept. 1962.

CHAPMAN, FREDERICK T., and ELTING JOHN R., "Brunswick Regiment of Dragoons 1776–1783," *Journal of the Company of Military Historians*, Vol. XII, No. 1, 1960.

CHERNOFF, ARNOLD MARCUS, "Screw-Barrel Pistols," *Guns and Ammo*, July 1965.

*Cook Collection Catalog*, Serven Gunroom, Santa Ana, Calif.

CUNEO, JOHN R., "Factors behind Raising the 80th Foot in America," *Journal of the Company of Military Historians*, Vol. XI, No. 4, 1959.

DEAN, BASHFORD, "On American Polearms," *Metropolitan Museum Studies*, Vol. I, Part I, 1928.

ENGLELHARDT, BARON A., "The Story of European Proof Marks," *The Gun Digest*, 1953.

GAMMAGE, RUSSEL, "British Naval Uniforms 1775–1783," *Journal of the Company of Military Historians*, Vol. XVI, No. 2, 1964.

GLASS, HERB, "The Long Long Rifle," *The American Gun*, Vol. I, No. 2, Spring 1961.

HAARMAN, ALBERT W., "The Hessian Army and the Corps in North America 1776–1783," *Journal of the Company of Military Historians*, Vol. XIV, No. 3, 1962.

HAARMAN, ALBERT W., and DONALD HOLST, "The Friedrich Von Germann Drawings of Troops in the American Revolution," *Journal of the Company of Military Historians*, Vol. XVI, No. 1, 1964.

HELD, ROBERT, "Fuzes, Flints, and Pyrites," *The American Gun*, Vol. I, No. 2, Spring 1961.

HOLST, DONALD W., and PETER COPELAND, "16th [Queens] Regiment of Light Dragoons, 1776–1778," *Journal of the Company of Military Historians*, Vol. XV, No. 4, 1963.

LATTIMER, JOHN K., "An Exhibition of Silver Hilted Swords by American Silversmiths of the Colonial, Revolutionary, and Federal Periods," *Bulletin of the Fort Ticonderoga Museum*, Vol. XI, No. 6, 1965.

———, "Sword Hilts by Early American Silversmiths," *Antiques Magazine*, Feb. 1965.

LELIEPVRE, EUGENE, "French Soissonnois Infantry 1780–1783," *Journal of the Company of Military Historians*, Vol. XI, No. 4, 1959.

MANDERS, ERIC, and GEORGE A. SNOOK, "New England Independent Companies 1675–1676," *Journal of the Company of Military Historians*, Vol. XVI, No. 2, 1964.

MEDICUS, PHILIP, "A Revolutionary Eagleheaded Saber," *Society of American Sword Collectors Bulletin*, May 1947.

PARKERSON, CODMAN, "Scottish Pistols," *The Gun Report*, Oct. 1964.

PETERSON, HAROLD L., "Brown Bess, the Standard Arm," *The American Rifleman*, Apr. 1954.

——, "Early Paper Cartridges," *The American Rifleman*, Feb. 1953.

——, "Firearms of the Pilgrims and Puritans," *The American Arms Collection*, July 1957.

——, "The Kentucky Rifle," *The American Rifleman*, Nov. 1964.

——, "Letter on American Horseman Sabers," *Society of American Sword Collectors Bulletin*, Oct. 1949.

RAY, FRED, JR., and FREDERICK P. TODD, "British 42nd [Royal Highland] Regiment of Foot, 1759–1760," *Journal of the Company of Military Historians*, Vol. VIII, No. 2, 1956.

SCOBIE, MAJOR L. H. MACKEY, "The Regimental Highland Pistol," *Army Historical Research*, Vol. VII.

SEVERN, JAMES E., "The Rifled Bore, Its Development and Early Employment," *The American Rifleman*, Mar. 1962.

SPRAGUE, RICHARD KIMBALL, "Revolutionary War Muskets," *Antiques Magazine*, July 1952.

WEBSTER, DON, "The Guns That Made Us Free," *Shooting Times*, Sept. 1964.

WEBSTER, DONALD B., JR., "American Wall Guns," *The American Rifleman*, Aug. 1963.

WELLER, JAC, "Principal Weapons of the American Revolution, Shoulder Arms," *The American Arms Collector*, July–Oct. 1958.

WHEELER, ROBERT F., "The Infantry Hanger during the Revolution," *The American Arms Collector*, Apr. 1957.

WOLF, PAUL J., "Powder Testers," *The American Arms Collector*, Oct. 1958.

# INDEX

*Page numbers in italic refer to illustrations.*